BEARING THE DEAD

LITERATURE IN HISTORY

SERIES EDITORS

DAVID BROMWICH, JAMES CHANDLER, AND LIONEL GOSSMAN

The books in this series study literary works in the context of the
intellectual conditions, social movements, and patterns of
action in which they took shape.

OTHER BOOKS IN THE SERIES

Lawrence Rothfield, *Vital Signs: Medical Realism in
Nineteenth-Century Fiction*
David Quint, *Epic and Empire: Politics and Generic
Form from Virgil to Milton*
Alexander Welsh, *The Hero of the Waverly Novels*
Susan Dunn, *The Deaths of Louis XVI: Regicide and the
French Political Imagination*
Sharon Achinstein, *Milton and the
Revolutionary Reader*

BEARING THE DEAD

THE BRITISH CULTURE OF MOURNING

FROM THE ENLIGHTENMENT

TO VICTORIA

Esther Schor

PRINCETON UNIVERSITY PRESS

PRINCETON, NEW JERSEY

PUBLISHED BY PRINCETON UNIVERSITY PRESS, 41 WILLIAM STREET,
PRINCETON, NEW JERSEY 08540
IN THE UNITED KINGDOM: PRINCETON UNIVERSITY PRESS,
CHICHESTER, WEST SUSSEX

LIBRARY OF CONGRESS CATALOGING-IN-PUBLICATION DATA

SCHOR, ESTHER H.
BEARING THE DEAD:
THE BRITISH CULTURE OF MOURNING
FROM THE ENLIGHTENMENT TO VICTORIA / BY ESTHER SCHOR.
P.   CM.—(LITERATURE IN HISTORY)
INCLUDES BIBLIOGRAPHICAL REFERENCES AND INDEX.
ISBN 0-691-03396-X

1. ENGLISH LITERATURE—19TH CENTURY—HISTORY AND CRITICISM.
2. MOURNING CUSTOMS—GREAT BRITAIN—HISTORY—19TH CENTURY.
3. ENGLISH LITERATURE—18TH CENTURY—HISTORY AND CRITICISM.
4. MOURNING CUSTOMS—GREAT BRITAIN—HISTORY—18TH CENTURY.
5. LITERATURE AND HISTORY—GREAT BRITAIN.
6. MOURNING CUSTOMS IN LITERATURE.
7. GRIEF IN LITERATURE. 8. DEATH IN LITERATURE.
I. TITLE. II. SERIES: LITERATURE IN HISTORY (PRINCETON, N.J.)
PR468.M63S36   1994
821'.009'354—dc20   94-11753 CIP

THIS BOOK HAS BEEN COMPOSED IN ADOBE SABON

SIX LINES FROM "FINAL SOLILOQUY OF THE INTERIOR PARAMOUR," FROM
COLLECTED POEMS BY WALLACE STEVENS. COPYRIGHT 1951 BY WALLACE STEVENS.
REPRINTED BY PERMISSION OF ALFRED A. KNOPF AND FABER AND FABER LTD.

SIX LINES FROM "IN MEMORY OF W. B. YEATS," FROM *COLLECTED POEMS*
BY W. H. AUDEN, ED. EDWARD MENDELSON. COPYRIGHT 1940 AND RENEWED 1968
BY W. H. AUDEN. REPRINTED BY PERMISSION OF RANDOM HOUSE AND
FABER AND FABER LTD.

PRINCETON UNIVERSITY PRESS BOOKS ARE PRINTED
ON ACID-FREE PAPER AND MEET THE GUIDELINES FOR
PERMANENCE AND DURABILITY OF THE COMMITTEE ON
PRODUCTION GUIDELINES FOR BOOK LONGEVITY
OF THE COUNCIL ON LIBRARY RESOURCES

PRINTED IN THE UNITED STATES OF AMERICA

1 3 5 7 9 10 8 6 4 2

This book is dedicated to

WALTER

and to the memory of

SANDRA

"Something so trifling in single instances that no
mathematical instrument, though capable of
transmitting shocks in China, could register the
vibration; yet in its fulness rather formidable and
in its common appeal emotional; for in all the
hat shops and tailors' shops strangers looked
at each other and thought of the dead;
of the flag; of Empire."
—Virginia Woolf, *Mrs. Dalloway*

CONTENTS

ACKNOWLEDGMENTS

I HAVE BEEN supremely fortunate in my editors: extensive comments from David Bromwich and Jim Chandler have simply left this a better book than it would otherwise have been. They were the best kind of editors, at once critical and encouraging, scrupulous and magnanimous. Their reading of my book, in short, helped me to read it much more acutely. To Lionel Gossman as well as Robert Brown and Bill Laznovsky of Princeton University Press I am also grateful.

This book was, in a narrow sense, a decade in the making, but I have been working toward it, if not on it, for much longer. For Harold Bloom's unparalleled teaching and Paul Fry's discerning comments on my dissertation, I am most appreciative. The John A. Annan Bicentennial Preceptorship from the Department of English at Princeton made it possible for me to make a sharp turn at a crucial moment; without that well-timed intervention, this would have been a different book. At Princeton, conversations with Maria DiBattista, Victoria Kahn, U. C. Knoepflmacher, Deborah Nord, and Elaine Showalter have been a great, ongoing, source of pleasure for me. For reading this manuscript, in part or in whole, I am grateful to Charles Altieri, Adrienne Donald, Fred Kaplan, Richard Kroll, Peter Manning, and Susan Wolfson. My debts become more diffuse as I thank the many insightful students I have had at Princeton, as well as receptive audiences at the Modern Language Association; the Center for Literary and Cultural Studies at Harvard; the North American Society for the Study of Romanticism; the International Association for Philosophy and Literature; and Southern Illinois University at Carbondale. The staff of the Rare Books and Manuscripts Division at Princeton's Firestone Library, in particular Stephen Ferguson, have helped more than they know, and my appreciation also goes to the staff of the New York Public Library.

When I review my debts, I am grateful not only for what I have been given, but for the very bonds of indebtedness; in this sense, our debts leave us the richer. I am grateful to Sally Goldfarb, Joseph Straus, Galit Pinsky Gottlieb, Barbara Bowen, Joanne Wolfe, Anne Barrett Doyle, Bernice Kliman, Phyllis Bolton, and Marilyn McGirr for their constancy during the vicissitudes of writing. My profoundest debts are to my loving family: to my father, Joseph Schor, whose sense of possibility has always been an inspiration; to Laura; to Joshua, Lori, and Gideon; to Bert, Bob, and Lily; to Ray, Rob, Ted, and Tess. My "caballeros," Daniel and Jordan, were my boon companions in this venture; Susannah was expected while I revised, and arrived to help me read page proofs. The dedication expresses, however reticently, two vast debts. My mother, Sandra Schor (1932–1990), is a presence throughout this book, as throughout my life; I have begun the book by introducing her role in it. Finally, a search through the galaxies would not turn up a husband more generous and true than Walter Greenblatt; my gratitude to him is that deep.

BEARING THE DEAD

INTRODUCTION

> Discourse about the past has the status of being the discourse
> of the dead. The object circulating in it is only the absent,
> while its meaning is to be a language shared . . . by living be-
> ings. Whatever is expressed engages a group's communication
> with itself through this reference to an absent, third party that
> constitutes its past. The dead are the objective figure of an
> exchange among the living.
> (Michel de Certeau [trans. Conley], *The Writing of History*)

THIS IS A BOOK about the persistence of the dead; about why they continue to matter long after we have emerged from grief and resigned ourselves to loss. I argue here for a conception of mourning that moves beyond the familiar notion of an individual's anguish in the immediate wake of bereavement. My methodological premise is that mourning as a cultural rather than psychological phenomenon has become opaque to us in the late twentieth century. A variety of sociological causes, documented in the extensive literature of thanatology, may be cited: the medicalization of death, the rise of the mortuary profession, the decline in mortuary arts such as photography, the attenuation of funeral rites and mourning rituals, among others.[1] But the problem is as much ideological as sociological; we persist in regarding mourning through Freudian lenses, which magnify the exquisite pain of bereavement while obscuring the calm commerce of condolence. For the purposes of this introduction, the difference between a psychological and a cultural approach to mourning may be described discursively: whereas a psychological account interprets mourning as a discourse between the living and the (imagined) dead, a cultural account interprets mourning as a discourse among the living.

Recent critics of textual mourning, using a therapeutic critical paradigm derived from Freud's 1917 "Mourning and Melancholia," have focused on elegiac lyrics.[2] They conceptually quarantine the mourner for examination as though such an interpretive practice would itself promote the "cure" for a condition that is declared, more or less explicitly, pathological. This gesture of isolation itself suggests a defense against the contagion of suffering. Clearly, the therapeutic paradigm of the "sick" mourner places critics of mourning in an odd position: even as they negotiate the text's requisite "resolution" of grief and pain, their practice itself stages mourning as an elaborate performance of suffering. The critic's own role—somewhere between sympathetic clinician and voyeur of pain—belies the paradigm of isolation under which therapeutic critics labor. Moreover, the diffusive structure of sympathy places the notion of an individual cure *autonomously achieved* in a dubious light. Because they focus on the individual psyche, psychological critics of mourning appear not to notice that mourning rarely, if ever, occurs in isolated instances; a single loss may generate multiple instances of mourning, as well as a manifold of sympathies that lessen in intensity—but stop where?—as one moves further from the wrought circle of grief.

If mourning must be redefined to accommodate the social diffusion of grief through sympathy, then that is what this book attempts. I interpret mourning as a phenomenon of far greater extension and duration than an individual's traumatic grief; as a force that constitutes communities and makes it possible to conceptualize history. Moreover, I believe that we lose sight of this sense of mourning at our personal and social peril. As we approach the millennium, our century continues to afford us cautionary reminders that we need the dead to be fully human: by the Holocaust deniers, on the one hand, and by the tenaciously political mourners of AIDS victims, on the other, we are reminded that both forgetting and remembering the dead have enormous consequences for the present and future of our world. Even as we give life to the dead, the dead shape the lives we are able to live.

This book sets out to recover, as de Certeau phrases it, a "discourse of the dead" within the textual and social practices of the British Enlightenment and its early nineteenth-century heirs. De Certeau's account of modern historical consciousness as a dialogue about the dead bears striking affinities to a developing secular theory of morals in Britain during the first half of the eighteenth century. My point of departure, like de Certeau's, is the dawn of a secular society, the late seventeeth-century removal of God from the position of historical "subject-king" and the substitution of "the past" in God's stead.[3] Moreover, de Certeau's identification of historical writing with an ethical imperative for the living resonates with the Enlightenment concept of mourning as a process that generates, perpetuates, and moralizes social relations among individuals. De Certeau's study of Enlightenment historiography and this study of mourning in the same period produce not parallel, but intersecting conclusions: just as Enlightenment historiography is an ethical enterprise, mourning is a historical one, making the past a crucial partner of the present.

Historians of the Enlightenment for more than a century have stressed its crucial displacement of divine authority with secular authority. J. B.

Schneewind's account of "Divine Corporation" theory and its legacy in the work of Kant and Bentham;[4] Philippe Ariès's chapters in *The Hour of Our Death* on the secularization of death and dying since the seventeenth century;[5] and de Certeau's chronicle of modern historiography are three histories of the Enlightenment among many that emphasize its secular, ethical revision of Christian morality. An alternative account is provided by J.G.A. Pocock, who narrates the demise of a classical, republican ideal of virtue in an age of commercial expansion. As Pocock observes in his seminal essay on the historiography of the Enlightenment, "Virtues, rights and manners,"[6] the juristically based discourse of liberalism and the republican discourse of the citizen's virtue describe distinct, if colliding, worlds. During the eighteenth century, Pocock argues, "Virtue was redefined . . . with the aid of a concept of 'manners.'"[7] Pocock identifies manners with the negotiation of an "increasingly transactional universe of 'commerce and the arts' . . . in which relationships and interactions with other social beings, and with their products, became increasingly complex and various, modifying and developing more and more aspects of his personality."[8]

The Enlightenment culture of mourning was instrumental in mediating between received ideas of virtue, both classical and Christian, and a burgeoning, property-based commercial society. In the first chapter of his *Theory of Moral Sentiments*, Adam Smith designates an originary act of sympathy for the dead as the motivation for all subsequent occasions of sympathy. The most urgent significance of this myth lies in Smith's *economic* metaphors for the relations between the living and the dead. According to Smith, sympathetic "tribute" "paid" to the dead is not given freely; rather it is an "indebted" consideration for the moral value with which the dead endow the living. Moreover, the diffusion of sympathy from the grave outward is characterized as a series of exchanges; sympathy is extended to the mourner by a disinterested party in exchange for a curbing of grief. Smith's theory of mourning, both as a theory of God's displacement by the dead, and as an ethical framework for the discipline of "manners," dramatizes the Enlightenment's translation of an ethics of virtue into an ethics of value.[9] Financial worth finds its moral correlative in "worthiness"; commodification in "dearness"; monetary expense, in the affections of "loss." The circulation of sympathies maps in a moral realm the dynamic process of exchange, negotiation, circulation—that is, the mechanisms by which both valued things *and values themselves* are distributed within a culture. Writing of the birth of political economy in Scotland, Pocock notes that "it appears to have had far more to do with morality than with science."[10] In the Enlightenment, mourning and sympathy provide the discursive means by which morals could be conceptualized as a moving force in a complex, diversified, capitalist society—a society which had survived both an inscrutably righteous God and the anachronistic republican ideal of the virtuous citizen.

．　．　．　．　．

Because this book interprets the cultural meanings of mourning from the Enlightenment to Victoria, its chapters are roughly chronological; chapter 1 begins with a discussion of the elegy in the context of Enlightenment moral philosophy, and the Epilogue considers Victorian death and mourning, and the relation between mourning and aestheticism. But since I argue that the meanings of mourning breach the boundaries between such contemporary disciplines as literature, philosophy, politics, and economics, the course of my argument is not linear; throughout, I have tried to demonstrate the efficacy of bringing a variety of analytical approaches to bear on the task of interpretation. Moreover, my idiosyncratic definition of "textual mourning," as the following summary of my argument should suggest, is not limited to lyrical elegies; indeed, I demonstrate in the first two chapters that the very construction of generic, formal terms like "elegy" and the broader "elegiac" are historically bound. In chapters 2 through 5, I attend to the assimilation of elegiac themes and conventions to a variety of literary and nonliterary forms: the sonnet, the topographical poem, the ode, and narrative forms such as the epic; as well as the political pamphlet and the sermon. Beyond these disparate literary traditions, the texts I study here draw on a variety of mourning traditions, among them pastoral elegy, funeral elegy, tragedy, classical funeral oration, Anglican funeral sermon, graveyard meditation, elegiac sonnet, effusion, epitaph, and eulogistic memoir. Some— the philosophical treatises, political pamphlets, sermons and mourning ephemera—are texts traditionally studied from within the specialized domains of philosophy, politics, theology, and social history. Given the interdisciplinary nature of my task, I have tried to develop a style of argument that will both make clear the contours of my historical account, and be capacious and flexible enough to support varied analytic approaches to a wide variety of texts. Should the drift of my argument at times seem wayward, the reader can consult the following brief summary of my argument and the premises from which it proceeds.

Part One, "A Century of Tears," studies the relation between mourning and morals during the British Enlightenment. A central preoccupation of Enlightenment thought is the conception of social identity on the basis of the intellect and the affections, rather than on the basis of physical desires or racial identity.[11] The philosophical theory of the moral sense—the theory of a natural and secular, rather than divine basis for moral life—plays a crucial role in the conceptual transition from a material to an immaterial link between individual and group. By basing an individual's moral judgements on a bodily act of perception, moral sense theory links one's bodily existence to one's morality; hence, the moral life is grounded within the physical life of individuals but not wholly determined by it.

The chief theoretical challenge to moral sense theorists was to establish a necessary link between the affections of individuals and the normative morals of a society. In chapter 1, "Elegia and the Enlightenment," I argue that such efforts culminate in Adam Smith's designation of sympathy for the dead as the basis of social sympathy. My treatment of Smith is preceded by a discussion of the changing representation of the elegy—a contested generic designation—during the first half of the eighteenth century. As the theory of moral sentiments develops, the elegy gains in esteem; it is increasingly associated with public virtue and masculinity. I follow my treatment of Smith with a reading of Gray's *Elegy Written in a Country Church-yard* as a poem that replaces a thematics of moral spectatorship with a thematics of moral circulation.

Sentimentalism is a pivotal term for the present study, since it refers simultaneously to a theory of how sentiments are evoked and circulated, and to the rhetorical praxis of evoking and circulating them. In chapter 2, "Written Wailings," my discussion turns from sentimental theory to sentimental praxis; here I examine the theoretical circulation of sympathies from the standpoint of rhetoric. As rhetoricians came to place greater emphasis on the evocation of pathos, critical interest came to focus on "the elegiac"—a mode, rather than a genre or form. At the same time, anxieties about the authorization of pathos—anxieties anticipated in the concluding stanzas of Gray's *Elegy*—become salient, particularly in elegiac sonnets. Gray's "Sonnet on the Death of Mr. West" performs an overwrought drama of authorizing pathos through appeals to sincerity (ethos) on the one hand, and to literary tradition (logos), on the other. In the cumulative sonnet cycles of Charlotte Smith and William Lisle Bowles, the effort to authorize pathos results in a rupturing of pathetic decorum. The chapter concludes with a reading of Wordsworth's youthful "Sonnet on Seeing Miss Helen Maria Williams Weep at a Tale of Distress," in which the fledgling poet reveals that sentimental sonnets evoke not social benevolism, but merely the solipsistic "virtue" of sensibility.

Chapter 3, "Burke, Paine, Wordsworth, and the Politics of Sympathy," represents the Revolution controversy as a crisis for both the theory and praxis of sentimentalism. The highly developed rhetoric of sympathy, which had only recently been viewed as a liability for the diffusion of virtue, became turned vigorously outward to a variety of political agendas—some activist; others, quietistic. The affections were approached as an avenue to the political will. In analyses of pamphlets by Burke, Paine, and Wordsworth, I attend to what I call "ethical style"—at once a rhetorical self-consciousness, and a rigorous attention to the ethical implications of style in critiques of the opposition. In one sense, the Revolution controversy was a debacle for sentimentalism, precisely because its proclivities for building a moral consensus were so easily exploited. But in another sense, the rhetoric of Burke and Paine ensured the endurance of sentimentalism by anticipating the two major rhetorical strategies for partisan politics in the post-Waterloo era: an appeal, from the right, to the sympathies of "moral nature" shared by a homogeneous nation; and a contrary appeal, from the left, to the particular sympathies of class and creed, to the end of progressing toward reform.

With chapter 4, the focus of this study narrows to the writing of William Wordsworth. Wordsworth is a central figure in Part Two, "Authentic Epitaphs," not simply because the Revolution was a watershed for his own moral consciousness, but because his changing *uses* of mourning anticipate the legacy of sentimentalism in the Victorian era. The Revolution controversy, which gave the lie to the sentimental dream of a moral consensus based on circulated sympathies, provided the impetus for William Wordsworth's sustained meditations on "the impotence of grief." In such meditations the sentimental trope of moral circulation is superseded by that of an individual's moral development, and the lyrical, lamentational rhetoric of sentimentalism is transmuted into autobiographical genealogies of ethical self-consciousness. During the decade between *The Ruined Cottage* (begun in 1797) and its extension into *The Excursion* (conceived as such in 1808), Wordsworth experimented with two alternative constructions of moral development, what I call in chapter 4 his two "Genealogies of Morals." In his "organicist" genealogy, Wordsworth invokes Hartley by arguing that morals develop necessarily, at the behest of nature; in his "elegiac" genealogy, on the other hand, he appeals to German idealism by arguing that morals develop as a consequence of the free, imaginative overcoming of the condition of loss. Wordsworth espouses both genealogies during the same decade; moreover, he has conceptual difficulty in keeping these positions distinct.

Wordsworth's moral genealogies are not a reaction against the Enlightenment so much as an assimilation of central Enlightenment values to a Romantic theory of selfhood. Not only did Wordsworth find it impossible to construct a self without according sympathy a central role; he is also the heir apparent to Adam Smith's notion that culture is founded at the grave. In *The Excursion*, moral autobiography is displaced by the writing of "authentic epitaphs," narratives about the dead; at the same time, Wordsworth's ambiguous theory of morals is transformed into a dialectical theory of history. In chapter 5 I argue that Wordsworth found in Burke's complex and at times contradictory thinking about history a way in which to reconcile his attraction to two divergent theories of morals, fatal and free. Burke provides Wordsworth not only with a defense of patriarchy and its inherited institutions; but also with a theory of how the living imaginatively bring the dead to life, and by so doing, invent history. "Bearing" the dead entails both "naturally" supporting them and imaginatively conceiving and giving birth to them. It is Wordsworth's meticulous evocation of the latter act that must qualify any characterization of *The Excursion* as Tory propaganda. By using tropes of gender—tropes that complicate Wordsworth's own epic claims to have "espoused" Nature in the Prospectus to *The Recluse*—Wordsworth presents these two theories of history as complementary, wedded to one another in his own British consciousness.

Wordsworth's *Excursion* effectively revives the sentimental tenet that public morals and private affections are continuous with one another. In chapter 6 I argue that this conviction, as well as Wordsworth's idiosyncratic tropes of gender, cut against the grain of the emerging doctrine of the separate spheres—public and private—for men and women, respectively. An even stronger challenge to the doctrine of separate spheres can be discerned in the aftermath of Princess Charlotte's death in childbirth in 1817. Chapter 6, "A Nation's Sorrows, A People's Tears: The Politics of Mourning Princess Charlotte," studies the conflation of the private and public realms in the strongly sentimental documents surrounding the Princess's death. While most of the Princess's mourners declared the "catastrophe at Claremont" to be above politics, such was demonstrably not the case: echoes of Paine in Percy Shelley's *Address to the People on the Death of the Princess Charlotte* and of Burke in a myriad of memoirs, sermons, and elegies identify this event as a moment of monarchical crisis strongly reminiscent of the turbulent days of the Revolution controversy. In her death, Princess Charlotte became a figure of both monarchical continuity and transition to an era of feminized monarchy.

Whereas Burke had entreated his readers to identify with the royal lineage, these documents seek to salvage monarchy by identifying it with the sympathetic "family" of Britain—and, by extension, with Britain's families. The revival of sentimental rhetoric during the mourning for Princess Charlotte would insert the family as a mediating force between the morals of the individual and those of the public realm. The achievement of Enlightenment morals was to conjure a phantom public in the private realm; its legacy was to bring to light in the public sphere the ghostly shapes of the heart.

Part II of this book, then, demonstrates the endurance of sentimental assumptions, conventions, and rhetoric beyond the cataclysm of the Revolution controversy. Since the period between the French Revolution and the accession of Victoria embraces what is called in literary studies the "Romantic" period, I want to dilate for a moment on the implications of the last three chapters for an interpretation of British Romanticism. Until recently, the attempt to "ground" British Romanticism in an Enlightenment context—particularly the work of Wordsworth and Coleridge following the 1798 *Lyrical Ballads*—resulted in a portrayal of Romanticism as a conservative reaction against a period of revolutionary violence and social upheaval. The attempt generated a picture of contrasts: against a turbulent background appears the stark, hawklike profile of Wordsworthian selfhood (also known, since the publication of Keats's letters, as "egotism"); and from its head springs the demonic image of Shelleyan Eros, failing signally to escape the contours of the self. According to the caricature I have sketched here, Romanticism forsakes the public realm which so preoccupied and galvanized the Enlightenment, and fetishizes the realm of the private. Wordsworth, whose career saw a radical youth become a conservative apologist for Toryism, seems to many to have lived a life allegorizing the Romantic turn to the right.

In the past decade the writings of such critics as Alan Bewell, James Chandler, and Alan Liu, among others, have done much to complicate this picture.[12] One result has been the replacement of political characterizations—radical, liberal, conservative—with detailed accounts of how Wordsworth's writing modulates between organicist and constructivist modes of representation. The result (to stay with my pictorial allegory) is a recursive figure in which poetics with different, sometimes contradictory political implications are held in a dynamic tension, and in which the viewer's image is recognized as a function of the particular critical perspective engaged. From my own reading of Wordsworth—of his dialectical thinking about both morals and history—another recursive figure emerges, one that looks back toward the Enlightenment and forward toward the era of Victoria.

While I have argued for the endurance of Enlightenment sentimentalism into the Romantic period and beyond, it is important to acknowledge that the Victorian period cast a pall over the term "sentimental," bringing it immeasurably closer to its modern connotations of tawdry, indulgent, shallow emotion.[13] During the Victorian era, the complexion of sentimentalism—indeed, the very meaning of the term—was left sallow by challenges coming from two directions. The arena of the affections, once entrusted to produce a morality superior to that conceived of through reason, was by the end of the eighteenth century increasingly subordinated to two distinct authorities: the authority of reason and that of religion. Reason, aligned with the public, masculine sphere, was thought to be a superior source of moral judgment than the affections, explicitly aligned with the private, or domestic sphere.[14] The authority of reason—insisting upon the authority of pleasure—undergirds the utilitarian challenge to sentimentalism, which took an aggregated material benefit, not a multiplicity of sympathetic exchanges, as its calculus of the good. Sentimentalism, from the perspective of utilitarianism, lay too much at the feet of individuals engaged in events of sympathy; the sentimental conception of a social group woven together by a delicate filigree of sympathies was exquisite but trivial. A more banal but far more robust conception of the social group—the number to benefit from a proposed course of action—was advanced by utilitarianism.

The religious critique, mounted chiefly by the Evangelicals, rejected the secular orientation of sentimental morals. Where utilitarianism took issue with an insufficient conception of the social group, the Evangelicals found sentimentalism to overemphasize the social group, neglecting an individual's personal salvation at the behest of a supreme deity. The phenomenon of sympathy became revised as a mundane visitation of divine pity and love; where sympathy did not invoke the divine, it was criticized as inadequate and superficial. Accordingly, the phenomenon of moral judgment, once annexed to the capacity for sympathy, became eclipsed by eschatological concerns with judgment and salvation.

Ultimately, the century of Malthus and Bentham, Lyell and Darwin—the century also of Reverend Cunningham and Canon Ryle—would annul the Shaftesburian marriage between nature and morals. As the "human" began to fall out of the language of nature, nature fell out of the language of morals, which took refuge on the one hand in utilitarianism, and on the other, in the rhetoric of Evangelical piety. Nature and morals were polarized; nature became necessary, amoral, wild, and inscrutable while the moral life became, by contrast, providential, pious, domestic, and illumined by a specifically Christian revelation.

Together, the utilitarian and religious critiques of sentimentalism changed the face of mourning in Victorian Britain. By the accession of Victoria, emphasis had begun to shift away from the mourner's participation, through sympathy, in the social fabric, toward the social recognition and patronizing of the individual mourner. A culture of mourning became a cult of mourning. Arguably, this situation was furthered by the mediating function of the family; by providing an institutional link between the individual and the social realm, the family provided the channels through which individual mourners obtained social preeminence. In my epilogue, I approach this phenomenon by contrasting the Enlightenment trope of circulation with the Victorian tropes of "high" (or in

George Eliot's term, "respectable") and "deep" grief. Most strikingly, in the Victorian era, the dead themselves have changed: where the dead of Adam Smith lay in the soil as an enduring, fertilizing provenance of sympathy, the dead of Tennyson and Mrs. Oliphant live on to enjoy the sublime fruits of immortality. From these latter dead, the epilogue turns away to consider Mary Shelley's *Last Man* as an allegory of the legacy of the Enlightenment culture of mourning. As prescient as it is ruminative, Mary Shelley's strange, prophetic novel figures aestheticism as the moral heir to the Enlightenment culture of mourning.

$\bullet \quad \bullet \quad \bullet \quad \bullet \quad \bullet$

This summary of my argument calls for some comments on my own critical method, particularly on my reading of textual mourning in a historical context. My insistence that mourning bears on issues of politics, economics, and sociology rightly suggests a dissatisfaction with existing accounts of textual mourning, which focus primarily on elegiac lyrics. What makes such readings inadequate, however, is not that they are too literary, too bound up with the parochial concerns of literary studies, but on the contrary, that they are not literary enough. I mean by this that existing treatments of textual mourning tend to veer away from discursive concerns, to engage either hermeneutic (in the case of psychoanalysis) or linguistic (in the case of deconstruction) frames of reference.[15] I have already discussed my qualms with psychoanalytic readings of mourning, which stake the analysis of particular texts on a system of normative, generalized assumptions about the psychological processes involved in mourning. The deconstructive approach to textual mourning, dwelling on how particular texts demonstrate the generalized conditions of language, is liable to a similar criticism. The essay that stands behind this approach—Paul de Man's 1969 "Rhetoric of Temporality"—is a sweeping reinterpretation of Romanticism from the perspective of the relation between symbol and allegory. De Man's literary history of Romanticism displaces the primacy of symbol by insisting on allegory as the authentic Romantic mode of signification. Unlike the symbol, which represses the temporal by insisting on a possible unity between the subjective mind and the objective forms of nature, allegory "always corresponds to the unveiling of an authentically temporal destiny."[16] Revelations of this destiny—that is, of human mortality—take the form of a "negative moment"; in British Romanticism, de Man's example is Wordsworth, who figures such moments as "the loss of self in death or in error."[17] (An alternative mode of representing the duality of the human and the natural, according to de Man, is irony, which locates dualism within the subject; in his discussion of allegory and irony, he implicitly characterizes the plot of Romanticism as a grim need to choose between death or madness.) The essay culminates in a reading of Wordsworth's "A Slumber did my Spirit Seal," in which the loss of Lucy is deemed an incidence of linguistic *différance* connected to the suddenly apprehended mortality of the subject. The eventual nature of mourning (and death, for that matter) is entirely eclipsed by its tropological function, to disrupt a mystified, symbolic poetics with the more authentic temporality of allegory. De Man's essay strikingly contracts the insights of Walter Benjamin in his seminal study of the German *trauerspiel*.[18] Where Benjamin views allegory as the encroachment of an ethico-historical consciousness on a specious transcendentalism, de Man insists on a "temporality" that is mute about history and a human condition—mortality—that is silent about ethics. That the deconstructive approach to textual mourning should have taken this turn away from Benjamin is ironic—or even, in light of de Man's own history, allegorical.

A few words are necessary, as well, about my own historicism. While I have found the historicist criticism of McGann, Levinson, and Simpson intellectually invigorating, I subscribe to a more dynamic sense of what writers do with and by means of language than I find present in their writing. In this study language—particularly figurative langauge—does more than displace or reveal a social or ideological reality; it shapes our sense of the real, as much in propagandistic advances on the will as in the rhetoric of lyric poetry. Like the work of the abovementioned historicist critics, however, my definition of textual mourning resists the text/context dichotomy endemic to the traditional historiography of ideas. Such a resistance aligns my method with the New Historicism, as I extrapolate its practices from the writings of its leading proponents—Stephen Greenblatt, Louis Montrose, and Catherine Gallagher. H. Aram Veeser, introducing a roundup of essays by New Historicists and their critics, places the New Historicism in relation to "the potted history of ideas" as follows:

> By forsaking what it sees as an outmoded vocabulary of allusion, symbolization, allegory and mimesis, New Historicism seeks less limiting means to expose the manifold ways culture and society affect each other. The central difficulty with these terms lies in the way they distinguish literary text and history as foreground and background. . . . New Historicism renegotiates these relationships between texts and other signifying practices, going so far. . . as to dissolve "literature" back into the historical complex that academic criticism has traditionally held at arm's length.[19]

What is "new" about the New Historicism, if anything, is this principle of textual selection. What is hardly new about it, as many have observed before me, is a practice of close reading whose genealogy extends back through post-structuralist criticism all the way to the old "New Criticism." My own readings of texts as diverse as Gray's *Elegy*, Burke's *Reflections*, Wordsworth's *Excursion*, or Shelley's "Address to the People" unapologetically depend on close scrutiny of strategically selected passages informed by a variety of intellectual traditions.

But does such a practice necessarily imply a traducing formalism? Is the close reading of texts where New Historicist practice ends?—is the "textualization of history," as Louis Montrose has called it,[20] the proper "end" of New Historicism? Reading Veeser's collection on the New Historicism, one finds a frank lack of consensus as to its "ends." If anything, Montrose's chiastic formulation—"a reciprocal concern with the historicity of texts and the textuality of history"[21]—suggests that New Historicism aspires to be a dialectic between metahistory and historiography. Indeed, Montrose's chiasmus informs the structure of this book: I have tried to balance my desire to tell a certain story about the vicissitudes of sentimentalism in the eighteenth and early nineteenth centuries with the need to expose the "texts" of history to skeptical analysis. For this reason, the structure of Parts One and Two are parallel and, internally, chiastic: whereas the first two chapters in each part "dissolve" literary texts into the texts of history, the third chapter in each part construes "history" textually. In this book, in other words, may be found the perverseness of New Historicism: precisely where one seeks "literature" (chapters 1, 2, 4, and 5), one finds "history"; precisely where one seeks "history" (chapters 3 and 6), one finds "literature." (The epilogue, just as perversely, reads a novel as a prophecy.)

But Montrose's own suggestion that New Historicism "[i]n effect . . . reorients the axis of inter-textuality, substituting for the diachronic text of an autonomous literary history the synchronic text of a cultural system"[22] seems to abandon the New Historicism to a metahistorical limbo. Such a statement places more pressure on the chiastic ideal of textual and historical reciprocity than it can withstand; it also reminds us that Greenblatt coined the term "Cultural Poetics"[23] and not "Cultural History" nor even "Cultural Fiction." What is apparently exhausted by the New Historicist penchant for the bizarre narrative is the historian's deviant desire to be the storyteller.

Thus, while my project has certain affinities with the premises and practices of the New Historicism, I am reluctant to temper this desire to tell a story—to write a history. My impulse is to synthesize Montrose's dialectic at the expense, perhaps, of a certain New Historicist skepticism. At any rate, I would like to think that in the right hands the methodological balancing acts of New Historicism need not yield a weightless equipoise, but rather an occasion for two ways of reading the past to take the positive measure of one another. De Certeau, who situates "history" between philosophy (which yields history an epistemology) and literature (which yields history a representational discourse), offers the present study a name for its procedure—to negotiate with "the dead" by telling the story of how we have lived among them and they among us. If de Certeau defines historiography as a dialogue between theory and narrative, then by his definition, what this study does is cultural history.[24]

. . . . .

In bringing this opening to a close, I find that my motive for writing this book is inseparable from my premises and purposes. In the spring of 1975, at the age of 42, my mother was diagnosed with breast cancer. I did not know then that her struggle with cancer was to endure, through repeated surgery and years of chemotherapy, for another fifteen years. My interest in elegiac texts goes back to these early days of my mother's illness, when I felt mourning to be at once necessary yet illegitimate. Paradoxically, as my mother's condition became more serious, my writing became increasingly abstracted from the experience of mourning. In my dissertation, I shifted my focus away from the pain of loss to analyze the sublimity of consolation; in revising, I deconstructed mourning as a condition of vacancy inherent in language. Both of these ventures now seem to me peculiarly defensive, exercises in intellectual homeopathy.

In July of 1990, after months of excruciating mental and physical suffering, my mother died. My license to mourn came from her, as she grieved for her daily losses of dexterity, memory, wit, physical beauty, and teeth. But only after her death did my family become, according to Jewish tradition, "mourners": the recipients of sympathy in the form of visits, cake, fruit, casseroles, old photographs, anecdotes, embraces; the ones obliged to *remember*. People we had never met left their homes to make the quorum necessary for our recital of the mourner's kaddish. For a week my sister-in-law cooked for us, leaving us free to preside, seated barefoot on hard benches, over a house full of mourners. The mirrors were covered, so we could not see ourselves; but wherever we looked were those who had gathered to comfort us.

In the weeks and months that followed, I received several hundred letters of condolence, each of which I answered. In writing these letters, I came to understand sympathy as the will to join a suffering person under the skin, conjoined with the sad knowledge that such a feat is not possible. I came to understand mourning as a recognition that the loneliness of death is something we are blessed with not being able to know in this life; mourning left me with a profound recognition—almost a physical sensation—of the difference between death and life.

This book began with the new questions I had come to ask as a mourner: What was the history of mourning? What were its social functions in the eighteenth and nineteenth centuries? How did mourning figure in the discourses of belles lettres? philosophy? politics? political economy? religion? How was the relationship between mourning and sympathy conceptualized? Was mourning understood as a communal or a psychological event or both? One way of life gave way to another; one view of mourning, abstracted and disembodied, gave way to another; one book grew into another book; and this, now, is that book.

PART ONE

A CENTURY OF TEARS

ONE

ELEGIA AND THE ENLIGHTENMENT

> When one is afraid to ask the wife of a tradesman whom she
> has lost of her family; and after some preparation endeavours
> to know whom she mourns for; how ridiculous is it to hear
> her explain herself, "That we have lost one of the house of
> Austria!"
>
> (Richard Steele, *Spectator #64 [1711]*)

Mourning, Morals, and Money

THIS CHAPTER interprets the cultural meanings of mourning in the Enlightenment. Since my analysis will invoke disciplines as diverse as literature, philosophy, politics, and economics, it seems a good idea to start by saying what I am *not* attempting here. First, although "the elegy" is my point of departure, I do not offer a comprehensive literary history of elegy per se; to show why such a history would miss both the point and the purview of mourning during the Enlightenment is one of the burdens of my argument. Second, while this chapter describes a shift in the representation of mourning during the first half of the eighteenth century, it necessarily anticipates developments more easily discerned in texts written during the latter half of the century. While such anticipations may seem to risk compromising what is historical about this account of the British Enlightenment, they also register the perils of narrating as developments what are more truly glimpsed as latencies and tendencies. Finally, a caveat about the eponymous personification of Elegia in this chapter's title. While my argument does not focus sustainedly on the vexed relations between gender and genre, it repeatedly demonstrates (and at moments, lingers over) the implication of gender in ostensibly formal generic categories. The Enlightenment shift toward the masculine gendering of mourning—a shift described in the change from Steele's "wife of a tradesman" to Gray's "rude forefathers of the hamlet"—accompanies a strengthening conviction in the public significance of mourning. Such masculinization of mourning was not reversed until the Victorian period; that the Victorians should at once have domesticated and refeminized mourning is not, as I shall argue at the end of this study, as retrograde a symmetry as it might seem. While I want to render the contours of this symmetry boldly, I have tried also to shade them with historical specificity, placing them in the context of larger debates about gender and power.

This chapter, first, makes claims for the increasing centrality of mourning during Britain's coming of age as an economic and political power; and second, anticipates the pressures—both extrinsic and intrinsic, historical and textual—countervailing this phenomenon in the final decades of the eighteenth century. What promoted mourning to this position of importance was the convergence of two needs, needs announced variously in the discourses of morals and money. First, moral philosophers such as Shaftesbury and Hutcheson sought to link an individual's "moral sense"—an inborn, natural basis for moral judgement—with the morals of the community. With Hume and later Adam Smith, attention became focused on the phenomenon of sympathy, on the possible ways in which individual sympathies might provide the basis for a public morality. In Adam Smith's *Theory of Moral Sentiments*, the need to theorize a public morality dovetails with the need to address the precariousness of an economy increasingly dependent on paper money and credit. Smith's theory suggests that the dead become, as it were, the gold standard for the circulation of sympathies within a society; at a single stroke, Smith both provides a theoretical account of the relation between private morals and public morality and suggests a role for mourning in remediating anxieties attending the proliferation of paper money in the British economy. Smith's metaphorical economy of British morals in the 1759 *Theory of Moral Sentiments*—as one might expect, corollary tropes of a moralized economy would appear in the 1776 *Wealth of Nations*—licensed a new esteem for literary mourning, for by promoting social homogeneity, mourning figuratively filled both the hearts and the coffers of the nation. This chapter argues that textual mourning is the rhetorical praxis for which Smith's concept of a dynamic, circulating, sympathetic culture of mourning is the theory.

An Unfortunate Lady

I want to approach the culture of mourning in the Enlightenment by taking up a point of debate in early eighteenth-century letters: the contested meaning of the formal term "elegy." Pastoral elegy, admired during the Renaissance in Britain and on the continent, had been out of vogue for nearly a century; in 1638 *Lycidas* became the sole pastoral elegy in the memorial volume for Edward King.[1] While the pastoral mode would survive into the eighteenth century as a satiric resource, the pastoral *elegy* would become an object of ridicule. By mid-century, Johnson's famous disparagement of *Lycidas*—"Where there is leisure for fiction, there is little grief"[2]—would apply a new critical standard of sincerity to pastoral elegy and find it absurdly wanting.

But the poem's "grosser fault," for Johnson, is the mingling of "trifling fictions" with "the most awful and sacred truths." Such "irreverend combinations" threaten to render the Christian apotheosis of the shepherd Lycidas yet another symptom of the poem's artifice. Johnson deems Milton "not to have been conscious" of such "impiety," though more recent critics, such as Sacks, have disagreed.[3] But that Johnson trembles for Milton's "sacred truths" suggests a reading public accustomed to sophisticated, "impious" readings of Christian poetry, and augurs the nineteenth-century revival of pastoral elegy in a resoundingly "impious" register.

The decline of pastoral elegy, along with its consolations of Christian apotheosis, was perhaps inevitable in an age that saw, in Ariès's words, a "decline in eschatological concern within the Christian faith."[4] This was, after all, an era in which the Christian ethos of rewarding the good after death was explicitly attacked as a self-interested basis for moral action; little wonder that the dominant idea of elegy ceased to rest on the consoling visions of Christian pastoral. Instead, theorists of the *belles lettres* turned to the Latin elegies of Tibullus, Propertius, and Ovid, which had a century earlier provided the elegiac models for Milton's seven Latin elegies and which would now shape what was known as "elegy" in the late seventeenth and early eighteenth centuries.[5]

If the Latin elegy was metrically well-defined by the elegiac distich—a hexameter followed by a pentameter—it was notoriously ill-defined in terms of its themes. Throughout the eighteenth century, English commentators sought alternately to redefine the elegy in nonmetric terms, and to establish an English metric analogue to the Latin distich. Attempting to reconceive the elegy formally, thematically, and stylistically, theorists of elegy such as Joseph Trapp (1712; Eng. trans. 1742), John Newbery (1762), William Shenstone (1764), an anonymous contributor to the *Annual Register* (1767), and Nathan Drake (1798) would transform the elegy from a function of meter and matter to a function of mind; by so doing, they would reinvent an objective form—the *elegy*—as a subjective mode—the *elegiac*.[6] But the terms "objective" and "subjective" are, in this connection, slightly misleading. For this transformation from form to mode, paradoxically, is subtended by a larger cultural transformation in the construction of private and public morality. The "elegy" becomes "elegiac" precisely when the public, moral significance of individual mourning becomes widely recognized. A closer look at the problematic theorizing of "elegy" in the early eighteenth century will show how a morally dubious poetic form was, in time, transformed into a morally beneficent discursive mode.

For Joseph Trapp, attempting to legitimate poetry, "venerable both for its Antiquity and its Religion"[7] in the first lectures on poetry at Oxford (1712), the elegy is a negligible—though, intriguingly, not neglected—topic. Adhering to the Horatian maxim that poetry should instruct and delight, Trapp asks, "What, in short, is [Poetry] else but the utmost Effort of the Mind of Man, that tries all its Nerves, while it infuses into it a Tincture of universal Learning temper'd with the greatest Sweetness" (9). Moral "profit," writes Trapp,

> may be the chief End of Poetry, and ought to be so, but for that very Reason Pleasure should be joined to it, and accompany it, as a Handmaid, to minister to its Occasions. When Children are allured with the sweeten'd Draught, or gilded Pill, they, as the Physician intended, consider nothing but the Beauty of the one, or the Taste of the other: But it is well known, this was not the chief intent of the Physician in his Prescription.
>
> This Rule relates principally to the more perfect and sublimer kinds of Poetry, and especially the Epic and Dramatic. For we don't pretend that Epigram, Elegy, Song and the like, conduce much to the Improvement of Virtue. It is enough, if these Writings keep within the Bounds of Chastity, and give no Offense in Good-manners. (25)

Moral "profit" may only be had from poetry when the balance of manly virtues exceeds that of feminine charms, as is the case in the "more perfect and sublimer kinds of Poetry." From the standpoint of "rais[ing] the mind to Virtue and Honour, by delivering down the Examples of Great Men to Immortality"(8–9), Trapp recommends the genres of epic and tragedy. Not surprisingly, Trapp identifies his own labors with that of the epic poet Milton: "I must own myself under some Concern, when I consider that I enter into a Province unattempted by others, and wherein I have no Footsteps to guide me" (1). Tragedy, like epic, typifies the power of poetry not only to "[celebrate] heroes, but [to make] them." Despite its exhibition of heroism, tragedy, like elegy, stirs the passions; but Trapp exonerates tragedy from moral dubiousness by designating Aristotelian catharsis as a masculine exercise: "[Tragedies] unbend the Mind, without debasing it to Softness, and Effeminacy"(323).[8] The elegy, as "the sweetest, the most engaging" type of poetry (163), epitomizes the "softer," morally uncertain, in short *feminine* qualities of poetry. From this gendered casting emerges a clear generic hierarchy. Trapp situates the elegy on the second rung of the generic ladder between lowest-ranked epigram and third-ranked pastoral; tragedy and epic, treated in the final lectures, occupy the ninth and tenth rungs, respectively.

Trapp's casting of elegy as feminine reflects less its capacity to stir emotion, than its refusal to be answerable to literary rules. Even in the mid-1740s, William Shenstone would note that "there have been few rules given us by the critics concerning the structure of *elegiac* poetry."[9] Elegiac poetry was more wayward even in its themes than in its structure, for the Latin elegy embraced both serious, moral, subjects and jocular, satirical ones. Worse yet, the Latin elegy at times addressed moral seriousness to erotic subject matter, confounding the moral categories of virtue and vice. Shenstone also mentions "the great variety of *subjects* . . . in which the writers of elegy have hitherto indulged themselves" (1:3–4).

It is telling that both Trapp and Shenstone attempt to mythologize this thematic variety as a moral lapse or deviation from a point of origin. Trapp asserts that while the elegy originates as a funeral poem, a wide variety of poems soberly cloaked in distiches go "under the Name of Elegies" (164). For Shenstone, extending the primordial elegiac object— the illustrious dead—to include "*absent* or *neglected* lovers" was a tolerable "indulgence." But once having

> obtained a small corner in the province of love, [elegists] took advantage, from thence, to overrun the whole territory. . . . They gave the name of *elegy* to their pleasantries as well as lamentation; till at last, through their abundant fondness for the *myrtle*, they forget that the *cypress* was their peculiar garland. (1:4–5)

Trapp and Shenstone both urge the chastening of elegy, though it must be noted that both consider this compatible with amorous subject matter. Shenstone defines the elegy by a certain "manner of treating" the subject—the sustenance of "a tender and querulous idea." Trapp, observing that "the chief Subjects to which Elegy owes its Rise, are Death and Love" (165), advocates extending the category to reflect "the larger sense of the Word, as it was used by the Ancients" and to include "Many very ingenious ones on Love, and others of a melancholy and soft Turn" (169). He summarily excludes from the elegiac category "epigrammatical, satirical, or sublime poetry"; "Elegy aims not to be witty or facetious, acrimonious or severe, majestic or sublime; but is smooth, humble, and unaffected; nor is she abject in her Humility, but becoming, elegant, and attractive" (169).

In Trapp's strict, gendered antithesis between elegiac softness and the firm muscle of tragedy, humility is the apex of elegiac morality. Shenstone, however, understands elegiac morality to be considerably more complex. He focuses the matter of gender on the audience, not the text, distinguishing between two types of elegies on the basis of their implied addressees:

Love-elegy therefore is more negligent of order and design, and, being addressed chiefly to the ladies, requires little more than tenderness and perspicuity. Elegies, that are formed upon promiscuous incidents, and addressed to the world in general, inculcate some sort of moral and admit a different degree of reasoning, thought, and order. (1:10)

By opposition to "the ladies," "the world in general" constitutes an implicitly masculine audience; as such, the worldly (as opposed to erotic) elegy incorporates the masculine values of "reasoning, thought, and order." Even if "formed upon promiscuous incidents," elegies are accountable to the "end of *all* poetry":

> . . . to encourage virtue. *Epic* and *tragedy* chiefly recommend the *public* virtues; *elegy* is of a species which illustrates and endears the *private*. There is a truly virtuous pleasure connected with many pensive contemplations, which it is the province and excellence of elegy to enforce. (1:6)

Far from being antithetical, elegy on the one hand and tragedy and epic on the other are leagued in the inculcation of virtue:

> [Elegy] magnifies the sweets of liberty and independence, that *endears* the honest *delights* of love and friendship, that *celebrates* the *glory* of a good name after death, that ridicules the futile arrogance of birth, that recommends the innocent amusement of letters, and insensibly prepares the mind for the humanity it *inculcates*.(1:6)

Whereas tragedy and epic propound public virtues, elegy is morally salutary for propounding private ones. By the 1740s, the elegy had absorbed many of the values previously in the domain of Renaissance pastoral— liberty, independence, friendship, reputation, modesty, and sober amusements.

Published in 1717, Pope's "Elegy to the Memory of an Unfortunate Lady," provides evidence for Shenstone's insistence on the moral potential of elegy. In his "Elegy," Pope elegantly sidesteps Christian eschatology by selecting as the mourned object of his elegy a suicide. Whereas *Lycidas* ends with a vision of the redeemed poet's succour among the "sweet Societies" of Saints, Pope's "Elegy" begins with a vision of the lonely reprobate's enduring suffering:

> What beck'ning ghost, along the moonlight shade
> Invites my step, and points to yonder glade?
> 'Tis she!—but why that bleeding bosom gor'd,
> Why dimly gleams the visionary sword?
> Oh ever beauteous, ever friendly! tell,
> Is it, in heav'n, a crime to love too well?
> To bear too tender, or too firm a heart,

To act a Lover's or a *Roman's* part?
Is there no bright reversion in the sky,
For those who greatly think, or bravely die?[10]

(lines 1–10)

Lycidas may enjoy a "large recompense," but the sky portends no "bright reversion" for this Lady. Having been buried outside the "sacred earth" of the churchyard, her ghost returns to the melancholy shades and glades from which she had been exiled by her guardian.

Keeping the Lady nameless—presumably an attempt to protect her reputation—Pope in fact lowers her reputation by linking this "Lover" with "bleeding bosom" to the pseudonymous women of pleasure yearned for and lamented in the Latin erotic elegy. While her own erotic passion is minimized, her "ruby lips," "cheeks, now fading," "breast which warm'd the world before," and "love-darting eyes" mark her as a provocative object of the poet's sexual interest. Johnson, who "sought with fruitless inquiry" the Lady's identity, was merely one of many readers who tried to "raise the lady's character" by identifying her (324). To ennoble this anonymous renegade from Christian virtue, Pope identifies her fault with that of "kings and heroes."

But her high aspirations, ambition, and glowing soul merely render "glorious" her indelible faults:

Why bade ye else, ye Pow'rs! her soul aspire
Above the vulgar flight of low desire?
Ambition first sprung from your blest abodes;
The glorious fault of Angels and of Gods:
Thence to their Images on earth it flows,
And in the breasts of Kings and Heroes glows!

(11–16)

Johnson, ever acute, would fault Pope for "condemn[ing] the uncle to detestation for his pride" (388–89) immediately after Pope praises the Lady for her Satanic ambition; Johnson also challenges this Lady's "claim to praise [or] to compassion," finding no reason to sympathize with this "impatient, violent, and ungovernable" woman (324). Indeed, because the guardian failed to sympathize with her, his family incurs the Furies' pitiless curse: "So perish all, whose breast ne'er learn'd to glow/ For others' good, or melt at others' woe" (45–46). Whereas pastoral elegy seeks to blame the perpetrator of the death, Pope curses the guardian not for killing the Lady (which he ostensibly did not), but for being—unforgivably—unsympathetic.

Precisely because there is no *reason* to sympathize with the Lady, Pope represents sympathy as a natural phenomenon.

What tho' no friends in sable weeds appear,
Grieve for an hour, perhaps, then mourn a year,
And bear about the mockery of woe
To midnight dances, and the publick show?
What tho' no weeping Loves thy ashes grace,
Nor polish'd marble emulate thy face?
What tho' no sacred earth allow thee room,
Nor hallow'd dirge be mutter'd o'er thy tomb?
Yet shall thy grave with rising flow'rs be drest,
And the green turf lie lightly on thy breast:
There shall the morn her earliest tears bestow,
There the first roses of the year shall blow;
While Angels with their silver wings o'ershade
The ground, now sacred by thy reliques made.

(59–68)

Having cut a dubious figure as a Roman hero, the Lady—in death—is now linked with the milder virtues of pastoral otium.[11] Derived from Latin epitaphs and Virgilian pastorals, Pope's nature provides the moral authority for ridiculing the arts and shows of mourning—the "sable weeds," ornate urns, funerary sculpture, and dirges of funereal rites. But, having expanded his scope beyond the Lady's death to consider the antithesis between "natural" and cultural mourning, Pope relinquishes an opportunity either to enlarge further the moral scope of his poem or to offer precepts for elegiac poetry.

Instead, after a perfunctory *sic transit gloria mundi*, he draws his poem like a curtain around himself:

Poets themselves must fall, like those they sung;
Deaf the prais'd ear, and mute the tuneful tongue.
Ev'n he, whose soul now melts in mournful lays,
Shall shortly want the gen'rous tear he pays;
Then from his closing eyes thy form shall part,
And the last pang shall tear thee from his heart,
Life's idle business at one gasp be o'er,
The Muse forgot, and thou belov'd no more!

(75–82)

It is the poet, finally, on whose sympathy the Lady's imperiled memory rests. Pointedly, the elegist is linked not to the monuments of funereal culture, but to the spontaneity of grief—singing, melting, and weeping. In lieu of "the bright reversion" which the sky refuses to provide the Lady, the poet pays a "gen'rous tear" which will, in turn, be due him when his own death arrives. By generously assuming and repaying heaven's debt, the elegist's exemplary sympathy motivates a legacy of poetic sympathy. Here elegiac poetry does not yield the moral "profit" afforded by epic poetry; on the contrary, a paucity of Christian virtue—the ghostly deficit that floats between an assumed debt and an expected tribute—makes possible the tender human relations between poet and lady, reader and poet.

While Pope's "Elegy" suggests the elegy's increasing distance from the structures, figures, and myths of Christian eschatology, it may well allegorize the career of Elegia, the eponymous muse of elegy, in Pope's century. During the first three decades of the century, the elegy's associations with femininity would be emphasized to argue that its virtue could not be secured, or, if secured, was limited to the private, or domestic sphere. Later, like Pope's Lady, Elegia would be helped to overcome her unfortunate associations with vice; her eroticism would be reinterpreted as domestic affection; and finally, if she made little reference to public morals, she would nonetheless be deemed capable of inculcating them in others. The century of tears would open with Trapp citing Horace on the elegy's shady origins,[12] but by mid-century, Elegia would preside—among her comforters—in the salon.

The Bowl and the Urn

Writing about elegy in the 1740s, Shenstone would analogize the pleasures of the urn with those of the bowl: "[Elegy] . . . has discovered sweets in *melancholy* which we could not find in *mirth*; and has led us with much success to the dusty *urn*, when we could draw no pleasure from the sparkling bowl" (1:6). But attempting to establish a necessary link between individual morals and public morality was the work of moral sense philosophers. As I will show later in this chapter, their attempt to conflate private and public virtue, culminating in Adam Smith's theory of sympathy, would be paralleled by the achievement of Gray's *Elegy*; accordingly, the contemporary philosophical context will help us to interpret both that poem and its immense popularity.[13]

Like Pope's "Elegy to the Memory of an Unfortunate Lady," the moral philosophy of Anthony Ashley Cooper, Third Earl of Shaftesbury (1671–1713), deflects rather than denies the burden of Christian eschatology. In the *Inquiry Concerning Virtue, or Merit*, published in the first edition of his *Characteristicks* (1711) and subsequently revised, Shaftesbury questions the moral, rather than metaphysical, value of Christian eschatalogy:

It may be consider'd withal; That, in this religious sort of Discipline, the Principle of *Self-Love*, which is naturally so prevailing in us, being no-way moderated, or restrain'd, but rather improv'd and made stronger every day, by the exercise of the Passions in a Subject of more extended Self-Interest; there may be reason to apprehend lest the Temper of this kind shou'd extend it-self in general thro all the Parts of Life.[14]

In Shaftesbury's reading, the morality of Christian eschatology fails to raise individuals above an almost Hobbesian desire for self-preservation. On the contrary, Shaftesbury fears for a society in which "Self-love" and the passions are actively trained from infancy by the desire for heaven; heaven, under this description, becomes little more than a quivering fantasy of satisfied desire. But Shaftesbury's attack on the morality of Christian "resignation" ushers Hobbesian "Self-love" into the eighteenth century, redefining it as economic self-interest:[15]

And if that which he calls *Resignation* depends only on the expectation of infinite Retribution or Reward, he discovers no more Worth or Virtue here, than in any other Bargain of Interest: The meaning of his Resignation being only this, "that he resigns his present Life, and Pleasures, conditionally for THAT which he himself confesses to be beyond an Equivalent; *eternal Living, in a State of highest Pleasure and Enjoyment.*" (36)

For Shaftesbury, the incommensurability between heavenly pleasures and sublunary sacrifice damns Christian eschatology as a "Bargain of interest." Though published in 1711, the *Characteristicks* was most likely written twenty years earlier; certainly Shaftesbury's sense of the immorality of interest sits uneasily beside Trapp's blithe figure of moral "profit." Still, Shaftesbury's moral critique of Christian eschatology expresses fears about a future for virtue in a mercantile, capitalist society—fears that would continue to inform moral thought throughout the century.

The father of "moral sense" philosophy, Shaftesbury locates the basis of virtue in the human mind, rather than in an extrinsic metaphysical authority; he posits an intrinsic "moral sense," an emotion of pleasurable approbation or painful disapprobation that arises from the mind's reflection on actions, emotions, or perceptions. By defining virtue as the promotion of a social "system" or "kind," Shaftesbury begs the question of how the moral sense yields moral imperatives; to bridge the gap between the moral "is" and the moral "ought," Shaftesbury simply invokes a "use of reason, sufficient to secure a right application of the affections" (20).

Bridging this gap more sturdily became the work of two generations of moral philosophers who followed Shaftesbury. Francis Hutcheson (1694–1746), in *Inquiry into the Original of our Ideas of Beauty and Virtue* (1725) and *Illustrations on the Moral Sense* (1728), reconceives the operation of the moral sense as occasioned by perception as well as by reflection; as such, on the analogy of Lockean epistemology, he develops what has become known as a "spectator" theory of morals. Such a theory empowers Hutcheson's thinking about how aesthetic phenomena—poetic and dramatic representations—implicate moral judgement: "We shall find [the moral] *Sense* to be the Foundation also of the chief Pleasures of *Poetry*. . . . *Dramatic* and *Epic* Poetry, are entirely address'd to this Sense, and raise our Passions by the Fortunes of *Character*, distinctly represented as *morally good*, or *evil*. . . ."[16] In the *Illustrations*, Hutcheson cites the *Iliad* and the *Aeneid* to demonstrate that moral approbation is not determined by self-interest:

> [Had] we no Sense of *moral Good* in *Humanity, Mercy, Faithfulness,* why should not *Self-love,* and our sense of *natural Good* engage us always to the victorious side, and make us admire and love the successful Tyrant, or Traitor? Why do not we love *Sinon,* or *Pyrrhus,* in the *Aeneid?* For had we been Greeks, these two would have been very *advantageous Characters.* Why are we affected with the Fortunes of *Priamus, Polites, Choreobus,* or *Aeneas?* (122)

Hutcheson even asserts that because the representations of poetry produce more lively ideas than the reflections of philosophers, poetry may be more efficacious than philosophy in promoting a normative morality:

> Where we are studying to raise any *Desire* or *Admiration* of an Object *really beautiful*, we are not content with a *bare* Narration, but endeavour, if we can, to present the *Object* itself, or the most lively *Image* of it. And hence the Epic Poem, or Tragedy, gives a vastly greater Pleasure than the Writings of *Philosophers*, though both aim at recommending Virtue. The representing the Actions themselves, if the Representation be *judicious, natural,* and *lively*, will make us admire the *good*, and detect the *Vitious*, the *Inhuman*, the *Treacherous* and *Cruel* by means of our moral Sense, without any *Reflections* of the *Poet* to guide our sentiments. (261)

Indeed, Hutcheson's thoughts on the power of Poetry to "recommend virtue" pull in two contrary directions. Hutcheson, drawn to the vividness of a moral stimulus that works immediately, by means of sensation, rather than mediately, by means of reflection, prefers a rhetoric of "image" to one of "narration." He prefers, in other words, tragic and epic representations, which *show* virtuous or vicious moral exempla, to philosophical or didactic treatises, which *tell* what is virtuous and what vicious.

At the same time, Hutcheson seems uneasy about the lack of discursive mediation in poetry and drama; counterfeited misery is dangerous because it calls on an audience to be compassionate regarding a sufferer of unknown morality in an unknown context. The lack of a mediating moral authority locates the responsibility for moral judgement with the spectator rather than with an authorized, mediating narrator. To compensate for this transfer of moral authority from author to spectator, Hutcheson insists on the significance of *context* to our perception of the object in question. Conversely, the spectacle of irremediable suffering threatens to take us out of our own context, threatening our social identity: "[I]f we see [that relief is] impossible, we may by *Reflection* discern it to be vain for us to indulge our compassion any further; and then *Self-love* prompts us to retire from the Object which occasions our Pain, and to endeavour to divert our Thoughts" (238). Because compassion can obscure the social identity of both sufferer and spectator, moral judgements based solely on compassion are viewed as a social threat. For Hutcheson, compassion can only give rise to normative virtue when the occasion of compassion is mediated.

Like Hume, who would note that tragedy makes use of historical people and places "to Procure a more easy reception of the whole," Hutcheson emphasizes the historical basis of most tragic representations. The context of tragic action and utterance is "the moral *Beauty* of the *Characters* and *Actions* which we love to behold. For I doubt," Hutcheson continues, "whether any Audience would be pleas'd to see fictitious Scenes of Misery, if they were kept stranger to the *moral Qualitys* of the sufferers, or their *Characters* and *Actions*" (239). Tragedy is morally beneficial not because its characters consistently exemplify virtue, but because their moral qualities, whether virtuous or vicious, are *already known* to the audience; based on historical events, tragic actions have already been normatively interpreted and assimilated. In Hutcheson's theory of moral spectatorship, tragic performance stages the culturally sanctioned rehearsal of the individual's moral judgement. While Hutcheson's spectator theory intuits tension between individual judgements and social norms, it neither analyzes nor theorizes relations between private morals and public morality.

With David Hume (1711–1776), the theory of moral spectatorship becomes considerably more rigorous, but at the same time less adequate as a theory of normative morality. In Book II of his *Treatise of Human Nature* (1742) ("Of the Passions"), Hume asserts that "sympathy is exactly correspondent to the operations of our understanding":[17]

> When any affection is infus'd by sympathy, it is at first known only by its effects, and by those external signs in the countenance and conversation, which convey an idea of it. This idea is presently converted into an impression, and acquires such a degree of force and vivacity, as to become the very passion itself, and produce an equal emotion, as any original affection. (317)

Our conversion of the idea into an impression depends on how closely the object of perception resembles ourselves; the locution of a "close" resemblance, Hume observes, uses spatial relations to metaphorize the vividness of a comparison. Since affliction and sorrow "have always a stronger and more lasting influence than any pleasure or enjoyment," (369) Hume analyzes tragedy as a showcase for sympathy:

> A spectator of tragedy passes thro' a long train of grief, terror, indignation, and other affections, which the poet represents in the persons he introduces. . . . As [the distinct passions] are all first present in the mind of one person, and afterwards appear in the mind of another; and as the manner of their appearance, first as an idea, then as an impression, is in every case the same, the transition must arise from the same principle. (369–70)

In tragedy, each spectator "passes thro' a long train" of affections; as each affection appears, it must in turn be imaginatively transformed from an idea into an impression. But the morality of the audience as a whole can only be expressed as the simple aggregate of each spectator's sympathies at a given moment.

While for Hume tragic performance remains the prime aesthetic example of the moral sense, his significant pairing of "a very play or romance" (470) alters significantly Hutcheson's (and Trapp's and Shenstone's) designation of tragedy and epic as the chief inculcators of moral virtue. For one thing, to substitute romance for epic is to select a domestic and feminine literary form as an aesthetic exemplar of the moral sense—in other words, to identify the moral sense with virtues associated with domesticity and privacy. This convergence of femininity and virtue is hardly coincidental to the development of moral sense theory; both Hutcheson and Hume evince the propensity of women and children to feel compassion as evidence that morality derives from an innate moral *sense*, rather than from custom or reason. For Hutcheson, "How independent this Disposition to *Compassion* is of *custom, education*, or *instruction*, will appear from the Prevalence of it in *Women* and *Children*, who are less influenc'd by these" (241). For Hume, the fact that "Women and children are most subject to pity, as being most guided by [imagination]"—that same "infirmity, which makes them faint at the

sight of a naked sword, tho' in the hands of their best friend" (370)—
suggests that pity is derived from the imagination rather than, say, from
"the instability of fortune and our being liable to the same miseries we
behold" (370).

But rather than relegate morals to the private realm, Hume's emphasis
on the morality of romance suggests an altered sense of how individual
moral judgements take on public significance. By citing romance—a
popular, vernacular, and widely circulated literary form—in lieu of epic
or tragedy, Hume draws attention to social intercourse rather than public performance as the arena of normative morality; to the interpersonal
phenomenon of conversation rather than the personal act of spectatorship.[18] For it is precisely the phenomenon of social intercourse on which
Hume would attempt to model his account of social morality in Book III
("Of Morals"). Here, Hume offers a far more nuanced account of the
relations between individual sentiments and the society's moral norms
than that afforded by spectator theory:

> [T]ho' sympathy be much fainter than our concern for ourselves, and a
> sympathy with persons remote from us much fainter than that with persons
> near and contiguous; yet we neglect all these differences in our calm judg-
> ments concerning the characters of men. . . . The intercourse of sentiments,
> therefore, in society and conversation, makes us form some general unalter-
> able standard, by which we may approve or disapprove of characters of
> manners. (603)

While our moral propensities may be innate, our moral standards derive
from "the intercourse of sentiments" within society. By acknowledging
the role of society in shaping an individual's moral judgements, Hume
undermines a strict distinction between individual morals and normative
morality. Furthermore, normative morality is not conceptualized, as
with Hutcheson, as an aggregate of individual moral responses, but
rather as the totality of moral converse within a society.

Hume's shift from a spectator theory to what we might call a "conversation" theory, ostensibly designed to offer a more flexible account of
the relationship between individual judgements and social norms, acknowledges that the commensurability of judgements and norms is
rarely absolute. Hypocrisy, for Hume, can be explained by the tendency
for social norms to dominate individual judgements: "And tho' the *heart*
does not always take part with those general notions, or regulate its love
and hatred by them, yet are they sufficient for discourse, and serve all
our purposes in company, in the pulpit, on the theatre, and in the
schools" (603). In addition to hypocrisy, Hume's scruple introduces the
bleak phantasm of a society whose moral discourse is wholly alienated
from the moral judgements of its members. With Hume, the absolute-

ness of a "moral sense"—Shaftesbury's unelaborated conviction that innate moral responses serve as the foundation of a public morality—falls to the possibility of a public morality "sufficient for discourse" but sensed by no one. Such a fantasy makes Hume's engagement with the Shaftesburian "moral sense" seem almost nugatory, beside the point of his inquiry into moral conversation.

Hume's skepticism merely states in an extreme form the perennial ethical objection to moral sense philosophy: its moral relativism. Even before Hume theorized moral conversation, Enlightenment moralists used metaphors to secure the moral sense against charges of relativism—used metaphors, that is, to do the work of argument.[19] Hutcheson, for example, conceptualizes moral approbation not as a cognitive function, but as an expressive one. Among a particular society's variegated moral signifiers—for example, terms like "virtue," "heroism," "judgment," "justification," "motivation," etc.—the approbation (or disapprobation) supplied by an innate moral sense functions as the transcendental signified to which these terms refer. While Hutcheson gives center stage to spectator theory, his implicit semiotics of morals suggests an awareness of moral conversation as a moving social force.

Conversation, for that matter, is only one way in which Hume renders the "intercourse of sentiments"; when he writes about the phenomenon of sympathy, his metaphor changes from conversation to "contagio[n]":

> The passions are so contagious that they pass with the greatest facility from one person to another, and produce correspondent movements in all human breasts. . . . [M]y heart catches the same passion, and is warm'd by those warm sentiments, that display themselves before me. Such agreeable movements must give me an affection to every one that excites them. (605)

In this passage, Hume's metaphor of contagion implicitly revives the ancient figure of the social body. While Hume assigns sympathy neither an etiology nor a teleology, he is insistent on its propensity to circulate; the "human breast" cannot resist it, nor can it prevent the transmission of sympathy to others. Tears, which "naturally start in our eyes" are symptomatic of the "excitation" and "movement" of our affections; the very perception of another's tears conveys the fever of "warm sentiments" to the observer's heart, which "catches the same passion." Metaphorizing sympathy as contagion, of course, bespeaks a stoical alignment of passions with moral corruption—or might, from the pen of a writer other than Hume, famous in his own day for acquitting the passions against just such stoical aspersions.[20] But Hume's metaphor—with its emphasis on social circulation and its whiff of corruption—strikingly anticipates Adam Smith's account of sympathy in the *Theory of Moral Sentiments* (1759). Smith succeeds, where his predecessors failed, in providing a secular basis for morals beyond the "human breast."

Adam Smith and the Tribute of Sympathy

Smith elaborates Hume's theory of sympathy by describing it as an imaginative act:

> Sympathy, therefore, does not arise so much from the view of the passion, as from that of the situation which excites it. We sometimes feel for another, a passion of which he himself seems to be altogether incapable; because, when we put ourselves in his case, that passion arises in our breast from the imagination, though it does not in his from the reality. We blush for the impudence and rudeness of another, though he himself appears to have no sense of the impropriety of his own behaviour; because we cannot help feeling with what confusion we ourselves should be covered, had we behaved in so absurd a manner.[21]

While Hume had observed that "indifference and insensibility" on the part of a sufferer increases our compassion, Smith analyzes this intensified response as a function of "put[ting] ourselves in his case." Sympathy does not consist, then, in having an affection identical to that of the sufferer; nor does it depend on the intensity of our resemblance to the sufferer. For Smith, sympathy derives from a feeling of dissonance between ourselves and the sufferer's situation; according to Smith, we do not imagine *being* that particular sufferer, but rather imagine being *ourselves* in the sufferer's situation. Smith's examples: the boor, because indifferent to propriety, will be unembarrassed whereas *we* would blush; the madman, having lost reason, will be "insensible" to his situation, whereas we "regard it with [our] present reason and judgment"; the infant, "knowing no future," cries for the agony of disease, whereas the mother cries with fear for "the unknown consequences."

Smith's fourth and most emphatic example—the dead—exemplifies what Alan Bewell has called "empiricist thanatology": "[T]he key to all our metaphors for death," writes Bewell, "the material substratum from which they all fundamentally derive, is to be found in what we see happening to or what we do with the bodies of the dead."[22] Smith, similarly, claims that in contemplating the dead, we put aside metaphysics in favor of our observations:

> We sympathize even with the dead, and overlooking what is of real importance in their situation, that awful futurity which awaits them, we are chiefly affected by those circumstances which strike our senses, but can

have no influence upon their happiness. It is miserable, we think, to be deprived of the light of the sun; to be shut out from life and conversation; to be laid in the cold grave, a prey to corruption and the reptiles of the earth; to be no more thought of in this world, but to be obliterated, in a little time, from the affections, and almost from the memory, of their dearest friends and relations. Surely, we imagine, we can never feel too much for those who have suffered so dreadful a calamity. (1:11)

Not confining himself, however, to "those circumstances which strike our senses," Smith imagines his own "dissolution," what he would sense in the position of the dead.[23] Smith's example of sympathizing with the dead crucially *reinscribes as self-sacrifice* the self-interest on which sympathy is based. Self-interest, an idea Shaftesbury strove to banish from the discourse of morals is now seen to lie at the heart of sympathy. In Gray's *Elegy*, for example, the fearsome fantasy of lying in a "narrow cell" beneath a "mould'ring heap" would yield a productive identification with the dead, a social identity designed to absorb and comfort the solitary mourner.

In sympathizing with the dead, then, we take up our place, imaginatively, in the grave. At the same time, the dead take up their places within our minds; we become, in Gray's apposite words, "mindful" of them. As the bodies of the dead tend to decompose, so, according to empiricist thanatology, do our ideas of the dead. Since, Smith asserts, there is no way in which we can remediate the situation of the corpse, we strive through continuous sympathy "artificially to keep alive" the idea of the dead:[24]

The tribute of our fellow-feeling seems doubly due to them now, when they are in danger of being forgot by every body; and, by the vain honours which we pay to their memory, we endeavour, for our own misery, artificially to keep alive our melancholy remembrance of their misfortune. That our sympathy can afford them no consolation seems to be an addition to their calamity; and to think that all we can do is unavailing, and that, what alleviates all other distress, the regret, the love, and the lamentations of their friends, can yield no comfort to them, serves only to exasperate our sense of misery. The happiness of the dead, however, most assuredly, is affected by none of these circumstances; nor is it the thought of these things which can ever disturb the profound security of their repose. The idea of that dreary and endless melancholy, which the fancy naturally ascribes to their condition, arises altogether from our joining to the change which has been produced upon them, our own consciousness of that change; from our putting ourselves in their situation, and from our lodging, if I may be allowed to say so, our own living souls, in their inanimated bodies, and thence conceiving what would be our emotions in this case. (1:11–12)

Paradoxically, the very "payment" of "tribute of our fellow-feeling" "doubly due" the dead, compounds their "misfortune" by "afford[ing]" them no consolatory "yield." Smith acknowledges that we cannot fully account for our sense of a "debt" to the dead by a meliorative motive, for we feel indebted to them in the full knowledge that our tribute brings the particular dead person no benefit.

I would suggest that Smith's sense of an unpayable debt to the dead reflects his conviction that the debt to the dead is not confined to the solitary sympathizer, but is rather distributed among the members of society at large. Smith, by using economic metaphors to figure sympathy for the dead, revises Hume's conversation theory of morals—itself a revision of Hutcheson's spectator theory—into a theory of moral *circulation*. Such a theory, I would argue, is presaged by Hume's metaphor of sympathy circulating within the social body. Smith's sympathetic mourner bent over the grave provides an originary moment for Hume's metaphor of contagion; taken together, the two figures of sympathy remind us that we catch something when we mourn at the grave—if not corruption, then a sympathetic twinge of death. For Smith, the dead communicate to the living a certain moral responsiveness that is, in turn, communicated to others.

In the fourth chapter of the first volume of *Theory of Moral Sentiments*, Smith provides an analysis of moral "conversation" as an exchange of sympathies between persons. The deep passions of grief, Smith maintains, threaten to make "conversation" itself impossible:

> [I]f you have . . . no indignation at the injuries I have suffered . . . we can no longer converse upon these subjects. We become intolerable to one another. I can neither support your company, nor you mine. You are confounded at my violence and passion, and I am enraged at your cold insensibility and want of feeling.(1:33)

Having redefined the "natural," affective sympathy of moral sense philosophy as a function of the imagination, Smith now, somewhat surprisingly, represents the imagination's inclination to failure when faced with the strong passions of grief. And where sympathy fails between individuals, Smith cautions, they become positively repellent toward one another.

What prevents this fracturing of society in the face of great grief is the grieving person's recognition of sympathy's value to afford relief. To the end of securing such sympathy, he counter-sympathizes with the perplexed spectators of grief:

> He must flatten, if I may be allowed to say so, the sharpness of [grief's] natural tone, in order to reduce it to harmony and concord with the emo-

tions of those who are about him. What they feel will, indeed, always be, in some respects, different from what he feels, and compassion can never be exactly the same with original sorrow; . . . These two sentiments, however, may, it is evident, have such a correspondence with one another, as is sufficient for the harmony of society. (1:35–36)

Smith's musical metaphors notwithstanding, he offers here an analysis of moral conversation as an exchange of sympathies between persons. The aggrieved individual, in order to secure the comfort of another's sympathy, imagines himself in the situation of the onlooker, an act that mutes his passion. The imagination of the onlooker, then, need not be strained beyond its capacities in figuring the onlooker in the situation of the aggrieved. While the aggrieved receives a tranquilizing comfort, the onlooker receives, quite literally, a consideration from the aggrieved that enfranchises him in a social bond.[25]

Elsewhere, Smith links these sympathies, respectively, to the complementary virtues of sensibility and amiability.[26] But in this context, individual virtue is secondary to the promotion of the "harmony of society." Smith's implication of social harmony in this act of moral conversation suggests a link between the scene of mourning—a sympathy with the dead—and the subsequent scene of sympathy between persons. More specifically, Smith's casting of both scenes as incidents of economic transaction shifts Hume's metaphor of moral conversation toward a metaphor of moral circulation. The mourner at the grave is merely one point in a network of emotional exchanges which constitutes the moral circulation of a society. The dead, because they cannot be remediated—because they both evoke and warrant our feelings of "dreary and endless" melancholy—provide the gold standard for the endlessly circulating currency of sympathy which constitutes a normative morality. For Smith, the moral authority of the dead, not of a transcendental God nor of the individual human body, "guarantees" the social circulation of sympathy, pity, compassion, approbation, and censure by which the living regulate their actions.

I want to argue that Smith's moral economy,[27] by theorizing relations between the sympathies of individuals and the harmony of a society, not only addresses a primary problem within Enlightenment moral philosophy; it simultaneously addresses a crisis in the socioeconomic sphere: the crisis of public confidence caused by the proliferation of paper money. Smith's consideration of money in Book II of *The Wealth of Nations* (1776) worries over precisely this issue. Just as sympathy transmutes the dead into a vital moral resource, paper money has the power to "convert this dead stock [of gold and silver currency] into active and productive stock; into materials to work upon, into tools to work with, and into provisions and subsistence to work for; into stock which produces something both to himself and to his country."[28] This "conversion," however, is more properly a liberation or dispersal of hard currency into ventures abroad, which greatly diminishes the security of domestic markets. The vast network of credit within Britain, whose economy, as Linda Colley notes, was more dependent on credit than that of any of its competitors,[29] converged on the twin issues of social harmony and public confidence. Colley understands the credit system to have been a promoter of domestic peace:

> All credit systems rely on confidence, confidence that interest payments will
> be made at the correct level and at the correct time, and confidence that
> debts will ultimately be repaid. So however much they disliked particular
> administrations, creditors and many of their clients were likely to regard
> any serious breach of the peace with alarm.[30]

And with good reason, for the credit system left Britain peculiarly vulnerable to any tremor in the social body that would threaten confidence in the circulating paper currency. Smith's fantasy of the dead as the moral debtor of the nation—like the Bank of England, a "great engine of the state"—provides the nation's morality with a backing that is fixed in the native soil, that is not to be dispersed in foreign speculations.

To push the analogy further—and to refer Smith's theory of sympathy to the literary practice of his contemporaries—we find a parallel between paper currency and the proliferating texts through which sympathy circulates at mid-century; for such texts, in order to place the moral resources of the nation into circulation—in order, that is, to be credited as both sympathetic and worthy of the reader's sympathy—demand a certain confidence in their authority. This difficulty, I grant, goes unresolved within Smith's *Theory of Moral Sentiments*. But Smith's economic remedy for an analogous difficulty within the sphere of banking has resonance for the career of sympathy in the second half of the century.

In *The Wealth of Nations*, Smith claims a direct relationship between public confidence and the visibility of hard currency in circulation. For Smith, the greatest nuisance to the credit system is the activity of "beggarly bankers" issuing small notes of dubious value. To counter this danger, he advocates disallowing bank notes smaller than five pounds, the result of which will be the maintenance of gold and silver coins in circulation. The visibility of such coins, even in small denominations, would promote confidence in the edifice of credit. What Smith argues for in the economic sphere has ramifications in the moral sphere, for it suggests that an overextended system of credit—whether overextended by trivial bank notes or by trivial elegies—incurs the dangers of relativism and, eventually, bankruptcy. Smith's admonition to keep small coins in circulation suggests the importance, at once, of a national dead and a local dead; of the circulation of texts of unspecified grief circulating among the graveyard poems of Blair, Hervey, Young, and Warton; and of the simultaneous transmission of sympathies through literature and the accessibility of the dead to citizens of small literary means. The continuities between Smith's theory of morals and his theory of money are highly suggestive; both hinge on nothing less than the endurance of society. For Smith, the notion of a moral economy was not a neat metaphor for a self-enclosed system, but rather a vision of morals and economics as interpenetrating systems, alternative accounts of the vitality of the social organism. If morals could be described as the interested exchange of sympathies, then by the same token, the fate of the nation's money could be seen to rest on its moral homogeneity.

With Adam Smith we find the culmination of the philosophical trends we have been tracing in this chapter: The turn in moral philosophy from tragedy and epic to popular and feminine literary forms such as the romance and the graveyard meditation; the empiricist search for a guarantor of moral culture; the attempt to generalize from a theory of moral conversation to a theory of moral circulation. But Smith is a crucial figure for this study not simply because he resolves a major philosophical problem of the first half of the century, but also because, more than any other Enlightenment thinker in Britain, he understood the increasing centrality of mourning and sympathy to be inextricably tied to the prosperity—indeed, to the identity—of the nation.

The moral liquidity ensured by tears, of course, had its cost in human felicity; the dead, in their nearness, would press upon the living. Fifty years after Shaftesbury discredited the Christian God's "large recompense" as a "bargain of interest," Smith's *Theory of Moral Sentiments* commends death—for Smith, the premonition of being dead—as the guardian and protector of society:

> It is from this very illusion of the imagination, that the foresight of our own dissolution is so terrible to us, and that the idea of those circumstances, which undoubtedly can give us no pain when we are dead, makes us miserable while we are alive. And from thence arises one of the most important principles in human nature, the dread of death, the great poison to the happiness, but the great restraint upon the injustice of mankind; which, while it afflicts and mortifies the individual, guards and protects the society. (1:12)

In *Tristram Shandy*, which began to appear during the same year as Smith's *Theory of Moral Sentiments*, Sterne familiarly calls death the "debt to nature," an ancient locution revived by a society which knew the ledger of its debt to death.[31] As I will argue next, Smith's sense of the grave as the source of moral life parallels Gray's inquiry into the nature of virtue within the graveyard framework of the *Elegy*; by mid-century mourning and morals stood together at the grave.

Their Artless Tale

To borrow the idioms that have developed from the preceding discussion of moral philosophy, a spectator theory of morals would be sufficient to account for the experience of Pope's elegist; Gray, however, writes an elegy whose "plot" is the transformation of moral spectatorship into moral circulation. Gray's achievement is to generalize the elegy's concerns by insisting on the interpenetration of individual moral experience and the morals of culture more generally.[32]

In Gray's day, few texts circulated as often and as widely as the *Elegy*. Having been liberally shared by Walpole while still in manuscript, it was precipitately published by Gray when a magazine he disdained sought to print it. Compared favorably to *Lycidas*, it saw five editions in its first year of publication (1751) and some seven more by 1763; anthologized and translated into Latin, it was reprinted by several periodicals.[33] In his *Life of Gray*, Johnson famously summed up its popularity—"The *Churchyard* abounds with images which find a mirror in every mind, and with sentiments to which every bosom returns an echo"—taking the occasion to define the common reader as "those uncorrupted with literary prejudices . . . the refinements of subtilty and the dogmatism of learning" (470). Commonly admired, it was admired by the "common," and revered for addressing what was common to all its readers: not their mortal fate, but their propensity to be moved by the fate of others. With Johnson, as with so many readers, the *Elegy* was popular not least of all for being popular. I agree with Henry Weinfeld that "the question of popularity is in a sense *thematized* in the poem"[34] but in the present context, I look beyond what Weinfeld calls the "fame-anonymity dialectic" to examine the problematic "thee" who is said to be "mindful of the unhonoured dead" in line 93. To anticipate my conclusion, the *Elegy*'s popularity remains an ironic comment on its own thematics of circulation, about which the poem turns at line 93, and toward which it is profoundly and perspicaciously ambivalent.

As we turn from morals back to mourning, it is worth pausing over the poem's title. In the Eton manuscript, as is well known, the poem is entitled "Stanza's Wrote in a Country Church-Yard." The word "elegy" appears nowhere in this manuscript; the original version of line 82 ("The place of fame and elegy supply") read "epitaph" for elegy. In his

Memoirs, Mason claimed to have suggested the title, noting that both alternate-rhyme meter (used by Hammond in his *Love Elegies* of 1742) and its graveyard matter rendered the poem "peculiarly fit" as an elegy.[35] Whether Shenstone's sober elegies, circulating in manuscript well before their 1764 publication, were in Mason's mind is debatable, but the fact is that by 1751, Trapp's and Shenstone's desire to establish the elegy as a decorous, reflective, meditative poem larger in scope than the funereal occasion had been realized, and a particular English metric form had become associated with it. It was this new sense of an elegy with which Mason, if his account is accurate, identified Gray's "Stanza's," and to which Gray was willing to attach his poem upon publication.[36] In light of this fact, it becomes easier to distinguish Gray's poem from the grave-yard meditation, typically written in meters other than alternate-rhymed quatrains (or, in the case of Hervey's *Meditations*, in prose). Whether in fact Gray's poem has much more than iconography and moral serious-ness in common with the graveyard meditation of the 1740s is open to debate. Let us consider two points of comparison between Gray's *Elegy* and Hervey's widely read *Meditations* (1746).[37] First, while Hervey uses the dead to urge his readers to "[consider] their latter end" and become virtuous, Gray uses sympathy for the dead as a means to speculate about virtue. Second, whereas Hervey tours the graveyard, providing exem-plary or cautionary narratives about each of the interred, Gray empha-sizes the speculative nature of his thoughts about the dead, who remain types, not individuals; each speculation rapidly shifts into the mode of moral generalization. In short, the graveyard meditation typically en-shrines melancholy within the firm framework of Christian eschatology, but Gray's *Elegy* both refuses to fetishize melancholy and refuses to admit a Christian telos.

As if to exhibit these facts, Gray begins his poem during the final mo-ments of the pastoral day. While *Lycidas* substitutes a rapt vision of heavenly brilliance for the gloom of night, and even Pope begins his elegy with a gloomy vision, Gray allows the gloom to gather like a film across the eye. The famous zeugma of line four—"to darkness and to me"—signals an identification of self and darkness; like the dead, the elegist has "Left the warm precincts of the chearful day"(87). By passing from day into night, however, the elegist identifies not with death, but with mortality, with the necessity of making this passage. In its opening stan-zas, the poem repeats this passage several times:

> The curfew tolls the knell of parting day,
> The lowing herd wind slowly o'er the lea,
> The ploughman homeward plods his weary way,
> And leaves the world to darkness and to me.

Now fades the glimmering landscape on the sight,
And all the air a solemn stillness holds,
Save where the beetle wheels his droning flight,
And drowsy tinklings lull the distant folds;

Save that from yonder ivy-mantled tower
The moping owl does to the moon complain
Of such as, wandering near her secret bower,
Molest her ancient solitary reign.

Beneath those rugged elms, that yew-tree's shade,
Where heaves the turf in many a mouldering heap,
Each in his narrow cell for ever laid,
The rude forefathers of the hamlet sleep.

The breezy call of incense-breathing morn,
The swallow twittering from the straw-built shed,
The cock's shrill clarion, or the echoing horn,
No more shall rouse them from their lowly bed.

$$(1-20)^{38}$$

The "darkness" of line four gives way to "the glimmering landscape"; the "solemn stillness" of line six gives way to "droning" and "tinkling" before subsiding into the owl's complaint; while the dead are "for ever laid" to rest, their "sleep" gives way to "The breezy call of incense-breathing morn." An inventory of Gray's allusions to both *L'Allegro* and *Il Penseroso* is unnecessary here, but I would insist that by linking and interspersing such allusions, Gray allegorizes the two temperaments as successive phases of existence. Only by having assimilated the pleasures of mirth does one earn the right to deep melancholy at the thought of mortality. Gray's *Elegy*, by repeating that passage from light to darkness, day to night, mirth to melancholy, begins by distancing its own meditative rhetoric from the cult of melancholy—or at very least, by reinterpreting melancholy as a masculine topos.[39]

For gender, as always in the poetics of elegy, provides a crucial nuance: the elegist, in other words, is not meditating for the sake of "divinest Melancholy," Milton's Goddess "sage and holy," but for the sake of the "rude forefathers of the hamlet." Like the sweet prince named in this line, the elegist's melting sorrow is framed by his participation in, rather than exemption from, patriarchy.[40] The "rude forefathers" differ from the traditional elegiac object—a youthful male poet—in three ways: they are multiple, unlettered, and associated with previous generations. Whereas Hervey refers to the dead as a "congregation," emphasizing their affiliation with the nearby church, Gray's perspective is predominantly secular, concerned less with "anthem" than with "annals."

Under his speculative eye come their labor, their domestic joys and burdens; seeing more figuratively and more deeply, he surveys their potential for heroic ambition, leadership, conflict, debate, revolution, economic stewardship, "noble rage," poetic genius, ruthlessness, pride, and guilt. Their piety goes unconsidered. The allegorical personifications of Ambition, Grandeur, Honour, and Flattery are out of place here partly because they appear in the wrong register; that they flock to this Churchyard suggests the numinous vacuum which, a century later, Victorian stonecutters would populate with angels.[41] The elegist identifies with the dead *not* because he fears for their souls, and *not only* because he shares their mortal destiny, but because he identifies his society as the heir to theirs. Written by a man whom Johnson introduces as "the son of Mr. Philip Gray, a scrivener of London," the *Elegy* expresses an idealized relationship to the dead which seeks to enlarge the idea of a cultural inheritance beyond class and local boundaries.[42] Despite generations of scholars who have attempted to specify a historical churchyard in or about which the *Elegy* was written, Gray has kept it—and himself—unnamed with good reason: the sense of duty evoked in these stanzas is not a function of locality, but rather of a cultural identity here epitomized (but not exhausted) by the community constellated around the country church.[43] Whereas Pope's expended tear signifies the poet's charity for a distressed ghost, here the "passing tribute of a sigh" constitutes the fulfillment of a civic duty.

And yet, in lines 81–97, it is the tenuousness of this connection that Gray emphasizes—not the duteous tribute, but the passing sigh. Having already indicated the pompous futility of "storied urn or animated bust," Gray reveals the pathetic reductiveness of the "uncouth rhymes and shapeless sculpture":

> Their name, their years, spelt by the unlettered muse,
> The place of fame and elegy supply:
> And many a holy text around she strews,
> That teach the rustic moralist to die.
>
> For who to dumb Forgetfulness a prey,
> This pleasing anxious being e'er resigned,
> Left the warm precincts of the cheerful day,
> Nor cast one longing lingering look behind?
>
> On some fond breast the parting soul relies,
> Some pious drops the closing eye requires;
> Ev'n from the tomb the voice of nature cries,
> Ev'n in our ashes live their wonted fires.

(81–92)

Precisely when Gray altered the word "epitaph" in line 82 to "elegy" is difficult to say, but the substitution signals a concrete sense of elegiac textuality and suggests that, with Gray, the elegy had come at last within striking distance of the public virtues. Whereas Trapp considered the literatures of fame (i.e., epic and tragedy) and elegy antithetical, and Shenstone found them dialectical, Gray associates them metonymically: "Fame and elegy" alike are unavailable to the rustic dead, who are "strewn" about with didactic "holy text[s]." Bearing merely names (perhaps misspelled) and numerals, the stones pathetically constitute "the short and simple annals of the poor"; their very inadequacy to provide a link to the "rude forefathers" itself implores "the passing tribute of a sigh." Similarly, the dying depend on the tenuous reliability of "some fond breast," and can be certain only of an uncertain number of tears— "some pious drops."

Whether the stanzas before us forge a more sturdy link to the dead than those stones and these tears, is the question. By relating "their artless tale," the elegist has related us both to himself, but more urgently, to the dead; the famous crux of line 93 may perhaps be understood as the figural collapse of those relationships in a spectacular performance of sympathy. Having become literally "mindful" of the dead, we imaginatively fuse with the sympathetic teller of their artless tale, and, in so doing, find that we have joined the dead:

> For thee who, mindful of the unhonoured dead
> Dost in these lines their artless tale relate;
> If chance, by lonely Contemplation led,
> Some kindred Spirit shall inquire thy fate,
>
> Haply some hoary-headed swain may say,
> "Oft have we seen him at the peep of dawn
> "Brushing with hasty steps the dews away
> "To meet the sun upon the upland lawn.
>
> "There at the foot of yonder nodding beech
> "That wreathes its old fantastic roots so high,
> "His listless length at noontide would he stretch,
> "And pore upon the brook that babbles by.
>
> "Hard by yon wood, now smiling as in scorn,
> "Muttering his wayward fancies he would rove,
> "Now drooping, woeful wan, like one forlorn,
> "Or crazed with care, or crossed in hopeless love.
>
> "One morn I missed him on the customed hill,
> "Along the heath and near his favourite tree;

"Another came; nor yet beside the rill,
"Nor up the lawn, nor at the wood was he;

"The next with dirges due in sad array
"Slow through the church-way path we saw him borne."

(93–114)

Like Smith, Gray understands sympathy as an imaginative act; as such, sympathy is autonomous and self-authorized. While the fragility of sympathy has already been made clear, it is only by placing ourselves in the grave that we understand the possible ironies of sympathy. Hence, the same poet who begins by distancing himself from the cult of melancholy, is recalled as a melancholic madman, muttering and babbling; the same poet who "in these lines" boldly links the rustics' furrow and the paths of glory alike to the grave is described as "wayward"; the same poet whose moral experience extends beyond the boundaries of locality and class is described as "crazed with care, or crossed in hopeless love." Sympathy becomes caricature as the poetic moralist becomes an effusive, mad solipsist.

The epitaph, by attaching the poet's career to the dictates of "holy text," merely redoubles the injuries of sympathy.

> *Here rests his head upon the lap of earth*
> *A youth to fortune and to fame unknown,*
> *Fair Science frowned not on his humble birth,*
> *And Melancholy marked him for her own.*
>
> *Large was his bounty, and his soul sincere,*
> *Heaven did a recompence as largely send:*
> *He gave to Misery all he had, a tear,*
> *He gained from Heaven ('twas all he wished) a friend.*
>
> *No farther seek his merits to disclose,*
> *Or draw his frailties from their dread abode,*
> *(There they alike in trembling hope repose)*
> *The bosom of his Father and his God.*

(117–28)

Here, the poet's sympathy for the "unhonoured dead" earns him a share in their "destiny obscure." Declining to characterize him by either his merits or his frailties, the epitaph fails to remember him as a poet; in stone, he is a maker not of verse but of tears. Instead, the epitaph traces the poet's deliverance from the false goddess of melancholy to a masculine deity: "his Father and his God." Having been "marked" by Melancholy, the poet is generously depicted as passively enthralled, rather than culpable of idolatry. The stilted diction of "bounty" and "recompence," giving and gaining, returns us from the idiom of civic circulation to that of Christian compensation. In Pope's "Elegy," the poet's tear signifies his generous assumption of heaven's unpaid debt to the Lady; here, the friend bestowed by heaven signifies a divine assumption of the world's unpaid debt to the sympathetic poet. Finally, the abode that transcends local and class boundaries is not that of the nation, but that of heaven; the dead poet abides with "his Father and his God" instead of with the "rude forefathers." Ironically, Gray's *Elegy* concludes by showing how easily a philosophy of sympathy may revert into an affirmation of the Christian doctrine of heavenly recompense—the very moral impasse that prompted Shaftesbury to theorize a moral sense.[44] A testament to grace, the epitaph is not a poem so much as yet another strewn and holy text.

· · · · ·

The profound influence of Gray's *Elegy* on the poetry of the next seventy-five years, I would argue, is largely a legacy of its first two dozen stanzas. As I will show, these stanzas extended the elegy's reach beyond the private virtues to embrace the public virtues as well; by expanding the object of the poet's sympathy from the unconscious dead to the self-conscious mortal, it replaced the notion of an elegiac occasion with that of an elegiac predicament, anticipating the Coleridgean dialectic between "life-in-death" and "death-in-life." Both John Newbery, author of *Art of Poetry* (1762) and the anonymous author of "An Essay on Elegies," published in the *Annual Register* for 1767, credit Gray's *Elegy* with earning a new respect and distinction for the elegy; for Newbery, the *Elegy* is simply "one of the best that has appeared in our language, and may be justly esteemed as a masterpiece."[45] The influence of a certain strain in Gray's *Elegy* would be felt most profoundly not in poetry, but in British anti-Jacobin politics: Burke's "philosophic analogy" between "the constitution of our country" and "our dearest domestic ties," and his conceit of English society as "a permanent body composed of transitory parts" are both richly anticipated by the spectacle of Gray's elegist contemplating the graves of the "rude forefathers of the hamlet."[46]

The poem's closing stanzas, however, expose the failure of sympathy to produce a rhetoric that will on the one hand *relate* the individual to the community and, on the other, *maintain* the individual within the community.[47] Once the poet stages the performance of sympathy by substituting the dead poet for the "rude forefathers" at the center of the poem, the evidence is far more dubious about the notion of sympathy as the moral liquidity of a society. The swain's recollection and the closing epitaph provide two alternative rhetorics of sympathy, each of which caricatures the alienation between the individual mourner and the culture at large. The swain, however sympathetic to the young poet, mistakes his sober musings for unintelligible ravings, his philosophical and political meditations for erotic pain. With the exception of line 109 ("One morn I missed him,") the swain speaks in the first person plural, as though speaking on behalf of the community; the youth frequents neither village, nor churchyard, but the nodding beeches, babbling brooks, woods, hills, heaths, trees, rills, and lawns that afford him a desired solitude. At home in nature, he exists at the margins of culture. Only in death does he rejoin the community centered on the church, his waywardness corrected by the "church-way path" down which he is borne. While the swain's words caricature the effusive poetry of melancholy, they also caricature the community's anxiety about this eccentric and wayward rhetoric, for the effusive, melancholic poet and the pious, narrow community are antithetical. The epitaph, on the other hand, relates the consequences of surrendering melancholic eccentricity to the centricity of inherited culture. Once buried in the churchyard, the youth's memory is awkwardly lashed to the "holy texts" strewn among the gravestones. The epitaph, by generalizing the youth's origins, predicament, and destiny, transforms his memory into a cultural artifact.

At mid-century, Gray's *Elegy* defines an uneasy and precarious position for the elegy between the marginalized rhetoric of the effusion and the traditional rhetoric of the epitaph. In so doing, it anticipates two competing strategies for authorizing elegiac poetry that will emerge in the second half of the century: on the one hand, defending the representation of grief by appeal to the cult of sincerity, and on the other, defending the elegiac text by appeal to its epitaphic, documentary affinities. The next major development in literary mourning—the elegiac sonnets of the 1780s and 1790s—would attempt to exploit as authorizing strategies the two rhetorical positions that for Gray represent the ironies of sympathy.

TWO

WRITTEN WAILINGS

The agony of grief which overpowered them at first, was voluntarily renewed, was sought for, was created again and again. They gave themselves up wholly to their sorrow, seeking increase of wretchedness in every reflection that could afford it, and resolved against ever admitting consolation in future.

(Jane Austen, *Sense and Sensibility*)

The Rhetoric of Sentiment

D URING the latter half of the eighteenth century, the fortunes of Elegia rose considerably. Gray's *Elegy*, by evincing both a collective, public object of mourning and a communal mourning persona, garnered a new esteem for literary mourning. In the pages of the *Annual Register*, Gray was credited with immeasurably broadening the elegy's scope:

> Elegy, it must be confessed, has often extended her province. . . . [a]s in the celebrated poem of Mr. Gray, written in a church-yard. For though she is generally the selfish mourner of domestic distress, whether it be upon the loss of a friend, or disappointment in love; she sometimes enlarges her reflections upon universal calamities, and with a becoming dignity, as in the inspired writers, pathetically weeps over the fall of nations.[1]

In 1711, as in the epigraph to the previous chapter, Richard Steele might mock a tradesman's wife as she laments a death in the house of Austria. But in the second half of the century, mourning for the remote in time and place was thought to signify moral elevation; sympathy for "the dead" had become the prerogative of ladies-in-waiting and tradesmen's wives alike.

While the elegy's extended purview earned it a new moral seriousness, the evocation of pathos took on a central role in the theory of rhetoric. George Campbell's *Philosophy of Rhetoric* (1776), the first comprehensive epistemological rhetoric, conceives of a gap, traditionally unacknowledged in rhetorical theory, between the conviction of the understanding and the persuasion of the will. Between the faculties of understanding and will, which Campbell believes to operate first and last, respectively, in the mental machine being persuaded, lie the faculties of the imagination (also called fancy) and the passions, which take on unprecedented importance in inducing the will toward the performance of a desired action. These faculties assume central importance in Campbell's rhetoric because their operation—or, more properly, *coop-eration*—encompasses that of the individual's moral sense. The virtues, writes Campbell,

> have this in common with passion. They necessarily imply an habitual propensity to a certain species of conduct, an habitual aversion to the con-trary: a veneration for such a character, an abhorrence of such another. They are, therefore, though not passions, so closely related to them, that they are properly considered as motives to action, being equally capable of giving an impulse to the will. . . . Accordingly, what is addressed solely to the moral powers of the mind, is not so properly denominated the pa-thetic, as the *sentimental*. The term, I own, is rather modern, but is never-theless convenient, as it fills a vacant room, and doth not, like most of our newfangled words, justle out older and worthier occupants, to the no small detriment of the language. It occupies, so to speak, the middle place be-tween the pathetic and that which is addressed to the imagination, and partakes of both.[2]

According to Campbell, one addresses the "moral powers of the mind" through rhetoric that calls emphatically on the faculties of imagination and the passions. For Adam Smith, the phenomenon of sympathy occu-pies the "middle place" between the imagination and the passions, the "vacant room" which Campbell assigns to the moral discourse of senti-ment. Smith, lecturing on rhetoric and belles lettres at Glasgow during the 1750s and 1760s, demonstrates the centrality of poetry in the rheto-ric of sentiment.[3] With the belletristic rhetorics of Smith and Hugh Blair, the previously "vacant room" of moral sentiment becomes filled with literary mourners.

During an era in which literary grief played so large a role in the moral life of the nation—was even equated, as Smith's *Theory of Moral Senti-ments* suggests, with the nation's moral liquidity—it is hardly surprising that attention should be turned to the rhetorical power to arouse sympa-thy. The belletristic criticism of the 1760s, 1770s, and 1780s, at once descriptive and prescriptive, offers an elaborate rhetoric of the elegy—a set of standards by which the persuasiveness of elegiac poetry can be judged. What emerges in these documents is an anxiety about such power, a sense that the rhetorical appeal to moral sentiment (through elegiac beauty and pathos) requires buttressing with other kinds of ap-peals. While Campbell's epistemological rhetoric theorizes alternately that the arousal of passions is the focus and the foundation of persuasion[4], belletristic criticism implicitly places the appeal to the passions in a familiar Aristotelian framework. Hence the appeal to the passions is mediated not by the other faculties per se, but by the traditional rhetorical appeals of *ethos* and *logos*. The moral necessity of evoking a pathetic response evokes emphases on the authority of the elegiac speaker (ethos) and on the authority of the elegiac text (logos). And, consistent with Smith's theory of sympathy, both authorizing appeals, in different ways, evoke the moral authority of the dead.

Ethos and *Logos*

As John Young, author of the Johnsonian *Criticism on the Elegy in a Country Church Yard* (1783), notes, the word "elegy" in the title of Gray's poem subjected it to "severer rules of criticism" than it would have met with had it borne a less generic title.[5] Whereas the chief elegiac "rule of criticism" for Trapp and Shenstone had been sobriety, now it had become sincerity, the ability of the elegiac text to persuade the reader of the elegist's grief. What Young fails to acknowledge is that such theoretical "rules of criticism" were largely derived from Gray's complex elegiac practice. Young's insistence on sincerity, in part, reveals anxiety about the extension of a form associated with privacy, domesticity, and femininity to more worldly, philosophical issues. Shenstone's observation that elegy "throws its melancholy stole over pretty different objects" (1:4) was unthreatening so long as those objects were pretty, trivial, or personal. "Elegy," in the words of the *Annual Register* essayist, ". . . has often extended her province, and the moral contemplations of the poet have sometimes worn her melancholy garb"(2:221). But once the moral and mortal contemplations of elegy became recognized as a rhetorical form, what was to ensure that Elegia not exchange her "melancholy garb" for flashier, more fashionable apparel?

The anxiety surrounding the extension of elegy's purview from private to public virtues coalesces around the issue of publishing grief. Critical qualms about sincerity reveal a residual uneasiness about the manliness of publicizing displays of emotion. Gray's *Elegy*, which bore a specious advertisement by Walpole (as "Editor") apologizing to the author for publishing his privately circulated poem, set a precedent for satisfying this critical qualm. But a generation after Gray's *Elegy* was published, Young rails against writers who persist in ignoring the impropriety of pressing the elegiac tear "on the general eye":

> If the writers of studied seriousness, and recorders of premeditated griefs, would employ one half of the time spent in preparing their sadnesses for the

public eye, in examining into the propriety of introducing them to the public at all, the journals of poetry would be less disgraced than they are with the *balance* of affectation against nature. . . . The sorrow, that is sorrow indeed, asks for not prompting. It comes without a call. It courts not admiration. It presses not on the general eye; but hastens under covert, and wails its widowhood alone. Its strong-hold is the heart. There it remains close curtained; *unseeing, unseen.* Delicacy and taste recoil at the publications of internal griefs. They profane the hallowedness of secret sadness; and suppose selected and decorated expression compatible with the prostration of the soul. (10–11)

Young's emphasis on "selected and decorated expression" both degrades elegiac rhetoric and acknowledges its profound influence. Young and others attempt the paradoxical project of offering an antirhetorical rhetoric of elegy; a set of standards that insists on a foundational sincerity—an authentic grief—and yet offers ways in which a poem can persuade a reader of sincerity *whether or not an authentic grief exists.*

To insist that the elegy was not written for publication, but was a spontaneous outpouring became a favored strategy. Like the tears it was ostensibly documenting, the elegy was customarily associated with fluidity. In 1712, Trapp had noted the elegy "to flow in one even Current" (167) aligning it with poetry's power to diffuse itself "like the Ocean . . . by a Variety of Channels, into Rivers, Fountains, and the remotest Springs"; Shenstone in the 1740s had characterized its style as "diffuse" and "flowing"; for Newbery, the elegy is "smooth and flowing"(70); for the *Annual Register* essayist, "flowing and harmonious"(2:221). Gray's desultory *Elegy,* according to Young, adulterates the desired fluidity of elegy. In 1755, Johnson's *Dictionary* would emphasize the elegy's fluency by defining *elegy* as "a short poem without points or turns." The term "Effusion," which Johnson used to say what *Lycidas* was *not,* had begun to be paired with "elegy" in the third quarter of the century and was the title Coleridge preferred for his elegiac sonnets of the 1790s. This common association of elegy with fluidity gives metaphoric life to the notion of sympathy as moral liquidity. By Goldsmith, this sea of tears was satirically observed to have depleted the nation's sentimental reserves: to the offer of an elegy, Dr. Primrose replies, "I have wept so much at all sorts of elegies of late that without an enlivening glass I am sure this will overcome me. . . ."[6]

In a similar vein, Young's antirhetorical rhetoric assails the preposterousness of "written wailings": "Who is there that says, or would be endured to say, 'I will take me pen, ink and paper, and get me out into a church-yard, and there write me an elegy; for *I do well to be melancholy?*'" (10) According to Young, Gray even *laid* his Meditation, at a time with which the idea of the operation of writing was incompatible. The "parting day;" the "glimmering landscape fading on the sight;" the "plowman returning home, and leaving the world to darkness;" are images consistent with the suppositions of a *thinking* muser, but irreconcileable with the process of *writing*, or even scrawling. (12)

As Trapp and Shenstone had attested, Elegia had not always worn widow's weeds; now she was repeatedly exhorted to dress simply and decently.[7] Newbury warns that the elegy, although "sweet and engaging, elegant and attractive," and "captivat[ing]," must forfeit frippery: "Elegy rejects whatever is facetious, satirical, or majestic, and is content to be plain, decent and unaffected. . . ."[8]

For the essayist of the *Annual Register*, the affected, overfigured elegies of his contemporaries are the subject of satire:

> The plaintive muse is generally represented to us, as *Passis elegia capillis*[;] as one that discards all shew, and appears in dishevelled locks; but the politer moderns are for putting her hair into papers; and whether the complaint turns upon the death of a friend, or the loss of a mistress, the passion must stand still, till the expression is got ready to introduce it. When we are truly affected, we have no leisure to think of art. . . . Then our language is unadorned, and unembarrassed with epithets; and perhaps, in that book, in which there are more instances of true and sublime simplicity, as in all the ancients together, there are less epithets to be met with than in any authors whatever. (2:220–21)

The ludicrous vision of the plaintive muse in curling papers is a fitting image for the ludicrousness of elegiac affectation. In such texts, not only does Elegia preen herself for public view; she also shows her primping hand. Pastoral elegy, its popularity reaching a nadir, is taken to epitomize poetry in which figures and allusions belie the claimed urgency of elegiac grief. Comparing the speaker of Gray's *Elegy* to Virgil's Corydon, Young parenthetically faults Virgil for "degrading [Corydon's] soliloquy into a *pastoral*" (6). Johnson, measuring *Lycidas*'s mournful rhetoric against its "remote allusions and obscure opinions," concludes of the poem's learnedness that "He who thus grieves will excite no sympathy."[9] Johnson's objection to *Lycidas* is premised on an assumption that the poem's allusiveness compromises the elegist's sincerity, the basis of his authorizing *ethos*; by Johnson's reasoning, one cannot be "mindful" of the dead and of Virgil at the same time.

But an alternative line of argument about elegiac rhetoric focuses not on the writer's authority but rather on that of the text; not on an appeal to *ethos*, but on an appeal to *logos*.[10] Whereas the appeal to *ethos* hinges on the writer's insistent concern with the dead, the appeal to *logos* rests on the text's affinities to literary tradition. To allude to Virgil, or even to emphasize the text's affinities to traditional generic categories, is to authorize the text through its relation to the literature of the past.

One symptom of the appeal to *logos* is the emphasis on affinities between elegy and epitaph, a poetic tradition of mortal inscription. For Young, the epitaphic quality of elegy could frankly redress the perennial problem of elegiac sincerity. Young would point to the case of Littleton, whose much-read elegy on the death of his wife endured like a monument in a world in which Littleton himself eventually remarried—presumably, with some embarrassment. That the poet may, like Littleton, survive his grief was a problem, though in the unusual case of Gray: "Whatever part self-deception or affectation may have originally had in the matter . . . [t]he features of his mind plied gradually to the cast of the mould his imagination had formed for it" (3). Gray's *Elegy*, after all, featured an explicitly epitaphic closure. While in 1712 Trapp had ranked the elegy between epigram and pastoral, Newbery in 1762 placed it between *epitaph* and pastoral in an extended list of poetic types; by 1787, Henry Headley would combine elegies and epitaphs under a single heading in his anthology *Select Beauties of Ancient English Poetry*.

Published during a period when generic rankings were becoming increasingly flexible and improvisational, Gray's *Elegy* also established the elegy's affinities to precisely those esteemed genres with which it had formerly been contrasted. As Gray's use of the churchyard as a synecdoche for the nation gained in influence, sublimity, once explicitly said to be beyond Elegia's reach, now seemed practically within her grasp. Newbery goes so far as to observe that "even the epic poem, with all its dignity, has sometimes the plaintive strain of the elegy" (155). The elegy's affinities to other genres are suggested in discussions of elegiac meter. While the elegiac quatrain remained the most popular form for explicitly elegiac poetry in the 1750s, 1760s and 1770s, it receives a new pedigree. Shenstone credits Hammond's *Love Elegies* as the source of the elegiac quatrain, but three decades later the *Annual Register* essayist would take it back to Dryden:

> The elegy, ever since Mr. Gray's excellent one in the church-yard, has been in alternate rhime, which is by many ridiculously imagined to be a new measure adapted to plaintive subject, introduced by that ingenious author, whereas it is heroic verse, and to be met with in Dryden's Annus Mirabilis. (2:221)

The same essayist recognizes a variety of other verse forms as "this kind of poetry":

The couplet is equally proper for this kind of poetry, as the alternate rhyme; and though Gray and Hammond have excelled in the last, Pope's elegy on the death of an unfortunate young lady will prove those numbers equally expressive and harmonious; nor shall I doubt to place our English ballads, such as have been written by Rowe, Gay and the natural, easy Shenstone, in the rank of elegy; as they partake more the simple pathetic, and display the real feelings of the heart, with less parade, than those affected compositions of classical labour. (2:221–22)

Despite his praise for Pope, the essayist makes clear that the problem of approximating the Latin elegiac distich in English was not solved by taut, highly wrought Popean couplets. Shenstone had already found the couplet inappropriate for elegy, since its frequent rhymes made for "scanty or constrained" expression. (*Lycidas*, by contrast, is said to feature rhymes too far apart for the ear to detect.) The alternate-rhymed quatrain was seen to mimic the diffuse, flowing quality of the elegy by lengthening the interval between a given rhyme, though Shenstone admitted that some might find it "too lax and prosaic." Young, for his part, disdains the alternate-rhymed stanza, which "possesses all the imperfections of blank verse, acquired with all the labour of rhime."

While the *Annual Register* essayist emphasizes the elegiac quality of "simple and pathetic" ballad form, Young, at the other end of the metric spectrum, observes that, "It is somewhat surprising that blank verse, improper in almost all other subjects, should never have been thought of as a vehicle for that species of excursive thinking which prevails so much in the elegiac strain"(7). Young's observation suggests an analogy between "the elegiac strain" and "that species of excursive thinking" found in the blank verse tradition of topographical poetry.[11] It also anticipates by two decades the flowering of elegiac blank verse in a topographical poem explicitly concerned with loss and its "abundant recompense"—published in 1798, Wordsworth's *Lyrical Ballads* would close with the consolations of "Tintern Abbey"—and by three decades the "excursive thinking" of Wordsworth's eponymous epic. But Wordsworth seems to have realized that accommodating blank verse within the literary house of mourning would mean evicting the metric form that, by the 1790s, had become its most clamorous resident—the ubiquitous elegiac sonnet; hence, the famous attack on Gray's "Sonnet on the Death of Richard West" in the Preface to the 1800 *Lyrical Ballads*. What Wordsworth was attacking, as I will argue shortly, was the Sonnet's failure *as rhetoric*; ten years before *Lyrical Ballads*, Wordsworth himself had written a sonnet impugning the ability of the elegiac sonnet to move its audience through pathos all the way to moral action.

But before discussing the elegiac sonnet and its discontents, we need to assess the implications of these various gestures extending Elegia's style, range, scope, occasions, and forms. What emerges from the critical discussion following Gray's *Elegy* is a shift from the formal discourse of "the elegy" to a modal discourse of "the elegiac." The rhetoric of elegy, in other words, had given the lie to a certain formalism and occasioned an alternative discourse in which "the elegiac" became an attribute of other belletristic forms or genres. Elegia, in wedding other forms, genres, and discourses, was to assume other names.

This development of the 1760s and 1770s coincides with a nascent English literary historicism that gradually begins to replace the French-influenced generic approaches of the first half of the century. In these literary histories and anthologies, the inventors of the literary dead typically pose as mourners erecting monuments to a lost heritage. One hardly needs to remark on the use of elegiac and epitaphic topoi in these works, so spectacularly are they displayed. Bishop Percy, for example, called his collection of "Ancient" English poems *Reliques* (1765). Thomas Warton, in *The History of English Poetry* (1775), regards poetry as "faithfully recording [and preserving] the features of the times," and of "transmitting to posterity genuine delineations of life in its simplest stages."[12] A glance at the title page of Headley's *Select Beauties of Ancient Poetry* reveals a weeping willow, a rectangular tomb bearing the inscription "*non omnis moriar*," and a subtitular epigraph by Davenant: "The monument of banish'd mindes." For Headley, to construct a literary history of English poetry, was to enshrine and entomb it:

> [I]s there not something that holds out a strong incentive to the lore of fame and the cultivation of the mind, when we thus see its works, though shrouded by occasional depressions, yet resting on the rock of Truth, insensible, as it were, to the lapse of Time and the wrecks of years, and surmounting at last every impediment, while the body to which they belonged has for ages been the plaything of the winds, or hardened with the clod of the valley?[13]

While the poet decays, the text endures, "resting on the rock of Truth" marking the place once occupied by the poet.

Headley, an anthologist rather than a narrative historian, finds himself in the peculiar position of trying to build a monument without a corpse to inter; constructing such a corpse would become his anthological work. Ten years before Mary Shelley's birth, Headley describes himself as an "anatomist" fashioning a composite corpse.

> Yet in thus playing the anatomist, every one who has sensibility, must, more or less, feel a melancholy reluctance at rejecting too fastidiously: the very reflection that the writers of these works upon which we now calmly sit in

judgment, have no longer the power of personally pleading for themselves, the temporary supports of prejudice, patronage and fashion, have long subsided forever; that in composing them, they might have forfeited their time, their future, and their health, and on many of those passages which we now by a random stroke of the pen deprive men of, might have fondly hoped to build their immortality; affords an irresistibly affecting specimen of the instability and hazard of human expectations. With the "disjecti membra poetae" before me, let me be pardoned then, if I have sometimes, as I fear I have, listened to the captivating whispers of mercy instead of the cool dictates of unsentimental criticism. (xi–xii)

But instead of emphasizing his invention of the corpus, Headley portrays himself as a mourner for the once-whole and vital body of English verse. His description of his labors focuses not on the hubristic satisfactions of construction, but on the pathos of "anatomizing" or dissecting; by excluding various "disjecti membra poetae," he consigns them to their "former oblivion." In a desultory meditation on the universal desire for immortality, the leveling accomplished by death, the lost labors of the unremembered dead, and "the instability and hazard of human expectations," Headley exhibits his own sympathy for the members of the corpus. On the basis of such sympathy, he asks to be indulged for listening to the "captivating" (a word Newbery and Trapp associate with elegy) appeal of mercy instead of the "cool dictates of unsentimental criticism." In the preface to *Select Beauties*, Headley's ostentatious sympathy asks English readers to read these poems as the relics of their own predecessors, identifying readers, editor, and corpus as part of a single literary community. Furthermore, it offers the corpus Headley has constructed as the natural guarantor of England's literary preeminence. Constructing "the dead," in elegiac literary history as in elegiac poetry, was a way of ensuring the moral consensus of the nation. As Shenstone writes of his own elegiac allusions to English texts, "[the author] builds his edifice with the materials of his own nation" (1:11).

Weeping in Vain

Curran has called Gray's "Sonnet [on the Death of Mr. Richard West]," published posthumously in 1775, "the motive force underlying the entire Romantic revival of the sonnet."[14] Ironically, the poem is perhaps more famous today as Wordsworth's unseemly display of the inheritance he chose to forfeit, that "large portion of phrases and figures of speech which from father to son have long been regarded as the common inheritance of Poets."[15] Wordsworth's announced forfeiture of Gray's legacy is disingenuous, not least because he would use the Sonnet's central figure of thought, the elegiac topos of the failed response, as the motivating trope of the Intimations Ode. But let us consider his objections, for a moment, on their own terms. Wordsworth's "canon of criticism" for deciding which of Gray's lines have "any value" is a distaste for a highly figured style that distances Gray's poem from "the language of prose when prose is well written"(1:132). The difference between Gray's poetry and Wordsworth's own, it appears, is the difference between "tears 'such as Angels weep' " and "natural and human tears"; what Wordsworth wants coursing through his poems are the "vital juices" of prose, for "the same human blood circulates through the veins of them both [poetry and prose]" (1:287). With such metaphors of lost fathers, human tears, and circulating blood, Wordsworth sacrifices Gray—and with him, the rhetorical tradition of the elegiac sonnet—so that the vitality of his own pathetic poetry may emerge. We must observe the strikingly sentimental terms in which Wordsworth announces that Gray is lost to the cause of poetry (as Francis Jeffrey would, in 1814, announce of Wordsworth). Such an announcement focuses on the divergence between Gray's putative rhetorical ambition—to evoke pathos—and the rhetorical effect of his inherited diction—to alienate the reader. When Wordsworth claims that Gray's style devalues his poem, his attack focuses on a gap between Gray's claimed sincerity and his artfulness. For Wordsworth, the ethical and logical appeals of Gray's poems compete with and finally undermine one another.

I think the opposite case can be made for Gray's Sonnet: that his logical appeal to literary tradition enhances, rather than undermines, his ethical appeal to sincerity. Making this case demands a more complex account than Wordsworth's of the fabulous reflexivity which was Gray's legacy to the elegiac sonneteers of the 1770s, 1780s, and 1790s—a reflexivity which Wordsworth mistook for solipsism. The matter, then, is not how Gray's rhetoric failed him, but rather what Gray stood to *gain* for his elegiac ethos by writing an Italian sonnet in an elevated, Miltonic diction. I want to suggest that Gray's Sonnet, in its form and its diction, alludes to a double inheritance—to the reflexive sonnets of Shakespeare, and to Milton's great elegies for paradise.

Writing in 1742 when it was unlikely that he had been exposed to Hammond's and Shenstone's elegiac quatrains, Gray composes alternate-rhyme quatrains within the framework of the Italian sonnet. But Gray's approach to the sonnet, reminiscent of that of the Renaissance "Englishers" Wyatt and Surrey, adapts the scheme and structure of the Italian sonnet to the uninflected fingertips of English words:

In vain to me the smiling mornings shine,
And reddening Phoebus lifts his golden Fire:
The birds in vain their amorous Descant join;
Or cheerful fields resume their green attire:
These ears, alas! for other notes repine,
A different object do these eyes require.
My lonely anguish melts no heart but mine;
And in my breast the imperfect joys expire.
Yet morning smiles the busy race to cheer,
And new-born pleasure brings to happier men:
The fields to all their wonted tribute bear:
To warm their little loves the birds complain:
I fruitless mourn to him that cannot hear,
And weep the more because I weep in vain.

A belated adapter, Gray reaches back through Shakespeare and Surrey to retrieve the octet-sestet structure of the Italians (and Wyatt); by so doing, he retains the Elizabethan quatrain, doubling it to form the octet (abababab); the sestet suggests an additional expanded quatrain (cdcdcd).

Gray's elegiac sonnet draws a portion of its force from the reflexive, epideictic tradition in which Joel Fineman has so brilliantly situated Shakespeare's sonnets.[16] Fineman's study of Shakespeare's rhetorical subjectivity suggests a reading of Gray's Sonnet as a melancholy blazon for a shattered self. Whereas humanity and nature are represented as collective and unconscious, the elegist is so isolated in self-consciousness that he cannot manage to collect himself for representation, torn asunder as he is into discrete ears, eyes, heart, and breast. To be in disharmony with the season is a topos used by medieval and Renaissance elegists alike; the elegist of *Lycidas*, desiring to "shatter your leaves before the mellowing year" provides an unusually violent example (and perhaps, by Milton's day, some violence is needed to render the topos even remotely moving). But Gray adapts this painful knowledge of nature's indifference by multiplying the sites of pain to suggest a profundity of feeling.

Lamenting a "fruitless" mourning, Gray's Sonnet also alludes powerfully to a Miltonic tradition of alienated reflexivity: Adam's lament for the Divine Presence following the fall:

> and if by prayer
> Incessant I could hope to change the will
> Of him who all things can, I would not cease
> To weary him with my assiduous cries:
> But prayer against his absolute Decree

No more avails than breath against the wind,
Blown stifling back on him that breathes it forth:
Therefore to his great bidding I submit.

(*PL* XI 307–14)[17]

Adam's lament goes on to catalogue the sites in the landscape—"this Mount," "this Tree," "these Pines," "this Fountain," "So many grateful Altars"—which, were he not expelled, he would revisit with his sons. For Adam's memorial tour of the lamented "Presence Divine," Gray substitutes the sites on his body—ears, eyes, heart, breast—which had once enjoyed the presence of his lamented friend. Whereas a young poet is typically mourned in pastoral elegy, Gray has chosen to mourn in West a young critic, an idealized reader whose death threatens to leave Gray's own poetic fruitfulness fallen, blasted. And yet Gray deemphasizes the identity of the lost West, telling us that losing him means losing Paradise; and that losing Paradise, for this Adam, means ending one's conversations with God. Nature's indifference, in this context, suggests its immunity to this personal fall; the birds persist in their amorous descants while the poet, "fruitless," mourns. Reiterating the vanity of his utterance in the final line of his poems, Gray's reflexivity becomes textual as well as psychological, at once logical and ethical. The first appearance of the word "I" in line thirteen at last signals a consciousness that represents—in the triple absence of a compassionate natural world, a sympathetic community and "him, that cannot hear"—the only possible ear for Gray's poetry.

Curran's reading of Gray's Sonnet as an "encoded" and "suppressed record of his unfulfilled secret life"[18] enhances our understanding of Gray's legacy. The provocative reticence of his sonnet—the "amorous Descant" and "little Loves" of the birds; the poet's melting and "fruitlessness"; even the lifting and "reddening" of Phoebus's fire—would come to exemplify an urgently suggested, but always inexplicit, context for grief. Death is never mentioned in the poem; both the precise nature and the occasion of the poet's anguish remain unspecified. One surmises that Mason's posthumous title was his only recourse for distinguishing this poem from a lover's complaint; West's death would be sufficient grounds for the poet's consummate anguish.

But what is boldest in this poem is not its admission of homoerotic loss into the elegiac tradition, but its admission that we learn how to grieve from the poets—specifically, from a pair of grieving fathers. Drydenic pedigrees aside, with a mere sonnet Gray places elegiac poetry firmly in the line of the lyrical Shakespeare and the epic Milton. His appeals to ethos and pathos, far from being mutually undermining, as Wordsworth judged them to be, are complementary, inventing a rhetoric whose very ethos lies in twinned traditions of impassioned loss. It was Gray's genius to render ethos and logos—counter to the prevailing wisdom of the day—inseparable.

Elegiac Sonnets

Coleridge, introducing an untitled collection of sonnets by several hands in 1796, derives his definition of the sonnet—"a small poem, in which some lonely feeling is developed"[19]—from the respective practices of Charlotte Smith and William Lisle Bowles. From Gray's Sonnet, Smith and Bowles received the impetus to represent a self deeply involved in an unspecified grief by means of broad, sometimes attributed, allusions to Shakespeare, Milton, and—not surprisingly—Gray himself. (Bowles sets one sonnet "Far from the stormy world's tumultuous roar"; Smith footnotes the line "And fruitless call on him—'who cannot hear'" to "*Gray's exquisite Sonnet*; in reading which it is impossible not to regret that he wrote only one.") While Smith and Bowles use the Elizabethan, rather than the Italian, sonnet form, Bowles in particular exploits the final couplet to achieve, following Gray, reflexive echoes:

> Like melodies which mourn upon the lyre,
> Wak'd by the breeze, and as they mourn, expire.
>> (Sonnet III [second edition])

> Ah! beauteous views, that hope's fair gleams the while,
> Should smile like you, and perish as they smile!
>> (Sonnet VII [second edition])

> Now here remov'd from ev'ry human ill,
> Her woes are buried, and her heart is still.
>> (Sonnet XII [first edition])

> Ah! be the spot by passing pity blest,
> Where, hush'd to long repose, the wretched rest.
>> (revised as Sonnet XV [second edition])[20]

With the sonnets of Smith and Bowles, it had become clear that Gray's Sonnet, in its reflexivity, allusiveness, indirectness, and contraction, had vastly expanded the purview of elegiac poetry in the closing decades of the century.

Smith and Bowles published their sonnets in cycles; according to Smith, each individual sonnet explores a "single sentiment" or moment in the complex and continuous emotional experience represented by the cycle as a whole. By so doing, Smith and Bowles, as Coleridge put it, "first made the Sonnet popular among the present English," and apparently *kept* it popular: Smith's *Elegiac Sonnets, and other Essays* (1784) went into its tenth edition in 1811, a decade after her death; Bowles's *Fourteen Sonnets, Elegiac and Descriptive* (1789) saw nine editions in fifteen years.[21] But the remarkable popularity of Smith's and Bowles's sonnets had several consequences. Just as Gray's *Elegy* both evoked concerns about the generic integrity of the elegy and licensed generic hybrids, the demand for subsequent editions requiring revision, amendment, and augmentation severely strained the unitary conceit of the sonnet cycle. The addition of new sonnets over a period of years, all ostensibly alluding to the same source of grief, called for new prefaces which would attest even more adamantly to the constancy and continuity of the poet's grief. In successive editions, both Bowles's and Smith's prefatory claims escalate, early poems are answered by later ones, and later poems are inflected by earlier ones.

In the course of its increasingly public career, the cumulative sonnet cycle undergoes a shift from the emotional unity of lyric into the dynamic transformations of narrative. A generation after Smith and Bowles, the legacy of their autobiographical narratives would appear anew in the elegiac biographies that form the center of Wordsworth's *Excursion*.[22] But what these sonnet cycles narrate, finally, is the difficulty of authorizing their pathetic appeal through ethical and logical strategies. The revisions prompted by these cycles' phenomenal popularity perplexed Smith's and Bowles's ability to assimilate ethical and logical appeals to the task of arousing pathos. The narratives of difficulty that emerge from these cycles, however, point in strikingly different directions. Whereas Smith's sonnets come to indict the moral authority of her audience, Bowles's sonnets come to invoke the moral authority of God. In each case, as we shall see, the decorum of the pathetic appeal is violated.

. . . . .

Smith's preface to the first edition of *Elegiac Sonnets* (1784) decorously establishes her intention to circulate her sonnets among a circle of intimates. Like Gray, however, she was forced to publish them when "they found their way into the prints of the day in a mutilated state" (1:iv). While not identifying the cause of her misery, she insists that "Some very melancholy moments have been beguiled by expressing in verse the sensations *those moments* brought" (my emphasis) (1:iv). In her preface to the third edition, Smith insists that the added sonnets are not necessarily new; she has augmented the volume with "Sonnets I have written since, or have recovered from my acquaintance, to whom I had given them without thinking well enough of them at the time to preserve any copies myself" (1:v). In her preface to the sixth edition, she inscribes possible objections from the audience within her text. A "friend" has advised her to include some poems "of a more lively cast"; " 'Toujours perdrix,' said my friend . . . ne vaut rien":

> "Alas!" replied I, "Are grapes gathered from thorns, or figs from thistles?" Or can the *effect* cease, while the *cause* remains? You know that when in the Beech Woods of Hampshire, I first struck the chords of the melancholy lyre, its notes were never intended for the public ear! It was unaffected sorrows drew them forth: I wrote mournfully because I was unhappy—And I have unfortunately no reason yet, though nine years have since elapsed, to *change my tone.* (1:x–xi)

Not until the sixth edition does Smith specify the continuing cause of her unhappiness: her disappointment by " 'the Honourable Men' who, *nine years ago*, undertook to see that my family obtained the provision their grandfather designed for them." But in closing, she alludes to other "domestic and painful" circumstances which must remain private—and no wonder; what place was there in an elegiac sonnet for a wastrel husband in debtor's prison, assiduously maintaining a relentless and legal claim on one's earnings?

In the early editions of *Elegiac Sonnets*, Smith frames her authorizing claim to a continuing, private source of pain within a variety of allusions to literary precursors. Like Hume and Gray, Smith understood our affections to be a dialogue between personal experience and the "intercourse of sentiments" that occurs in culture. Moreover, as a published sentimental novelist, Smith had no doubt that her own mourning was mediated by a culture that valued sensibility and melancholy. The cycle's opening manifesto of sincerity reviews the "cost" of the "Muse's favours":

> The partial Muse, has from my earliest hours
> Smiled on the rugged path I'm doom'd to tread,
> And still with sportive hand has snatch'd wild flowers,
> To weave fantastic garlands for my head:
> But far, far happier is the loss of those
> Who never learn'd her dear delusive art;
> Which, while it decks the head with many a rose,
> Reserves the thorn, to fester in the heart.
> For still she bids soft Pity's melting eye
> Stream o'er the ills she knows not to remove,
> Points every pang, and deepens every sight
> Of mourning friendship, or unhappy love.
> Ah! then, how dear the Muse's favours cost,
> *If those paint sorrow best—who feel it most!*
>
> (Sonnet I)

The muse's gift—fantastic garlands for the head—exacts its price in the heart's pain. Smith conceives of the burden of melancholy as a mark of her learning, her literacy; unlike Hume, she conceives of the unlettered classes as exempt from the cultural intercourse of "sentiments." (In another sonnet, the sight of a shepherd calls forth both the reflection that he has never felt the indignities she has, and that "those fine feelings" are "children of Sentiment and Knowledge born" [Sonnet IX].) The self-authorizing final couplet, by echoing the conclusion of Pope's *Eloisa to Abelard*, declares the inextricability of Smith's mourning from literary grief. At its extreme, this allusion to prior mourners involves the appropriation of a literary mourner's voice. The very counterfeiting of grief that Hutcheson had deemed a moral threat and Young had disdained is here redeemed with a known context—only now the context itself is also counterfeit. Smith offers, for example, a series of suicidal sonnets "supposed to be spoken by Werther," which was expanded in subsequent editions, as well as another series based on Petrarch's sonnets. She even includes a series of sonnets spoken by a character in her own novel, *Celestina*. Smith's appropriation of her own novelistic voice underscores the highly mediated quality of her elegiac laments.

In later editions, however, Smith betrays a sense of alienation from the texts of her own mourning. For Smith, revising her sonnets for yet another edition, a sense of divergence begins to intrude between the pain she claims still to feel and that rendered in the sonnets. Her sonnets, she avers defensively, have not exhausted her well of grief. In the later sonnets Fancy, like Sleep and Hope, becomes increasingly a delusive, mirthful, even seductive betrayer of the grieving poet. Volume one of the fifth edition concludes with a sonnet that begins:

> No more my wearied soul attempts to stray
> From sad reality and vain regret,
> Nor courts enchanting fiction to allay
> Sorrow that sense refuses to forget:
> For of calamity so long the prey,
> Imagination now has lost her powers,
> Nor will her fairy loom again essay
> To dress affliction in a robe of flowers.

> (Sonnet XLVIII)

These flowers that "dress affliction" seem to be thornless, as if plucked from a fantasy of Eden. Smith seems to be registering her sonnets' disappointment of the "rules of criticism" by which sincerity and artfulness are competing—and mutually undermining—strategies.

Smith's sonnet cycle, taken together with its prefaces (which are all cumulatively included), narrates an increasingly pessimistic tale of her own rhetorical failure to evoke pathos. Such a tale can only be called ironic, for it was, after all, Smith's popularity that prompted her several revisions and prefatory remarks. But I would suggest that Smith's sense of rhetorical failure is a displacement of her failure to move her well-placed friends to ameliorate her situation: the continuing oppression of enforced dependence on the husband whose livelihood, in fact, depended on her earnings. Neither authorial success nor even patronage could dislodge her husband's legal rights or give her those she needed. (A late sonnet "To Dependence," published the same year as Wollstonecraft's *Vindication of the Rights of Woman*, anticipates the mordant political sonnets of Shelley.)

One index of Smith's pessimism is the negative recasting of figures that appear early in the sonnets. In Sonnet XXVII, for example, Smith addresses childhood as "O happy age!"; children appear collectively as "yon little troop at play,/By sorrow yet untouch'd; unhurt by care." In a sonnet first published in the tenth edition, however, a child's misery on discovering that his beloved glowworm has become, next morning, "rayless as the dust," illustrates a dismal moral: "So turn the World's bright joys to cold and blank disgust." Another example: in an early sonnet, Smith regards the moon as a comforter: "And oft I think—fair planet of the night,/That in thy orb, the wretched may have rest" (Sonnet IV). The final, remarkable sonnet in the tenth edition describes the moon's sublime indifference to a storm-wracked earth:

> While in serenest azure, beaming high,
> Night's regent, of her calm pavilion proud,
> Gilds the dark shadows that beneath her lie,
> Unvex'd by all their conflicts fierce and loud.
> —So, in unsullied dignity elate,
> A spirit conscious of superior worth,
> In placid elevation firmly great,
> Scorns the vain cares that give Contention birth;
> And blest with peace above the shocks of Fate,
> Smiles at the tumult of the troubled earth.
>
> (Sonnet LIX)

While the earlier sonnet recognizes the moon's sovereignty—"Queen of the silver bow!"—it also emphasizes her femininity: "thy mild and placid light/Sheds a soft calm upon my troubled breast." In the later sonnet, the trappings of royalty—its exaltation, its pageants, and its pavilions—cast the moon as imperious and inclement, hoarding the blessings of peace. In Smith's sonnets, virtually each correspondent breeze, storm, moon, or nightingale is echoed in a later palinode in which the addressed figure fails to sympathize with the poet.

Nor does the human world afford sympathetic listeners. That these sonnets are well populated with personifications, suggests the need to create an interlocutor who will open a space for speech. While Smith does address several sonnets to personal friends, more urgent affinities link her to disenfranchised figures of alienation: wanderers, shipwrecked mariners, madmen, exiles, pilgrims, and fugitives. An allusion to the "exertions" of anonymous friends in the fifth edition gives way in the sixth to vituperations upon "'Honorable Men.'" Her role as Authoress, finally, has become mortifying to her; she has come to be "well aware that for a woman—'The Post of Honor is a Private Station.'"

Ultimately, Smith reckons her failure as a gendered exclusion from the moral authority of the "rude forefathers"—from Gray's cult of sympathy for the patriarchal dead. Her most incisive meditation on her failure to authorize pathos lies in her own churchyard poem:

> Press'd by the Moon, mute arbitress of tides,
> While the loud equinox its power combines,
> The sea no more its swelling surge confines,
> But' o'er the shrinking land sublimely rides.
> The wild blast, rising from the Western cave,
> Drives the huge billows from their heaving bed;
> Tears from their grassy tombs the village dead,
> And breaks the silent sabbath of the grave!
> With shells and sea-weed mingled, on the shore
> Lo! their bones whiten in the frequent wave;
> But vain to them the winds and waters rave;
> *They* hear the warring elements no more:
> While I am doom'd—by life's long storm opprest,
> To gaze with envy on their gloomy rest.
>
> (Sonnet XLIV)

Like pregnant women who begin to labor at the full moon, the sea, "no more its swelling surge confines" at the behest of this "mute arbitress." As the land "shrinks" under the sea's fearsome power, the sea violates the sanctity of the churchyard; whereas Gray fancies the "rude forefathers" to sleep "for ever" in their narrow cells, Smith watches as the churchyard yields up its bones to the wild fate of Milton's Lycidas. Ingeniously alluding to Gray's sonnet, Smith notes that "vain to them the winds and waters rave; /*They* hear the warring elements no more"; turning, as Gray does, to her own misery, she identifies not with the narrow cells of the predecessors, but with the whitening bones strewn among the shells. Just as Gray's sonnet circles back to the declaration of vanity with which it begins, Smith's final couplet hovers around a reprise of its open-

ing word, "Press'd," reading in it both "oppression" and the "rest" that
is death. In this poem, Smith does not simply offer an ironic critique of
Gray's idealized community centered on the grave. She also authorizes
her poem by invoking a feminine goddess hostile to the sanctity of
Gray's "unhonoured" dead. If Smith's sonnets have a story to tell, it is
that Elegia's marriage to the cause of public morality may be a darker,
more obscuring "doom" than she had supposed.

•   •   •   •   •

Smith's radical, ironic narrative contrasts sharply with that which
emerges from Bowles's sonnets. As Curran has noted, Bowles uses the
topos of the journey as a structuring principle; at the farthest point in the
voyage out, the poet returns in thought to his point of origin, anticipating his literal return.[23] The editor's advertisement to the first edition of
Bowles's *Fourteen Sonnets*, on the model of Walpole's advertisement to
Gray's *Elegy*, characterizes the poet as a "Traveler": "The following
Sonnets (or whatever they may be called), were found in a Traveller's
Memorandum-Book. They were selected from amongst many others,
chiefly of the same kind. The Editor has ventured to lay a few of them
before the Publick. . . ." The preface to the second edition, written by
the "Author," links the poet's travel to topographical poetry, emphasizing his appreciation for the fashionable picturesque:

> The following Trifles were chiefly suggested by some Picturesque Objects
> which presented themselves to the Author in a Tour to the Northern Parts
> of this Island, and on the Continent. They were before committed too hast-
> ily to the Press; but the favourable Reception which they experienced, has
> induced him to revise them, and, with the Addition of a few more, to make
> them less unworthy of the Publick Eye.
>
> It having been said that these Pieces were written in Imitation of the little
> Poems of Mrs. Smyth, the Author hopes he may be excused adding, that
> *many* of them were written prior to Mrs. Smyth's Publication. He is con-
> scious of their great Inferiority to those beautiful and elegant Composi-
> tions; but, such as they are, they were certainly written from his own
> Feelings.

Five years after the publication of Smith's *Elegiac Sonnets*, her name has
become synonymous with "elegance," a code word for affectation; here,
Smith's acknowledgment that her grief is mediated by culture is turned
against her. By contrasting Bowles with Smith, this preface insists on the
authenticity of Bowles's response to nature. As late as the eighth edition,
Bowles continues to work within the conventions of topographical poetry while insisting on the spontaneity and sincerity of his compositions:

[T]he greatest part of those originally committed to the press were *written down, for the first time, from memory.*

This is nothing to the publick, but it may serve in some measure to obviate the common remark on melancholy poetry, that it has been very often gravely composed, when possibly the heart of the writer had very little share in the distress he chose to describe.

But there is a great difference between *natural* and *fabricated* feelings, even in poetry:—To which of these two characters the Poems before the reader belong, the author leaves those, who have felt sensations of sorrow, to judge. (vii)

Whereas Smith's tenth edition attaches her grief to her precarious position as a woman pleading against the designs of a treacherous husband—declares that her grief has, in other words, a pervasive, ongoing cause, not an occasion—Bowles's eighth edition narrows his grief toward a traditional elegiac occasion: "The sudden death of a deserving young woman." While Bowles's biography suggests that he actually wrote from erotic disappointment, his fabrication of a funereal motive suggests the conservatism of his elegiac poetics.

But just *how* conservative can best be indicated by a glance at the two sonnets which Bowles prefixed to the second edition, published scant months after the first. Instead of beginning with a sonnet "Written at Tinemouth, Northumberland, after a tempestuous voyage," Bowles begins with two sonnets which present himself as a figurative, rather than literal, traveler. In the first, "To a Friend," he represents himself "on life's wide plain/Cast friendless, where unheard some sufferer cries / Hourly, and oft our road is lone and long"(Sonnet I). The second generalizes the predicament of wandering:

> Languid, and sad, and slow from day to day,
> I journey on, yet pensive turn to view
> (Where the rich landscape gleams with softer hue)
> The streams, and vales, and hills, that steal away.
> So fares it with the children of the earth:
> For when life's goodly prospect opens round,
> Their spirits beat to tread that fairy ground,
> Where every vale sounds to the pipe of mirth.
> But them, vain hope, and easy youth beguiles,
> And soon a longing look, like me, they cast
> Back o'er the pleasing prospect of the past:
> Yet fancy points where still far onward smiles
> Some sunny spot, and her fair colouring blends,
> Till cheerless on their path the night descends.
>
> (Sonnet II)

In this Bunyanesque allegory of travel, "Life's wide plain" appears to give onto "life's goodly prospect," but the transient, deceptive light of fancy yields to the falling night. By prefacing his travel poems with these two sonnets, Bowles instructs his readers to interpret his travels as *figures* of his own spiritual journey, in the course of which he yearns for a more stable source of illumination than that provided by fancy. While Bowles sometimes uses the sonnet's turn contrastively (now versus then, here versus there), he quite often uses the turn to signal dualistic levels of interpretation (space suggesting time, outer suggesting inner), calling on the reader to *allegorize* by interpreting the material data of the first section in the spiritual terms of the second.

The solitary traveler, then, is properly understood to be existentially alone on a journey not of the body but of the soul. Rather than explore his affinities with various human beings, as Smith does, he seeks out the "loneliest haunts all desolate," peopled only by the "unfriended Virtues"—Pity, Patience, Piety, Content, Genius, and Sorrow. Although Coleridge in 1796 understands Bowles's sonnets to "create a sweet and indissoluble union between the intellectual and the material world" (543), what emerges from Bowles's sonnets is the *insufficiency* of nature as a correlative of humanity. Accordingly, Bowles's sonnets crave divine authorization for our "natural" propensity for moral response. For companionship Bowles turns, as do Gray and Smith, beyond both nature and society; unlike Gray and Smith, he turns *toward* God.

Sonnet XI, "On Dover Cliffs," offers the most explicit evidence of this traveler's origin and destiny:

> On these white cliffs, that calm above the flood
> Uplift their shadowing heads, and, at their feet,
> Scarce hear the surge that has for ages beat,
> Sure many a lonely wanderer has stood;
> And, whilst the lifted murmur met his ear,
> And o'er the distant billows the still Eve
> Sail'd slow, has thought of all his heart must leave
> To-morrow,—of the friends he lov'd most dear,—
> Of social scenes, from which he wept to part:—
> But if, like me, he knew how fruitless all
> The thoughts that would full fain the past recall,
> Soon would he quell the risings of his heart,
> And brave the wild winds and unhearing tide,
> The World his country, and his GOD his guide.
>
> (Sonnet XI)

Fittingly, the second edition concludes with a sonnet "To the River Cherwell," a locale in which "erewhile I stray'd." Here, the poet rests "till the bright sun /Of joy returns, as when Heaven's beauteous bow/

Beams on the night-storm's passing wings below" (Sonnet XXI). This is a poem of covenant, in which elegiac sorrow is redeemed by grace: "yet something have I won/Of Solace." Ethos, in a sense undreamed of by Gray, has become Logos: not the word of literature, but the Word of God. With Bowles, the decorum of the elegiac sonnet is violated by a hunger for Christian consolation. His rhetoric, finally, is that of prayer; his audience is not located in the "vacant room" of mourning, but in the house of God.

The project of arousing the sentiments, then, is peculiarly vexed in the sonnet cycles of Smith and Bowles. Smith, taking the measure of her rhetorical success not in the sustained popularity of her verse but in her enduring economic and marital oppression, announces her alienation from a moral order based on the moral capital of the "forefathers." Bowles, in seeking to ground his appeal in divine authority, creates the illusion of forsaking rhetoric in favor of prayer; in the end, he turns from his audience to face his God. In the authorizing strategies of Smith and Bowles culminate the rhetorical tensions of ethos and logos within the elegiac sonnet, tensions brought to a head in the sentimental ordeal of the cumulative sonnet cycle. The rhetoric of sentiment found its own most eloquent critics in its most eloquent practitioners; but it would have others. The rhetorical critique of sentimentalism, spectacularly mounted within the sonnet cycles themselves, would be both complemented and complicated by a critique from without; an answering critique of the consensual ethics of sentimentalism from the world of politics. That critique, as it emerges in Britain from a variegated "politics of sympathy" surrounding the French Revolution, is the subject of the following chapter. But as elegiac sentimentalism reached its decadent phase in the late 1780s, it was for a fledgling poet to assess what ethical powers remained to poetic tears.

The Wanderer Recalled

Wordsworth's first published poem, which appeared in 1787 under the Latin pseudonym "Axiologus" (meaning "words' worth"), is a sonnet whose title announces its inspiration by the lachrymose verse of Helen Maria Williams. The "Sonnet On Seeing Miss Helen Maria Williams Weep at a Tale of Distress," is one of many youthful poems Wordsworth wrote as exercises in the rhetoric of sentiment. Composed at Hawkshead and at Cambridge, these poems bear titles or first lines alluding broadly to their sources: "[In Part from Moschus's Lament for Bion]" (Moschus's "Lament for Bion"); "The Death of a Starling" (Catullus's Verse III); "The Dog: An Idyllium" (Milton's *Lycidas*); "To Melpomene" (Milton's *Il Penseroso*); "On the Death of an Unfortunate Lady" (Pope's

"Elegy to the Memory of an Unfortunate Lady"); "The Vale of Esth-
waite" (Gray's *Elegy Written in a Country Church-yard*); "[A Ballad]"
(Percy's *Reliques*).[24] In a pastoral elegy entitled "The Dog," for example,
a comic, almost gnomic attenuation of *Lycidas* culminates in a sublime
consolation situated within "the calm Ocean of my mind."[25] From the
perspective of the Christian pastoral elegy tradition, the poem, in both
its tone and its secular, autonomous consolation, is nothing if not inde-
corous; Wordsworth might well have said of his pathetic precursors, as
he said of his childhood landscapes in *Home at Grasmere*, "I loved to
stand and read/Their looks forbidding, read and disobey."

By using the word "Seeing" in the title of his sonnet on Williams,
suggesting his perception of and proximity to the weeping poet, Wordsworth casts himself not as a writer but as a *reader* of sentimental verse.
Weeping, formerly considered a feminine act, has become in these final
decades of the century, the poetic inheritance of the young male poet;
Williams's sympathetic weeping over a "tale of distress" is easily absorbed across gender lines as William's own "swimming eyes" brim accordingly. At the same time, however, Wordsworth internalizes and
heightens this accustomed response by tracing the current of pathos into
his own streaming blood:

> She wept.—Life's purple tide began to flow
> In languid streams through every thrilling vein;
> Dim were my swimming eyes—my pulse beat slow,
> And my full heart was swelled to dear delicious pain.
> Life left my loaded heart, and closing eye;
> A sigh recalled the wanderer to my breast;
> Dear was the pause of life, and dear the sigh
> That called the wanderer home, and home to rest.
>
> (1–8)[26]

In the meticulous somatic details of the octet—the purple tide, the thrilling vein, the slow pulse, the swollen, "loaded" heart, the closing eye—
we find Wordsworth making literal the sentimental trope of the life
"within"; in a current locution, the poem is not about how one feels
"inside," but rather about how one's "insides" feel. In the stark dispro-
portion between the brief statement "She wept" and the elaborate response, Williams's suffering is eclipsed by Wordsworth's; eclipsed, that
is, by his reflexive fascination with his own viscera. Emblematically, the
dash linking the weeping "she" with the poet is superseded by another
that connects him more intimately to the sensations coursing through
his body. The oxymoron "dear delicious pain," the juxtaposition of
"languid" and "thrilling," the swollen heart and the small death (the
dear "pause of life") provocatively conflate a Petrarchan, erotic diction

with the poet's self-absorption. Not only are the poet's senses (his "closing eye") dimmed by his acute attention to his inner life; his will is
thoroughly suspended in this "dear . . . pause of life." And in this pause,
the read sonnet's power to move that will toward virtuous action remains entirely suspended. In this moment of self-consummation, the
poet's moral agency is consumed, and with it, the rhetorical success of
Williams's sonnet.

Only when the inner wanderer is recalled, does the poet trouble to
record the "proclamation" of "That tear":

> That tear proclaims—in thee each virtue dwells,
> And bright will shine in misery's midnight hour;
> As the soft star of dewy evening tells
> What radiant fires were drowned by day's malignant power,
> That only wait the darkness of the night
> To cheer the wandering wretch with hospitable light.
>
> (9–14)

In the ambiguous phrase "That tear" (reminiscent of the crucial "thee"
in line 93 of Gray's *Elegy*), the tears of the two poets swim together,
jointly proclaiming the virtue of Williams—and, by implication, Wordsworth's. Such virtue must be proclaimed, we might say, because it is not
demonstrated. Williams's shining virtue is said to defy her own dark
melancholy; Wordsworth compares it to the "soft star of dewy evening"
capable of cheering "the wandering wretch with hospitable light." But
unlike the poet's own internal wanderer, this "wandering wretch" is not
called home by the dewy star of evening; nor is it conceivable that star-
light, however "hospitable," would be more welcome to such a vagrant
than sunlight. Moreover, Williams's virtue is compared to a weak, involuntary phenomenon, one that requires the support of darkness before its
efficacy can be proclaimed. It illuminates spontaneously, uncommanded
by her will—as involuntary, say, as the dropping of a tear or the flowing
of the blood. Williams's *agency*, like that of Wordsworth's, is a vexed
matter. Her tear does not persuade the reader to take virtuous action, so
much as "proclaim" her own quiescent virtue. The precise social impact
of Williams's tear is said to be the propagation of cheerfulness, a strange
conclusion for a poem that begins by proclaiming Williams's virtually
lethal effect on the poet.

If what one lingers over is a sign of what one deems important, then
it is true, as James Averill says of this sonnet, that "the 'wanderer' within
each reader is more important than 'the wandering wretch.'"[27] Certainly
the vitality and intensity with which the poet reflects on his response
exposes as stagnant and somnolent the "virtue" that sympathy is said to
entail. And certainly, as Averill recognizes, Wordsworth's exquisite play

between self-forgetfulness and self-consciousness, albeit circumscribed by a coy Petrarchanism, is a harbinger of a poetry that would make consciousness itself a fruitful subject for poetry.

But I would like to place emphasis not on what the poem prophesies, but on what it observes: an uneasy dualism in the rhetoric of sentiment between a vital psychology of reflection and an exhausted ethics of benevolent social response. In this sonnet, Wordsworth provides an anatomy of pathos that impugns the rhetoric of sentiment as an ethical force. More important, Wordsworth's impulse to recall this inner wanderer to the demands of a world peopled with wandering wretches suggests an anxiety lest the moral dimension of sentimentality—the legacy of the theory of moral sentiments—should drop out entirely. In short, the psychologistic excesses of Wordsworth's sonnet crave the revival of an ethos of social virtue within the domain of sympathy.[28] For all the critical acuity of the Williams sonnet, however, Wordsworth in 1787 could not have anticipated the upheaval that the culture of sympathy was about to undergo. As the following chapters will show, he was to have no small role in ushering sympathy into a new century.

THREE

BURKE, PAINE, WORDSWORTH, AND

THE POLITICS OF SYMPATHY

"Your tale has moved me much and I have been
I know not where."
(William Wordsworth, *Adventures on Salisbury Plain*)

Ethics and Politics

IN *The Ethics of Romanticism*, Laurence Lockridge refers to "the usual understanding that ethics deals with obligation and moral value as they pertain to individuals in their relatedness to themselves and to others; politics deals with larger groups or governments wherein expediency may or may not—depending on which politics is invoked—properly override moral objections."[1] The logic of Lockridge's distinction notwithstanding, a sharp distinction between ethics and politics makes no sense at a historical moment at which the relations between governments and persons are themselves radically in question; at which the very institutions through which governments are represented by persons and persons by governments are hotly contested. That the French Revolution brought on a crisis in British domestic politics is well known; but I want to offer an account of this crisis that addresses the interpenetration of politics and ethics in the writings of the Revolution's supporters and detractors alike. This chapter proposes not only that the debate over the French Revolution in Britain occurs within the discourse of sentimentalism, but also that the Revolution controversy was, in large part, a crisis *about* sentimentalism. From that fierce debate about the sovereignty of monarchy in France and Britain, emerges another about the sovereignty of feeling within the public order. I argue here that the rhetoric of sentimentalism, as well as alternative modes of evoking pathos, were both the means and the method, the terms and the topic, of the debate. By so arguing, I necessarily focus both on the readings of revolution produced by British political writers of the 1790s and on how these writers tried, rhetorically, to make their readings persuasive. Just as Wordsworth "saw" Helen Maria Williams in the throes of anguish, Britain "saw" France in the throes of revolution—that is to say, *rhetorically*.

But what did Britain "see"; what "tale of distress" did Britain read?[2] What the British public read was not one but multiple tales of distress, tales whose tellers competed strenuously for their sympathies. I find the very terms in which the young Wordsworth signals the rhetorical failure of the sentimental sonnet—the disjunction between pathetic reflection and ethical response—highly suggestive for an account of how both sides in the controversy maneuvered sentimental rhetoric to specific partisan ends, even when sentimentalism was itself under criticism. Burke, among others, saw clearly that any response to events across the channel would necessarily entail a reflection on the composition and viability of Britain's own monarchy; as Ronald Paulson has noted, Burke confessed shortly before the publication of the aptly titled *Reflections* that "in reality, my object was not France, in the first instance, but this Country."[3] He might as well have written not "my object" but "my subject," for in the *Reflections* the "late conduct" of members of the Revolution Society quickly supplants the "late proceedings in France" as the focus of his remarks.[4]

The Revolution controversy, which saw the rhetoric of sentiment become a powerful political instrument, eventuated in a crisis in the meaning and value of sympathy that would resonate well into the Victorian era. In 1789, the word *sympathy*, which had widened in the eighteenth century to include the sense of "commiseration with suffering" had not yet come to mean an explicitly political inclination or predisposition; during the Revolutionary-Napoleonic period, however, the rhetoric of political favor would become soldered to the discourse of morals. One legacy of this conjunction is the term "political sympathy"; the OED cites Southey's *History of the Peninsular War* (1823) as the first reference in English to a political "sympathy," but the transition can be glimpsed a good deal earlier. In Wordsworth's *Convention of Cintra* (1809), for example, the provenance of "sympathy" is ambiguous: "[E]very person . . . would carry both into his conflicts with the enemy in the field, and into his relations of peaceful intercourse with the inhabitants, not only the virtues which might be expected from him as a soldier, but the antipathies and sympathies, the loves and hatreds of a citizen—of a human being—acting, in a manner hitherto unprecedented under the obligation of his human and social nature" (1:225). When Wordsworth finds sympathy emerging from one's "human and social nature," he emphatically identifies humans as "citizen[s]," not members in some theoretical social order.[5] The notion of a specifically *political* sympathy is also broached in the Cintra pamphlet via Wordsworth's allegory of "the British and Spanish Nations, with an impulse like that of two ancient heroes throwing down their weapons and reconciled in the field, cast[ing] off at once their aversions and enmities, and mutually embrac[ing] each other" (1:228). Figuring nations as persons, the allegory implicitly figures persons as nations—"if even their loyalty was such as . . . we could not thoroughly sympathize with" (1:229)—vigorously mediating between the notion of personal and political sympathies. In such passages we witness the transition from the "natural" sympathies of the Enlightenment to the "political" sympathies of a revolutionary age.

To speak of a "political sympathy," of course, is to have moved beyond the dream of a moral consensus that lies at the heart of sentimental theory; the extended ordeal of British response and reaction to the changing shapes of the French Revolution put the lie to such a dream. During this period alliances formed, parties shifted, factions erupted, and coalitions altered with a rapidity never before experienced in the lifetime of most of the Revolution's observers. The lesions in the British body politic discerned by Burke and, despite his attempts to treat them, widened by him, were nothing compared to the gashes that sundered the revolutionary National Convention in the fall of 1792 over the fate of Louis XVI. During the five-year interval between the fall of the Bastille in 1789 and the fall of Robespierre in 1794, the Revolution surrendered its phantasm of apocalyptic, benevolent, universal *fraternité* to a harsh reality of factionalism, imperialism, intrigue, and terror. As if in sympathy, Britain entered the darkest period of self-division over the issue of a proper response to regicide. When British Jacobins quaked over Pitt's draconian bills, repressive arrests, and militarism, they were merely expressing movement in fault lines that had long run through the base of the British polity. Among those Britons who favored the Revolution, divisions ran deep and, midway through the decade, proliferated; republicans debated reformists, and rifts opened between Godwinians and those who favored the modes of activism made familiar by Thelwall and the London Corresponding Society.[6]

If sentimentalism could no longer teach the British that they were cut of the same moral cloth, it could, however, be put in the service of building and consolidating a particular ethico-political consensus. The uneasiness with which elegiac sonneteers regarded their own sentimental rhetoric gives way in the 1790s to frank and bold recognitions of the rhetorical powers of sympathy. Once it was acknowledged that pathos could be produced and then deployed, sympathies were evoked, organized, and directed to serve a variety of political goals.

The three figures on whom I dwell in this chapter each experimented rhetorically with a different conception of the relation between feeling and political action. Burke, desiring to stay the British from sympathizing with the fortunes of the French revolutionaries, makes reflection not only the method of his treatise, but its rhetorical goal. Paine, impatient with what he took to be the vanity of Burke's reflections, demands that his reader move beyond reflection and embrace the French cause. Wordsworth, in *Adventures on Salisbury Plain*, provides a narrative commentary on the rhetorical projects of both Burke and Paine, for he demonstrates that a climate of harsh political repression can disable the will, placing a possible audience for revolution beyond the reach of rhetoric. In *Adventures on Salisbury Plain*, Wordsworth's Jacobin purpose—to move his reader in the direction of empowerment and change[7]—succumbs to the sentimental drama of reflection. As these disparate projects and purposes attest, an early casualty of the Revolutionary period was the sentimental ethos of a moral consensus constituted by sympathetic response and kept in circulation by a shared dead. By the end of the decade, it would become the work of poets to assess what meanings the rhetoric of sympathy could yet sustain.

Burke: "This Great Drama"

At the heart of Burke's attack on Price in his *Reflections on the Revolution in France* (1790) lies an attack on Price's heart:

> Why do I feel so differently from the Reverend Dr. Price, and those of his lay flock, who will choose to adopt the sentiments of his discourse?—For this plain reason—because it is *natural* that I should; because we are so made as to be affected at such spectacles with melancholy sentiments upon the unstable condition of mortal prosperity, and the tremendous uncertainty of human greatness; because in those natural feelings we learn great lessons; because in events like these our passions instruct our reason; because when kings are hurl'd from their thrones by the Supreme Director of this great drama, and become the objects of insult to the base, and of pity to the good, we behold such disasters in the moral, as we should behold a miracle in the physical order of things. We are alarmed into reflexion; our minds (as it has long since been observed) are purified by terror and pity; our weak unthinking pride is humbled, under the dispensations of a mysterious wisdom. (93–94)

To Burke, the "sentiments of his discourse" reveal Price's heart to be aberrant, unnatural; Price and his adherents are simply not made as "we are . . . made." As Chandler and others have observed, Burke makes it difficult to decide what he intends by terms like "nature" and "natural." According to Chandler, Burke uses the term "natural" to refer both to the realm we commonly call "nature" and to that which we know as "culture." To complicate matters further, he refers to them at times alternatively; at other times, simultaneously. What Burke gains by this ambiguity, Chandler argues, is a dialogue between the two realms.[8] The ambiguity of Burke's "natural feelings," I would suggest, parallels that which resides in the discourse of eighteenth-century sentimental theory. The sentimental term "moral nature," in pointing resolutely away from a divinely authorized moral order, points simultaneously in two other directions: toward an innate "moral sense" and toward the cultural codes by which morals are influenced, and which morals, in turn, shape. These two directions are intertwined, for, as Hume and Adam Smith argue, the functioning of the moral sense is influenced by our experience. A similar constellation of meanings clusters around Burke's use of such terms as "natural feelings" (or, elsewhere, "inbred sentiments") to betoken feelings produced by "prejudices" and feelings which serve as the teachers of "great lessons." In the passage just cited, "nature" points toward a state of being into which we are born, the way "we are . . . made"; yet Burke is here, as elsewhere, keenly concerned with the *cultural* instruction our affections afford.

Burke, asserting Price's unnaturalness, takes issue with the latter's transformation of his pulpit into an arena of political dissent: "[P]olitics and the pulpit are terms that have little agreement. No sound ought to be heard in the church but the healing voice of Christian charity" (23). Price's rhetoric, a "porridge" of religion and politics, is itself an equivocal sign of interests impinging on vocation. Not only had Price, whom Burke calls a "spiritual doctor of politics," substituted rhetoric for prayers, his own rhetorical authority for the transcendental authority of God; Price had also exploited his position for ungodly ends. Burke's own gesture toward a Providential "Supreme Director" suggests an anxious attempt to authorize *his* rhetoric by appeal to Divine will, if not to Divine truth. But this attempt suggests that Burke's reaction to Price emerges from a more fundamental discontent with Price's authority than that it abuses his pulpit. I understand Burke's reaction to Price as a reaction against what Burke understood as the implicit politics of sentimental discourse. Briefly recapitulating the argument of my first chapter may help to illuminate Burke's reading of sentimental politics.

Hume, viewing Shaftesbury's and Hutcheson's spectator theory of an innate moral sense as overly absolute, emphasizes the role of social "conversation" in moral judgement. Adam Smith's analysis of mourning for the dead develops Hume's conversation theory of morals into a theory of how morals circulate within a society. Smith, while analyzing the process of identification that evokes an individual's sympathy with the dead, designates the corporate dead as the moral capital of a culture: because the dead cannot be compensated for their privations, they warrant more sympathy than their immediate circle of mourners can supply. By means of a system of sympathetic exchanges—exchanges of sympathy for consideration—moral affections circulate throughout a society. By implication, a society may be defined as those who share a common dead. With Adam Smith, the "nature" of moral sentiments becomes, ineluctably, an affair of cultural circulation authorized only in the sense that a currency is "backed" by a standard. Published the same decade as Smith's *Theory of Moral Sentiments*, Gray's *Elegy Written in a Country Church-yard* identifies the graves of the "rude forefathers of the hamlet" as the crux of a polity uniting the living and the dead, and extending beyond the borders of the hamlet. Though neither Smith nor Gray troubles over the particular ways in which the dead shape the moral judgements of a culture, they both demonstrate that a communal sympathy with the dead is essential for the survival and maintenance of that group's moral order.

Burke's attack on Price's heart, I would suggest, is neither an attack on his morals, nor on his rationalist theory of morals, but on his *rhetoric* of morals, which Burke here associates with the left-wing politics of religious dissent (23). When Jacobin *fraternité* supplants Christian charity as the teaching of the dissenting church, then, for Burke, the church has pronounced its hostility to established authority. Price's sermon "in a strain which I believe has not been heard in this kingdom, in any of the pulpits which are tolerated or encouraged in it, since the year 1648" (23), by linking the dissenting church to the cause of republicanism, renders the politics of sentimental theory explicit. In despising Price's heart, Burke despises the democratization of feeling licensed and abetted by what he understands as a nonauthoritarian culture of moral sympathies.[9]

As a consequence of his stance on sentimentalism, Burke undertakes a threefold task. First, he must provide an account of the authorized sympathies on which a pathetic appeal might prudently be based; second, he must establish the basis for his own rhetorical authority; and third, he must take pains to distinguish the character of his rhetorical appeal from that of Price. Let me consider these in sequence.

Burke's scruples about the authority of sympathy in the *Reflections* find him reconsidering his earlier writing about sympathy in his 1757 *Philosophical Enquiry into the Origins of our Ideas of the Sublime and the Beautiful*. In the *Philosophical Enquiry*, Burke reaches the topic of sympathy by way of a brief discussion of beauty, introduced as a "social quality."[10] For Burke, the perception of beauty determines the difference between animal lust and human love; it transforms an individual's passion to mate into a tamer, superior passion for society. The object of attention, no longer a sexual lure, can now be chosen for the particular aesthetic pleasures it provides.

When Burke remarks, however, that "Men are carried to the sex in general . . . but they are attached to particulars by personal *beauty*" (1:x), we understand him to be speaking not of all individuals, but of males, for both aesthetic choice and sympathy are introduced as adjuncts of male sexual choice. The phenomenon of sympathy, for Burke a domestication and dispersal of male sexual desire, entails an explicit curbing of male power with respect to women. As men mute the force of their desire—as they are transformed by beauty from "man" into "men"—their objects are simultaneously transformed from "females" into feminine "women." Not surprisingly, once Burke develops his contrasting categories of the beautiful and the sublime in Parts Three and Four, the beautiful object is consistently feminized as curving, small, delicate, quiet, calm, and unimposing; its inferiority to the perceiver is always emphasized. But in light of Burke's discussion of sympathy in Part One, we can see that this emphasis on the feminine weakness of the beautiful object is designed, in part, to address two points: first, that feminization itself mitigates the powerlessness of the female object by elevating her from female to woman; and second, that the act of sympathy entails the effeminization of the perceiver.

In the *Reflections*, however, Burke aims for a definition of sympathy that is secured against this potential confounding of categories—categories at once of gender and of power. He seeks a new definition of the sympathetic man, a definition that will provide a middle way between sympathy's propensity to feminize the sympathizer and its power, simultaneously, to tempt him into lust and brutalize him. What prompts this change is that Burke knew himself to be facing evidence of both corruptions of sympathy, in England and in France, respectively. The first type, which he identifies with Price, is a sympathy whose method is the authorization of individual feeling, whose consequence is the leveling of difference, and whose end is the dissolution of both authorized tradition and traditional authority. The second, which Burke identifies with the French Jacobins, is a kind of sympathy that takes as its object not an individual, but a group. Burke's thinking about sympathy in the *Reflections* is complex because he wants to argue that these two modes of sympathy are, at base, corrupted by the same indifference to tradition; moreover, that fluent English sympathies, left to congeal and harden, can and will become more like French ones. Burke argues that both modes of sympathy—libertarian sentimentalism and revolutionary pity—founder on their indifference to authority.

Burke's rhetorical *strategy* for distinguishing between licit and illicit sympathies, which I want to consider as distinct from his argument, is to demonstrate that both the dissenting and Jacobin abuses of sympathy swerve from the "natural." Burke's strategy, in other words, is precisely *not* to take issue with the sentimental commonplace, derived from moral sense theory, that morality begins and ends in the breast. We have already seen Burke portray Price as a sport of moral nature, an ethical aberration. As he turns to consider French morals, he stresses, as with Price's morals, their unnaturalness:

> All your [French] sophisters cannot produce any thing better adapted to preserve a rational and manly freedom than the course that we have pursued, who have chosen our *nature* rather than our speculations, our breasts rather than our inventions, for the great conservatories and magazines of our rights and privileges. (47)

> In England we have not yet been completely embowelled of our *natural* entrails; we still feel within us, and we cherish and cultivate, those inbred sentiments which are the faithful guardians, the active monitors of our duty, the true supporters of all liberal and manly morals. We have not been drawn and trussed, in order that we may be filled, like stuffed birds in a museum, with chaff and rags, and paltry, blurred, shreds of paper about the rights of man. We preserve the whole of our feelings still native and entire, unsophisticated by pedantry and infidelity. We have real hearts of flesh and blood beating in our bosoms. (99–100)

> The worst of these politics of revolution is this; they temper and harden the breast, in order to prepare it for the desperate strokes which are sometimes used in extreme occasions. But as these occasions may never arrive, the mind receives a gratuitous taint; and the moral sentiments suffer not a little, when no political purpose is served by the depravation. This sort of people are so taken up with their theories about the rights of man, that they have totally forgot his *nature*. Without opening one new avenue to the understanding, they have succeeded in stopping up those that lead to the heart. They have perverted in themselves, and in those that attend to them, all the well-placed sympathies of the human breast. (my emphases) (77)

Throughout, Burke equates "natural" sympathies with "manly" ones, taking pains in his metaphors to immunize British sympathy against the feminine taint of sensibility. Hence, British passions are not only susceptible of discipline; they *inculcate* discipline. Based in "our breasts rather than our inventions," British morals conduce to "preserve a rational and manly freedom"; the British "breast," figured as a "conservatory" and "magazine" of "rights and privileges," suggests a fort stocked with provender and arms. "[O]ur natural entrails" harboring "inbred" rather than "inborn" sympathies, perform a variety of active roles: they are "faithful guardians . . . active monitors" and "true supporters" of all liberal and manly morals. Finally, if it is in the British "nature" to allow passion to prevail over reason, it is because passion is recognized as reason's esteemed *instructor*.

Anticipating later Jacobin defenses of the terror, Burke points out that revolutionary politics tend to disable natural responses, leaving the "well-placed sympathies of the human breast" perverted and depraved. Here, Burke's less extreme metaphors—hardening and stopping, rather than disembowelment—are the more resonant. Revolutionary toughness—understood as a desparate attitude intended to support desperate measures—becomes itself a progressive disease of the revolutionary state; what may be good for decisive action makes for intolerable politics. What Burke anticipates is a politics of desperation, a systematic implementation of violence in lieu of a functional polity. French sophistry does not eviscerate the seat of morals so much as allow it to wither over time; moreover, it habituates the individual to life with a moral disability, bringing on a secondary moral amnesia. What substitutes for fellow-feeling, according to Burke, is a conviction about "the rights of man," a conviction that has no clear relation to "the understanding."[11]

And yet Burke's insight that the understanding is apt to be passed over in moral affairs reveals much about his own paradoxical attempt to reveal to the British people their own moral "nature." While he insists on the authority of a British moral "nature," Burke offers his readers a simulacrum of moral "nature"—both an image of an essential moral responsiveness with which his readers were to identify, and a function for such a "moral nature," were it to exist. By so doing, Burke reconstructs the deficient sympathies of his fellow Britons. The rousing theme of difference between the English and the French, in other words, at once obscures and remedies the fragmentation of the British polity.

With this observation, I move to Burke's second task: to establish the basis for his own rhetorical authority. Ironically, the passage that most keenly reveals Burke's rhetorical ingenuity is his attempt to align his own ethos with an inherited tradition:[12]

> Our political system is placed in a just correspondence and symmetry with the order of the world, and with the mode of existence decreed to a permanent body composed of transitory parts; wherein, by the disposition of a stupendous wisdom, moulding together the great mysterious incorporation of the human race, the whole, at one time, is never old, or middle-aged, or young, but in a condition of unchangeable constancy, moves on through the varied tenour of perpetual decay, fall, renovation, and progression. Thus, by preserving the method of nature in the conduct of the state, in what we improve we are never wholly new; in what we retain we are never

wholly obsolete. By adhering in this manner and on those principles to our
forefathers, we are guided not by the superstition of antiquarians, but by
the spirit of philosophic analogy. In this choice of inheritance, we have
given to our frame of polity the image of a relation in blood; binding up the
constitution of our country with our dearest domestic ties; adopting our
fundamental laws into the bosom of our family affections; keeping inseparable, and cherishing with the warmth of all their combined and mutually
reflected charities, our state, our hearths, our sepulchres, and our altars.
(45–46)

Burke's famous "philosophical analogy" for the British polity—a "permanent body composed of transitory parts"—may in part be understood as a scruple about his own moral authority. But I want to suggest
that Burke's attempt thus to authorize himself is also an attempt to authorize the moral sentiments by appeal to cultural codes inherited from
antiquity. I am suggesting here that Burke's resonant conceit revises the
libertarian politics he thought implicit within sentimentalism by displacing the figure of synchronic circulation with a figure of diachronic transmission: inheritance.

What Burke perceived in the ethics of sentimental circulation, was,
very simply, the vitality of the dead. If the dead, by virtue of our feeling
for them, are essential to the moral sanity of the society, might it not be
said that they retain their membership in that society even in death?
Might it not even be said that they are, despite the ghostly status of their
membership, the crucial component of the enduring body politic? The
consequences of such thinking inform not only Burke's propounding of
the English moral "nature," but also his execration of the French revolutionaries. If, as Burke claims, the ways of the English dead are a living
part of English social life, the Revolution in France raises the spectre of
a people who, having "murdered" their dead, are able and willing to
murder their living priests and kings. "Liberty," writes Burke, "when
men act in bodies, is *power*"; according to Burke, English liberty differs
from French liberty insofar as the powers English liberty confers are
organized by inherited institutions:

[T]he succession of the crown has always been what it now is, an hereditary
succession by law: in the old line it was a succession by the common law; in
the new by the statute law, operating on the principles of the common law,
not changing the substance, but regulating the mode, and describing the
persons. Both these descriptions of law are of the same force, and are derived from an equal authority, emanating from the common agreement and
original compact of the state, *communi sponsione reipublicae*, and as such
are equally binding on king, and people too, as long as the terms are observed, and they continue the same body politic. (32–33)

When Burke remarked that "I should therefore suspend my congratulations on the new liberty of France, until I was informed how it had been combined with government"(20), he knew that without the damping effect of tradition, the combination of liberty and government might be explosive.

The import of Burke's "philosophical analogy," becomes clearer when we consider one feature of his defense of monarchy, a recognition that institutions "can . . . be embodied, if I may use the expression, in persons; so as to create in us love, veneration, admiration, or attachment"(91). If persons represent institutions by embodying them, then by a corollary process institutions represent persons by *disembodying* them, allowing both their own survival beyond bodily death and immortalizing their dearest attachments. Thus, Burke's conceit punningly "mould[s] together" the buried generations into a permanent "whole." The dead, far from being lost, are constantly retained, their graves annexed to a community defined by "our hearths, our sepulchres and our altars." One arm of the body politic is itself a dead hand which clutches traditions "grasped as in a kind of mortmain for ever"(45). For Burke, the grave is a place of warning, not of mourning; taking the eighteenth-century graveyard meditation back to its Calvinist roots, he admonishes the Enlightenment with a time "after the grave has heaped its mould upon our presumption, and the silent tomb shall have imposed its law on our pert loquacity" (99). The grave, here, is not a sign of divine judgment, but of the judgment of the "forefathers"; joined in this way to the past, we figuratively "adhere" to them. As Burke elides the radical, angular shape of Christian history (and, with it, the intervention of grace), he figures forth a body politic that endures "perpetual decay, fall, renovation, and progression." Of this conceit, Paine would note trenchantly in *The Rights of Man* that "It is the nature of man to die, and he will continue to die as long as he continues to be born. But Mr. Burke has set up a sort of political Adam, in whom all posterity are bound for ever. . . ."(280). In lieu of divine authority, Burke's obstreperous figure suggests a human lineage redeemed by a "stupendous wisdom," simultaneously human and transcendental.

Crucially, Burke constructs the British nation not on the expansive model of Christendom, but on the contracted model of the family, an institution that straddles the disparate realms of nature and culture. Arguing that the British political system, modeled on familial inheritance, preserves "the method of nature in the conduct of the state," Burke in turn constructs the moral "nature" of families on the model of their legal existence. Burke's tacit assumption, of course, is that such legal institutions were originally shaped in accordance with the natural affections, but it is one thing to suggest that affections may shape institutions and another to deduce the former from the latter. What needs to be stressed is that while nature prevents the survival of the individual, the so-called "method of nature" as encoded in the body of law and applied by social institutions, ensures the survival of the family. Burke does not dispute that the parts are indeed "transitory"; still, his figure of the "permanent body" supposes the survivals of legal inheritance fully to redeem the losses of nature. And once sympathy ceases to be transmitted among contemporaneous individuals, the generation, organization, and regulation of the affections come to lie entirely within the domain of cultural authority.

It was for Paine to object that what Burke had mistaken for "the method of nature"—primogeniture—was "a law against every law of nature, and nature herself calls for its destruction. Establish family justice, and aristocracy falls" (320). "Nature herself" goes hand-to-hand with what Paine refers to as Burke's "political Adam."[13] Even in 1795, when his son, Richard, predeceased him, Burke was at pains to maintain that the "method of nature" had not been violated; in "Letter to a Noble Lord," he appeals to "a disposer whose power we are little able to resist, and whose wisdom it behoves us not all to dispute. . . ."[14] Still, in the doctrine of the "permanent body of transitory parts" Burke recasts the circulation theory of morals—a theory of moral indebtedness—as a theory of entailed moral inheritance; in Burke's figure, the currency of mournful emotion is replaced by the currency of affections celebrating the simultaneity of present and past, of the living and the dead. Thus, whereas Smith constructs moral culture as a perpetual mourning for the dead, Burke constructs it as a celebration of the nation's perpetual life.

· · · · ·

We turn now to the character of Burke's rhetorical appeal; to how Burke characterizes his own appeal by comparison to the competing appeal of Price. If the nation's dead are known to *endow* the living rather than *bereave* them, then it would seem that the "well-placed sympathies of the human breast" are so placed to express a sense of continuing attachment to the dead, rather than a sense of their absence. Burke appeals to the affections not for the establishment of a moral consensus within the British nation—this he customarily asserts, whether literally or allegorically—but in order to inculcate sympathy for the revolution's victims. Accordingly, Burke attempts to arouse *pathos* not by evoking the British dead, but by evoking the imperiled remains of what Burke in 1790 already understood as the posthumous French monarchy: Louis XVI and Marie Antoinette. For Burke, "this great drama" of revolution, "purif[ying]" the mind "by terror and pity" (94), was unequivocally a tragedy. While Burke's own representation of the revolution—part *Annual Register* sketch, part passion play, part elegy, part sermon—employs a variety of literary modes, it centers on a representation of the tragic fall of the French monarchy.[15]

By invoking Aristotelian tragedy, Burke harks back to early eighteenth-century literary treatises such as Trapp's *Lectures on Poetry* (1712; trans. 1742), in which the emotions of terror and pity were seen to lie within the domain of the tragic, and had not yet come to reside, as they would later in the century, in the modes of the gothic and sentimental romance. I understand Burke's appeal to tragedy not simply as a retrograde gesture, but as an implicit critique of the literary modes associated with sentimentalism: most notably, the lyric, the gothic romance, and the novel. By identifying sympathetic response with the pity and terror evoked by tragic catharsis, Burke seeks to circumvent the democratization of morals that circulate freely within sentimentalism, and he does so, effectively, by *reviving a spectator theory of morals*.

In the idiom of Shaftesbury, Hutcheson, Hume, and now Burke, we contemplate the scenes in France as "spectacles." Our affections arise in the gap between who we are and what we see, and, "instructing our reason" with "great lessons," provide the basis for moral discourse. In tragedy, an audience's affections are trained—are both educated and directed—on the actions of monarchs and nobles; pity and terror occur under the aegis of "a mysterious wisdom" that evokes the "stupendous wisdom" whose disposition "mould[s] together the great mysterious incorporation of the human race"(46). Burke invokes the moral authority of his tragedy, in part, by ridiculing that of Price's sermon, which he likens to melodramatic, popular entertainment. Of Price's audience, he remarks:

> A cheap, bloodless reformation, a guiltless liberty, appear flat and vapid to their taste. There must be a great change of scene; there must be a magnificent stage effect; there must be a grand spectacle to rouze the imagination, grown torpid with the lazy enjoyment of sixty years security, and the still unanimating repose of public prosperity. The Preacher found them all in the French revolution. (77–78)

Burke's initial strategy is to cast Price's sober spectacle of revolutionary Enlightenment as a cheap and trivial entertainment. To this end, he casts the National Assembly in the role of comic "actors." Far from representing, in Price's words, "the dominion of kings changed for the dominion of laws,"[16] the National Assembly becomes in Burke's hands a "monstrous tragi-comic scene" (22): "The Assembly . . . acts before them the farce of deliberation with as little decency as liberty. They act like the comedians of a fair before a riotous audience. . . ."(81). And yet Burke's need to denigrate these public spectacles signals his recognition of their rhetorical power: "Indeed the theatre is a better school of moral sentiments than churches, where the feelings of humanity are thus outraged" (94) he writes, with an irony that is deadly serious.

Such a recognition of the didactic power of tragedy emerges clearly in his discussion of revolutionary theater:

> It was but the other day that they caused [the St. Bartholomew's Day massacre] to be acted on the stage for the diversion of the descendants of those who committed it. In this tragic farce they produced the cardinal of Lorraine in his robes of function, ordering general slaughter. Was this spectacle intended to make the Parisians abhor persecution, and loath the effusion of blood?—No, it was to teach them to persecute their own pastors; it was to excite them, by raising a disgust and horror of their clergy, to an alacrity in hunting down to destruction an order, which, if it ought to exist at all, ought to exist not only in safety, but in reverence. . . . The author was not sent to the gallies, nor the players to the house of correction. (157)

As the preceding passages suggests, the St. Bartholomew's Day massacre might well have been narrated as a parable about insurrection and inhumanity instead of as an object-lesson in the clergy's depravity. The difference, as Burke clearly recognizes, is one of narration, a process that conflates the interpretation of historical "event" and a rhetorical argument on behalf of that interpretation.

As Burke's comments on revolutionary drama suggest, the teaching of tragedy hinges not only on the specific narrative that constitutes it, but on that narrative's exclusion of alternative versions. Burke's own tragic history of the revolution suppresses alternatives through a series of substitutions: a revolution in "sentiments, manners, and moral opinions" for one in government; the sixth of October for the fourteenth of July; the creation of a "bastile for Kings" for the storming of the Bastille; orgies of blood for rituals of purgation and sacrifice; the passion of the monarchs and crucifixion of the nobles for the prophesied millennium; tragedy for triumph. To make his ethos as historian compelling, Burke effaces his own shaping interests, describing the events of the revolution as though they had already been taken up within the realm of the historical:

> History will record, that on the morning of the 6th of October 1789, the king and queen of France, after a day of confusion, alarm, dismay, and slaughter, lay down, under the pledged security of public faith, to indulge nature in a few hours of respite, and troubled melancholy repose. (84)

According to Burke, his own narrative is not a fictive invention, but a superfluous gloss on "history, who keeps a durable record of all our acts, and exercises her awful censure over the proceedings of all sorts of sovereigns. . . ."(84). Pointedly, Burke figures the stratagems of the revolutionaries as the sketching of an as-yet-unfinished "history-piece":

> A groupe of regicide and sacrilegious slaughter, was indeed boldly sketched, but it was only sketched. It unhappily was left unfinished, in this great history-piece of the massacre of innocents. What hardy pencil of a great master, from the school of the rights of men, will finish it, is to be seen hereafter. (86)

Beyond revealing a damning palimpsest—the massacre of the innocents—Burke's figure of a "history-piece" presents a historicism as abstract as "the school of the rights of men"; the denouement of the early moments of the revolution are figured here as but the completion of a sketch. In Burke's dour pun, to complete this piece of history will be "to finish" off both the sketch and its sketchers.

In his tragic narrative of the imprisonment of the royal family, Burke pauses to lament the sorrows of Marie Antoinette: "[S]he bears the imprisonment of her husband, and her own captivity, and the exile of her friends, and the insulting adulation of addresses, and the whole weight of her accumulated wrongs, with a serene patience, in a manner suited to her rank and race. . . ."(88). After this lament, the narrative abates in favor of an elegiac recollection of the queen in her former glory; "revolution," here figured as a tragic turn of the wheel of fortune, brings forth a fall:

> It is now sixteen or seventeen years since I saw the queen of France, then the dauphiness, at Versailles; and surely never lighted on this orb, which she hardly seemed to touch, a more delightful vision. I saw her just above the horizon, decorating and cheering the elevated sphere she just began to move in,—glittering like the morning-star, full of life, and splendor, and joy. Oh! what a revolution! and what an heart must I have, to contemplate without emotion that elevation and that fall! Little did I dream when she added titles of veneration to those of enthusiastic, distant, respectful love, that she should ever be obliged to carry the sharp antidote against disgrace concealed in that bosom; little did I dream that I should live to see such disasters fallen upon her in a nation of gallant men, in a nation of men of honour and of cavaliers. I thought ten thousand swords must have leaped from their scabbards to avenge even a look that threatened her insult.—But the age of chivalry is gone. —That of sophisters, oeconomists, and calculators, has succeeded; and the glory of Europe is extinguished for ever. (89)

Whether or not Burke's "morning star" alludes to the Platonic epigram which would afford Shelley's *Adonais* an epigraph and Tennyson's *In Memoriam* a poignant figure of transfiguration, his narrative of the revolution here blossoms into a lyrical elegy not only for the queen's glory, but for the *ancien régime*.[17] The lamented queen serves as a metonymy for "the age of chivalry," her personal glory for that of Europe. What has passed, with the old order, is a culture empowered by its transfigurations—those same transfigurations brought about by the power of sympathy. Burke's own metaphors, in this lyrical lament for the piteous queen, are themselves suggestive of such transfiguring power.[18] The same idealizing order that transforms a woman into a glittering vision of femininity[19] transforms masculine desires—simultaneously sexual and aggressive—into noble aims. If chivalry is Burke's accustomed name for an ethos balancing masculine aggression and feminine taming, we are reminded how much more insistent Burke is in the *Reflections* than in his aesthetic writing on the *virile* practice of sympathy: "I thought ten thousand swords must have leaped from their scabbards to avenge even a look that threatened her insult"(89).

With the passing of the old order, however, pass such transfigurations; Burke resolves the figure of the morning star ironically, pointing out that the queen's fate is not to set gently like an evening star, but to be yanked untimely from the realm of astral comparison: "On this [new] scheme of things, a king is but a man; a queen is but a woman; a woman is but an animal; and an animal not of the highest order"(90). Stripped of chivalry's idealizing accoutrements—of the "ideas, furnished from the wardrobe of a moral imagination"—the "defects of our naked shivering nature"(90) are exposed. Not only do Burke's metaphors in his elegy for the *ancien régime* locate the metaphorical principles of chivalry; the elegy is also metaphorical in a larger sense: it transforms history into a war between the human impulse toward glory and our permanently defective human "nature."

By casting his historical narrative as a tragedy, Burke aspires not to "rouze the imagination" but to "alarm" the mind into "reflecting" on its own reliance on the "dispensations of a mysterious wisdom." But by submitting this tragedy to the incursions of lyric, Burke associates his own transforming imagination with the "mysterious wisdom" of the ages. To move his audience to sympathize with the deposed queen is, paradoxically, to arrest them in a reflection on their own moral nature. By so doing, Burke rejects as subversive the theory of moral circulation and deploys a politics of sympathy to consolidate the moral authority of the British monarchy.

Paine: "Figures in a Magic Lantern"

Several points of my analysis of Burke are anticipated by Paine's blistering critique of the *Reflections*. I want to review the central points of this critique before assessing Paine's rhetorical strategies for the writing of sympathetic history. As Burke attacks Price's heart, Paine attacks Burke's:

> Not one glance of compassion, not one commiserating reflection, that I can find throughout his book, has he bestowed on those who lingered out the most wretched of lives, a life without hope, in the most miserable of prisons. . . . Nature has been kinder to Mr. Burke than he is to her. He is not affected by the reality of distress touching his heart, but by the showy resemblage of it striking his imagination. He pities the plumage, but forgets the dying bird. (288)

While Burke purports to derive his sympathies from his moral nature—a "nature," that is, disposed by prejudice toward that with which it sympathizes[20]—Paine focuses on Burke's mediating imagination. Paine's focus is doubly ironic. Not only does it undermine Burke's claims for his own historiography, but—in terms that echo Price's critique of Shaftesbury and Hutcheson—it indicts Burke for a sympathy linked more closely to aesthetic than to moral judgement. As Burke's lament for chivalry indeed suggests, his moral imagination—that is to say, his sympathy—is stirred by plumage; his moral *indignation*, by animals. Morals, under this critique of the moral sense, are but a cult of taste. For Paine, Burke's particular entanglement of ethics and aesthetics tainted Burke's judgements in both spheres.

But that Burke's imagination corrupts his morals is less disturbing to Paine than that it corrupts his history: "I cannot consider Mr. Burke's book in scarcely any other light than a dramatic performance; and he must, I think, have considered it in the same light himself, by the poetical liberties he has taken of omitting some facts, distorting others, and making the machinery bend to produce a stage effect" (296). Burke's omissions, distortions, and machinations here come under the rubric of his own literary "performance"; contra Burke, Paine shrewdly implicates him as an actor in the tragedy he writes. After quoting Burke's announcement that "History will record" the sufferings of the King and Queen, Paine takes issue with Burke's historiographical style: "This is neither the sober style of history, nor the intention of it. It leaves everything to be guessed at, and mistaken" (298). Paine's immediate complaint, in this passage as in that cited above, is directed at

Burke's substitutions: there, Burke focuses on the monarchs rather than on the prisoners in the Bastille; here, Burke's focus on the monarchs is said to repress mention of the provocations of the *Garde du Corps*.

But Paine's assault widens to include Burke's strategies of representation:

> As to the tragic paintings by which Mr. Burke has outraged his own imagination, and seeks to work upon that of his readers, they are very well calculated for theatrical representation, where facts are manufactured for the sake of show, and accommodated to produce, through the weakness of sympathy, a weeping effect. But Mr. Burke should recollect that he is writing history, and not *plays*. (286)

Paine impugns Burke's invocation of tragedy as a strategy calculated to wring tears from the audience. Here, tragedy works not on the audience's heart, but on its imagination; it produces not weeping but "a weeping effect." Paine mentions Burke's "tragic paintings" to reveal both Burke's artistry and the two-dimensional superficiality of his colorful—and colored—rendering. But whereas Burke indicts the Jacobin "history-piece"—an unfinished sketching of regicide—for its abstraction, Paine's comment emphasizes the manner in which Burke frames his material:

> It suits his purpose to exhibit consequences without their causes. It is one of the arts of the drama to do so. If the crimes of men were exhibited with their sufferings, the stage effect would sometimes be lost, and the audience would be inclined to approve where it was intended they should commiserate. (297)

For Paine, drama is an art that frames actions by repressing their causation. Dramatic emphasis falls on the *grand geste*, rendering acts illegible as "consequences." The "arts of drama," for Paine, are tantamount to those of tableau. The "stage effect" of such framing is a pathetic appeal to the audience; but Paine identifies this pandering after effects as a moral fraud. Were the King's "crimes" included along with his sufferings, the audience's judgement might well *approve* his travails, and sympathy would be forfeited.

Paine's attack on Burke, like Burke's on Price, merges ethical impeachment with an analysis of style; both these attacks on what we might call "ethical style" recognize that rhetorical style is not neutral, but is inflected with intention.[21] Paine's own ethical style must show itself to be immune to the charges he levels at Burke: it must be antitheatrical; eschew blatant, fraudulent appeals to sympathy; liberate actions from their Burkean frames by linking consequences to causes, and causes to consequences; avoid "theatrical exaggerations" (296); and emphasize depth and detail rather than color and veneer. I want now to consider what constitutes Paine's ethical style; what type of representation Paine offers in lieu of—and as a rebuttal to—Burke's invocation of tragedy.

While Paine's comments sometimes run toward melodrama or gothic romance—"[Burke's] hero or his heroine must be a tragedy-victim expiring in show, and not the real prisoner of misery, sliding into death in the silence of a dungeon"(288)—we may understand such gestures as an attempt to liberate his account from the aristocratic cultural authority of tragedy. Paine's more original gestures in this direction, I would argue, evoke a style that twentieth-century readers can conveniently refer to as "cinematic."[22] To begin with, Paine does not select a single climactic scene to represent (analogous to Burke's taking of the King and Queen). Whereas Burke privileges the events of 5–6 October over those of the 14th of July, Paine includes both. By presenting two linked scenes of conflict—the fall of the Bastille, which Paine dubs "this plot against the National Assembly" (293) and the taking of the royals, which Paine gingerly refers to as "the expedition to Versailles"—he suggests an ongoing, unresolved struggle.

Paine launches his account of the taking of the Bastille by emphasizing the visual and isolating the perceiving mind: "The mind can hardly picture to itself a more tremendous scene than [that] which the city of Paris exhibited at the time of taking the Bastille, and for two days before and after, nor conceive the possibility of its quieting so soon" (288). The scene is not perceived by an audience but by a lone mind, as if in darkness, asked to "picture to itself" the scene. After this prologue, Paine offers a flashback which balances the convened National Assembly with a burgeoning conspiracy, headed by the Count de Broglio [Duc de Broglie], "'an high-flying aristocrat, cool, and capable of every mischief.'" Turning to the Assembly, Paine represents the poignant passing of the revolutionary mantle from the elderly Archbishop of Vienne, "a person too old to undergo the scene that a few days, or a few hours, might bring forth" (290), to Lafayette.

Paine's announcement that "the event was freedom or slavery" (290) identifies the two sides with these abstractions. Whereas Burke focuses on individuals, Paine's eye scans the assembled forces: "On one side, an army of nearly thirty thousand men; on the other, an unarmed body of citizens. . . ."(290). As the crisis draws near, the long-range view gives way to a close-up—"In his march, [the Prince de Lambsec] insulted and struck an old man with his sword"—which, in turn, yields to a panning of the crowd: "The French are remarkable for their respect to old age, and the insolence, with which it appeared to be done, uniting with the general fermentation they were in, produced a powerful effect, and a cry of *To arms! to arms!* spread itself in a moment over the whole city"(291). Among Paine's "powerful effects" lies his evocation of the fervid arming of the citizens during the night; he scans the narrow "streets of Paris," the "loftiness of the houses," and passes his gaze over "every sort of weapon they could make or procure: guns, swords, blacksmith's hammers, carpenter's axes, iron crows, pikes, halberds, pitchforks, spits, clubs, etc." (291–92). The following morning a numberless "body of unarmed citizens [dares] to face the military force of thirty thousand men"(292). Emphasizing the perspective of the citizens—"All was mystery and hazard"—Paine breaks off the account before describing the actual attack. In lieu of showing citizens on the offensive, he declares his intention simply to "[bring] into view the conspiracy against the nation which provoked it, and which fell with the Bastille"(293). Burke's tragic fall of the Queen is answered by the fortunate fall of Broglio.

Paine's account of the events of October employs many of the same techniques: panoramic comparison of forces; crowd scenes; sudden changes in perspective; flashback; evocations of passing time through repeated actions; the use of drumbeats and cries providing sound effects; and rapid "cutting" from one location to another. In this account, Paine demonstrates the dramatic irony that attends revealed causation: "[T]he circumstance which serves to throw this affair into embarrassment is, that the enemies of the Revolution appear to have encouraged it, as well as its friends" (298). Whereas the July narrative shows Paine speeding up, as it were, the pace of time, the October narrative shows his ability to slow time down. To increase suspense, he gives frequent indications of time: "He arrived at Versailles between ten and eleven at night" (299); "It was now about one in the morning" (300); "at two o'clock the King and Queen retired" (300). Such temporal indicators allow Paine to expose Burke's compression of events into a single day, a fraud compelled by Burke's "arts of [tragic] drama," which require unity of time. Paine's attentions to the clock allow him to attest that "this scene took up the space of two days, the day on which it began with every appearance of danger and mischief, and the day on which it terminated without the mischiefs that threatened. . . ." (301). Within this difference lies the meaning of M. Bailley's words, "un bon jour"—to Burke, words of brutality; to Paine, words of peace.

Paine's emphasis lies not only on the provocations to the citizens—the plot to spirit the King to Metz; the taking on of the counter-cockade by the *Garde du Corps*; the imprudent decision of a guard to fire on the crowd—but on the revolutionaries' scruples for the safety and well-being of the King and Queen. While Burke allows the Queen center stage, Paine mentions her only to suggest that her alarm was not singular: "not the Queen only, as Mr. Burke has represented it, but every person in the palace, was awakened and alarmed. . . ." (300). Whereas Burke represents the Queen's female person as a celestial body, Paine zooms in on "a very numerous body of women, and men in the disguise of women, collected around the Hotel de Ville or town-hall of Paris, and set off for Versailles" (299). Burke celebrates sexual difference in his lament for chivalric sympathies, for the old order's passive, ethereal women and aggressive, virile, men; Paine cites the abuses of chivalry as the occasion for "the irregularity of such a cavalcade." Before the tyranny of the old order, gender difference gives way to a sense of human wrong; men and women are joined in the march on the *Guard du Corps*. Burke considered the chivalric idea as the "wardrobe of a moral imagination"; but for Paine, even women's garments worn by men en route to Versailles could constitute a "moral wardrobe."

In his concluding remarks about the events of October, Paine contrasts Burke's representational strategy with his own. Impeaching the authority of Burke's eyewitness informer, Lally Tollendal, Paine denies that the populace called for the hanging of the bishops:

> The bishops have never been introduced before into any scene of Mr. Burke's drama: Why then are they, all at once, and altogether, *tout à coup et tous ensemble*, introduced now? Mr. Burke brings forward his bishops and his lantern, like figures in a magic lantern, and raises his scenes by contrast instead of connection. (301)

Who better than Paine to recognize Burke's images of revolution as projections? But whereas Burke's projections are static and contrastive, Paine's projective art is one of connection and motion. His is the art of the *moving* picture; an art of images whose frames are invisible to the eye. In its mobility, Paine's art suggests inclusiveness and comprehensiveness; more important, it models a mode of engaged, enfranchised responsiveness, which its audience is invited to imitate. Paine moves his readers not by evoking pathos, but by sweeping them into the kinetic force field of his narrative. In images of urgency, immediacy, and access, Paine seems to have captured what *must* be recorded, not what *would* be recorded. Burke has faith that "History will record" these fateful events; but Paine claims to leave it to the perceiving mind to "picture to itself" images of revolution. Whereas Burke's tragedy laments the absence of chivalric glory, Paine's magic lantern celebrates the presence of an irresistible force. But if Paine's art succeeds in persuading its audience of their own unmediated relation to the revolution, it is because he is a master of the perspectival manipulations that comprise the art of cinema. Burke might appeal to a divine "Supreme Director" to authorize his tragic revolution; Paine's own direction has produced these moving images of revolution.

Wordsworth: Mixed Feelings

With Jacobin and Tory propagandists alike usurping the role of "Su-preme Director of this great drama," it is hardly surprising that, in the fall of 1791, a young British eyewitness to the Revolution should have felt himself attending

> a theatre of which the stage
> Was busy with an action far advanced.
> Like others I had read, and eagerly
> Sometimes, the master pamphlets of the day,
> Nor wanted such half-insight as grew wild
> Upon that meagre soil, helped out by talk
> And public news; but having never chanced
> To see a regular chronicle which might shew—
> If any such indeed existed then—
> Whence the main organs of the public power
> Had sprung, their transmigrations, when and how
> Accomplished (giving thus unto events
> A form and body), all things were to me
> Loose and disjointed, and the affections left
> Without a vital interest.
>
> (*Prelude* 9:94–108 [1805])[23]

So assiduously do the "master pamphlets of the day" construct their readers as spectators that an eerie aesthetic distance intrudes between the young Wordsworth and the revolution. While the Revolution could be viewed, like ("Among other sights") "the Magdalene of le Brun/A beauty exquisitely wrought" (9:78–79), it was sublimely impossible to *take in*; even a relic from the Bastille, once pocketed, produces no influx of emotion. Writing of his arrival in France some thirteen years later, Wordsworth attributes his lack of "vital interest" to both the unintelligi-bility of events and the incoherence of the revolutionary body politic. In this Burkean retelling, the Revolution has left both the plots and the members of a civilization "loose and disjointed." Such "regular chroni-cles" as Burke and Paine offer are precisely what Wordsworth remem-bers lacking as he attempted to assimilate the phenomena of revolution. As Wordsworth grows progressively closer to violence the figure of the missing "chronicle" becomes radicalized:

> I crossed—a black and empty area then—
> The square of the Carousel, few weeks back
> Heaped up with dead and dying, upon these
> And other sights looking as doth a man

Upon a volume whose contents he knows
Are memorable but from him locked up,
Being written in a tongue he cannot read,
So that he questions the mute leaves with pain
And half upbraids their silence.

(10:46–54)

By September of 1792 at the Place de Carrousel, Wordsworth has taken in too much rather than too little. He rejects the bodies of the "dead and dying" as foreign texts; and yet the violence, like an untranslatable idiom, has taken hold of him.

But when would he take hold of it? As it happened, Wordsworth grasped the plot of the Revolution not through a chronicle but, in the celebrated passage about the "hunger-bitten girl," through a body. The diachronic structure of this passage—percept followed by concept—has led many readers to explore its affinities with those passages in *The Prelude* collectively known as the "spots of time." A recent reading of this passage, for example, casts it in the role of precursor, an unsublimated, politically explicit prototype of such passages as the crossing of the Alps in Prelude VI, in which "banners militant" are borne by minds, not armies.[24] But while the events narrated here take place well before the composition of *The Prelude*, their composition *follows* closely on that of the Alps passage.[25]

Why does Wordsworth, writing in 1804, insist on casting this moment of decisive political significance on the diachronic model of the spots of time? I would suggest that the hunger-bitten girl provides a crucial link between the sentimental paradigm of sympathy and the characteristic diachronism of the Wordsworthian sublime. The vision of the hunger-bitten girl is at once a moment of moral conviction and of political commitment. It occurs under the aegis of Michel Beaupuy, a romantic figure attractive to Wordsworth for his combination of aristocratic noblesse and revolutionary ideals. The landscape through which Beaupuy leads Wordsworth provides the backdrop for the passage—the chateaux and villages of the Loire valley—evoking the traditional romance of a lady whose "high-seated residence" finds her "bound to him [François I] in chains of mutual passion." This romance of an aristocratic lady imprisoned by love—a tale of "cressets and love beacons"—calls forth a sympathetic "gleam" from the young Wordsworth, in whom "chivalrous delight" vies with "virtuous wrath and noble scorn" of aristocratic vices. Using the term "imagination" to name a dualistic power that both enflames him against the aristocracy and mitigates his wrath even to the point of pleasure, Wordsworth attempts to dissolve contradictory political leanings into a single, recognizable moral impulse—sympathy:

> Imagination, potent to enflame
> At times with virtuous wrath and noble scorn,
> Did also often mitigate the force
> Of civic prejudice, the bigotry,
> So call it, of a youthful patriot's mind,
> And on these spots with many gleams I looked
> Of chivalrous delight. Yet not the less,
> Hatred of absolute rule, where will of one
> Is law for all, and of that barren pride
> In those who by immunities unjust
> Betwixt the sovereign and the people stand,
> His helpers and not theirs, laid stronger hold
> Daily upon me—mixed with pity too,
> And love, for where hope is, there love will be
> For the abject multitude.
>
> (9:497–511)

Wordsworth suggests here that his "chivalrous delight" in the aristocratic romance did not decrease his "hatred of absolute rule"; on the contrary, just as the tour of the Loire prepares for the return to Paris, the story of the desirous lady ripens Wordsworth for the claims of liberty.

The term "pity"—one more appropriate to tragedy than to romance—suggests a certain aesthetic distance between Wordsworth and those he contemplates. In accord with sentimental theory, how strong the hatred and how intense the pity depends on how vivid an image Wordsworth is offered. Hume, concluding Book I of the *Treatise of Human Nature*, states with some trepidation that "The memory, senses, and understanding are, therefore, all of them founded on the imagination, or the vivacity of our ideas."[26] The relation between judgement and sense being axiomatic in moral sense theory, Hume can thus assert that "every kind of opinion or judgment, which amounts not to knowledge, is deriv'd entirely from the force and vivacity of the perception. . . ."[27] In the passage just quoted, despite Beaupuy's daily tutelage in the injustices of the *ancien régime*, the claims of a passionate lady out of chivalric romance weigh heavily against the massed claims of "the people," an "abject multitude."

In the person of the hunger-bitten girl, however, arrives a competing stimulus for Wordsworth's sympathies:

> And when we chanced
> One day to meet a hunger-bitten girl
> Who crept along fitting her languid self
> Unto a heifer's motion—by a cord
> Tied to her arm, and picking thus from the lane

> Its sustenance, while the girl with her two hands
> Was busy knitting in a heartless mood
> Of solitude.

$$(9:511-18)$$

It is Wordsworth who is "bitten" by the girl's hunger; she, on the contrary, seems benumbed by it. Tied to a heifer, the girl's degradation is signaled by the "fit" between her "languid self" and the "heifer's motion." Furthermore, the heifer's successful foraging is juxtaposed with her knitting; while the heifer is sensible enough to secure "sustenance," the girl's knitting hands reflect her distracted self-absorption. The hunger-bitten girl might well have been found not in the Loire valley, but in the pages of Smith's *Theory of Moral Sentiments*; her animal movements and "heartless mood/Of solitude" place her among those children and madmen whose insensibility to suffering, according to Smith's taxonomy of sympathetic objects, heightens pathos. As Hume puts it, "[the force and vivacity of the perception] constitute in the mind, what we call the BELIEF of the existence of any object."[28] In Wordsworth's case, perceiving the hunger-bitten girl delivers an intuition of the degradation and poverty which she signifies. In short, the hunger-bitten girl provides a fiercely particular image of suffering that attaches sympathy, under Beaupuy's tutelage, to the work of revolution. Here Wordsworth's great teacher becomes the voice of an authentic revolutionary sympathy, one that escapes Burke's charge of stopping and hardening the heart.

Wordsworth is also at pains here to represent a mode of sympathy in which ethical response is an adjunct of feeling. In this passage, the dual task of sympathetic response and reflection are split between Beaupuy and Wordsworth; together they comprise an ideal of revolutionary sympathy, in which feeling flowers into action and action is nourished by feeling. Context and response are provided by a single agitated statement of Beaupuy's—"at the sight my friend/In agitation said, 'Tis against that/Which we are fighting' "—while reflection is taken up by Wordsworth:

> I with him believed
> Devoutly that a spirit was abroad
> Which could not be withstood, that poverty,
> At least like this, would in a little time
> Be found no more, that we should see the earth
> Unthwarted in her wish to recompense
> The industrious, and the lowly child of toil,
> All institutes for ever blotted out
> That legalized exclusion, empty pomp
> Abolished, sensual state and cruel power,

Whether by edict of the one or few—
And finally, as sum and crown of all,
Should see the people having a strong hand
In making their own laws, whence better days
To all mankind.

(9:520–34)

While Beaupuy responds by focusing attention on the political movement within which he battles injustice, Wordsworth reflects on the mobilization of his own apocalyptic hopes. Poverty, exploited labor, insti-
tutionalized oppression, and disenfranchisement will be expunged not
by violence but by a "spirit . . . which could not be withstood"; it is a
vision of "better days/To all mankind," not specifically to the hunger-
bitten French peasantry. A fertile, willing earth will become an active
partner of human industry in this redeemed polity,[29] in which sovereignty, "the sum and crown of all," has passed to the people. While
Beaupuy is often thought to play the man of action to Wordsworth's
man of contemplation (and, shortly thereafter, perplexity), it should be
noted that like Beaupuy's response, Wordsworth's reflection comes to
rest in an image of action, in the figurative "strong hand" of democratic
autonomy.

In this image culminates what may be called an apocalypse of sympathy, an idealized representation of sympathy as the spontaneous amelio-
ration of the world. Response and reflection are no longer represented
dualistically; instead, reflection spontaneously brings about ameliorative response—in a finer tone. What is clarified by the vision of the
hunger-bitten girl is not a political stance but rather a conviction that
the moral scope of sympathy could be extended to a realm traditionally
identified with the moral authority and intervention of a divine re-
deemer. What Wordsworth, writing in 1804, would want to rescue
from the debacle of revolutionary politics, was the dream of sympathy as
an apocalyptic moral force. By structuring this passage as a sublime
spot of time, Wordsworth identifies his own sympathetic imagination
as redemptive. A decade later, in *The Excursion* (to anticipate one
phase of the argument of chapter 5), the reformational powers of sympathy would become severely circumscribed—regionalized; even per-
sonalized.

•   •   •   •   •

As the passage on the September massacres of 1792 suggests, however,
the mixed feelings resolved here in the discourse of sympathy were soon
to give way to a deeper perplexity. In 1791 Paine could still decry
Burke's misplaced sympathies, still insist that Burke's jaundiced gaze

had passed over the true victim of the drama. By the time Louis XVI had been executed in January of 1793, the tragic narrative at the heart of Burke's *Reflections* had come to seem a prophecy of regicide; considerably more was now at stake in the politics of sympathy. Following the regicide by a mere ten days, Bishop Watson's "Appendix to a Sermon Preached before the Stewards of the Westminster Dispensary" would deploy Burkean pathos to represent regicide as the inevitable culmination of revolutionary violence:

> And are there any men in this kingdom, except such as find their account in public confusion, who would hazard the introduction of such scenes of rapine, barbarity, and bloodshed, as have disgraced France and outraged humanity, for the sake of obtaining—What?—Liberty and Equality.[30]

Wordsworth could not have responded to Watson's Appendix at a more difficult time; his 1793 "Letter to the Bishop of Llandaff" went unpublished.

In the "Letter," debating Watson's "principles" takes a back seat to examining "some incidental opinions found at the commencement of your political confession of faith."[31] Among Watson's "opinions" are the following:

> With respect to the means by which this new republic has been erected in France, they have been sanguinary, savage, more than brutal. They not merely fill the heart of every individual with commiseration for the unfortunate sufferers, but they exhibit to the eye of contemplation an humiliating picture of human nature, when its passions are not regulated by religion, or controlled by law. I fly with terror and abhorrence even from the altar of Liberty, when I see it stained with the blood of the aged, of the innocent, of the defenceless sex, of the ministers of religion, and of the faithful adherents of a fallen monarch. My heart sinks within me when I see it streaming with the blood of the monarch himself. (1:25)

Watson, an apostate from the ranks of revolutionary support, observes that "It is one thing to approve of an end, another to approve of the means by which an end is accomplished" (1:24); he focuses his remarks on the savagery of the Revolutionary process. Building on Burke's myth of British moral nature, Watson seeks "commiseration for the unfortunate sufferers" in "the heart of every individual"; going Burke one better, he metaphorizes Burke's spectacle as "an humiliating picture of human nature" exhibited to "the eye of contemplation." The sentimental catalogue of sufferers reliably contains "the aged and the innocent," as well as women and priests. At the fall of the monarch, the sympathetic Bishop's "heart sinks within. . . ."

Like Paine's reply to Burke, Wordsworth's reply to Watson maneuvers between irony and invective:

At a period big with the fate of the human race, I am sorry that you attach so much importance to the personal sufferings of the late royal martyr and that an anxiety for the issue of the present convulsions should not have prevented you from joining in the idle cry of modish lamentation which has resounded from the court to the cottage. . . . [T]here was not a citizen on the tenth of august who, if he could have dragged before the eyes of Louis the corse of one of his murdered brothers, might not have exclaimed to him, Tyran, voilà ton ouvrage. Think of this and you will not want consolation under any depression your spirits may feel at the contrast exhibited by Louis on the most splendid throne of the universe, and Louis alone in the tower of the Temple or on the scaffold. (1:32)

Wordsworth follows Paine's lead in gesturing toward a more appropriate occasion for sympathy than the murdered king—the king's murderous "ouvrage." He devotes more attention, however, to debunking the pathos that laces Watson's "Appendix." Just as Paine mocks Burke's "violence and grief" ("Mr. Burke is sorry, extremely sorry, that arbitrary power [is] pulled down" [288]), Wordsworth mocks Watson's "depression" by offering to console him with the corpse of a *sansculotte*. Only the image of such a corpse, a murdered "brother" of the citizenry, might defuse the sensational "contrast exhibited by Louis on the most splendid throne of the universe, and Louis . . . on the scaffold"; still, Wordsworth's tableau is haunted by Burke's vignette of the two Marie Antoinettes, angel and animal.[32] Again like Paine, Wordsworth indicts Burke's own moral "nature," calling him an "infatuated moralist," and depicting him seducing Watson with an "intoxicating bowl." Sounding the harshest note in a thoroughly ungentle document, Wordsworth subverts Burke's own attack on the democratic circulation of sympathy:

Mr Burke rouzed the indignation of all ranks of men, when by a refinement of cruelty superiour to that which in the East yokes the living to the dead he strove to persuade us that we and our posterity to the end of time were riveted to a constitution by the indissoluble compact of a dead parchment, and were bound to cherish a corse at the bosom, when reason might call aloud that it should be entombed. (1:48)

While Burke speaks of the legacy of chivalry as that which "distinguished [Europe] from the states of Asia," Wordsworth answers mordantly that reverence for a "dead parchment" is tantamount to the exquisite perversions of "the East." As Edward Said points out, "Orientalism is a style of thought based upon an ontological and epistemological distinction made between 'the Orient' and (most of the time) 'the Occident.'"[33] On either side of the debate, Orientalism is deployed to provide extra leverage for the wielding of moral distinctions.

Whereas Burke sought to move his audience through tragedy and Paine through cinematic narrative, Wordsworth quite radically shapes the revolution as a comedy. Burke and Watson may identify the revolution with the fall of monarchy, but Wordsworth traces the arc of revolution in the era's pregnancy, calling it a "period big with the fate of the human race." Burke and Watson attend the scaffold; Wordsworth, the childbed, anxious "for the issue of the present convulsions." Ridiculing "the idle cry of modish lamentation which has resounded from the court to the cottage," Wordsworth instead announces "a fairer order of things" about to "spring" from the birth-pangs of revolution.

But the satire points toward a crucial intuition about the politics of sympathetic circulation. For Wordsworth the (short-lived) republican, circulation itself is not enough; suddenly the precise path of circulation is at issue. A cry that travels "from the court to the cottage" represents the moral indebtedness of the underclass to the aristocracy; but what of a cry from cottage to cottage? Might sympathy be directed toward consolidating class identity in the interest of reform? Whereas Burke's "tales of distress" had attempted to control sympathy vertically by identifying the "stupendous wisdom" of the dead as a higher moral authority, Wordsworth's *Adventures on Salisbury Plain* would attempt to shape sympathy horizontally by representing how a network of told tales among the oppressed might consolidate "the bond of nature."

But the telling of this tale—or the attempt to tell it—lay two years in the future. Instead of mounting such a tale, Wordsworth's "Letter" takes a strikingly different tack: it baldly attempts a defense of the Terror. Surprisingly, Wordsworth appears to concede Burke's point that revolutionary politics can permanently disable moral response:

> [T]his spirit of jealousy, of severity, of disquietude, of vexation, indispensable from a state of war between the oppressors and oppressed, must of necessity confuse the ideas of morality and contract the benign exertion of the best affections of the human heart. Political virtues are developed at the expence of moral ones; and the sweet emotions of compassion, evidently dangerous where traitors are to be punished, are too often altogether smothered. But is this a sufficient reason to reprobate a convulsion from which is to spring a fairer order of things? (1:34)

How was a period "big with the fate of the human race" to "contract the benign exertion of the . . . human heart"? Having left the child-bed of revolution for England, Wordsworth had already feared that the "present convulsion" might well leave the infant Revolution "altogether smothered." In defending the development of political virtues "at the expence of moral ones," Wordsworth cannot mask his uneasiness; expressing his own mixed feelings about the grim course of the Revolution, he displaces moral virtues onto a redeemed future when the moral re-education of society could begin.

If the reunion of moral and political virtues lay in the future, the future could not begin soon enough. Six months later, in the summer of 1793, Wordsworth would hurry that future into being, writing the poem that would "rectify the erroneous notions which a habit of oppression, and even of resistance, may have created, and to soften this ferocity of character proceeding from a necessary suspension of the mild and social virtues. . . ." (1:34). Aside from tempting him to tempt personal danger, debating the Tory politics of sympathy had forced Wordsworth into an untenable moral position. Abandoning the attack on Tory pathos in the suppressed "Letter," Wordsworth turned instead to "tales of distress" that would evoke sympathy with the cause of reform.

"Tales of Distress": On Salisbury Plain

Representing the Revolution as a tragedy, Burke seeks to evoke a cathartic reflection on the negligible stature of his audience's moral wisdom: "We are alarmed into reflexion; our minds (as it has long since been observed) are purified by terror and pity; our weak unthinking pride is humbled, under the dispensations of a mysterious wisdom" (94). Paine, as I have suggested, impugns Burke's politics of sympathy; he moves his audience toward active response by making them wise partners in the "production" of revolution: "As it is not difficult to perceive . . . that revolutions on the broad basis of national sovereignty, and government by representation, are making their way in Europe, it would be an act of wisdom to anticipate their approach, and produce revolutions by reason and accommodation, rather than commit them to the issue of convulsions" (385). Wordsworth's Salisbury Plain poems, spanning the tumultuous decade of the 1790s, document a shift in Wordsworth's attitude toward the politics of sympathy. In *Salisbury Plain*, written in 1793, Wordsworth frames his sentimental "tale of distress" with a diatribe against the extrinsic causes of his character's oppression. For while such sentimental evocations of sympathy may suggest a democratic distribution of moral authority, they also construct suffering as an effect of reflection rather than as a consequence of circumstance. Wordsworth's frame suggest an emerging sense of uneasiness with the use of sentimental narrative to forge a Jacobin politics of sympathy. Revising the poem as *Adventures on Salisbury Plain* (1795–99), Wordsworth brings this insight to bear on a world in which circumstance not only causes suffering, but now also impedes the "natural" ability to sympathize.

In *Salisbury Plain*, written in 1793, Wordsworth writes a "tale of distress" designed to evoke sympathy for cause of reform. Unlike Burke, who conceals his own framing of history, Wordsworth adds a highly visible frame: a rhetorical polemic that indicates the political context for the "Exile, Terror, Bonds and Force" represented in the narrative. That the "Oppressor's dungeon" may be stormed, the ground of suffering is carefully mapped. As my reading of Charlotte Smith's late, vituperative sonnets suggests, political invective tends to disrupt the decorum of sentimentality; in *Salisbury Plain*, however, the problem is more than simply a breaking of decorum. Wordsworth seems to recognize that the sentimental conventions governing his tale—the very ground on which it makes its pathetic appeal—suggest an intrinsic, rather than extrinsic, provenance for the female vagrant's considerable suffering.[34]

Wordsworth's curiously indirect prologue begins by echoing Rousseau's *Second Discourse*. The comparison between the "Hungry savage" and those who live amid "Refinement's genial influence" appears to indict the civilized evils of inequality and greed for "thoughts which bow the kindly spirits down/And break the springs of joy"(*SP* 19).[35] But the comparison actually demonstrates that suffering is not measurable in absolute, objective terms; suffering, on the contrary, is an effect of perceived difference:

> The thoughts which bow the kindly spirits down
> And break the springs of joy, their deadly weight
> Derive from memory of pleasures flown
> Which haunts us in some sad reverse of fate,
> Or from reflection on the state
> Of those who on the couch of Affluence rest
> By laughing Fortune's sparkling cup elate,
> While we of comfort reft, by pain depressed,
> No other pillow know than Penury's iron breast.
>
> (*SP* 19–27)

In this stanza, Wordsworth aligns two types of difference with a Miltonic "or": that created in the mind when memory juxtaposes two periods of time, and that which exists objectively between the "couch of Affluence" and the unpillowed domain of Penury. By linking the objective difference of social class so casually with the subjective difference of memory, Wordsworth virtually structures the pain of class difference as a function of the reflecting consciousnesss. Suffering may well be caused by "foes more fierce than e'er assail/The savage," but it is represented here as an effect of reflection.

A similar phenomenology of suffering emerges in the narrative of the female vagrant.[36] Wordsworth, calling the vagrant's tale an "artless story," recalls the plangent prefaces of the sonnets of sensibility; the female vagrant is framed both as the subject of her own narrative and as an object of sympathy. Her elegiac refrain ("Can I forget") focuses the lens of memory not on the difference between classes, but on the temporal difference between an idyllic past and a miserable present. She expresses her father's misfortunes ambiguously as an amalgam of "cruel chance and wilful wrong": cleaving to the passive tense, she ascribes his sufferings to "oppression," leaving the specific perpetrator (stanza 34) anonymous. Although the vagrant is directly victimized by the dispossession of her household, she represents her suffering as an "oppression" "by human grief" borne of sympathy for her father:

> "Can I forget that miserable hour
> When from the last hill-top my sire surveyed,
> Peering above the trees, the steeple-tower
> That on his marriage-day sweet music made?
> There at my birth by mother's bones were laid
> And there, till then, he hoped his own might rest.
> Bidding me trust in God he stood and prayed:
> I could not pray, by human grief oppressed,
> Viewing our glimmering cot through tears that never ceased."
>
> (*SP* 262–70)

The father's pathetic prayer reveals a double dispossession: from the Cottage by the Derwent, and, proleptically, from the churchyard in which his wife's bones rest. The link between the living and the dead must now be supplied by the frail language of prayer. The daughter's "human grief" makes such prayer impossible, but binds her more strongly to her father as they begin their exile. To the end of preserving the decorum of pathos, Wordsworth continually elides the matter of agency in the vagrant's narrative; her allegorical assay against the "dog-like" "brood/That lap, their very nourishment, their brother's blood," seems to have strayed into the narrative from the Spenserian rhetoric of the epilogue.

But nowhere is the elision of agency more striking than in the narrator's interjected lament:

> And are ye spread ye glittering dews of youth
> For this,—that Frost may gall the tender flower
> In Joy's fair breast with more untimely tooth?
> Unhappy man! thy sole delightful hour
> Flies first; it is thy miserable dower
> Only to taste of joy that thou may'st pine
> A loss, which rolling suns shall ne'er restore.
> New suns roll on and scatter as they shine
> No second spring, but pain, till death release thee, thine.
>
> (*SP* 217–25)

Here, the premature loss of hope, signified by the elegiac topos of the frosty flower, obtains in the "miserable dower" of "Unhappy man"; Wordsworth's Augustinian cadences compress the sin of Eden into a single act of tasting joy and pining loss. In the final couplet, Gray's much-echoed lament from the Eton College Ode—"No second spring"—aligns this stanza with the reflexive lamentations of sensibility.

Just as the narrator's lament ends with no hope of restored happiness, the vagrant imagines no comfort for her suffering and certainly no seizing upon restitution from the agents of her oppression. Instead, her final stanzas describe a release from pain:

> "Peaceful as this immeasurable plain
> By these extended beams of dawn impressed,
> In the calm sunshine slept the glittering main.
> The very ocean has its hour of rest
> Ungranted to the human mourner's breast.
> Remote from man and storms of mortal care,
> With wings which did the world of waves invest,
> The Spirit of God diffused through balmy air
> Quiet that might have healed, if aught could heal, Despair."
>
> (SP 352–60)

The ocean's eerie quiet offers healing by erasing the consciousness of difference: that between the homeless and those at home; that between the hungry and the fed; and finally, that between the present and the past. "I seemed," says the vagrant, "transported to another world." To "[Roam] the illimitable waters round" is to make a lack of fixity, direction, and destination the paradoxical ground of one's existence; the vagrant's dream of unceasing travel on the ceaseless waves is more truly a dream of stupor, trance, and the fixed gaze.[37] Suicide, ever an alluring possibility, signifies chiefly an end to consciousness. In a literary mode in which suffering is an effect of consciousness, the logical remedy for suffering is to obliterate consciousness.

The female vagrant's movement from ruined spital to cottage suggests a movement from the vacant sites of Christian charity into the institutions of secular benevolism. But her narrative is less securely housed within the structure of Wordsworth's angry meta-narrative. In his conclusion, Wordsworth leaps away from the particularities of the narrative to adopt a magisterial, Johnsonian perspective:

> Nor only is the walk of private life
> Unblessed by Justice and the kindly train
> Of Peace and Truth, while Injury and Strife,
> Outrage and deadly Hate usurp their reign;

From the pale line to either frozen main
The nations, though at home in bonds they drink
The dregs of wretchedness, for empire strain,
And crushed by their own fetters helpless sink,
Move their galled limbs in fear and eye each silent link.

(SP 442–50)

Like Godwin, who undertakes in *Caleb Williams* "a general review of the modes of domestic and unrecorded despotism by which man becomes the destroyer of man,"[38] Wordsworth argues that the personal is political; what impedes the motions of social progress are self-imposed fetters fully as "mind-forg'd" as Blake's manacles. And yet Wordsworth's vehemence seems to acknowledge that these crippling fetters are tempered in part by the painful heat of sentimentalism, in which suffering points not outward to the agents of oppression, but inward to the self's quiet dramas of reflection. The strained, overwrought translations of the poem's final stanza—particular to general, oppressed to oppressor, private to public, effect to cause—betray the "gulf of separation" between the discourse of sentimentality and that of Jacobin protest. Calling on the "Heroes of Truth" to "uptear /Th'Oppressor's dungeon from its deepest base," Wordsworth levels "the herculean mace/Of Reason" squarely at the very assumptions on which the female vagrant's narrative relies to move its audience.[39] If his agenda is, indeed, to "rectify the erroneous notions which a habit of oppression, and even of resistance, may have created," he does so at the expense of his own ethos as a teller of sentimental tales.

· · · · ·

In his biography of Wordsworth, Stephen Gill summarizes Wordsworth's revision of *Salisbury Plain* as follows: "*Salisbury Plain* had sandwiched an illustrative episode between opening and closing declamations that pointed up its significance. *Adventures on Salisbury Plain* works entirely through interlocking human stories."[40] Gill, among others, has observed that the didactic frame of *Salisbury Plain* has collapsed. The revised narrative of the female vagrant is now precariously positioned between sorrow and anger; her prodigious griefs now signify prodigious wrongs. If the female vagrant absorbs a measure of the metanarrative's anger, the poem's "Hero of truth" appears to be the sailor, whose exhortations to "the bond of nature" substitute for the narrator's harsh diatribe against "Exile, Terror, Bonds and Force":

> Then with a voice which inward trouble broke
> In the full swelling throat, the Sailor them bespoke.

> " 'Tis a bad world, and hard is the world's law;
> Each prowls to strip his brother of his fleece;
> Much need have ye that time more closely draw
> The bond of nature, all unkindness cease,
> And that among so few there still be peace;
> Else can ye hope but with such num'rous foes
> Your pains shall ever with your years increase."
>
> (*ASP* 658–66)

The sailor's speech, insofar as it supplies a nexus for the "interlocking stories" of multiple sufferers, seems to be the testing ground for this poem's version of class consciousness. Indeed, the proliferation of narratives suggests less the variety than the commonality of suffering among the oppressed; the poem does indeed seem to send up a cry of lamentation "from cottage to cottage."

But the sailor's "homely truth" of the affections, coming as it does on the lips of a murderer, has hardly a suggestion of the earlier poem's moral absoluteness. More to the point, it is ironically inflected by the sailor's harrowing guilt. The import of this irony is not to subvert the sailor's wisdom, but rather to argue that a particular historical moment of political tyranny and domestic repression has placed the ethos of sympathy in jeopardy. For *Adventures on Salisbury Plain* is written from within the crucible of 1794–95, an era of treason trials, of the suspension of habeas corpus, of a direct assault upon the king's carriage, and finally, of the iron-fisted "Treasonable practices" and "Seditious Meetings" bills of December 1795. What has changed from *Salisbury Plain* to *Adventures*, in other words, is the nature of the "numerous foe." In *Adventures*, the counterforce to the "bond of nature" is not the fetter of intellectual error, but rather the "withering grasp" of fear.

Wordsworth, working from Godwin's necessitarian insights, on the basis of which he seconds Godwin's critique of the penal system in *Caleb Williams*, dramatizes a historical moment in which every cause is a result, and every result a cause; in which public and private crimes are so deeply intertwined as to vex profoundly the task of moral judgement.[41] It is fear, not guilt, that brings on the sailor's crippling affliction. The "good cottage pair" who shelter, succor, then bury the sailor's wife have rational powers sufficient to deduce "He is the man!" but forfeit the task of moral judgement to "the law."[42] In *Adventures*, Wordsworth thematizes the telling of sentimental tales, for such tales themselves tell that the "withering grasp" of fear corrupts the "bond of nature." In lieu of offering a meliorative sympathetic response, the sailor's sympathies, corrupted by fear, place him in the grasp of crippling, paralyzing reflections.

Two interpolated episodes that precede the sailor's arrival at the Spital (stanza 21) sketch, respectively, normative and corrupt paradigms of sympathetic response. In the sailor's meeting with the old man in stanzas 1–5, Wordsworth gives us a vignette of normative sympathetic response. In accordance with Hume's and Smith's theories of sympathy, the ragged, diseased, and impoverished "aged Man with feet half bare," is the more pathetic for not being wholly sensible of his suffering:

> "And dost thou hope across this Plain to trail
> That frame o'ercome with years and malady,
> Those feet that scarcely can outcrawl the snail,
> These withered arms of thine, that faltering knee?
> Come, I am strong and stout, come lean on me."
>
> (*ASP* 10–15)

With "melting heart," the old man relates his intention to assist his daughter, a story that moves the sailor not to "quit his helpless friend" until a post chances to overtake them. Having alleviated the old man's suffering—he is now accompanied and resting comfortably on a cushion—the sailor goes on his way "self-satisfied." Quite schematically, the sailor's sympathy leads primarily to his comforting, meliorative response, and secondarily to his own self-approbating reflections.

A different reaction is evoked by the sight of a man hanging on the gallows:

> The proud man might relent and weep to find
> That now, in this wild waste, so keen a pang
> Could pierce a heart to life's best ends inclined.
> For as he plodded on, with sudden clang
> A sound of chains along the desart rang:
> He looked, and saw on a bare gibbet nigh
> A human body that in irons swang,
> Uplifted by the tempest sweeping by,
> And hovering round it often did a raven fly.
>
> It was a spectacle which none might view
> In spot so savage but with shuddering pain
> Nor only did for him at once renew
> All he had feared from man, but rouzed a train
> Of the mind's phantoms, horrible as vain.
> The stones, as if to sweep him from the day,
> Roll'd at his back along the living plain;
> He fell and without sense or motion lay,
> And when the trance was gone, feebly pursued his way.
>
> (*ASP* 109–26)

If the opening vignette of sympathy derives its momentum from Hume and Smith, the encounter with the gallows derives its force from the Burkean sublime. As Burke observes in the *Philosophical Enquiry*, death is the ultimate referent of all sublime terrors: "what generally makes pain itself, if I may say so, more painful, is, that it is considered as an emissary of this king of terrours. When danger or pain press too nearly, they . . . are simply terrible" (1:vii). Because "the great ought to be dark and gloomy" (3:xxvii), the ear is often the avenue of terror; a "sudden clang" initiates the encounter, delaying the vision of the gallows for a heart-stopping moment. The hanging body, uplifted by the "sweeping" tempest and encircled by the hovering raven, has passed from humanity into the realm of a "savage spot" in nature. The fear generated by these "dire phantasms" is so paralyzing as to "cross" the sailor's sense, disabling emotion altogether; he drops, senseless and motionless, into a trance.[43] That the "train/of the mind's phantoms" entails an image of identification is strongly suggested by the poem's closing image of the sailor on the gallows; if the former image is a premonition of the latter, the latter completes the act of sympathy aborted here.

Listening to tales of other sufferers, the sailor shows a pattern of disabled response in which the familiar token of moved sympathies—the flowing tear—is replaced by a paralyzing, reflective trance. After hearing the vagrant's account of her sea-journey, the sailor becomes figuratively dislocated by his own phantasms; though moved by her tale, he becomes utterly removed from her. In *Salisbury Plain*, the breaking dawn offers the traveler a sign of progress; he "temper[s] sweet words of hope" to comfort the vagrant, as the dawn transfigures her wan face. In *Adventures*, however, the sailor is impervious to the promise of dawn:

> "But come," she cried, "come after weary night
> Of such rough storm the breaking day to view."
> So forth he came and eastward look'd: the sight
> Into his heart a [   ] anguish threw;
> His wither'd cheek was ting'd with ashy hue.
> He stood and trembled both with grief and fear,
> But she felt new delight and solace new,
> And, from the opening east, a pensive chear
> Came to her weary thoughts while the lark warbled near.
>
> (*ASP* 568–76)

While in *Salisbury Plain*, the rosy dawn shown by the sailor "ting'd with faint red smile her faded hue" (338), here it is the vagrant who offers the "eastward" glance to the sailor; dawn, however, merely renders the sailor's face more ashen. While the vagrant "did with a light and chearful step depart," the sailor remains anguished and troubled:

But deep into his vitals she had sent
Anguish that rankled like a fiery dart.
She with affectionate and homely art
His peace of mind endeavour'd to restore:
"Come let us be," she said, "of better heart."
Thus oftentimes the Woman did implore,
And still the more he griev'd, she loved him still the more.

(*ASP* 588–94)

Notably, both the female vagrant and the abusive father recognize the sailor's disturbance as a symptom of sympathy; ironically, the sailor, espouser of the "bond of nature," has now become the occasion for, rather than the donor of, sympathy. Placing the sentimental "bond of nature" in the context of class identity only serves to blind these observers to how inextricably the moral judgement of the working classes is tied up with the abuses of the "num'rous foes." The vagrant's fragile consolation—" 'Why should you grieve," she said "a little while/ And we shall meet in heaven"—suggests the impotence of this natural bond as an instrument of social change. Another sentimental reader, the abusive father, finds "self-reproach" prompted by the weeping sailor, not by his own bleeding son. Even as the sailor shapes the incident of the battered child into a sign of his own wretchedness, the sight of his tears are said to have "beguil'd" the father of his anger.

The deathbed scene that follows, superimposing the bond of marriage upon "the bond of nature,"[44] produces an "extreme distress"—but not sufficiently extreme to unsettle this pattern of aborted (and abortive) sympathies. The sailor does not respond; instead, he reflects, demanding, not offering, comfort: "He cried, 'O bless me now, that thou should'st live/I do not wish or ask: forgive me, now forgive.'" By no means is this guilty outburst to be mistaken for a confession; thereafter, the sailor's wrenching somatic symptoms and hallucinations intensify, leading him to seek the respite from consciousness—"Oh God that I were dead"—that only the gallows can offer.

As an attempt to use sympathy to represent and promote the consolidation of class interest, *Adventures on Salisbury Plain* is a failure. Wordsworth's attempt to mobilize a community of sorrow is thwarted by the sailor's paralyzing implosions of consciousness. As a Godwinian act of persuasion, however, the poem succeeds in laying blame for the corruption of "the bond of nature" (rather than reason, as Godwin would have it) at the feet of a politically repressive, judicially corrupt and militaristic government. If the "bond of nature" in spite of Burke's desire to sustain it, has been ravaged by repressive Tory policy, Wordsworth also shows its limitations as a politics of reform. In both Salisbury Plain poems, Wordsworth implicitly questions certain quietistic assumptions that lie behind sentimentalism and impair it as a rhetorical instrument of reform. Wordsworth's conservative construction of sentimentalism provides a sharp reply to Burke's nightmare of unmanaged sentimental circulation. Later, in the apocalyptic vision of the hunger-bitten girl, Wordsworth would attempt to transcend the gap between reflection and response. But upon this gap, variously exploited by both Burke and Paine to different ends, Wordsworth's Jacobin politics of sympathy foundered.

Politics and Ethics

The sympathetic spectacles produced by Burke and Paine foreshadow the two major rhetorical strategies for partisan politics in the decades after Waterloo; after 1815, the immediate task for Britain was to decide whether to celebrate or renovate itself. The contrary positions of Burke and Paine became revived and enmeshed in dialectic of sympathies: an appeal, from the right, to the sympathies of "moral nature" shared by a homogenous nation; and a contrary appeal, from the left, to the particular sympathies of class and creed, to the end of progressing toward reform.

But the immediate legacy of the conscription of sentimentalism for propaganda in the 1790s was a deep, nostalgic pessimism concerning the moral value of sympathy. After a decade in which sympathy was recruited alternately for the moral renovation or preservation of society, it was now being collapsed into the psychologism of sensibility—a development prophesied and, I would emphasize, resisted by Wordsworth's youthful sonnet on Helen Maria Williams. Whereas in early 1795 the Godwinian Wordsworth understood ruinous grief as a symptom of governmental intervention in the imagination, such grief would soon be understood as a symptom of the imagination's need for government:

> Starting from the dream of youth, [man] turns disgusted from the loathsome scene; perhaps, retires to commune with himself, to pause upon the lot of mortality.
>
> To this important crisis, many of the characters which adorn or blot the records of humanity, owe their origin. . . . [S]ome there are, gifted with an imagination of the most brilliant kind; who are accustomed to expatiate in all the luxury of an ideal world, and who possess a heart glowing with the tenderest sensations. These men too frequently fall a sacrifice to the indul-

gence of a warm and vigorous fancy, and which is, unhappily, not sufficiently corrected by a knowledge of mankind, or the rigid deduction of
scientific study.[45]

Here, in "The Government of the Imagination" (1798), Nathan
Drake displaces the debacle of the revolutionary ideals onto what we
might call the growth of an individual mind. "Knowledge" and "science," proposed here as neutral, apolitical pursuits, offer an implicit
tonic to the rampant pathology of politics. In an essay on melancholy,
Drake makes clear that the ungoverned imagination leads directly from
the dissolution of the individual, to that of society:

> That this amiable and tender sorrow so frequently the concomitant of the
> best disposition and principles, and the certain test of a generous and sus-
> ceptible heart, that this should be so often carried to an extreme, should so
> often militate against our social and domestic duties, is an event which
> merits the most serious attention. It is not however uncommon; he, to
> whom these sweet but melancholy sensations have been once known, will
> not easily be persuaded to relinquish them; he shuns society, and, dwelling
> on the deprivations he has suffered, seeks to indulge what, when thus cher-
> ished, is but childish imbecility. (1:61)

For Drake, the "generous and susceptible heart" is more likely to even-
tuate in a voluptuousness of melancholy than in the bettering of society.
In an oblique history of the fall of melancholy, the politicization of sympathy in the 1790s is tenderly lamented:

> [T]he melancholy of Milton, Young, and Gray, was so repressed by the
> chastening hand of reason and education, as never to infringe upon the
> duties of life; the spirit, the energy of Milton's comprehensive soul, the
> rational and sublime piety of Young, the learning and morality of Gray,
> powerfully withheld the accession of a state of mind so inimical to the rights
> of society. (1:82)

Unable to accord any ethical value to the discourse of politics, Drake's
retrograde essay calls on Milton's sublimity, Young's piety, and Gray's
learning as moral insurance against solipsism. Urging the restriction of
sympathy to grief, rather than grievance, Drake warns against unwar-
ranted indulgences in "the luxury of grief."

The year 1798 would find Drake attacking grief as a cover for self-
pleasure and Wordsworth writing a long narrative poem—*The Ruined
Cottage*—on the "impotence of grief"; clearly the role of sympathy in
what Burke had called "liberal and manly morals" was in some doubt.
But if the rhetorical politics of sympathy had cast a long shadow on the

morality of sympathy, it had also focused attention on the rhetoric of morals. In an unfinished "Essay on Morals," written in 1798 or 1799, Wordsworth abandons the dualistic discourse of sympathetic response and reflection of sympathy in favor of an inquiry into moral "habits." Excoriating "systems of morality" that set "an undue value . . . upon that faculty which we call reason," Wordsworth advises that "our attention ought principally to be fixed upon that part of our conduct and actions which is the result of our habits" (1:103). Because "in a strict sense all our actions are the result of our habits," moral action can be regarded as an effect of habit. Habit, it appears, is formed by a process independent of reflection:

> Now, I know no book or system of moral philosophy written with sufficient power to melt into our affections[?s], to incorporate itself with the blood & vital juices of our minds, & thence to have any influence worth our notice in forming those habits of which I am speaking. . . . Can it be imagined by any man who has deeply examined his own heart that an old habit will be foregone, or a new one formed, by a series of propositions, which, presenting no image to the [? mind] can convey no feeling which has any connection with the supposed archetype or fountain of the proposition existing in human life? (1:103)

What Wordsworth desires of this type of moral writing is that it act on us as something *other* than writing; as something that "influences" us immediately and spontaneously by melting and flowing within us. Wordsworth's characterization of this type of writing recalls the sentimental insistence on spontaneous and immediate writing as a sign of the author's sincerity—only Wordsworth has displaced the elegist's claims onto the text, said here to "produce" its own influential meanings. More important, this influential process displaces and annuls the reader's reflective powers; what the idiom of reasoned reflection might render a self-conception, is here rendered as the engendering of a reading by the text.

At the same time, Wordsworth replaces rationalist "system and proposition" with image and description, rhetorical modes that "inform" us by *referring* to "human life."

> [Rationalist systems] contain no picture of human life; they *describe* nothing. They in no respect enable us to be practically useful by informing us how men placed in such or such situations will necessarily act, & thence enabling us to apply ourselves to the means of turning them into a more beneficial course, if necessary, or of giving them new ardour & new knowledge when they are proceeding as they ought. (1:103–4)

Moral writing is given the task of "enabling us to be practically useful" by multiplying our experience of moral judgement beyond our own biography. We make judgements, as it were, as though we had the benefit of multiple selves. Becoming informed, then, consists in acquiring the habits of many selves; being influenced, in giving over self-consciousness to the formation of a habitual self. In both cases, the price of rescuing sympathy from the realm of rhetoric—the price of moving beyond the dualism of reflection and response—is to render sympathy an unconscious phenomenon.

In essence, this essay could be abandoned because, with *The Ruined Cottage*, the project it attempts had already been achieved: begun in 1797 and revised in 1798 and 1799, *The Ruined Cottage* boldly gives over the attempt to ground an ethos of sympathy in action by evoking a moral ideal of "natural sympathy." In the following chapter, we will see how Wordsworth's acknowledgment of "the impotence of grief" in *The Ruined Cottage* leads him to discover new names for grief's estimable powers.

·PART TWO·

AUTHENTIC EPITAPHS

FOUR

"THE IMPOTENCE OF GRIEF": WORDSWORTH'S
GENEALOGIES OF MORALS

For poetry makes nothing happen: it survives
In the valley of its saying where executives
Would never want to tamper; it flows south
From ranches of isolation and the busy griefs,
Raw towns that we believe and die in; it survives,
A way of happening, a mouth.
　　　　　　　　　　(W. H. Auden)

For me, nature that lacks compassion is the most beautiful: a
cold world in another world.
　(Zbigniew Herbert, trans. John and Bogdana Carpenter)

Powers "To Virtue Friendly": Two Faces of Grief

WHAT GIVES *The Ruined Cottage* its peculiar quality of being unforgettable—to the young man listening by the cottage; to Coleridge, Lamb, and others of Wordsworth's circle; to readers of our own day who continue to hold it in high esteem[1]—is the abyss between Margaret's deep suffering and the Pedlar's deeply felt sympathy for her. Students who ask me why the Pedlar "didn't do more for her" are asking both the right and the wrong question. Surely we need to notice that the Pedlar's sympathy for Margaret is wholly as inefficacious as Margaret's anguish for her lost Robert. On the other hand, we notice also that the uselessness of sympathy functions as a principle of plot: in this narrative of "partings welded together" (to borrow Dickens's memorable phrase), sympathy routinely, even ritually, fails to alter a world of bad harvests, rural dislocation, deserting husbands, negligent mothers, and starving children. As a result of the "impotence of grief," grief accumulates. Not only does the Pedlar's sympathy fail to ameliorate Margaret's lot materially; it barely comforts her. Only one of their conversations, having "built up a pile of better thoughts" (D279),[2] can be called constructive; from the start, the Pedlar confesses that "I had little power/To give her comfort" (D275–76). Sympathy fails, in part, because Margaret's character is defined by her refusal of comfort—"She thanked me for my will, but for my hope/It seemed she did not thank me" (D385–92)—a refusal that restricts her human connections to an endless series of comfortless meetings:

> Yet ever as there passed
> A man whose garments shewed the Soldier's red,
> Or crippled Mendicant in Sailor's garb,
> The little child who sate to turn the wheel
> Ceased from his toil, and she with faltering voice,
> Expecting still to learn her husband's fate,
> Made many a fond inquiry; and when they
> Whose presence gave no comfort were gone by,
> Her heart was still more sad.
>
> (D462–70)

In *The Ruined Cottage*, the failure of sympathy is *structural*: both in terms of narrative and character, sympathy is bereft of power to bring forth an ameliorating response.[3]

And yet in *The Ruined Cottage* it is not true that grief, as Auden says of poetry in his elegy for Yeats, makes nothing happen. In default of the ameliorative myths of sentimental benevolism, Wordsworth nonetheless draws from "the impotence of grief" an ethical self-consciousness that he identifies with power:

> "It were a wantonness and would demand
> Severe reproof, if we were men whose hearts
> Could hold vain dalliance with the misery
> Even of the dead, contented thence to draw
> A momentary pleasure never marked
> By reason, barren of all future good.
> But we have known that there is often found
> In mournful thoughts, and always might be found,
> A power to virtue friendly."
>
> (D221–29)

In the Pedlar's "mournful thoughts," grief and sympathy are linked; Wordsworth, like Adam Smith, recognizes grief as a type of sympathy, sympathy as an incidence of grief. As the previous chapter suggests, Wordsworth's reevaluation and reconstitution of the moral meanings of these crucial sentimental terms results from his Jacobin experiments in the politics of sympathy. Undertaken from within the ruins of sentimental theory, Wordsworth's bracing reassessment of grief and sympathy in

The Ruined Cottage issues, as I will argue in this chapter and the next, in his thinking about morals for two decades to follow, and ultimately in the "authentic epitaphs" of *The Excursion*.

·   ·   ·   ·   ·

Let us begin by asking what the Pedlar takes to be the "power" of "mournful thoughts," and how or why such thoughts are "friendly" to virtue. For the Pedlar, "mournful thoughts" have two distinct powers— powers he presents as contradictory, indeed competing, modes of conso- lation. First, they can produce what the Pedlar calls "the strong creative power/Of human passion" (D78–79):

> The Poets in their elegies and songs
> Lamenting the departed call the groves,
> They call upon the hills and streams to mourn,
> And senseless rocks, nor idly; for they speak
> In these their invocations with a voice
> Obedient to the strong creative power
> Of human passion.
>
> (D73–79)

Wordsworth's reference to "elegies" is significant for evoking not the sentimental sonnets of the 1770s and 1780s, but classical pastoral elegy.[4] Here, Wordsworth revives a tradition that lay dormant through- out much of the eighteenth century, but which—owing in part to Words- worth's pastoral elegiac allusions in the "Intimations Ode"—was to un- dergo a revival in the hands of such nineteenth-century poets as Shelley, Arnold, Swinburne, and Yeats. A fuller account of Wordsworth's use of the pastoral elegy tradition will appear later in this chapter; for now it will suffice to observe that the Pedlar's tale of Margaret begins by insis- tently evoking several pastoral elegiac conventions:

> O Sir! the good die first,
> And they whose hearts are dry as summer dust
> Burn to the socket. Many a passenger
> Has blessed poor Margaret for her gentle looks
> When she upheld the cool refreshment drawn
> From that forsaken spring, and no one came
> But he was welcome, no one went away
> But that it seemed she loved him. She is dead,
> The worm is on her cheek, and this poor hut,
> Stripp'd of its outward garb of houshold flowers,

Of rose and sweet-briar, offers to the wind
A cold bare wall whose earthy top is tricked
With weeds and the rank spear-grass. She is dead. . . .
(D96–108)

In these thirteen lines, we hear an elegiac refrain ("She is dead") as well as the elegiac exclamation that would resonate ironically in Shelley's ear as he composed the Preface to *Alastor*[5] fifteen years later: "O sir! the good die first. . . ."(D96). Wordsworth focuses (as Ruskin would in his discussion of "the pathetic fallacy"[6]) on nature's phenomenal sympathy for the human condition. While he emphasizes the poet's "calling" voice, he evokes not a responsive voice of "senseless" rocks, but rather an *image* of nature's feeling for humanity. This image, soon to be contrasted with that of a blithe natural world in the heyday of the cottage, gives onto another pair of contrasting images. As in the great pastoral elegies of the Renaissance—among them, Spenser's *November* eclogue from *The Shepheardes Calender* and Milton's *Lycidas*—the "strong creative power" of passionate grief presents both an image of Margaret *then*, pictured ministering, like Spenser's Dido and Milton's Lycidas; and Margaret *now*, pictured—also like Dido and Lycidas—as a wasted corpse.

Like the elegiac speakers of Spenser and Milton, each of whom acknowledges the brutality of mortal change, the Pedlar risks "sinking" under the terrible burden of negotiating among these images:

—You will forgive me, Sir,
But often on this cottage do I muse
As on a picture, till my wiser mind
Sinks, yielding to the foolishness of grief.
(D116–19)

Having touched "bottom," the speakers of *November* and *Lycidas* have recourse to at least the rhetoric of transcendental consolations;[7] from their elegiac despair rise consoling images, however fragile, of transcendental succor. The Pedlar, of course, makes no such transcendental gesture. But at precisely the point where a vision of elegiac consolation might begin, he inaugurates his narrative of Margaret's tale with images of the living, suffering Margaret: "She had a husband, an industrious man. . . ." (D120). Such images both expose elegiac visions of transcendence as human artifacts, and replace them with redemptive visions of human life. What the "creative power of human passion" brings forth is the passion of human history, a narrative of contingency, both textual and thematic. In *The Ruined Cottage*, the "consolation" for brutal images of mortal change is the mortal narrative which such images make

possible. Wordsworth's consolation is neither transcendental nor immanent; it is rather a process of textual revival that neither celebrates nor
denies the change of death. In Wordsworth's hands, elegiac hymn becomes elegiac history.

But "mournful thoughts" have a second "power to virtue friendly."
While grief's power to "sink" the mind may suggest the "foolishness" of
elegiac despair, it also suggests that "mournful thoughts" are empowered to lead the mind into its depths—that they have a second "power to
virtue friendly":

> "Sympathies there are
> More tranquil, yet perhaps of kindred birth,
> That steal upon the meditative mind
> And grow with thought. Beside yon spring I stood
> And eyed its waters till we seemed to feel
> One sadness, they and I. For them a bond
> Of brotherhood is broken. . . .
>
> . . . .
> . . . . When I stooped to drink,
> A spider's web hung to the water's edge."
>
> (D79–89)

These "kindred" sympathies do not originate in passion; rather, they
emerge from habits of meditation and mature with thought. Unlike passionate sympathies, these sympathies do not call on nature for response,
nor do they yield an image of nature responding. This second type of
grief appears to value nature for precisely the tranquility that passionate
grief cannot tolerate. Moreover, such grief interprets what Zbigniew
Herbert has called "a cold world within another world" not as a sign of
indifference, but as a sign of sympathy; as a sign, that is, of nature's
moral value. Within nature's apparent inertia, "mournful thoughts"
may discover a life that signifies ministering, comfort and—most important—continuity. Stooping to drink, the Pedlar celebrates his own communion with these sad waters.

For the Pedlar, this sympathy is distinctly superior to that imagined by
the impassioned elegist; it draws comfort not from the narratives that
emerge from images of change, but from a sense of penetrating the
changing *appearances* of nature to reach a changelessness within, indifferent to human mortality. Paradoxically, this indifference is said to provide comfort:

> "Be wise and chearful, and no longer read
> The forms of things with an unworthy eye.
> She sleeps in the calm earth, and peace is here.

> I well remember that those very plumes,
> Those weeds, and the high spear-grass on that wall,
> By mist and silent rain-drops silver'd o'er,
> As once I passed did to my heart convey
> So still an image of tranquillity,
> So calm and still, and looked so beautiful
> Amid the uneasy thoughts which filled my mind,
> That what we feel of sorrow and despair
> From ruin and from change, and all the grief
> The passing shews of being leave behind,
> Appeared an idle dream that could not live
> Where meditation was. I turned away
> And walked along my road in happiness."
>
> (D510–25)

Admonishing the young Poet "no longer [to] read/The forms of things with an unworthy eye," the Pedlar invests nature with his own moral worth; not surprisingly, he finds nature richly "silver'd o'er." In an analogous act of displacement, the Pedlar denies his own creative power; hence, an "image of tranquillity" is *conveyed* to him, not *produced* by him. Such images, like "A spider's web hung to the water's edge" are autonomous, generated by nature, not by the human observer.

Accordingly, this denial of creativity is simultaneously a denial of contingency. So deeply does the Pedlar invest in the image of nature's tranquility, that its human origins become obscured; this image of nature comes to signify a deeper reality than that of human experience. The Pedlar's "chearfulness and happiness" express not a facile, aesthetic delight in nature—for such is Browning's critique of Wordsworthian "silvering o'er" in *Andrea del Sarto*—but rather a consolation of immanence. Whereas the former "power" of grief arrives at consolation by recognizing the power of images, this second "power" of grief arrives at consolation by *seeing through images*. Within the very phrase lies a crucial ambiguity. On the one hand, "seeing through images" may mean penetrating nature to reveal the immanence of the buried Margaret: "she sleeps in the calm earth." Alternately, "seeing through images" may mean using them as a filter or lens for perception. Seen *through* the image of natural tranquility, human experience breaks down into fragile images that are uncongenial to narrative; to the Pedlar, the "passing shews of being" appear "an idle dream that could not live/Where meditation was." The image of a tranquil nature, transmuted into an immanent, even sacramental presence, vanquishes—even nullifies—the sorrowful images of human history, bound up as they are in disruption and mortality.

Perhaps the widespread critical uneasiness with the Pedlar's consolation rests on the young Poet's perplexed reception of the old man's "natural wisdom." For such wisdom seems to arise as a defense against the power of narrative images. The Pedlar's six returns to Margaret's cottage (before and after her death) both prophesy and allegorize Margaret's propensity to return, unbidden, to his thoughts. Manuscript D (1799), to which Wordsworth added the Pedlar's consolation, also contains new lines on Margaret's haunting presence:

> "Sir, I feel
> The story linger in my heart. I fear
> 'Tis long and tedious, but my spirit clings
> To that poor woman: so familiarly
> Do I perceive her manner, and her look
> And presence, and so deeply do I feel
> Her goodness, that not seldom in my walks
> A momentary trance comes over me;
> And to myself I seem to muse on one
> By sorrow laid asleep or borne away,
> A human being destined to awake
> To human life, or something very near
> To human life, when he shall come again
> For whom she suffered."
>
> (D362–75)

Neither Margaret nor mortality, as the young Poet seems to notice, is so easily buried within nature. If the Pedlar is haunted, it is because he is a conjuror, whose "busy eye" creates not simply images, but apparitions:

> He had rehearsed
> Her homely tale with such familiar power,
> With such a[n active] countenance, an eye
> So busy, that the things of which he spake
> Seemed present, and, attention now relaxed,
> There was a heartfelt chillness in my veins.
> I rose, and turning from that breezy shade
> Went out into the open air and stood
> To drink the comfort of the warmer sun.
>
> (D208–16)

The Pedlar's "familiar power" renders Margaret a virtual "familiar" of his narrative sorcery. The Poet, compelled to "review that Woman's suff'rings," senses Margaret's presence with a "chillness in my veins," which he moves to shun; blessing Margaret "with a brother's love," he becomes an initiate into that somber magic, another "familiar."

The Pedlar's "natural wisdom," then, can be read as a defense against the grip of his own elegiac images; his response to this trance is to bury the mortal images of his narrative within nature, releasing Margaret— into the ground, into sleep, into death, into unconsciousness, or into human life repeated, as Keats would say, "in a finer tone." However defensive the Pedlar's strategy—and however readily we recognize it as a mode of moral imagination—it is presented in this poem as a movement that *subsumes and moves beyond* images of the dead past and the grieving present that constitute the elegiac power of "mournful thoughts." Though the Pedlar strives toward a consolation of immanence, we discern here the temptation to transcend one's own arresting, even paralyzing images. Having "buried" Margaret, the Pedlar exhorts the Poet to do the same: "My Friend, enough to sorrow have you given, The purposes of wisdom ask no more" (D508–9). The young Poet is asked to pass beyond the "strong creative power of human passion"— albeit a power "friendly" to virtue—and trust in the moral life of nature.

. . . . .

The two faces of grief in *The Ruined Cottage*—the distinct powers generated by "mournful thoughts"—suggest two theories of ethics that inform Wordsworth's writing in the decade following *The Ruined Cottage*. On the one hand, several of Wordsworth's lyrics align him with the young Poet of *The Ruined Cottage*, for whom the emergence of ethical "wisdom" results from both recognitions of loss and redemptive narratives of human history. In such elegiac poems as "Tintern Abbey," "The Intimations Ode," and *Elegiac Stanzas Suggested By a Picture of Peele Castle*, the haunted youth of *The Ruined Cottage* becomes the poet who advances morally by returning to his own scenes of ruin and of hope. On the other hand, Wordsworth, like the Pedlar, can be found arguing that morals "[grow] with thought," identifying a human sympathy with (and faith in) nature as the ground of ethical consciousness. In Book 8 of *The Prelude*, as well as in several crucial early fragments, Wordsworth represents his progression from "love of Nature" to "love of Mankind" as the fulfillment of an ethical potential immanent within himself.

But if *The Ruined Cottage* shows us these two different faces of grief, it also allows us to glimpse resemblances between them. The Pedlar's "natural wisdom" provides a defense against his own passionate images. The young Poet embraces the elegiac image of Margaret as a resistance to the Pedlar's sublime attempt to bury her within nature. By casting this correspondence in terms of defense and resistance, I want to urge a certain skepticism regarding Wordsworth's narrative, which associates the elegiac genealogy of morals with callow youth, the organicist genealogy with a seasoned and wise maturity. In other words, this juxtaposition of young Poet and aged Pedlar suggests that one genealogy can be subsumed, over time, into the other. But I would argue that this sequence represents not only the Pedlar's discomfort with his own imaginary powers, but Wordsworth's own desire to see these two theories of morals reconciled to one another. At the conclusion of this chapter, I will return to the matter of Wordsworth's desire to see his two genealogies—and the historicism that underwrites them—coalesce. But in the next two sections, I will argue that representing these genealogies as successive stages in the path to an ethical life is merely one way among several in which Wordsworth strove to establish the mutual resemblance of the two faces of grief. By the end of the decade following *The Ruined Cottage*, Wordsworth had come to recognize both faces of grief as his own.

Elegiac Genealogy: "A Deep Distress Hath Humanized My Soul"

Wordsworth's elegiac genealogy of morals—the tracing of moral development to an incidence of loss—takes shape as a revision of the Christian pastoral elegy tradition. As Ellen Lambert and Renato Poggioli have suggested, Christian pastoral is less a tradition, than a traditional *problem* that centers on the assimilation of a Christian metaphysics to a classical literary mode.[8] One is reminded of the old sophomore survey question: "Can there be a Christian tragedy?"[9] Can pastoral mourning be reconciled with the Christian faith in redemption? Can pastoral consolations, for that matter, possibly serve Christianity's apocalyptic resolutions? Medieval Christian poets had felt acutely both the limitations and resources of Virgilian pastoral; as Annabel Patterson has pointed out, medieval readers of Virgil's Fifth and Tenth Eclogues focused on interpreting them as allegories of Christ's passion.[10] Renaissance poets, by extending pastoral conventions to evoke and mourn the Edenic condition, afforded a more central place to pastoral in western literary consciousness than it had previously enjoyed. Still, as Books XI and XII of *Paradise Lost* suggest, the limited purview of pastoral lamentation would ill support the sweeping apocalyptic perspective inherent in the Christian worldview. To render and sustain the Christian myth of history, the support of a pastoral source beyond Virgil's Fifth and Tenth Eclogues was required.

It was found not in Virgil's pastoral elegies, but in his Fourth Eclogue, the Pollio. As Poggioli has observed, medieval commentators conflated imagery derived from Virgil's Pollio with evocations of the Nativity in Luke and Matthew through the process of *contaminatio*.[11] But more important than the Pollio's enhancement of the commentary tradition was the specific cluster of images it offered—a child-saviour, his divine mother, a Providential divinity, the defeat of original sin, the vision of a golden age—imagery that dovetailed with the Christian mythology of redemption. With its Virgilian origins divided between the retrospective Fifth Eclogue and the prospective Fourth Eclogue, Christian pastoral elegy glances, Janus-like, back toward an Edenic past and ahead toward a new heaven and a new earth; that is, toward a future in which a lost Paradise shall be redeemed and regained.

As the foregoing discussion suggests, Christian pastoral elegy is tripartite in structure: it retrieves an image of the deceased, passionately laments an image of the privative present, and celebrates the transcendence of the dead through a visionary evocation of grace, an event which in turn promises the redemption of humanity. The retrieval of Christian pastoral in the nineteenth century follows a revolutionary period in which secular politics and religious apocalypse are frequently merged by writers at both ends of the political spectrum. But the most influential meditation on pastoral elegy for nineteenth-century poets was not written until the long days of the Terror. Friedrich von Schiller, in *On Naive and Sentimental Poetry* (1795), found the tripartite structure of the pastoral elegy tradition suggestive for a theory of how individuals—not a National Assembly and not a Committee for Public Safety—may advance a progressive humanism through the creation of aesthetic images. Schiller's most significant revision of Christian pastoral elegy is to adapt it to the mourning of an internal sense of loss or lack. What was traditionally described as an explicit event observed within a public sphere— as explicit, say, as the death of Spenser's Dido or Milton's Lycidas—now becomes an implicit, private sense that something *has been* lost. After all, the pastoral elegiac contrast between images of the present and the past already elides the catastrophic event of loss. It is not so great a step from this practice of contrasting images to the internalization of elegiac loss. Schiller's revisionary internalization of elegy under the rubric of the "sentimental" temperament leads Coleridge to observe that, "Elegy is the form of poetry natural to the reflective mind. It *may* treat of any subject, but it must treat of no subject *for itself*; but always and exclusively with reference to the poet himself. . . ."[12] But for all of Schiller's theorizing—and all of Coleridge's losses—it was Wordsworth who would develop the profoundly influential rhetoric of subjective loss in lyrics that remain today at the center of British Romanticism. In Wordsworth's elegiac poems—among them, "Tintern Abbey," the "Intimations Ode," and "Elegiac Stanzas Suggested By a Picture of Peele Castle," what is lamented is always recognizably an image of the self.[13] In the context of such elegies, Wordsworthian autobiography—that brood-

ing sense of "Two consciousnesses" in *The Prelude* (2:32)—is more saliently a phenomenon of self-haunting than of self-making; it brings the
subject face to face with its own "other being."

The essential difference between Schiller and Wordsworth lies in their
respective revisions of elegiac consolation. Schiller, calling for a new
"Elysium," appeals to the transcendentalism of Christian pastoral elegy
as a potent trope for a secular, aesthetic redemption; he models his aesthetic utopianism on the new heaven and new earth of Christian mythology. *The Ruined Cottage* finds Wordsworth close to Schiller in substituting the artifact of narrated human history for the visionary consolations
of Christian pastoral. But after *The Ruined Cottage*, Wordsworth's
poems of loss veer away from displacing salvific religious images with
redemptive secular ones. In the "Intimations Ode," for example, Wordsworth replaces Christian transcendence with *descendental* tropes evoking necessity, rather than redemption. Such tropes confirm the inevit-
ability of such curtailments of self as the Ode mourns. While Schiller's
ethical consolation resides in the individual's aesthetic freedom, Wordsworth identifies the ethical not with an aesthetic recovery from loss, but
rather with a sober recognition of the human propensity to be fatally
diminished. In this section, I want to argue that Wordsworth's elegiac
poems approach the very *generation* of elegiac imagery—not simply images of consolation—as a problem. If Wordsworth's elegiac poems are
essentially elegies for the self, it should not surprise us that elegiac imagery represents a threat, for such images are necessarily entangled with
the mortality of the poet. When the elegiac image depicts a former self,
it evokes the posthumous quality of autobiographical narrative.

· · · · ·

First, a brief consideration of "Tintern Abbey" will suggest how
problematic elegiac images are by showing how systematically Wordsworth displaces and suppresses them in this poem. In "Tintern Abbey,"
Wordsworth defines the sympathetic imagination *against and by contrast to* the image-producing faculty of the mind. Since four distinct
types of loss and recovery are considered within the poem, we can readily observe Wordsworth's reluctance to produce elegiac images of his
own life story. After the initial meditation on the appearance of the landscape after an absence of five years, Wordsworth considers first a loss of
place:

> These beauteous forms,
> Through a long absence, have not been to me
> As is a landscape to a blind man's eye:

But oft, in lonely rooms, and 'mid the din
Of towns and cities, I have owed to them
In hours of weariness, sensations sweet,
Felt in the blood, and felt along the heart;
And passing even into my purer mind,
With tranquil restoration. . . .

(22–30)

While Wordsworth contrasts his own powers of perception with those of "a blind man's eye," the "beauteous forms" of the regretted place do not appear to him as images, but rather take the form of "sensations sweet/Felt in the blood, and felt along the heart"; oddly, they are perceived not by the senses, but within the body. To the influence of these nonvisual sensations, Wordsworth attributes a certain compensating "gift," the "best portion of a good man's life,/His little, nameless, unremembered, acts /Of kindness and of love"(33–35). The "nameless, unremembered" quality of such acts suggests the facelessness of their recipients; no clear image of a beneficiary is registered. Indeed, the affections are as likely to lead in a different direction, toward a sublime vision beyond images of life, "into the life of things." This state is achieved when the eye is "made quiet by the power /Of harmony and the deep power of joy." In this peculiar locution, the discord between impassioned images of present and past is obliterated by a harmony that puts out, as well, the clamorous eye of grief.

Despite Wordsworth's insistence on the utter sufficiency of his youthful eye, he forfeits an attempt to "paint" (a term that will be retrieved in "Peele Castle") the scenes of his youth. In lieu of a two-dimensional "painting," Wordsworth invokes the deep "sounding" of the cataract, and suggests his greedy, appetitive consumption (rather than perception) of the "colours and forms" of the landscape:

—I cannot paint
What then I was. The sounding cataract
Haunted me like a passion: the tall rock,
The mountain, and the deep and gloomy wood,
Their colours and their forms, were then to me
An appetite; a feeling and a love,
That had no need of a remoter charm,
By thought supplied, nor any interest
Unborrowed from the eye. —That time is past,
And all its aching joys are now no more
And all its dizzy raptures. Not for this
Faint I, nor mourn nor murmur; other gifts
Have followed; for such loss, I would believe,

> Abundant recompense. For I have learned
> To look on nature, not as in the hour
> Of thoughtless youth; but hearing oftentimes
> The still, sad music of humanity,
> Nor harsh nor grating, though of ample power
> To chasten and subdue.
>
> (75–93)

The interest "borrowed" from the eye is sufficient to render nature valuable to the child. Maturity, however, brings this need to borrow nature's value from some other source, a need declared satisfied by the "abundant recompense" of line 88. But the loss of "that [past] time" is felt as nature's loss, and the recompense must be invested precisely there. The poet's "elevated thoughts," his sense of "something far more deeply interfused," exchange the picturesque particularities of landscape for the elemental generalities of sun, ocean, air, sky, and finally "the mind of man." As the greedy eye of youth gives way before the "language of the sense," perception is displaced by a *discourse* of perception.

A loss of place, a loss of time; one senses Wordsworth drawing the coordinates of his subject, then circling it. The third loss of "Tintern Abbey"—that of "my former heart" (111–46)—finally touches on the figure of the poet:

> Nor perchance,
> If I were not thus taught, should I the more
> Suffer my genial spirits to decay:
> For thou art with me here upon the banks
> Of this fair river; thou my dearest Friend,
> My dear, dear Friend; and in thy voice I catch
> The language of my former heart, and read
> My former pleasures in the shooting lights
> Of thy wild eyes. Oh! yet a little while
> May I behold in thee what I was once,
> My dear, dear Sister!
>
> (111–21)

While Dorothy may seem to be an image of the poet's "former heart," she is better described as a kind of dynamo, spontaneously generating the "language of my former heart" and projecting the legible text of his "former pleasures." Wordsworth must *read* Dorothy, in other words, if he wishes to "behold" in her his youthful self. Dorothy's intelligibility serves here to annul the "heavy and the weary weight/Of all this unintelligible world"(39–40), now expressed in terms of human unscrupulousness: "evil tongues,/Rash judgements, . . . the sneers of selfish men,/. . .

greetings where no kindness is" (128–30). The ethical, as in lines 88–92, arises in the assignment of value; as Wordsworth performs his benediction for Dorothy, he simultaneously reckons her worth: "my dearest Friend,/My dear, dear Friend." While the ethical does not veer toward the metaphysical here, it does "look through death"—at least through the demise of Dorothy's present dynamism:

> and, in after years,
> When these wild ecstasies shall be matured
> Into a sober pleasure; when thy mind
> Shall be a mansion for all lovely forms,
> Thy memory be as a dwelling-place
> For all sweet sounds and harmonies; oh! then,
> If solitude, or fear, or pain, or grief,
> Should be thy portion, with what healing thoughts
> Of tender joy wilt thou remember me,
> And these my exhortations!
>
> (137–46)

Wordsworth conceives of Dorothy's mature mind as both a monument to her youthful powers, and as a mausoleum for her stilled thoughts. Through the agency of these preserved and preserving thoughts, Wordsworth expects Dorothy to fashion her own consolation for suffering.

But these anticipations of Dorothy's great loss deliver Wordsworth to his final meditation on his own death:

> Nor, perchance—
> If I should be where I no more can hear
> Thy voice, nor catch from thy wild eyes these gleams
> Of past existence—wilt thou then forget
> That on the banks of this delightful stream
> We stood together; and that I, so long
> A worshipper of Nature, hither came
> Unwearied in that service: rather say
> With warmer love—oh! with far deeper zeal
> Of holier love. Nor wilt thou then forget,
> That after many wanderings, many years
> Of absence, these steep woods and lofty cliffs,
> And this green pastoral landscape, were to me
> More dear, both for themselves and for thy sake!
>
> (146–59)

Against this intimation of mortality, Wordsworth points emphatically to his own renewed presence in the landscape, attempting to ground himself decisively "after many wanderings, many years/Of absence"(156–

57). But it is not a zealous, devotional image of nature that proves to "anchor" the poet's presence, but rather his own feet: "on the banks of this delightful stream/We stood together." In gesturing to these feet, Wordsworth gestures as well to the poetic feet of his text, feet that wander toward and away from the premonition of his own demise. Rather than investing nature with the power to go on without him—of nature indeed empowered to betray "the heart that loved her"—Wordsworth leaves us with the poem that empowers him to return, at will, to the scenes of his dearest and deepest lessons. But whereas Wordsworth expends the value of such lessons on nature midway through the poem, and appears to lavish another portion on Dorothy, he now confers value upon his textual relation to the reader. Indeed, in this concluding elegy for the self, Wordsworth masters the haunting elegiac image of his own death by contriving to haunt the reader. The topos of the traveler's return with which the poem begins is transformed into the textual return of the poet in the reader's hands as the haunted reader returns to the poem.

In "Tintern Abbey," the poet's ethical investments in nature and Dorothy are jeopardized by his closing investment in the text and, by extension, the reader. The text does not cherish the poet's "dear" ones so much as compete with them for assignments of value. In the "Intimations Ode," however, such investments are predicated not on an urgent need to disburse the "abundant recompense" of imagination, but on a sober assessment of the imagination's value. Helen Vendler's reading of the Ode as an elegy locates a durable consolation in the poem's climactic ninth stanza.[14] My reading registers the temptations of this position, but identifies the poem's "consolation" not in the conversions of metaphor (a displacement of Christian elegiac transcendence?) but in the poet's advance to sharper reckonings of his loss.

In the opening stanzas of the "Intimations Ode," Wordsworth radicalizes the problem of elegiac imagery. Like the pastoral elegiac mourner, his initial gesture is formally to declare and repeat his loss. He appears to contrast images of the past with those of the present. But whereas the pastoral elegist is content to compare images of a plenary past and an impoverished present, Wordsworth laments his inability to *imagine* loss; it is as though he wants, in the words of Shelley's *Defence of Poetry*, "the creative faculty to imagine that which [he knows]."[15] Unable to render images of an event of loss, he laments this inability as a crucial *lack of images* that might empower him to fix the place or time of the disaster. After all, it is easier to find something if one knows where and when it was lost. He multiplies dichotomies as though they were coordinates on the map of loss: then-now in the first stanza gives way to a split between the seen and the known in the second, which in turn gives way to a gap between "all the earth" (including nature, beasts, and children) and the self in the third and fourth stanzas. But the problem of imagining loss is not by these means "put by"; by lamenting his inability to imagine the occasion of loss—a moment of figurative death—Wordsworth acknowledges the threatening nature of elegiac imagery more generally. Unable to place his loss, Wordsworth is pressed by haunting questions—"Whither is fled the visionary gleam? /Where is it now, the glory and the dream?"—that rise up out of the earth.

And "the earth" is, indeed, the answer demanded by the stanzas that follow. A synopsis of Wordsworth's descendental strategy in the Ode would go something like this: In the central stanzas of the Ode, the celestial infant descends from the imperial palace of "God, who is our home," to become the "foster-child" of earth, to become finally imprisoned in the deterministic social world. In stanza nine, memory seems to provide a trapdoor for this prison, recalling "those obstinate questionings/Of sense and outward things,/Fallings from us, vanishings" (142–44):

> Hence in a season of calm weather
> Though inland far we be,
> Our Souls have sight of that immortal sea
> Which brought us hither,
> Can in a moment travel thither,
> And see the Children sport upon the shore,
> And hear the mighty waters rolling evermore.
>
> (162–68)

It is tempting to discover in this stanza the sort of redemptive aesthetic image that Schiller sponsors in *Naive and Sentimental Poetry*. The return produces a spontaneous image of origins—or, rather, of *origination*; the mighty waters, having brought these children "hither," continue to lap soulfully at their feet. In this reading, the child's juxtaposition with immortal waters remedies the deficiency of images in the poem's opening stanzas. It is as though the image of the child in stanza IV—the image of one's own lost nature—were successfully penetrated to reveal its metaphysical grounds; here Wordsworth once again "sees through images." Furthermore, with this image of flux-in-fixity, Wordsworth casts aside fluctuating images of the self's history in favor of a stable, authenticating image of origins.

But against this redemptive, aesthetic reading of stanza IX, I would argue that the "consolation" of stanza IX is the conviction that such recollections of immortality *must inevitably* fade into the light of common day. Like the sporting children and the mighty waters, recovered origins and fatal process are juxtaposed; they are not contradictory, but continuous. Inscribed in stanza IX is an emblem of memory as a meeting place between the earth and the sea; memory entails not immersion in these waters—no, that way madness lies—but rather, *emergence* from them onto the dry land of earth. The "soul," we discover, is fated to return even from its immortal rendezvous; it is only *natural* for it to do so. Memory may be the mother of the muses, but the foster-mother of memory is earth.

The final stanzas of the Ode, modulating from memory of past consciousness to a reflexive consciousness of the present self, celebrate our habituation to the limitations of self allegorized in the mythic central stanzas. It is this curtailment of self in favor of the external world that defines the ethical. In ethical terms, the contrast between stanzas IX and stanzas X and XI is striking. In stanza IX, Wordsworth significantly revises the image of the child in stanza V by substituting the "immortal sea" for God as the child's provenance. By so doing, Wordsworth emphasizes the pre-ethical nature of childhood sublimity: the revision at once effaces parental and filial affections (rendering the waters' "might" slightly ominous), and portrays childhood sublimity as a matter of pleasurable "sport"—not moral education, and not duty. This is not the second-level civil innocence imagined by Schiller and Blake, but an amoral innocence that is prior to civility.

Stanza XI, however, identifies the ethical as the poet's sympathy for a natural world from which sublimity has escaped. Such is the price of Wordsworth's descendentalism, which identifies nature with mortal process, not with sublime changelessness. Even as he vows to "grieve not," his urgent attention to "what remains behind" suggests that the poet faces, at last, an elaborate image of nature's mortal body. The "remains" in question lie all about him, among the "Fountains, Meadows, Hills, and Groves" of the landscape.[16] From this sacrifice of sublimity— from his willingness to embrace the pathetic image of a physical, mutable natural world—"springs" the discourse of sympathy in stanza X. His empathic response to nature is predicated on a mental act of imagination: "We in thought will join your throng,/Ye that pipe and ye that play,/Ye that through your hearts today/Feel the gladness of the May!"(172–75). The tender affection for nature that his loss releases in him teaches that the moral value of memory lies in the power to relinquish it. This lesson is not, I would insist, of the "immortal sea"; that lesson, as Stevens said, is "inhuman, of the veritable ocean." Hence, the attempt, in stanza XI, to align elegiac sympathy ("the soothing thoughts that spring/Out of human suffering") both with an innate "moral sense" (the "primal sympathy/Which having been must ever be") and with a metaphysical moral order ("the faith that looks through death,/In years that bring the philosophic mind") is severely strained.

While the Ode prefers the consolations of mortal process to those of vision, it nonetheless closes with a visionary gesture: the mortal eye and the human heart endow nature's "remains" with the ghostly power to teach us to feel:

> The Clouds that gather round the setting sun
> Do take a sober colouring from an eye
> That hath kept watch o'er man's mortality;
> Another race hath been, and other palms are won.
> Thanks to the human heart by which we live,
> Thanks to its tenderness, its joys, and fears,
> To me the meanest flower that blows can give
> Thoughts that do often lie too deep for tears.
>
> (197–204)

If *The Ruined Cottage*, "Tintern Abbey," and the Ode trace the origins of the human capacity to value that which lies beyond ourselves, it might be said that Wordsworth is less an elegiac revisionist than an elegiac *fundamentalist*. In these poems, he arrives at the "zero degree" of elegy. In "Tintern Abbey" and the Ode, the ethical is finally identified not with a traumatic lack within the self, but with a recognition of one's ability to be diminished *by a loss of that which lies beyond the self*, whether that recognition be felt as the sadness of humanity, the dearness of Dorothy, or the tenderness of wildflowers. Wordsworth's Romantic revision of pastoral elegy, like Schiller's, seeks ultimately to identify elegiac imagery with a deliverance from subjectivity; or, as a reading of Wordsworth's "Elegiac Stanzas Suggested By a Picture of Peele Castle" will suggest, with the redemptive possibility of a common mourning. Unready to "mourn nor murmur," and pledging yet to "grieve not," "Tintern Abbey" and the Ode are not elegies but rather meta-elegies, proto-elegies, rehearsals for loss.

While "Peele Castle" has often been read as a palinode for the "Intimations Ode," such readings focus on Wordsworth's repudiation of the visionary gleam as "the light that never was, on sea or land." But as I have already argued, the Ode itself anticipates this swerve away from the transcendental in its figuration of memory. "Peele Castle," far from being a palinode, does not depart from the Ode so much as extend it, consolidating its harsher lessons about nature, loss, and the elegiac image.

In "Peele Castle," a poem in which nature proves to have betrayed "the heart that loved her," the Ode's valedictory investment in the physical forms of nature is no longer necessary. But although "Peele Castle" does not echo the affection for nature that closes the Ode, the Ode's closing revival of an *attachment* as a suitable elegiac subject provides a crucial pretext for the loss Wordsworth here "deplores." John Wordsworth, ostensibly elegized following his 1805 drowning in the shipwreck of the *Abergavenny*, figures here chiefly as an attachment of the poet's. The historical John Wordsworth—here rendered nameless, faceless, and inspecifically related to the poet[17]—is submerged within the poet's "deep distress." While Coleridge's axiom regarding elegiac subjectivity still obtains—Wordsworth's most explicit statement about his loss calls it "[a] power . . . which nothing can restore" (35)—the self is now diminished not by a natural process, but by being catastrophically deprived of an attachment *in the world*.

If the agency of loss is natural process in "Tintern Abbey" and the "Intimations Ode," what then is the agency of catastrophe in "Peele Castle"? While Wordsworth stops short of representing the actual shipwreck of the *Abergavenny*, he acknowledges the mortality of these waters, their "deadly swell." By refusing to cite the specific storm—the specific incident—in which the vessel capsized, Wordsworth points away from the dramatic fatalism of tragedy, toward an understanding of nature itself as fatal. Nature, indeed, is the cause of loss, but a version of nature that presses on the human from without, rather than from within, as does the foster-mother of the Ode. Just beneath the surface of Wordsworth's "trampling waves" surge the "whelming tides" and "sounding seas" of *Lycidas* which brutally "hurl" the shepherd's bones to all points of the compass. In *Lycidas*, at "the bottom of the monstrous world," we glimpse the face of evil; Wordsworth takes us to no such depths. But the awful, sublime force that convulses the waters of "Peele Castle" intimates that nature may be in league with the sublime in a way that the poet of "Tintern Abbey" and the Ode had not suspected; that in the shape of the "deadly swell," the "immortal sea that brought us hither" lays on us a mortal claim. If the face of nature has darkened from "Tintern Abbey" and the "Intimations Ode," we may predict that this poem's genealogy of morals will turn aside from nature in a search for the origins of ethical consciousness. Indeed, loss may occur through the agency of nature; but the ethical arises, Wordsworth argues, through the production and dissemination of elegiac imagery.

Let us look more closely at elegiac imagery in "Peele Castle." While "Peele Castle," in its antithetical structure, may seem to imitate closely the pastoral elegiac dualism of "now" and "then," it must be stressed that Wordsworth's poem does not produce images, so much as meditate on their production. Wordsworth takes pains to insist on the "serenity" of his present mind; we are not to seek here for passionate images of elegiac loss. Nor does Wordsworth offer a fully embodied image of a better past; rather than simply produce an image recalling Peele Castle's erstwhile appearance, he considers how he would once have represented it.

Wordsworth's meditation on the production of elegiac imagery issues in a new poetics of the elegiac image. At the outset, Wordsworth meditates on his own former aesthetic:

> I was thy neighbour once, thou rugged Pile!
> Four summer weeks I dwelt in sight of thee:
> I saw thee every day; and all the while
> Thy Form was sleeping on a glassy sea.
>
> So pure the sky, so quiet was the air!
> So like, so very like, was day to day!
> Whene'er I looked, thy Image still was there;
> It trembled, but it never passed away.
>
> How perfect was the calm! it seemed no sleep;
> No mood, which season takes away, or brings:
> I could have fancied that the mighty Deep
> Was even the gentlest of all gentle Things.
>
> (1–12)

Wordsworth begins by emphasizing the consistency of this image; he beheld the castle "Every day," "day to day," for "four summer weeks." His reluctance to let it out of his sight suggests a childlike sense of his control over the image, as though his blinking were enough to make it vanish. His own propensity for "fancy" is indicated in his desire to think the "mighty Deep" "the gentlest of all gentle Things" by virtue of its stillness during one calm month. While he seems not to have been fully aware of his own image-making powers, he was conscious of the castle's; its reflection in the water introduces a tremulous capacity for difference: "It trembled, but it never passed away."

Image-making becomes the explicit subject of the poem at line 13, when Wordsworth considers the result "if mine had been the Painter's hand/to express what then I saw." The word "painting," of course, gestures toward the sister art of his friend Beaumont. But it also reaches back to a sister poem, "Tintern Abbey," in which Wordsworth claims to have been unable to "paint/What then I was." In describing his former aesthetic, Wordsworth in fact paints "what then [he] was":

> Ah! THEN, if mine had been the Painter's hand,
> To express what then I saw; and add the gleam,
> The light that never was, on sea or land,
> The consecration, and the Poet's dream;

> I would have planted thee, thou hoary Pile
> Amid a world how different from this!
> Beside a sea that could not cease to smile;
> On tranquil land, beneath a sky of bliss.
>
> Thou shouldst have seemed a treasure-house divine
> Of peaceful years; a chronicle of heaven;—
> Of all the sunbeams that did ever shine
> The very sweetest had to thee been given.
>
> A Picture had it been of lasting ease,
> Elysian quiet, without toil or strife;
> No motion but the moving tide, a breeze,
> Or merely silent Nature's breathing life.
>
> (13–28)

What will be later indicted as "the fond illusion of my heart," is here granted the dignity of "the poet's dream"; the "gleam,/The light that never was, on sea or land," is projected onto the landscape by the poet. The keenest expression of the poet's self is his depiction of the elemental harmony of the surrounding world: the anthropomorphic sea "that could not cease to smile," the "tranquil land," and the "sky of bliss." The central focus of this idyllic image, however, is the castle, which here serves as a surrogate for the lost brother, who even now remains submerged. Just as Dorothy was to become a "mansion for all lovely forms . . . a dwelling place/For all sweet sounds and harmonies" (140–42), Wordsworth would have had the castle become a repository of a precious past: "Thou shouldst have seemed a treasure-house divine,/Of peaceful years"(21). Dorothy's heightened value—her *dearness*—is paralleled by the treasured castle; her proximity to Nature is here answered in the castle's closeness to heaven. Whereas in "Tintern Abbey" Wordsworth was to "read/My former pleasures in the shooting lights /Of [Dorothy's] wild eyes," here the castle is a similarly legible "chronicle of heaven."

I am suggesting that what Wordsworth repudiates in "Peele Castle" as "the fond illusion of my heart" is his own sense of the past in "Tintern Abbey" (and, with some qualifications, in the Ode) as authentically available through memory. In lieu of the "present past," he announces his perpetually present loss:

> So once it would have been,—'tis so no more;
> I have submitted to a new control:
> A power is gone, which nothing can restore;
> A deep distress hath humanized my Soul.

Not for a moment could I now behold
A smiling sea, and be what I have been:
The feeling of my loss will ne'er be old;
This, which I know, I speak with mind serene.

(33–40)

In "Peele Castle," as in the Ode, loss does not exist as an *event*; rather, the phenomenon of loss replaces "him whom I deplore" as a vital *attachment* of the poet's. This attachment to loss expresses itself, by contrast to the "painted" illusion of lines 13–28, as a new perspective, one that transforms "the gleam that never was" to "lightning"; the tidal "breeze" into "the fierce wind"; "a glassy sea" into a "sea in anger"; the "moving tide" into "trampling waves." In representing this altered perspective, Wordsworth offers a counter-image to that which he would once have painted.

It is not an image "borrowed" from his own eye, however, but from another's; if "a power is gone, which nothing can restore" this must be, in part, the power to place faith absolutely in one's own poetic images. Instead, Wordsworth assesses the aesthetic *and* moral value of Beaumont's "passionate work":

Then, Beaumont, Friend! who would have been the Friend,
If he had lived, of Him whom I deplore,
This work of thine I blame not, but commend;
This sea in anger, and that dismal shore.

O 'tis a passionate Work!—yet wise and well,
Well chosen is the spirit that is here;
That Hulk which labours in the deadly swell,
This rueful sky, this pageantry of fear!

And this huge Castle, standing here sublime,
I love to see the look with which it braves,
Cased in the unfeeling armour of old time,
The lightning, the fierce wind, and trampling waves.

(41–52)

Indeed, unlike Wordsworth's forsaken image of "Elysian quiet, without toil or strife," Beaumont's painting gestures toward an awareness of a human struggle against the fatal forces of nature. Beaumont's painterly sympathy for the "Hulk which labours in the deadly swell," may well suggest to Wordsworth Beaumont's fitness as a friend toward the lost sailor. But more important, Beaumont's gesture of sympathy prompts in Wordsworth a sympathetic embracing of the painter's image as his own.

In Beaumont's painting, the spirit of John Wordsworth is not to be sought in the castle, but rather within "The Hulk which labours in the deadly swell"(47). What, then "remains behind" of the castle? Recalling the aesthetic values of Burke's *Enquiry*, Wordsworth finds the castle's sublimity antithetical to beauty; here, sublimity derives not from benignity, but from the castle's specifically inhuman capacity to "brave" the elements. In a stunning turn, Wordsworth appropriates Beaumont's sublime, unfeeling castle as an image of his former self:

> Farewell, farewell the heart that lives alone,
> Housed in a dream, at distance from the Kind!
> Such happiness, wherever it be known,
> Is to be pitied; for 'tis surely blind.
>
> But welcome fortitude, and patient cheer,
> And frequent sights of what is to be borne!
> Such sights, or worse, as are before me here.—
> Not without hope we suffer and we mourn.
>
> (53–60)

The final stanza of "Peele Castle" is often read as the culmination of the poem's turn away from "the gleam that never was"; such a gleam has come to illuminate only the poet's moral blindness. His summer "dwelling" proves to have been the protective housing of "a dream"; his ceaseless vision, benightedness. But Wordsworth's famous valediction to "the heart that lives alone," is nonetheless an embrace of a certain kind of vision—a vision shared, a common art of suffering and of loss. In "Peele Castle," Wordsworth's elegiac art moves beyond the lyric to define a scene of moral instruction, a rhetoric of common and communal sorrow.

Just as the Pedlar seeks in *The Ruined Cottage* to subsume elegiac images into a theory of natural sympathy, Wordsworth's poems of loss veer away from the burden of imagining their own redemption. Given the opportunity to argue for the redemptive power of images, as Schiller does, Wordsworth abjures an aesthetic salvation. In "Tintern Abbey," elegiac images provide a harassing presentiment of the poet's own demise; in a defensive gesture reminiscent of the Pedlar's burial of Margaret, Wordsworth leaves Dorothy to comfort herself, pointing to the rhetorical power of his own poetic feet to persuade the reader of his continued presence within the poem. In the Ode, and more explicitly in "Peele Castle," Wordsworth strains to recover the rhetorical power of elegiac images—to recover, that is, their use in composing narratives of human suffering that might constitute the texts of a community's moral instruction. His descendentalism in the central stanzas of the Ode is most urgently a critique of the aestheticization of the elegiac image. *Even within the Ode,* I would insist, Wordsworth finds this displaced transcendentalism a liability. But the descendental myth also reveals Wordsworth's need to frame the transmission of elegiac images within a naturalistic—and mortal—context. In "Tintern Abbey," the "Intimations Ode," and "Peele Castle," Wordsworth's elegiac genealogy of morals makes a strong appeal to organicism to limit the considerable powers of elegiac imagery. Paradoxically, Wordsworth's alternative genealogy of morals—the organicist genealogy—gestures, conversely, toward the liberating mediations of the elegiac image.

Organicist Genealogy: "Love of Nature Leading to Love of Mankind"

Wordsworth's first revision of the 1797 tale of Margaret—a long passage on the background of the Pedlar added in 1798—entails what has been called his first attempt at poetic autobiography.[18] In light of Francis Jeffrey's later criticism of the philosophic Pedlar (or Wanderer, as he was later called),[19] it is worth noting that Wordsworth's initial revisions in Manuscript B try to account for the Pedlar's moral authority. Though low-born and self-educated, the Pedlar is a "chosen son":

> Why should he grieve? He was a chosen son:
> To him was given an ear which deeply felt
> The voice of Nature in the obscure wind,
> The sounding mountain and the running stream.
> To every natural form, rock, fruit, and flower,
> Even the loose stones that cover the highway,
> He gave a moral life; he saw them feel
> Or linked them to some feeling. . . .
>
> (B76–83)

The Pedlar's moral life arises not from what he lacks but, on the contrary, from his gifts; why, indeed, "should he grieve?" Retrieving the aesthetic emphasis of moral sense theory, Wordsworth sketches a type of moral imagination that is partly perceived and partly created: "feeling" sound, the Pedlar takes his moral life from nature; "seeing" feeling, he seems to endow nature with a moral life.

The Pedlar's very sensitivity to nature, however, appears to leave him insensible to the human community. Instead of engaging with individuals, he responds to "every natural form, rock, fruit, and flower,/Even the loose stones that cover the highway. . ."(B80–81); instead of concerning himself with his own kindred and community, he contemplates "kindred multitudes of stars":

> Such sympathies would often bear him far
> In outward gesture, and in visible look,
> Beyond the common seeming of mankind.
> Some called it madness—such it might have been,
> But that he had an eye which evermore
> Looked deep into the shades of difference
> As they lie hid in all exterior forms,
> Which from a stone, a tree, withered leaf,
> To the broad ocean and the azure heavens
> Spangled with kindred multitudes of stars,
> Could find no surface where its power might sleep,
> Which spake perpetual logic to his soul,
> And by an unrelenting agency
> Did bind his feelings even as in a chain.
>
> (B90–103)

This perfect reciprocity, which "Did bind his feelings even as in a chain," defines the ligatures that attach the Pedlar so keenly to nature; making his "own" world out of nature, the Pedlar becomes so self-sufficient as to appear deviant. It is easy to see how the rural community's fearfulness could become, in the hands of the urbane reviewers of *The Excursion*, derision.[20] The Pedlar seems yet to awaken to the demands and constraints of life within a human community. Emblematically, the young Poet next comes upon the Pedlar asleep; even his face, dappled with the "forms of nature," has yet to assume its human identity.

A contemporaneous fragment from the Alfoxden notebook boldly asserts the missing link between this intuition of nature's moral life and ethical concerns:

> And never for each other shall we feel
> As we may feel till we [?find] sympathy
> With nature in her forms inanimate
> With objects such as have no power to hold
> Articulate language. In all forms of things
> There is a mind[21]

Elaborating on this crucial fragment (which would eventually become part of the Wanderer's "eloquent harangue" in *The Excursion* IV), Wordsworth asks how "we shall acquire the . . . habits by which sense is made/Subservient still to moral purposes." In the following fragment from Manuscript B, which proclaims natural sympathy to be "not useless," the acquisition of ethical habits is largely a negative process:

> Not useless do I deem
> These quiet sympathies with things that hold
> An inarticulate language for the [man]
> Once taught to love such objects as excite
> No morbid passions no disquietude
> No vengeance & no hatred needs must feel
> The joy of that pure principle of love
> So deeply that unsatisfied with aught
> Less pure & exquisite he cannot choose
> But seek for objects of a kindred love
> In fellow-natures & a kindred joy
> Accordingly he by degrees perceives
> His feelings of aversion softened down
> A holy tenderness pervade his frame
> His sanity of reason not impaired
> Say rather all [h]is thoughts now flowing clear
> From a clear fountain flowing he looks round
> He seeks for good & finds the good he seeks. . . .[22]

The "pure principle of love" is promulgated by Nature's "inarticulate" language, which excites "no morbid passions no disquietude/No vengeance & no hatred." Just as Nature's inarticulateness is considered a boon, its inability to motivate the passions is deemed fortuitous, allowing "all his thoughts [to flow] clear/From a clear fountain flowing." If to "seek for good" is to find "the good [one] seeks," then seeking and finding must be a unitary act. That seeking and finding comprise a single act of projection is not denied, but this act is identified as a rational, not imaginative, function; reason, in turn, is motivated by the energy of a "clear fountain"—an image of transcendental origins.

This narrative of active sympathy, passive "softening," and active "seek[ing] for good" is collapsed in the practice of "habits":

> All things shall sp[ea]k of man & we shall read
> Our duties in all forms & general laws
> And local accidents shall tend alike
> To quicken & to rouze & give the will
> And power which by a chain of good
> Shall link us to our kind. No naked hearts
> Nor naked minds shall then be left to mourn
> The burthen of existence.[23]

Here, the chain that "did bind [the Pedlar's] feelings" has become "a chain of good" that "Shall link us to our kind." Wordsworth's shift in emphasis from sense to reason evokes the diction of civil institutions—of duty, law, will, and power. Hearing and seeing give way to "reading," an acknowledgment that experience is mediated by interpretation;[24] for such interpretations as clothe "naked hearts" and "naked minds" are supplied from the Burkean "wardrobe of a moral imagination." Existence, thus mediated by morals, ceases to be an occasion for mourning.

While Nature ostensibly leads toward an appreciation of the value of other human beings, in the passage just considered it chiefly reveals the powers of the poet's own mind. As a canceled passage from Book 8 of *The Prelude* suggests, this heightened valuing of self may lead, ironically, to a devaluing of humanity. After a lengthy celebration of the child's reciprocity with nature—"the universe in which/He lives is equal to his mind"—Wordsworth asks:

> If upon mankind
> He looks, and on the human maladies
> Before his eyes, what finds he there to this
> Framed answerably? —what but sordid men,
> And transient occupations, and desires
> Ignoble and depraved. Therefore he cleaves
> Exclusively to Nature, as in her
> Finding his image. . . .[25]

Defensively, Wordsworth adds that the child's "spiritual sovreignty" is merely "in *apparent* slight/Of man and all the mild humanities" (my emphasis), but the harsh, antisocial implication is not so easily softened. That the child finds "his image" in Nature suggests that the idea of nature moralized is an image of his own making, and a projection of his idealized self.

Perhaps Wordsworth did recognize an unresolved problem here; the climax of *The Prelude* 8—Wordsworth's apocalyptic consciousness of himself as a moral agent—revises this passage by "retrac[ing] the way that led me on/Through Nature to the love of human-kind. . ."(8:587–89). But I would argue that this path, like others Wordsworth treads in *The Prelude*, proves to have "broken windings" (2:176). Wordsworth's organicist genealogy of morals suggests a tension between his commitment to "telling time" (stressing a causal link between his sense of the "awful powers and forms of nature" and his growing awareness of "man suffering") and his transcendental ambitions (the moral universe being "One galaxy of life and joy"—nature unbound). For Wordsworth's organicism, like Burke's "nature," straddles two disparate, not easily reconciled, realms: on the one hand lies the mutable, the temporal, and the rhetorical; on the other lies the eternal, the transcendental, and the metaphysical.

I want to examine now the manner in which Wordsworth allows the faculty of fancy to mediate between these competing principles in *The Prelude*:

> Nor could I with such object overlook
> The influence of this power [fancy] which turned itself
> Instinctively to human passions, things
> Least understood—of this adulterate power,
> For so it may be called, and without wrong,
> When with that first compared.
>
> (8:589–94)

In recognizing fancy's influence, Wordsworth recognizes it as morally suspect, "adulterate," in fact, dangerous: "From touch of this new power/Nothing was safe" (8:525–26). Among its several dangers, fancy exposes the conceit of nature as a moral guide, and insists on the presence of death and loss in the plenum that is Nature.

Throughout Book 8 of *The Prelude*, Wordsworth worries over the precedence of fancy in his moral "preparation." In elevating the rural shepherd to supernatural proportions (8:391–428), for example, he worries that his adoration of the shepherd might appear delusional. Though he insists on the shepherd's reality, he does however recognize the role played by his own childhood imagination:

> But images of danger and distress
> And suffering, these took deepest hold of me,
> Man suffering among awful powers and forms:
> Of this I heard and saw enough to make
> The imagination restless—nor was free
> Myself from frequent perils. Nor were tales
> Wanting, the tragedies of former times,
> Or hazards and escapes, which in my walks
> I carried with me among crags and woods
> And mountains. . . .
>
> (8:211–20).

If the child himself is powerless to tell the provenance of these images, the adult poet is not. Wordsworth describes himself as gripped by "images of danger and distress/And suffering," but acknowledges that it was he who "carried with [him]" such images from "tales. . . the tragedies of former times" to the "crags and woods/And mountains. . . ." of Nature. In the version of 1850, the child's "images of danger and distress" have rendered the rocks and streams "speaking monuments," that vividly express the presence of death in nature.

Though Wordsworth insists later in Book 8 that the hour of humanity "had not yet come" till he was twenty-three (or twenty-two in the 1850 version), the narrative of its coming picks up precisely where the child's "imagination restless" had left off:

> But when that first poetic faculty
> Of plain imagination and severe—
> No longer a mute influence of the soul,
> An element of the nature's inner self—
> Began to have some promptings to put on
> A visible shape, and to the works of art,
> The notions and the images of books,
> Did knowingly conform itself (by these
> Enflamed, and proud of that her new delight),
> There came among these shapes of human life
> A wilfulness of fancy and conceit
> Which gave them new importance to the mind—
> And Nature and her objects beautified
> These fictions, as, in some sort, in their turn
> They burnished her. From touch of this new power
> Nothing was safe: the elder-tree that grew
> Beside the well-known charnel-house had then
> A dismal look, the yew-tree had its ghost
> That took its station there for ornament.
>
> (8:511–29)

The child's projection of images onto nature is here recapitulated under the sign of fancy. The difference between the child's "plain imagination and severe" and fancy, it seems, is in part the difference between orality and textuality; between the child's access to "traditionary tales" and his access to books.[26] Because texts, unlike oral tradition, are not bound by a locality, they fail to "place" images for the child, as the Matron's tale does; instead, they authorize the child to place images where he will. Fancy is menacing, in part, because it privileges individual will and desire over the fatedness of place, "adulterating" traditional spaces with alien imaginings.

But the chief source of suspicion about fancy lies in its relation to "human passions, things/Least understood." Crucially, fancy exposes the limits of reason in moral discourse, rushing in where reason fears to tread. Through the faculty of fancy, the poet creates *images of passion* with which he "touches" nature—as, presumably, his affections had been "touched" by Gothic, sentimental tales:

Then, if a widow staggering with the blow
Of her distress was known to have made her way
To the cold grave in which her husband slept,
One night, or haply more than one—through pain
Or half-insensate impotence of mind—
The fact was caught at greedily. . . .

(8:533–38).

As the widow beds down with the dead in this necrophiliac encounter, "wetting the turf with never-ending tears," her mental "impotence," contrarily, evokes the erotic potency of sympathy. In consideration of the poet's "cravings," fancy transforms the denuded foxglove and the "slender blades of grass/Tipped with a bead of rain or dew" into a "drooping" bower for a "lorn" vagrant and her "babes." Wordsworth's emphasis on the tactile, his admission that such fancies "enflamed" and "delighted" him, and his association of "adulterate" fancy with his twenty-second year—the year in which he met Annette Vallon—suggest that fancy's "new importance to the mind" (8:522) is attributable to its conflation of desire and death.[27]

Indeed, Wordsworth takes such pains to chastise his overvaluation of fancy that he protests too much: "Then common death was none, common mishap,/But matter for this humour everywhere,/The tragic super-tragic, else left short"(8:530–32). He refers to fancy not as a faculty but, retrieving a medieval idiom, as a "humour"(8:531), noting later that it "rises in worth" when engrafted onto imagination. Nature, he insists, "beautified/These fictions, as, in some sort, in their turn/They burnished her"(8:523–25); but the value of fancy's images has been inflated, "the tragic super-tragic, else left short." Wordsworth's confessed overinvestment in such images strongly recalls Adam Smith's moral economy,[28] in which one accrues moral capital through one's sympathetic investments:

Yet in the midst
Of these vagaries, with an eye so rich
As mine was. . . I had forms distinct
To steady me. These thoughts did oft revolve
About some centre palpable, which at once
Incited them to motion, and controlled,
And whatsoever shape the fit might take,
And whencesoever it might come, I still
At all times had a real solid world
Of images about me. . . .

(8:594–605).

Indeed, Wordsworth's sympathetic eye becomes "so rich" that he positively lavishes his imaginings on nature; he perceives nature aesthetically, as a series of structures and forms to which his own fanciful images might be anchored. Thus anchored, the poet's fancy produces an oxymoronic "real solid world of images."

This phrase, merging the envisioned and the material, anticipates the moral apocalypse that follows:

> There came a time of greater dignity,
> Which had been gradually prepared, and now
> Rushed in as if on wings—the time in which
> The pulse of being everywhere was felt,
> When all the several frames of things, like stars
> Through every magnitude distinguishable,
> Were half confounded in each other's blaze,
> One galaxy of life and joy. Then rose
> Man, inwardly contemplated, and present
> In my own being, to a loftier height—
> As of all visible natures crown, and first
> In capability of feeling what
> Was to be felt, in being rapt away
> By the divine effect of power and love—
> As, more than any thing we know, instinct
> With godhead, and by reason and by will
> Acknowledging dependency sublime.
>
> (8:624–40)

"A time of greater dignity" than that presided over by fancy, this era witnesses the emergence of the ethical "Man" within. This internal human figure—a familiar romantic archetype of the imagination—is identified with a reasoned will, rather than with fanciful desires. No longer "enflamed" by fancy's eroticism, Wordsworth celebrates the blaze in which "the several frames of things" become "one galaxy of life and joy" (8:631). Once sober reason displaces passionate fancy within the moral imagination, there is less need for the structures and forms of nature. With impunity Wordsworth dissolves the "solid world of images" into the ubiquitous pulse of being and the eternally visible stars. This consecration of the imagination to reason acknowledges "dependency sublime" on an extrinsic divinity, and by so doing, forfeits the legacy of fancy in this genealogy of morals.

Reading this genealogy, we may be tempted to insist that it is not Nature, but fancy, with its passionate images of death and erotic loss, that brings on the poet's mature moral self-consciousness; that the organicist narrative is simply a screen through which elegiac imagery may be seen to play. Indeed, the organicist genealogy is only persuasive when fancy is repudiated in favor of reason. But this is only one conceptual problem with Wordsworth's organicist genealogy of morals; another resides in the moral implications of its implicit transcendentalism. For the import of this particular apocalypse is a paradoxical transcendence of morals; "the divine effect of power and love" hushes the discourse of moral sympathies, habits, judgments, and actions. To put it slightly differently, Wordsworth identifies himself as a moral agent at precisely the same moment at which he identifies himself with spirit; the imagination, at once a moral and a metaphysical agent, has made this paradox inescapable. But if we consider that Book 8 is the threshold to the French books of *The Prelude*—books in which Wordsworth witnesses the demise of the ethical and humanistic ideals fostered by the dawning Revolution—we can understand this apocalypse to foreshadow Wordsworth's insistence on the imagination as the epic consolation for this epic loss. The moral apocalypse of Book 8, I am suggesting, is at once retrospective, pointing back toward Wordsworth's dreams for humanity, and prospective, pointing forward to the sublime reveries of Snowdon. The transcendence of a discourse of morals by one of imagination proves to be the epic destination of *The Prelude*.

Or, as Lockridge has suggested, of Romanticism more generally: "The Romantic imagination is so extended in its range of function that it effectively supplants moral sense, reason, and conscience as the principal moral faculty."[29] However normative the Romantic displacement of a moral discourse onto that of imagination, Wordsworth's case is idiosyncratic in two respects. First, imagination enters the arena of morals specifically to usurp the imaginary operations of fancy, whose passionate images of loss overwhelm both the integrity of human life and that of the landscape. Second, the discourse of morals is placed in the service of a larger structure of loss and compensation; like the Miltonic language of innocence, which we know only through its post-lapsarian counterpart, the sentimental discourse of morals is *that which is lost* in the crucial French books of *The Prelude*. Imagination may transcend morals in Book 8, but it arrives there in the guise of a sublime consolation for moral failure. Hence, while Wordsworth's organicism attempts to "trace" how love of nature leads necessarily to love of man, the attempt is disrupted both figurally, by the images of fancy; and structurally, by the strongly elegiac pattern of Wordsworth's epic.

From Genealogy to History

In the decade following *The Ruined Cottage*, Wordsworth's answer to the discursive crisis of the "Essay on Morals" was to undertake—on many occasions, and in many forms—the historiography of the moral self. The two faces of grief in *The Ruined Cottage* prove to be but alternative histories of the moral self. The elegiac genealogy of morals links ethical consciousness to a sober understanding of history's contingency, and historical consciousness to the imagination of death. Embracing the task of narrating history—of passionately creating the historical artifact—itself constitutes an ethical commitment framed by the exigencies of mortality. The organicist genealogy, on the other hand, argues on behalf of a continuous process of moral growth, a "love of nature leading to love of man"; with meditative thought, the mind is said to "grow," like a body, into ethical consciousness. Though this genealogy dispenses with historical narrative as so many fragile images, it is nonetheless a narrative. But just as it argues for both a tranquility immanent within nature and an inborn potential for ethical life, this genealogy strains to transcend its narrative status; it strains against its own images of moral development, breaking into a lyric celebration of a power not contingent on the human.

This account of Wordsworth's alternative genealogies should now allow us to recognize more readily the resemblance between the two faces of grief in *The Ruined Cottage*. The elegiac genealogy curbs its salvific powers by framing its narratives within natural limits. The organicist genealogy, conversely, employs the mediations of elegiac imagery to strain against natural limits, toward transcendental powers. By way of exploring this resemblance, I want to suggest that the two faces of grief share an intellectual parentage in the dual influence of British empiricist and German idealist ethical theories.

Wordsworth's insistence on a natural progression from a sensory engagement with nature into ethical consciousness bespeaks the lingering influence of associationist moral philosophy. As late as 1887, Nietzsche attributed the genealogical impulse to "English psychologists" who are "always. . . looking for the effective motive forces of human development in the very last place we would wish to have them found, e.g., in the inertia of habit, in forgetfulness, in the blind and fortuitous association of ideas."[30] In his reading of "English psychology," Nietzsche may have underestimated the influence of another line of argument about habit running from Hume to Hazlitt; it is far from true that habit is universally linked to the association of ideas. Still, behind such "English psychology"—and behind Wordsworth's organicism—lies Hartley's insistence in *Observations on Man* (1749) on the moral sense as a mature result, a summa of all previous "pleaures and pains." According to Hartley, the moral sense "employs the force and authority of the whole nature of man against any particular part of it, that rebels against the determinations and commands of the conscience or moral judgment."[31]

On the other hand, Wordsworth's Romantic revisions of pastoral elegy, as I have already suggested, are mediated by his engagements, through Coleridge, with German idealism. From the post-Kantian idealist tradition, with its developing account of the supplement of consciousness, arrives the notion of a mature ethics that results from striving to overcome a lack of psychological wholeness. For Schiller, the elegiac mode allegorizes the sentimental difference between "two conflicting representations and perceptions—with actuality as a limit and with his idea as infinitude. . . ."(116). On either side of a privative present, lie (respectively) a lamented natural past, associated by Schiller with literary pastoral, and a visionary, ideal future, associated by him with the aesthetic imagery of idyllic poetry. It was Wordsworth's achievement in *The Prelude* to recast Schiller's theory of elegiac poetry as a personal elegy of epic proportions.

That Wordsworth's thinking about ethics following the "Essay on Morals" enacts a dialectic between the continental and British ethical traditions is largely borne out by the intimate relations between his two moral genealogies.[32] And it is no small achievement to have placed the German and English ethical traditions in dialogue; such an achievement might only be found in a poet whose arguments are no less passionate for being undogmatic. Unlike critics who have focused on the fluctuating balance of power between mind and nature, I have been concerned here with Wordsworth's search for a moral discourse adequate to the complexity of his dialectical perspective. Hence, what I have tended to represent in this chapter as conceptual instabilities within Wordsworth's two approaches to moral development will shortly require a more positive account. For the dual parentage of Wordsworth's ethics informs not only the poet's ethical positions during the so-called "great decade," but also the complex cultural politics of *The Excursion*. The perplexed conversation between fate and freedom that Wordsworth records within his moral histories of the self would become an achieved dialectic in his moral histories of the dead—the "authentic epitaphs" of *The Excursion*.

FIVE

"THIS PREGNANT SPOT OF GROUND":

BEARING THE DEAD IN *THE EXCURSION*

> The case of Mr Wordsworth, we perceive, is now manifestly
> hopeless; and we give him up as altogether incurable, and be-
> yond the power of criticism. We cannot indeed altogether
> omit taking precautions now and then against the spreading
> of the malady;—but for himself, though we shall watch the
> progress of his symptoms as a matter of professional curiosity
> and instruction, we really think it right not to harass him any
> longer with nauseous remedies,—but rather to throw in cor-
> dials and lenitives, and wait in patience for the natural termi-
> nation of the disorder. . . . We now see clearly, however, how
> the case stands;—and. . . consider him as finally lost to the
> good cause of poetry. . . .
>
> (Francis Jeffrey)

Jeffrey's Wordsworth; Wordsworth's Burke

DISCHARGING Wordsworth from the clinic of criticism in this
review of *The Excursion*, Francis Jeffrey admits him to the hos-
pice of moribund poets—to be sustained, presumably, by more
charitable readers than Jeffrey. But Jeffrey's diagnosis of Wordsworth,
in its emphasis on bodily disease, differs strikingly from his pathology of
The Excursion as "a tissue of moral and devotional ravings."[1] Wordsworth the poet is figured not as a madman, his insanity a late complica-
tion of hypertrophic morals, but rather as *physically* corrupt; Jeffrey
cites the "spreading" of the malady, the "nauseous remedies" of purgation.[2] As I suggested in chapter 3, such metaphors of physical corruption
enjoyed wide currency in the Jacobin propaganda of the 1790s, where
they impugn Burke's conservative conceit of "a permanent body composed of transitory parts" as a cover for Burke's trafficking with the
dead. In the unpublished "Letter to the Bishop of Llandaff," for example, Wordsworth likens Burke's attachment to the dead to the "exquisite
perversions of the East." Two decades later, Jeffrey indicts the Wordsworth of *The Excursion* for a similar "perversion" of his "powers"(51)
by figuring his poetical corruption as a reactionary embrace of the Burk-

ean dead: in writing a poem that hovers over the putrefying graves of the dead, Wordsworth has become poetically corrupt and moribund.

Jeffrey's medical allegory, then, is more than rhetorical virtuosity. Nor is it simply a sly recuperation of Jacobin propaganda at its most morbid. Published in the pages of the *Edinburgh Review*, Jeffrey's attack on Wordsworth is part of a larger cultural enterprise with a twofold aim: to promulgate and advance the theory of political economy; and simultaneously to defend vigorously the economic cornerstone of Whig ideology—what Pocock has called the "'miscibility' of landed and monetary property."[3] Whether blasting the Lake poets or championing the theories of Smith and, after 1817, Ricardo, the *Edinburgh* reviewers undertook to blend the piquant rhetoric of partisan politics with that of rigorous scientific inquiry; that Jeffrey's Whiggish swipe at Wordsworth's Toryism wears a veneer of critical, even clinical, disinterestedness shows how easily the *Edinburgh*'s rhetorical hybrid could be turned to a grave kind of satire.[4]

While Jeffrey's diagnosis of Wordsworth reveals the etiology of Jeffrey's own virulence, what can it tell us about Wordsworth? More specifically, what does it have to say about Wordsworth and Burke? The crucial relation between Wordsworth's poetry and his ideology has occupied critics of *The Excursion* from Wordsworth's contemporaries—Jeffrey and Hazlitt[5]—to our own: Hartman and, more recently, Johnston and Chandler.[6] It has become a truism that the poem's critical fortunes in our own time have been no richer than they were during the decade of its original publication. Recent attempts to defend the poem or simply to take its seriousness seriously—which usually amount to the same thing—tend to set as the criterion of their success the presentation of evidence contravening, or at least qualifying and placing in context, the poem's putative ideological conservatism. Johnston's nuanced, contextual reading of *The Excursion*, which foregrounds the Wanderer's heterodox and unassimilable "eloquent harangue" in Book 4, is emblematic of this tendency.

This chapter may at moments suggest the temptations of such an approach, for my argument takes shape around the claim that Wordsworth's Burke is hardly the Tory ideologue Jeffrey takes him to be. Wordsworth's Burke is, in fact, highly idiosyncratic; idiosyncratic—yet, since Pocock's 1982 essay "The Political Economy of Burke's Analysis of the French Revolution," a Burke whom it has become of late easier to recognize. Arguing against Cobban's portrait of Burke "in revolt" against the Enlightenment, Pocock presents Burke's economic analysis of the French Revolution as strongly Whiggish and rooted in diverse assumptions central to the theory of political economy. In emphasizing the menace of the French national debt, Pocock claims, Burke is largely consistent with the Whiggish analysis of the Scottish historians—Hume, Robertson, Smith, and Millar. Placed in this intellectual tradition, even Burke's esteem for aristocracy and for established religion can be accounted for by Pocock by the Whig conviction that feudal chivalry and clerical learning are alike precursors to a commercial age.

The matter on which Burke clearly diverges from the intellectual tradition of the Scottish Whigs, according to Pocock, is the relation between commercial society and the moral constraint of manners:

> [A] strictly progressive theory of manners, such as Burke might have derived from his Scottish acquaintances, presented them as arising, and fulfilling the natural sociability of man, only in the course of the commercialization, refinement and diversification of society. In outlining his differences with "our oeconomical politicians," Burke declared that manners must precede commerce, rather than the other way round, and that modern European society needed and must not sever its roots in a chivalric and ecclesiastical past. This move . . . was historicist and traditionalist, but it was not reactionary. It anchored commerce in history, rather than presenting it as the triumph over history. . . . Burke proposed to keep the past actual, but he did not propose to return to it.[7]

Pocock's Burke, in these sentences, is not far from Wordsworth's. For both, the essence of Burke's moral thought lies in his insistence that a commercial age must bear historical witness to the institutions which gave rise to it; but Wordsworth intuited beyond this that the essence of Burke's historicism lay in his recognition that the past has but an ideal existence. For Pocock, Burke's insistence on the historicity of commerce—that is, on the crucial role of prejudice and prescription to a developing commercial society—represents a gesture toward the civic humanist ideal (a more subtle conclusion than the familiar view of Burke as altogether hostile to political economy). But Wordsworth understands Burke's historicism to point in a different direction; for he sought in Burke an understanding of how the ideal existence of the past could nonetheless produce a field of moral force that would at once define and preserve the customary life of England's communities. In *The Excursion*, Wordsworth's particular interest centers on how the past is to be kept "actual" in a post-revolutionary age in which rupture, not continuity, determines the ragged outline of the past. Hence, we can see that Wordsworth found in Burke a thinker congenial to his own moral dilemma: how to reconcile a theory of necessary (or in Burke's rhetoric, "natural") morals with an understanding that morals arise from the imaginative recovery from a crisis of loss. It is Burke's self-consciousness as a historian, rather than his historiography, that attracts Wordsworth; Wordsworth's Burke theorizes not how history forms the generations, but instead, the generation of history.

In this chapter, I argue that in *The Excursion*, Wordsworth attempts to wed Burke's patriarchal and pragmatic use of the dead as a site of moral authority to a complementary theory of how we conceive of—and, indeed, create—"the dead." Wordsworth's "way" toward this dualism, traced by the career of the Solitary, is negative. Through the Solitary, an antitype to Burke, Wordsworth theorizes the predicament of a culture that has turned on its dead, a culture caught between its utopian visions and its satirical observations. But this turn away from the dead—and from Burke—proves necessary for determining how we may, as self-conscious, rather than "natural" individuals, turn back to the dead and avail ourselves of their moral "uses." In his treatment of the Solitary, Wordsworth appeals to Schiller's *On Naive and Sentimental Poetry* for a theory of the "sentimental" temperament which, in imagining "authentic epitaphs" of the dead, provides a feminine counterplot to Burkean patriarchy. While the Solitary yields to the temptations of a solipsistic transcendence, his moral failure is instructive, for it motivates Wordsworth's own imaginary negotiations with the dead in Books 6 and 7. My argument, in short, is that Jeffrey was correct all along—Wordsworth *is* committed to a Burkean embrace of the dead; but my diagnosis of the poet is different. Where Jeffrey finds the moral corruption of reaction, I discern a sane liberalism that heals the "soft infections of the heart."

Bearing the Dead

The range of ideas that Wordsworth offers under the aegis of Burke can be synopsized by examining the ideological play within his allusions to Burke. Specifically, I want to examine his revisions of Burke's figure of the British polity in the *Reflections on the Revolution in France* as a "permanent body composed of transitory parts." As in the "Genius of Burke" passage added to *The Prelude* in 1832,[8] Wordsworth glosses, almost interlinearly, this central Burkean figure in the Pastor's tribute to the genius of Oswald in Book 7:

> "The vast Frame
> Of social nature changes evermore
> Her organs and her members, with decay
> Restless, and restless generation, powers
> And functions dying and produced at need,

And by this law the mighty whole subsists:
With an ascent and progress in the main;
Yet, oh! how disproportioned to the hopes
And expectations of self-flattering minds!"

(7:999–1007)

Here Burke's "permanent body composed of transitory parts" becomes "the vast Frame/Of social nature," and its transitory "organs" and "members"; Burke's "stupendous wisdom" becomes "the law" through which "the mighty whole subsists"; and Burke's "varied tenour of perpetual decay, fall, renovation, and progression" becomes "decay/Restless, and restless generation." Wordsworth's rhetorical coda even invokes the mortifying terms in which Burke insists that his model is progressive.

But what concerns me here is not Wordsworth's scriptural use of Burke to advance an explicit Tory politics, but his more exploratory allegorizations of Burke, those passages in which he seeks not to promulgate Burke, but to interpret him. The funeral procession of Book 2, the passage through which Wordsworth himself returned to *The Recluse* in 1807, signals its obliquity by offering a resonance, rather than an image, of Burkean multiplicity within unity:

[F]rom out the heart
Of that profound abyss a solemn voice,
Or several voices in one solemn sound,
Was heard ascending; mournful, deep, and slow
The cadence, as of psalms—a funeral dirge!

(2: 372–76)

Unlike Snowdon's "streams innumerable, roaring with one voice," (*Prelude* 13:58–59), this abyss intimates an insistently social unity. Here, the "heart" of the abyss is not silent, but vocal. If the abysmal voice of Snowden's waters is "homeless," this ascending voice emanates from the community that makes its home in that rift.

The Wanderer, praising the funeral procession as an enduring instance of "precious rites/And customs of our rural ancestry/. . . gone, or stealing from us" (2:550–52), focuses on the mourners' curtailment of mourning in an embrace of their customary duties:

"But most of all
It touches, it confirms, and elevates,
Then, when the body, soon to be consigned
Ashes to ashes, dust bequeathed to dust,
Is raised from the church-aisle, and forward borne
Upon the shoulders of the next in love,

The nearest in affection or in blood;
Yea, by the very mourners who had knelt
Beside the coffin, resting on its lid
In silent grief their unuplifted heads. . . .

. . . . .

—Have I not seen—ye likewise may have seen—
Son, husband, brothers—brothers side by side,
And son and father also side by side,
Rise from that posture:—and in concert move,
On the green turf following the vested Priest,
Four dear supporters of one senseless weight,
Form which they do not shrink, and under which
They faint not, but advance toward the open grave
Step after step—together, with their firm
Unhidden faces. . . ."

(2:566–88)

Bearing the dead, then, evokes Burke's sense of the enduring *presence* of the dead in the body politic; these mourners achieve a stoic consolation as they lift their heads from the coffin in order to begin the procession. By so doing, they temporarily detach themselves from the dead only to reattach themselves under the aegis of the group. This movement of identification with the community is also a movement from self-consciousness to unconsciousness, as the individual mourner "in silent grief" becomes a member of the pallbearing troupe. The adjacency of "Son, husband, brothers" signals both the endurance of patriarchy and its consolation; moving "in concert," these men display their membership in a hierarchical body politic, presided over by the dead and led by the moral authority of the "vested Priest." Their horizontal adjacency is balanced by their vertical contiguity to the corpse, who links them all and advances, with them, "toward the open grave." In true Burkean fashion, the procession at once expansively registers pride and purges it.

At the same time, this passage represents a movement from church to churchyard; from an institution *intrinsic* to the official Church to another *extrinsic* to it—adjacent, but set apart. Whereas the Church derives its authority from scripture and the hierarchy of the archbishops, bishops, and priests who minister, the churchyard lies within two spheres of influence: that of the Church, and that of the local community. Despite the patriarchal assemblage of mourners, affection here is said to give an equal claim as blood, privileging "the nearest in affection *or* in blood" (my emphasis). In this passage, bearing the dead entails actively supporting and maintaining them; it is the living who hold the power to exert and sustain the traditional authority of the community.

Paradoxically, the funeral procession of Book 2 eventuates not in a scene of burial, but, in Books 6 and 7, in the figural exhumations of the churchyard; in *The Excursion*, the work of "bearing" the dead entails the figurative work of "baring" them. In Book 5, the Pastor meditates on this paradox:

> "True indeed it is
> That they whom death has hidden from our sight
> Are worthiest of the mind's regard; with these
> The future cannot contradict the past:
> Mortality's last exercise and proof
> Is undergone; the transit made that shows
> The very Soul, revealed as she departs."
>
> (5:661–67)

For the Pastor, this paradox is Christian in nature, analogous to that whereby the soul finds immortality only in death. Death may hide the corpse, but the soul is "revealed as she departs." In death, the mobile, protean self is stilled, at last rendering the dead accessible to our "regard": "with these/The future cannot contradict the past."

But in practice, the Pastor's work of "baring the dead" hardly bespeaks the spontaneity of grace. On the contrary, "baring the dead" bespeaks the concerted effort entailed in the moral imperative to discover and reveal virtue. If the Pastor deems the revelation of virtue a matter of grace, the Wanderer has quite another sense of it:

> "The mine of real life
> Dig for us; and present us, in the shape
> Of virgin ore, that gold which we, by pains
> Fruitless as those of aëry alchemists,
> Seek from the torturing crucible. There lies
> Around us a domain where you have long
> Watched both the outward course and inner heart:
> Give us, for our abstractions, solid facts;
> For our disputes, plain pictures.
>
> . . . . .
>
> Or rather, as we stand on holy earth,
> And have the dead around us, take from them
> Your instances; for they are both best known,
> And by frail man most equitably judged."
>
> (5:630–49)

Though Burke believes the dead to be eternally within our regard, and the Pastor believes the baring of the dead to be accomplished by grace, the Wanderer understands the necessity of "mining" the earth in order to bare the dead—and mining is, as *Paradise Lost* informs us, a fallen, Satanic art. For the Wanderer, in other words, the "baring" of the dead is accomplished by human labor. Though the dead are "best known" and "most equitably judged," the value in their lives, according to the Wanderer *contra Burke*, is unapparent; one must "dig" for this mortal gold, robbing the grave, as it were, for moral worth. And in Wordsworth's epistemology of virtue, the "aery alchemy" of theory and debate fails to produce gold precisely where the mining of the Pastor succeeds. "Bearing the dead" (supporting them) entails the work of "baring" them (revealing their value).

This homonymic excursus suggests that "bearing" the dead is not simply a matter of representation; to use the Burkean idiom of Wordsworth's fragmentary "Essay on Morals," it entails more than offering "plain pictures" in lieu of abstractions. Nor is it a matter of reanimation; for, unlike the "faded garlands dangling" from the Maypole (2:137), the dead do not beg revival. In *The Excursion*, "bearing" the dead is accomplished through the labor of conceptually "bearing" them—*conceiving and giving imaginative life to them*. In the central books of *The Excursion*, the graveyard doubles as a childbed, as the Pastor performs the feminine labor of conceiving and birthing narratives amid the fertile ground of the churchyard. To the poet, a metonymist, the churchyard is "this pregnant spot of ground" (5:371). The Pastor, on the other hand, discreetly allegorizes this necrophiliac intercourse between a "mysteriously-united pair":

> "To a mysteriously-united pair
> This place is consecrate; to Death and Life
> And to the best affections that proceed
> From their conjunction; consecrate to faith
> In Him who bled for man upon the cross;
> Hallowed to revelation; and no less
> To reason's mandates; and the hopes divine
> Of pure imagination. . . .
>
> (5:903–10)

Somewhat less "mysteriously," the Pastor feminizes the institution of the churchyard, which signifies the "tender" and "motherly" acceptance of all human "children":

> "And blest are they who sleep; and we that know,
> While in a spot like this we breathe and walk,

That all beneath us by the wings are covered
Of motherly humanity, outspread
And gathering all within their tender shade,
Though loth and slow to come!"

(5:922–27)

The sympathetic, inclusive Pastor, speaking *ex cathedra* from within the churchyard's "tender shade," proves to be the poem's most significant "mother"; but I want to insist that it is his conceptual, imaginative labor, not only his tender sympathies, that are represented here by the feminine trope of "bearing the dead."

Wordsworth's particular understanding of this feminine labor may be clarified by the Pastor's observation that the "conjunction" of Death and Life results in a multiple birth, among the offspring of which are the affections, Christian faith, reason, and "the hopes divine of pure imagination." Wordsworth's insistence on distinguishing imagination from these other faculties has marked *The Excursion* as divergent from the current of British Romanticism. The imagination is hardly the totalizing mental function which it is held to be in Wordsworth's own earlier poems, such as "Tintern Abbey" or even the 1805 *Prelude*. And yet one of Wordsworth's least recognized achievements in *The Excursion* is his insistence that the imagination is a *sibling* of faith (as well as of reason and of the affections). In the broadest terms, they share a genealogy: the mind contemplating death. Perhaps because of this shared parentage, the siblings faith and imagination, like the two faces of grief in *The Ruined Cottage*, resemble one another, operating in the analogous spheres of metaphysics and ethics, respectively.

In *The Excursion*, Wordsworth analogizes metaphysics and ethics by structuring both faith and virtue as epistemological problems. The Solitary's skepticism evokes the Poet's observation

"But, after all,
Is aught so certain as that man is doomed
To breathe beneath a vault of ignorance?
The natural roof of that dark house in which
His soul is pent! How little can be known—
This is the wise man's sigh; how far we err—
This is the good man's not unfrequent pang!"

(5:586–92)

According to the Pastor, the problem of knowing grace is compounded by the difficulty of knowing our own capacity for faith:

"Knowledge, for us, is difficult to gain—
Is difficult to gain, and hard to keep—

As virtue's self; like virtue is beset
With snares; tried, tempted, subject to decay.
Love, admiration, fear, desire, and hate,
Blind were we without these: through these alone
Are capable to notice or discern
Or to record; we judge, but cannot be
Indifferent judges. 'Spite of proudest boast,
Reason, best reason, is to imperfect man
An effort only, and a noble aim. . ."

(5:492–502).

Reason, according to the Pastor, has been overestimated; the affections, which shape perception itself ("We see, then, as we feel"), underestimated. Notably, the Pastor does not recommend the imagination as an avenue or substitute for faith—that task has already fallen to the Wanderer in Book 4. But introducing virtue (that is, exemplary, educative virtue) as an analogue for knowledge, he admits an ethical function for imagination far exceeding that accorded it by Adam Smith. As Wordsworth writes in the *Essays Upon Epitaphs*, virtue must be "bared" because it is by nature hidden:

> [T]he virtues, especially those of humble life, are retired; and many of the highest must be sought for or they will be overlooked. . . . The afflictions which Peasants and rural Artizans have to struggle with are for the most part secret; the tears which they wipe away, and the sighs which they stifle,—this is all a labour of privacy. In fact their victories are to themselves known only imperfectly: for it is inseparable from virtue, in the pure sense of the word, to be unconscious of the might of her own prowess. (2:64–65)

If the virtues of the living are, by definition, hidden and unconscious, how much more difficult of access must be the virtue of the dead. Thus, while Wordsworth insists on a *natural* inclination to honor, revere, and sustain the dead, he also emphasizes the self-conscious intentionality of "knowing" the dead to be virtuous. Such knowledge, in other words, is made possible by the imagination.

Wordsworth's dualistic "bearing" of the dead in *The Excursion*—his patriarchal pallbearing and his matriarchal conception and parturition—links *The Excursion* to the genealogies of morals that develop in the decade that precedes it. But whereas those genealogies show Wordsworth unable to advance a coherent dualism of the moral self, *The Excursion* shows him subsuming both necessity and self-consciousness, fate and freedom, into a single ethico-political stance. I will have more to say presently about Wordsworth's use of tropes of gender within this dualism; in particular, about the adumbration of femininity within this intellectual scheme. For now, it will do to suggest that for Wordsworth, the Burkean stance of bearing—actively supporting—the dead is complementary to and continuous with the labor of conceptually bearing them.

In *The Excursion*, Wordsworth evokes the dualistic "bearing" of the dead by way of the fruitless Solitary, whose own erotic preference—an embrace of death—brings his sexuality into the arena of aberration. Ironically, Wordsworth holds the Solitary accountable for much the same perversion for which Jeffrey censured him in the *Edinburgh Review*. In Books 2–5 of *The Excursion*, Wordsworth theorizes a psyche that has turned away from the patriarchal attachment to the dead, but has also stopped short of fruitful reconception. Wordsworth's "negative way" to the imaginative deliverance of the dead is through the intellectual miscarriage of the Solitary.

"The Sublime Attractions of the Grave"

The nature of the Solitary's malady, of course, does not concern Jeffrey, who declines to diagnose him. On the contrary, for Jeffrey, the Solitary's narrative, "the most spirited and interesting part of the poem," suggests Wordsworth's poetic acuity, his "fine perception of the secret springs of character and emotion."[9] But if Jeffrey declines to diagnose the Solitary, his "inward malady" is diagnosed within the poem threefold: by the Wanderer, by the Solitary himself, and by Wordsworth.

In Book 2, the Wanderer alerts us to the Solitary's function as an antitype to Burke. Here the Wanderer traces the Solitary's pathological despondency to a motivating catastrophe—the sudden loss of his daughter, son, and then wife:

> "[M]iserably bare
> The one Survivor stood; he wept, he prayed
> For his dismissal, day and night, compelled
> To hold communion with the grave, and face
> With pain the regions of eternity.
> An uncomplaining apathy displaced
> This anguish; and, indifferent to delight,
> To aim and purpose, he consumed his days,
> To private interest dead, and public care.
> So lived he; so he might have died."
>
> (2:201–9)

The Wanderer interprets the Solitary's travail (to be psychologically anachronistic) through the implicit paradigms of displacement and repression. The Solitary's turn to the grave displaces a desire for communion with his wife, the "partner of [his] loss" (3:669); his apathy, an embrace of affective and spiritual death, represses the anguish of his compounded losses. "Dead" to both public and private concerns—"So lived he; so he might have died"—the Solitary's posthumous existence foretells the death-in-life in which the travelers first encounter him in Book 2. At moments, the Solitary's own narrative of his displacements—both figurative and literal—seems to support the Wanderer's psychological diagnosis. During the Solitary's French sojourn, for example, he both displaces and represses his erotic and paternal anguish by embracing "society":

> "Thus was I reconverted to the world;
> Society became my glittering bride,
> And airy hopes my children.—From the depths
> Of natural passion, seemingly escaped,
> My soul diffused herself in wide embrace
> Of institutions, and the forms of things;
> As they exist, in mutable array,
> Upon life's surface."
>
> (3:734–41)

In an effort to "escape" "the depths of natural passion," the Solitary takes Society, in lieu of his lost wife, as his "glittering bride"; takes to himself "airy hopes" instead of children.

According to the Wanderer, the French disaster centers not on the Solitary's skeptical faithlessness to Christianity, but on his faithlessness to the dead. For the Solitary had *never* been a man of ready faith; by his own account, an "immense . . . space" had stood between him and his pious wife: "The eminence whereon her spirit stood,/Mine was unable to attain." In France, the Solitary displaces his belief in his wife's faith onto a worship of Liberty:

> "[T]here arose
> A proud and most presumptuous confidence
> In the transcendent wisdom of the age,
> And her discernment. . . .
>
> .   .   .   .   .
>
> An overweening trust was raised; and fear
> Cast out, alike of person and of thing.
> Plague from this union spread, whose subtle bane
> The strongest did not easily escape;

And He, what wonder! took a mortal taint.
How shall I trace the change, how bear to tell
That he broke faith with them whom he had laid
In earth's dark chambers, with a Christian's hope!"

(2:234–48)

To the Wanderer, the Solitary's spiritual investment in French Liberty cancels and betrays his links to his dead wife. The repressed returns as the "dimness" that had crept over his wife's face as she died reappears on the aspect of Liberty: "humbled Liberty grew weak,/And mortal sickness on her face appeared." En route to America, though beyond the contagion of the Terror, he becomes smitten with the "plague" of memory, which exacerbates the pain of his own wounded pride.

To the Wanderer, the Solitary's return to England is a repatriation in bad faith. His decision to "[fix] his home . . . /Among these rugged hills," is merely another displacement of the psychological fixity once offered by his wife's faith. In fact, the Wanderer construes this "fixing" not as a reattachment to English soil, but as a turning away from the turf in Devon where his wife's body lies:

"[I]nwardly opprest
With malady—in part, I fear, provoked
By weariness of life—he fixed his home,
Or, rather say, sate down by very chance,
Among these rugged hills; where now he dwells,
And wastes the sad remainder of his hours,
Steeped in a self-indulging spleen, that wants not
Its own voluptuousness;—on this resolved,
With this content, that he will live and die
Forgotten,—at safe distance from 'a world
Not moving to his mind.'"

(2:305–15)

With this repressive turning from the dead, the Solitary grounds himself in English earth, to embrace the prospect of—indeed, to anticipate—the hour of his death. In lieu of a Burkean identification with the dead, he identifies himself with death, and morbidly "remains" to "waste" his hours. Comparing his life to that of a troubled stream, the Solitary seeks his personal displacement in death to "the unfathomable gulf, where all is still."

The Solitary's account of himself, on the other hand, refutes the Wanderer's charge of bad faith by establishing the philosophical and intellectual context for his behavior.

> "I called on dreams and visions, to disclose
> That which is veiled from waking thought; conjured
> Eternity, as men constrain a ghost
> To appear and answer; to the grave I spake
> Imploringly;—looked up, and asked the Heavens
> If Angels traversed their cerulean floors,
> If fixed or wandering star could tidings yield
> Of the departed spirit—what abode
> It occupies—what consciousness retains
> Of former loves and interests. Then my soul
> Turned inward,—to examine of what stuff
> Time's fetters are composed; and life was put
> To inquisition, long and profitless!
> By pain of heart—now checked—and now impelled—
> The intellectual power, through words and things,
> Went sounding on, a dim and perilous way!"
>
> (3:686–701)

Following his loss, the Solitary calls, conjures, speaks, and asks for response, appealing indiscriminately to dreams and visions, ghosts, "eter-
nity," angels, the grave, and the stars; clearly the metaphysical complexion of the respondent is secondary to the desire for dialogue. Whereas
the Wanderer views the Solitary's turn inward as self-indulgent apathy,
the Solitary represents it as an exertion of "intellectual power" in which
this ordeal of petition culminates.

With these differing accounts of the Wanderer and the Solitary before
us, we might ask how Wordsworth diagnoses the Solitary's despondency—as pathology or as power? Wordsworth is most explicit in telling
us what it is not: the Christian sin of despair. Like Milton's *Ode on the
Morning of Christ's Nativity*, *The Excursion* inscribes the melancholy
gods of an old order, only to banish them from its precincts. The Solitary's soliloquy nods simultaneously toward Spenser's Despaire and
Milton's Penseroso:

> "If I must take my choice between the pair
> That rule alternately the weary hours,
> Night is than day more acceptable; sleep
> Doth, in my estimate of good, appear
> A better state than waking; death than sleep:
> Feelingly sweet is stillness after storm,
> Though under covert of the wormy ground!"
>
> (3:275–81)

Most urgently, these lines on behalf of night, sleep, and death recall the mellifluous seductions of Spenser's Despaire: "Sleep after toile, Port after stormy seas." But if despair, for a Christian, is the unforgivable sin, it is so because it suggests a conviction in the nonexistence of grace. Spenser's Despaire does not tempt the faithless; instead, "dispairing" the testaments, he relies on a competing theology that implicitly denies salvation, drawing from that effete denial some rather florid conclusions. If the Solitary resembles Despaire, it is because his speech is similarly seductive. Wordsworth, by invoking both Spenser's Despaire and Milton's prolusive Penseroso, indicates the *rhetorical* appeal of these Renaissance figures of melancholy. More an intellectual exercise than a credo of skepticism, the Solitary's lines claim the leisure of rhetorical choice—"If I must take my choice between the pair"—and seem to invite an interlocutor's debate.

Wordsworth's Solitary and Spenser's Despaire, however, share a striking resemblance to that ambiguous corrective for despair, Contemplation:

> that godly aged Sire,
> With snowy lockes adowne his shoulders shed,
> As hoarie frost with spangles doth attire
> The mossy braunches of an Oke halfe ded.
> Each bone might thorugh his body well be red,
> And euery sinew seene through his long fast:
> For nought he car'd his carcas long vnfed;
> His mind was full of spirituall repast,
> And pyn'd his flesh to keep his body low and chast.[10]

In the Solitary, Wordsworth creates a secular analogue for the contemplative hermit of medieval Christianity. The Solitary's age and "hollow cheek," his "lowly" dwelling, his surprising vigor for one "halfe ded" and his distance from "worldly business" (*FQ* I x 46) all liken him to Spenser's figure of Contemplation. Whereas Contemplation dwells in a "litle Hermitage," the secular Solitary urbanely adduces "my hermitage, my cabin, what you will" (2:651); his sustenance is had from earthly, rather than spiritual sources. This image of the Solitary as secular hermit is compelling even to the Wanderer, whose exclamation bears Spenserian undertones:

> "—Hail Contemplation! from the stately towers,
> Reared by the industrious hand of human art
> To lift thee high above the misty air
> And turbulence of murmuring cities vast;

> From academic groves, that have for thee
> Been planted, hither come and find a lodge
> To which thou mayst resort for holier peace,—
> From whose calm centre thou, through height or depth,
> Mayst penetrate, wherever truth shall lead;
> Measuring through all degrees, until the scale
> Of time and conscious nature disappear,
> Lost in unsearchable eternity!"
>
> (3:101–12)

For the Wanderer, the true place of secular hermitage proves not the cabin, but the landscape—in the Wanderer's words, the "boundless depth" of "the chasm of sky above my head" and the "abyss in which the everlasting stars abide." Contemplation, then, is to be rescued from the "stately towers" of cities and academic groves" and ruralized within the "calm centre" of this landscape. This concentering, however, describes both the Solitary's topography and his contemplative *attitude*. Whereas Spenser's Contemplation has been virtually blinded as a result of seeing "God . . . from heauens hight" (*FQ* I x 47), the Solitary, in a familiar Romantic gesture, takes his locus of transcendence as the depths, not the heights. The secular hermitage is the landscape *as it is taken up within the contemplating mind*.

In the hermitical landscape occupied by the Solitary—a landscape bounded by the "sweet recess" in which he lives, and by the "hidden nook" to which he leads his visitors—the contemplative life of the secular hermit lies revealed. To the Poet, the Solitary's landscape signals both the ideality of the Solitary's mind, and its deathlike stasis:

> Before us; savage region! which I paced
> Dispirited: when, all at once, behold!
> Beneath our feet, a little lowly vale,
> A lowly vale, and yet uplifted high
> Among the mountains; even as if the spot
> Had been from eldest time by wish of theirs
> So placed, to be shut out from all the world!
> Urn-like it was in shape, deep as an urn. . . .
>
> (2:326–33)

Appearing "all at once . . . beneath our feet," the valley startles the Poet, recalling Wordsworth's sudden apprehension of brightness, then mist, "at my feet" in the approach to Snowdon. Initially, the Poet seems unsure as to whether the valley is visionary or real. "Shut out from all the world," the valley suggests a region of the mind; its "lowness" indicates the depths of inwardness. "Urn-like," the valley mimics a mind full of death. Still, "throwing down [his] limbs at ease/Upon a bed of heath," the Poet interprets the valley's morbidity as transcendental stillness:

> Far and near
> We have an image of the pristine earth,
> The planet in its nakedness: were this
> Man's only dwelling, sole appointed seat,
> First, last, and single, in the breathing world,
> It could not be more quiet: peace is here
> Or nowhere; days unruffled by the gale
> Of public news or private; years that pass
> Forgetfully; uncalled upon to pay
> The common penalties of mortal life,
> Sickness, or accident, or grief, or pain.
>
> (2:359–69)

"Pristine" and paradisal, the valley enjoys a benign weather of uneventfulness; it is ahistorical, indifferent. To the poet, this might easily be "man's only dwelling."

But in the "hidden nook," to which the Solitary escorts both his visitors, both Poet and Wanderer become disturbed by the landscape of the mind espousing death:

> Upon a semicirque of turf-clad ground,
> The hidden nook discovered to our view
> A mass of rock, resembling, as it lay
> Right at the foot of that moist precipice,
> A stranded ship, with keel upturned, that rests
> Fearless of winds and waves.
>
> (3:50–55)

In this compressed allusion to "Peele Castle," Wordsworth locates a petrified simulacrum of the fatal ship *Abergavenny*; like Beaumont's painting, this landscape is stained by the presence of death. Here the castle's "unfeeling armour" is displaced onto the ship, whose "fearlessness" suggests that this nook, like the castle, lies "at distance from the kind." This nook, "That seemed for self-examination made; Or/for confession, in the sinner's need,/Hidden from all men's view," calls into question whether contemplation is not merely an avoidance of confession; whether it is a haven for transgression, rather than transcendence.

What the hermitic landscape reveals is a certain blankness between the deathward gaze of despondency and the redemptive vision promised by contemplation. While both Wanderer and Poet intuit (and are unsettled by) this discrepancy, it remains for the Solitary to articulate it:

"Ah! what avails imagination high
Or question deep? what profits all that earth
Or heaven's blue vault, is suffered to put forth
Of impulse or allurement, for the Soul
To quit the beaten track of life, and soar
Far as she finds a yielding element
In past or future; far as she can go
Through time or space—if neither in the one,
Nor in the other region, nor in aught
That Fancy, dreaming o'er the map of things,
Hath placed beyond these penetrable bounds,
Words of assurance can be heard; if nowhere
A habitation, for consummate good,
Or for progressive virtue, by the search
Can be attained,—a better sanctuary
From doubt and sorrow, than the senseless grave?"

(3:209–24)

The Solitary's considerable mental powers may well span the profundi-
ties of "imagination high" and "question deep," the sublimity of
"heaven's blue vault," and the unconscious boldness of Fancy, "dreaming o'er the map of things." But they do not equip him to cross the gap
between the mind's visionary powers and the spirit's powerlessness to
embrace them for consolation; a gap between "the unvoyageable sky. . .
stretched overhead" and the "subterraneous magazine of bones"
(5:345) on which he takes up his stance. For all his rhetorical brilliance,
rooted in the melancholic persuasions of Spenser, Milton, and Shakespeare, the Solitary defines his lack as "words of assurance"; he is unable
to find, in the Wanderer's memorable phrase, "conceptions equal to the
soul's desires" (4:137).

•　•　•　•　•

To elaborate this discussion of the Solitary's "inward malady," I want to
place Wordsworth's diagnosis of the Solitary in the context of Schiller's
diagnosis of the contemporary *zeitgeist* as "sentimental." In *On Naive
and Sentimental Poetry*, Schiller defines the sentimental as an effect of
difference, a negotiation between

> two conflicting representations and perceptions—with actuality as a limit
> and with [the sentimental poet's] idea as infinitude; and the mixed feelings
> that he excites will always testify to this dual source. . . . For now the ques-
> tion arises whether he will tend more toward actuality or toward the
> ideal—whether he will realize the former as an object of antipathy or the

latter as an object of sympathy. His presentation will, therefore, be either *satirical*, or it will be (in a broader connotation of the word which will become clearer later) *elegiac*. (116–17)

With Schiller's dichotomous definition of the sentimental in mind, we may understand the Wanderer's agenda to be the conversion of the Solitary—but not from skepticism to Christianity; such will be the work of the Pastor. Rather, within the domain of the sentimental, the Wanderer seeks to convert the Solitary from the satirical sensibility to an elegiac one. Schiller, whose dichotomies always entail implicit moral hierarchies, advocates a movement from satire to elegy; the satirical poet is urged to embrace the visionary mode of the elegiac. In Schiller's terms, the Wanderer seeks to move the Solitary from "senseless" satire to sympathetic vision.

Within the domain of the elegiac sensibility, Schiller constructs another dichotomy:

> [The elegiac,] too, like satire, comprehends two species. Either nature and the ideal are an object of sadness if the first is treated as lost and the second as unattained. Or both are an object of joy represented as actual. The first yields the *elegy* in the narrower sense [or lamentation], and the second the idyll in the broader sense. (125)

If the lamentational[11] poet "seeks nature, but as an idea and in a perfection in which she has never existed" (127), the idyllic poet is charged with *reimagining* and thus reinventing nature. What Schiller intends by this becomes clearer when he designates bucolica as falsely idyllic, for such poems "unhappily . . . place that purpose *behind* us, *toward* which they should, however, lead us" (149). It is the task of the idyllic poet to

> undertake the task of idyll so as to display that pastoral innocence even in creatures of civilization and under all the conditions of the most active and vigorous life, of expansive thought, of the subtlest art, the highest social refinement, which, in a word, leads man who cannot now go back to Arcady forward to Elysium. (153)

The idyllic poet, in other words, is to invent the pastoral of *civilization*. I will consider in the following section how Schiller's prescription for the sentimental poet compares with the remedies offered the Solitary by the Wanderer and the Pastor. But I want now to argue that Wordsworth's sentimental Solitary constitutes an ethical critique of Schiller's theory of sentimentality.

To Schiller, the most decisive difference between the naive and sentimental temperaments lies in their relation to experience:

The naive genius is thus dependent upon experience in a way unknown to the sentimental. The latter, we know, only begins his function where the former concludes his; his strength subsists in completing an inadequate subject *out of himself* and by his own power to transform a limited condition into a condition of freedom. Thus the naive poetic genius requires assistance from without, whereas the sentimental nourishes and purifies himself from within. (157–58)

The sentimental poet's radical transformation of "a limited condition into a condition of freedom"—his transcendence of experience, in other words—is achieved when experience becomes obviated by an internal sense of "actuality"; in lieu of the naive poet's dialogue with nature, the sentimental poet conducts an internal dialogue between (again) "actuality as a limit and . . . his idea as infinitude" (116). Presumably the idyllic vision arises as the fruit of this dialectic within the self, a Yeatsian "dialogue of self and soul."

But the Solitary's own theory of contemplative hermitage, embedded within his remarks about the medieval hermit, both disappoints and criticizes Schiller's theory of sentimental transcendence. He imagines the hermit "compassed round by pleasure, sigh[ing]/For independent happiness" (3:380–81):

> [C]raving peace,
> The central feeling of all happiness,
> Not as a refuge from distress or pain,
> A breathing-time, vacation, or a truce,
> But for its absolute self; a life of peace,
> Stability without regret or fear;
> That hath been, is, and shall be evermore!
>
> . . . . .
>
> —What but this,
> The universal instinct of repose,
> The longing for confirmed tranquillity,
> Inward and outward; humble, yet sublime:
> The life where hope and memory are as one;
> Where earth is quiet and her face unchanged
> Save by the simplest toil of human hands
> Or seasons' difference; the immortal Soul
> Consistent in self-rule; and heaven revealed
> To meditation in that quietness!—
>
> (3:381–405)

The hermitic self, as the Solitary himself conceptualizes it, proves to be a *hermetic* self; its radical autonomy is enacted not as dialogue, but as silence—not as freedom, but as limitation. Denying the vacancy of the

hermit's life, the Solitary celebrates it for "its absolute self"; and a concentric sense of stable, absolute self, apparently, is what the hermit enjoys as peace. The hermit seeks, more urgently than the "simplest toil"
of Eden, "confirmed tranquillity," an alignment of "Inward and outward," "hope and memory" around the axis of the self. His "transcendence" denies rather than surpasses the differentials of space and time;
of history and politics; of God and nature; and of the human community. To the Solitary, "the universal instinct of repose" finally speaks of
nothing more than "the sublime attractions of the grave."

Perhaps nowhere is this deathlike self revealed more spectacularly
than in the Solitary's narrative of his vision.

> "[A] step,
> A single step, that freed me from the skirts
> Of the blind vapour, opened to my view
> Glory beyond all glory ever seen
> By waking sense or by the dreaming soul!
> The appearance, instantaneously disclosed,
> Was of a mighty city—boldly say
> A wilderness of building, sinking far
> And self-withdrawn into a boundless depth,
> Far sinking into splendour—without end!
>
> . . . . .
>
> Right in the midst, where interspace appeared
> Of open court, an object like a throne
> Under a shining canopy of state
> Stood fixed. . . ."
>
> (2:829–64)

The Solitary's vision of civilization-in-nature—or nature *as* civilization—does not suggest the sublime architecture of a New Jerusalem,
Christian or secular. It reveals, on the contrary, a solipsistic[12] shrine to
the sovereign self. Rather than figuring the self as a space for contemplative, fruitful, philosophical dialogue, the Solitary figures it as an en-
throned icon; he evokes an *idolatry*, rather than a dialectic or even a
theology, of selfhood. "[S]inking far/And self-withdrawn into a boundless depth,/Far sinking into splendour—without end" (2:837–38), this
vision reveals the severity of the Solitary's "self-withdrawn" solipsism.
While the vision atop Snowdon in *Prelude* 13 argues for the sublime
substantiality of vapor, the Solitary's vision fixes upon a vacancy; at its
center lies an "interspace" within which "a shining canopy of state/
Stood fixed." Unable to image forth the mobility of the body politic, the
Solitary's sublime vision imagines a fixity of the interior. To exclaim "I
have been dead!" is to acknowledge a dead silence at the heart of the
sovereign self.

This silence exists, perhaps, because for all the Solitary's rhetorical brilliance, the contemplative self remains unspeaking; or perhaps, judging from the Solitary's biography, *unspeakable*.[13] For the Solitary's ideal of interiority stops perilously short of the self-communion that is the primal motive of such diverse Romantic lyrics as Wordsworth's "Intimations Ode," Coleridge's "Dejection: An Ode," Shelley's *Mont Blanc*, and Keats's Odes. The true "impotence of grief" is expressed in the Solitary's refusal to engage with (as a later poet would put it) an "interior paramour":

> This is, therefore, the intensest rendezvous.
> It is in that thought that we collect ourselves,
> Out of all the indifferences, into one thing. . . .
>
> .   .   .   .   .
>
> Out of this same light, out of the central mind,
> We make a dwelling in the evening air,
> In which being there together is enough.[14]

Wordsworth's diagnosis of the Solitary, I would insist, does not identify the sentimental temperament as a pathology. On the contrary, Wordsworth credits the Solitary's claims for his secular hermitage as a condition of intellectual striving born of a difference within the self. But in exposing his idealized transcendence as solipsism—in exposing the tyranny of the sovereign self—Wordsworth convicts the sentimentalist of a disabling egoism that compromises his potential as a sentimental visionary. Though the Solitary endures in the poem through the ninth book—escapes, in fact, its pageantry of closure—his psychic predicament is frozen in the pivotal fifth book:

> [L]ooking down the darksome aisle
> I saw the Tenant of the lonely vale
> standing apart; with curvèd arm reclined
> On the baptismal font; his pallid face
> Upturned, as if his mind were rapt, or lost
> In some abstraction;—gracefully he stood,
> The semblance bearing of a sculptured form
> That leans upon a monumental urn
> In peace, from morn to night, from year to year.
>
> (5:209–17)

"Housed in a dream, at distance from the kind," the Solitary's solipsism gives on to an abstraction verging on mindlessness. His own psychic fixation is externalized as he takes on "The semblance . . . of a sculptured form." In this tableau of the Solitary, he becomes a monument to the deathlike fixity and vacancy that haunts the sentimental temperament, a work of funerary art instead of a deathless artist.[15]

Idylls of the Dead

Schiller's theory of the idyll is enormously suggestive as a framework for interpreting the Wanderer's and the Pastor's respective remedies for the Solitary's "malady."[16] While the Wanderer's prescription, as Johnston has argued, is heterodox from a Christian perspective, its insistence on humanizing nature through the "imaginative will" (4:1128) makes him a rather orthodox disciple of Schiller. Like Schiller, the Wanderer insists on the striving that lies at the heart of the sentimental idyll which, in Schiller's words, "obtains its value . . . by approximation to an infinite greatness." While I do not wish to rehearse the Wanderer's "eloquent harangue" here, it bears noting that his invocation of the mythopoetic Greek mind precisely parallels Schiller's discussion of Greek culture as an exemplification of the naive: "The whole structure of their social life was founded on perceptions, not on a contrivance of art; their theology itself was the inspiration of a naive feeling, the child of a joyous imaginative power. . . . [T]he Greek had not lost nature in his humanity" (104). In the end, however, the Wanderer's injunctions recommend a *revival*, not a surpassing, of the mythopoetic imagination. Schiller deems such a revival retrograde, not to say inaccessible for the sentimentalist who, like the poet Klopstock, "witnesses the matter out of everything he touches so as to transform it into spirit. . . ." (135). Even the Wanderer's invocation of Providence reproving a "Vain-glorious generation"(4:278) privileges nature over human history: " 'By nature's gradual processes be taught;/By story be confounded' "(4:288–89). As the Wanderer closes his "eloquent harangue," Wordsworth figures the naive Wanderer as Rousseau's noble savage:

> Here closed the Sage that eloquent harangue,
> Poured forth with fervour in continuous stream,
> Such as, remote, 'mid savage wilderness,
> An Indian Chief discharges from his breast
> Into the hearing of assembled tribes,
> In open circle seated round, and hushed
> As the unbreathing air, when not a leaf
> Stirs in the mighty woods.
>
> (4:1276–83)

For Wordsworth, the Wanderer is insufficiently self-conscious to offer an idyllic remedy; his mental life, like that of Greeks and "primitives," is as spontaneous as a "continuous stream."

Whereas the Wanderer's remedy bespeaks the naiveté of "savage wilderness," the Pastor, on the other hand, is associated with an idyllic "sweet civility on rustic wilds":

> "As 'mid some happy valley of the Alps,"
> Said I, "once happy, ere tyrannic power,
> Wantonly breaking in upon the Swiss,
> Destroyed their unoffending commonwealth,
> A popular equality reigns here,
> Save for yon stately House beneath whose roof
> A rural lord might dwell."—"No feudal pomp,
> Or power," replied the Wanderer, "to that House
> Belongs, but there in his allotted Home
> Abides, from year to year, a genuine Priest,
> The shepherd of his flock; or, as a king
> Is styled, when most affectionately praised,
> The father of his people."
>
> (5:92–104)

Like Mary Shelley, who in 1816 set *Frankenstein* in the pre-Napoleonic Republic of Geneva, Wordsworth retrieves the nostalgic ideal of the Swiss "commonwealth." This is a valley in which "a popular equality reigns," not the Pastor. His authority is domesticated, located not in a "stately House," but in an "Allotted Home"; his paternalism is acknowledged with and *as* affection.

In Book 5, the egalitarian churchyard is both a synecdoche and an epitome of the "popular equality" of the valley. In the Pastor's words:

> "[C]harity, and love, that have provided,
> Within these precincts, a capacious bed
> And receptacle, open to the good
> And evil, to the just and the unjust;
> In which they find an equal resting-place:
> Even as the multitude of kindred brooks
> And streams, whose murmur fills this hollow vale,
> Whether their course be turbulent or smooth,
> Their waters clear or sullied, all are lost
> Within the bosom of yon crystal Lake,
> And end their journey in the same repose!
>
> (5:911–21)

The churchyard accepts "the good and evil. . . the just and the unjust." Nor, as becomes clearer in the catalogue of the dead that follows (5:946–77), does the churchyard discriminate on the basis of baptism, age, social class, gender, or mental firmness. Whereas the poet compares the valley to the secular ideal of the Swiss commonwealths, the Pastor seeks a metaphysical analogue for mortal equality; his image of "kindred brooks and streams" entering "the bosom of yon crystal Lake" redeems for Christianity the Solitary's skeptical figure of "particular current[s]" running alike into "[T]he unfathomable gulf, where all is still" (3:991).

Wordsworth's idyll of the churchyard seconds Burke's assertion that, "to love the little platoon we belong to in society, is the first principle (the germ as it were) of public affections. It is the first link in the series by which we proceed towards a love to our country and to mankind"(59). In the first of the *Essays Upon Epitaphs*, Wordsworth describes "a parish-church, in the stillness of the country, as a visible centre of a community of the living and the dead; a point to which are habitually referred the nearest concerns of both"(2:56). The remark is prompted by Addison's view (echoed in *The Excursion* by the Solitary) that many pious epitaphs unwittingly satirize the dead. Wordsworth offers a geometric corrective: the churchyard is not defined by the spread vectors of rectitude and perversity, but by the concentric pull it exerts upon the community:

> As in these registers the name is mostly associated with others of the same family, this is a prolonged companionship, however shadowy. . . . Such a frail memorial then is not without its tendency to keep families together; it feeds also local attachment, which is the tap-root of the tree of Patriotism.(2:93)

Quoting Gray's *Elegy* as the epigraph to the second of the "Essays," Wordsworth pays homage to the "rude Forefathers of the hamlet"(2:69): "[I]n these evidences I have seen a proof how deeply the piety of the rude Forefathers of the hamlet is seated in their natures, I mean how habitual and constitutional it is. . . ."(2:69).

But this Burkean insistence on the churchyard's centrality recalls the hermetic perils of centricity; the cult of the churchyard, unless it admits its own utopian status as a balm for a world of suffering and inequality, is no better than that of the sovereign self. The Poet derives the significance of the churchyard from its juxtaposition with an imperfect world:

> "And, in the centre of a world whose soil
> Is rank with all unkindness, compassed round
> With such memorials, I have sometimes felt,
> It was no momentary happiness
> To have *one* Enclosure where the voice that speaks
> In envy or detraction is not heard;
> Which malice may not enter. . . ."
>
> (6:634–40)

From the Poet's perspective, the cult of the churchyard proves a radically unstable idealization, threatening to tumble into a sentimental abyss between actuality and the ideal; like Burke's "permanent body composed of transitory parts," it risks, even courts, dismemberment. In a similar passage in the *Essays Upon Epitaphs*, a churchyard idyll breaks down into a haunted skepticism:

> Amid the quiet of a Church-yard . . . I have been affected by sensations akin to those which have risen in my mind while I have been standing by the side of a smooth Sea, on a Summer's day. It is such a happiness to have, in an unkind World, one Enclosure where the voice of detraction is not heard; where the traces of evil inclinations are unknown; where contentment prevails, and there is no jarring tone in the peaceful Concert of amity and gratitude. I have been rouzed from this reverie by a consciousness, suddenly flashing upon me, of the anxieties, the perturbations, and, in many instances, the vices and rancorous dispositions, by which the hearts of those who lie under so smooth a surface and so fair an outside must have been agitated. The image of an unruffled Sea has still remained; but my fancy has penetrated into the depths of that Sea—with accompanying thoughts of Shipwreck, of the destruction of the Mariner's hopes, the bones of drowned Men heaped together, monsters of the deep, and all the hideous and confused sights which Clarence saw in his Dream!(2:63–64)

In both passages, the "one Enclosure" fails to provide a psychic center of gravity. Wordsworth identifies churchyard utopianism, as he did the hermetic landscapes of Book 3, with the defensive and facile illusions of "Peele Castle": "Housed in a dream," the poet "could have fancied that the mighty Deep/Was even then gentlest of all gentle Things" (11–12). The "one Enclosure" of the churchyard takes on the anaesthetic circularity of the "huge Castle. . . . Cased in the unfeeling armour of old time." The "hideous and confused" dream of Clarence merely revives the nightmare of loss commemorated in Peele Castle.

Both the "eloquent harangue" of the Wanderer, in which idyll gives way to unself-conscious naiveté, and the churchyard idyll presided over by the Pastor, in which utopianism forgets its provenance as critique, suggest Wordsworth's resistance to the Schillerian remedy of the idyll. What Wordsworth describes in the passage just quoted as the giving way of "reverie" to "consciousness," suggests a reluctance to invest in the idyllic transcendence of sentimental difference. While the stalwart Solitary reneges on the utopian impulse—"Not for a happy land do I enquire,/Island or grove" (5:349–50)—his cult of selfhood may be recognized as an attempt to transcend sentimental self-consciousness. Hence, the Solitary's solipsism is not a failed transcendence so much as a critique of transcendence for its solipsistic denial of difference within the self.

The *Essays Upon Epitaphs* suggest a mode of recovery from sentimental crisis that is not predicated on idyllic investments in transcendence. Wordsworth, invoking the Solitary's sentimental mode, describes this recovery as "contemplation":

> Nevertheless, I have been able to return, (and who may not?) to a steady contemplation of the benign influence of such a favourable Register lying open to the eyes of all. Without being so far lulled as to imagine I saw in a Village Church-yard the eye or central point of a rural Arcadia, I have felt that with all the vague and general expressions of love, gratitude, and praise with which it is usually crowded, it is a far more faithful representation of homely life as existing among a Community with which circumstances have not been untoward, than any report which might be made by a rigorous observer deficient in that spirit of forbearance and those kindly prepossessions, without which human life can in no condition be profitably looked at or described. (2:64)

Wordsworth recovers not by designating the churchyard as a "rural Arcadia," but by recognizing it as a "Register," a "representation" of "homely life." The solipsistic investments of idyll are countered by the morally "profitable" enterprise of sympathizing with the dead. In a moral economy reminiscent of Adam Smith's, mortal deposition conjoined with sympathy for the dead becomes a moral deposit on behalf of the community. The dead "Are here deposited, with tribute paid/Various, but unto each some tribute paid" (5:971–72). For Smith, the tribute paid to the dead partially compensates an unpayable debt; the dead are our moral creditors *in perpetuum*. But *The Excursion* focuses on the self-conscious and "various" *acts of valuation* that set this process in motion; on the imaginative payment of tribute that establishes the worth of the dead. If, as Wordsworth writes in the first *Essay Upon Epitaphs*, "[T]he composition of an epitaph naturally turns . . . upon departed worth"(2:56), then we must turn to Wordsworth's theory of the epitaph to see what role such tribute plays in *The Excursion*.

"Authentic Epitaphs"

In response to the Pastor's resonant questions, "And Whence that tribute? wherefore these regards?" (5:988), Wordsworth appended the first of the *Essays Upon Epitaphs* (1810) as an extended footnote. In this first *Essay*, such questions yield Wordsworth an opportunity to establish a sublime intuition of immortality. But within the text of *The Excursion*, however, the Pastor responds to his own queries with a commentary on the provenance of memory:

"Not from the naked *Heart* alone of Man
(Though claiming high distinction upon earth
As the sole spring and fountain-head of tears,
His own peculiar utterance for distress
Or gladness)—No," the philosophic Priest
Continued, "'tis not in the vital seat
Of feeling to produce them, without aid
From the pure soul, the soul sublime and pure;
With her two faculties of eye and ear. . ."

．　．　．　．　．

Not without such assistance could the use
Of these benign observances prevail:
Thus are they born, thus fostered, thus maintained;
And by the care prospective of our wise
Forefathers, who, to guard against the shocks,
The fluctuation and decay of things,
Embodied and established these high truths
In solemn institutions. . . ."

(5:979–1001)

While denying that such tribute comes solely from the affections, the Pastor cites a collaboration between the "naked *Heart*" of feeling and the "soul sublime and pure." By so doing, he recognizes sympathy in the tradition of Adam Smith as a phenomenon conflating the affections and the imagination; a "philosophic *Priest*" (my emphasis), he gives sympathy, unlike Smith, a sublime cast.

But despite this insistence on epitaphic sublimity, we observe that Wordsworth's inquiry into the significance of epitaphs has shifted from a metaphysical register to a cultural one. At the same time, Wordsworth distinguishes between two gendered types of human activity. First, the feminine soul is said to stand in an aesthetic relation to divinity, gaining access to "the WORD" "with her two faculties of eye and ear." Hence, the "benign observances" which the soul promotes are both the cultural practice of preserving memory and a witness to a divine power. The soul, even as she observes divine benignity, gives birth to "benign observances" that sustain the dead; through these observances, she "foster[s]" and "maintain[s]" them. Hence, while Wordsworth's figure may seem to emphasize the soul's aesthetic perception of divinity, the birth, fostering, and maintenance of "benign observances" strongly identify the soul's activity as an act of conception. It is a type of contemplation—a contemplation both of divine immanence and of transcendence—that Wordsworth assigns to the feminine soul.

Second, Wordsworth cites the paternity of "our wise forefathers, who . . . embodied and established" the value of the dead in "solemn institutions."[17] If institutions of embodiment and establishment constitute a masculine type of epitaphic discourse, enshrining the mores, traditions, and prejudices of the past within stable institutions, its feminine counterpart focuses on the observances that bridge the divine and human realms, bringing new life out of the dead. While such patriarchal institutions as the Church, Schools, Government, and Monarchy are the prime concern of Book 8 (which might be said to begin in Book 7 with the narratives of Oswald and Sir Alfred Erthyng), the serial narratives of Books 5–7 perform the "benign observances" that Wordsworth assigns to a feminine, maternal principle. In this phase of the poem, Wordsworth's emphasis falls on the speech through which the dead are brought forth for the edification of the living:

> "Epitomize the life; pronounce, you can,
> Authentic epitaphs on some of these
> Who, from their lowly mansion hither brought,
> Beneath this turf lie mouldering at our feet:
> So, by your records, may our doubts be solved;
> And so, not searching higher, we may learn
> *To prize the breath we share with human kind;*
> *And look upon the dust of man with awe.*"
>
> (5:650–57)

Wordsworth uses tropes of gender to distinguish between the masculine *products* of civic tradition and the feminine *process* by which the dead provide the moral resource of tradition.

But when he works toward a definition of his own epitaphic mode in *The Excursion*, Wordsworth relies on the trope of "authenticity" to develop a comparison between the institutional, scriptural epitaphs discussed in the *Essays Upon Epitaphs* and the orally transmitted epitaphs of *The Excursion*.[18] At the heart of this difference lies that between the criterion of epitaphic "sincerity" in the *Essays*, and that of epitaphic "authenticity" in *The Excursion*. Let us consider these by turns. Wordsworth's criterion of epitaphic sincerity is derived from the neoclassical and late-eighteenth-century rhetorical criticism of elegiac verse discussed in chapters 1 and 2. Epitaphic "sincerity" rests on the ethos of the author:

For, when a Man is treating an interesting subject, . . . no faults have such a killing power as those which prove that he is not in earnest, that he is acting a part, has leisure for affectation, and feels that without it he could do nothing. This is one of the most odious of faults; because it shocks the moral sense: and is worse in a sepulchral inscription, precisely in the same degree as that mode of composition calls for sincerity more urgently than any other.(2:70)

One hears an echo of Johnson's own blast at *Lycidas*—"Where there is leisure for fiction, there can be little grief."[19] Whereas eighteenth-century critics such as Johnson scour elegies for an apparent deficit of sincerity, however, Wordsworth's poetics of the epitaph focuses on the impropriety of flamboyant sincerity:

> The very form and substance of the monument which has received the inscription, and the appearance of the letters, testifying with what a slow and laborious hand they must have been engraven, might seem to reproach the author who had given way upon this occasion to transports of mind, or to quick turns of conflicting passion. (2:60)

Effusiveness may be at home in the monody or elegy or even the funeral oration, but because the epitaph is a written or engraved form, the epitaphic author must eschew the transient transports of emotion. The "engraven record" demands a certain gravity.

But the *Essays Upon Epitaphs* emphasize that the "engraven record" entails an unusual kind of writing that is legible to those at the margins of literate culture:

> [A]n epitaph is not a proud writing shut up for the studious: it is exposed to all. . . : the stooping old man cons the engraven record like a second hornbook;—the child is proud that he can read it;—and the stranger is introduced through its mediation to the company of a friend: it is concerning all, and for all. (2:59)

The "authentic" epitaph, however, does not presuppose a written text. Insofar as it is oral, it transmits traditions more broadly across the social spectrum than does the written epitaph. This broad reach, of course, carries tradition to unlettered sectors of the population, to regions and among classes where literacy is the exception rather than the rule. Like Wordsworth's lyrical ballad, "The Brothers," *The Excursion* explicitly values the oral epitaph as a superior "depository" for mortal tribute:

> Green is the Churchyard, beautiful and green,
> Ridge rising gently by the side of ridge,
> A heaving surface, almost wholly free
> From interruption of sepulchral stones,
> And mantled o'er with aboriginal turf
> And everlasting flowers. These Dalesmen trust
> The lingering gleam of their departed lives

> To oral record, and the silent heart;
> Depositories faithful and more kind
> Than fondest epitaph: for, if those fail,
> What boots the sculptured tomb?

(6:605–15)

The oral epitaph, Wordsworth claims, is more "faithful and more kind" than the written epitaph. "Faithfulness," the central attribute of "authenticity," aligns the aesthetic and the moral in a theory of epitaphic representation. But the degree of "faithfulness" differs from written to oral epitaph as differs the "proportion of the common or universal feeling of humanity to sensations excited by a distinct and clear conception . . . of the individual"(2:57). Exactly what proportion of generality to specificity is considered "due" in the written epitaph is suggested in the follow passage:

> What purity and brightness is that virtue clothed in, the image of which must no longer bless our living eyes! The character of a deceased friend or beloved kinsman is not seen, no—nor ought to be seen, otherwise than as a tree through a tender haze or a luminous mist, that spiritualises and beautifies it; that takes away, indeed, but only to the end that the parts which are not abstracted may appear more dignified and lovely; may impress and affect the more.(2:58)

According to Wordsworth's poetics of the epitaph in the *Essays*, a written epitaph ought not to give us images of the dead, but rather a "tender haze or a luminous mist" that improves upon their character. Generality is not merely to be emphasized; it is to subsume particularity.

The oral epitaphs of *The Excursion*, on the other hand, promise "[c]lear images before your gladdened eyes/Of nature's unambitious underwood,/And flowers that prosper in the shade" (6:652–54). Instead of supplying a mediating "haze" or "mist," the Pastor describes himself as "lifting up a veil, /A sunbeam introducing among hearts/Retired and covert"(6:649–51). "Faithfulness," for the oral epitaph, suggests an aesthetic of particularity, idiosyncrasy, detail, one that contrasts sharply with the neoclassical emphasis on the general, the abstract, the universal. In the *Essays*, Wordsworth claims to have derived this ideal of "faithful" representation from a seventeenth-century source: William Weever's *Ancient Funeral Monuments* (1638). Indeed, eschewing neoclassical theories of epitaph, he cites Weever for providing the model for a "perfect Epitaph":

> [In Weever's] conception an Epitaph was not to be an abstract character of the deceased but an epitomized biography blended with description by which an impression of the character was to be conveyed. Bring forward the

one incidental expression, a kind of commiseration, unite with it a concern on the part of the dead for the well-being of the living made known by exhortation and admonition, and let this commiseration and concern pervade and brood over the whole so that what was peculiar to the individual shall still be subordinate to a sense of what he had in common with the species—our notion of a perfect Epitaph would then be realized. (2:89)

Wordsworth's "perfect Epitaph" balances the general and particular by summoning the latter to illustrate "a sense of what [the dead] had in common with the species." Hence, the universal is represented not by obscuring the particular through a "haze" or "veil," but by contextualizing the particular within a narrative illustrative of moral virtue. Such an epitaph is emphatically biographical; it elaborates the character of the dead by representing his or her acts—and their consequences—within a human community framed within a secular, temporal world.

Moreover, in this account of the "perfect Epitaph," the term "character" points in two directions. On the one hand, it points toward the written abstract of a "moral character"—a documentary account of "what he had in common with the species." On the other hand, it points toward idiosyncrasy, toward the "incidental expression" that conveys "what was peculiar to the individual"; points, finally, even toward the invention of the dead as fully realized, psychologically plausible *characters*. Wordsworth's notion of epitaphic "character," in other words, is in transition between the eighteenth-century discourse of morals and the nineteenth-century discourse of psychology; between the documentary genre of the moral "character" and the novel of psychological realism. Reviving Weever as his example, Wordsworth seeks to redress the neoclassical balance in favor of the general with an art of "epitomized biography blended with description by which an impression of the character was to be conveyed." He quotes Weever, in other words, from the perspective of the century that would witness the birth of such "characters" as Jane Eyre, Heathcliff, Becky Sharp, and Pip. Through such psychological "characterization," Wordsworth recognized, the moral and universal receives a considerable rhetorical impetus, the power to "give to universally received truths a pathos and spirit which shall re-admit them into the soul like revelations of the moment" (2:83).

In broader terms, these shifts from image to narrative, from moral "character" to psychological "character"—developments recapitulated in moving from the theory of the *Essays Upon Epitaphs* to the praxis of *The Excursion*—suggest a shift in the discourse of human lives from the general and normative to the personal, particular, and peculiar. Such a change is already apparent, of course, in the writing of Johnson, whose commentary in the "Life of Pope" on Pope's epitaph for Sir

William Trumbull laments Pope's failure to include the name of the deceased: "The end of an epitaph is to convey some account of the dead; and to what purpose is anything told of him whose name is concealed? An epitaph and a history of a nameless hero are equally absurd, since the virtues and qualities so recounted in either are scattered at the mercy of fortune, to be appropriated by guess"(406). Johnsonian biography, like Wordsworth's *Essays on Epitaphs*, places the particular in the service of illustrating general moral truths; and if Johnson implicitly suggests an analogy between biography, epitaph, and history, it remained for Wordsworth's *Excursion* to identify explicitly these three discursive forms. *The Excursion* witnesses a change of emphasis within the discourse of human lives from human *nature* to human *history*.

· · · · ·

In *The Excursion*, keeping faith with the dead entails bringing them to life within the vivid converse of the living. I want to close this chapter with a reading of the story of Ellen (6:778–1052), for it is in this story that Wordsworth explicitly conjoins the trope of feminine conception with the "authentic epitaphs" of history. In the story of Ellen, the feminine does not reside in the landscape of Nature, nor, specifically, in the "nature" of the affections, but in the darker realms of the interior—an interior in which the mind and the grave are conjoined. Then, through the metonymic agency of the Pastor, Ellen's experience—a personal experience of "bearing the dead"—is brought forth into the community.

What is allegorized in the story of Ellen is one striking implication of Wordsworth's dualistic approach to the past: the attachment of femininity—even of maternity—to the public sphere. This conjunction calls for a few remarks, not least because Wordsworth's tropes of gender in *The Excursion*—masculinity for inherited tradition, femininity for the imagining of the past—imply an equation of mind with femininity and nature with masculinity; and such an equation directly contradicts the famous gendering of masculine mind and feminine nature in the "spousal" Prospectus to *The Recluse*. This contradiction is, above all, a strong reminder that the Romantic discourse of gender is more flexible, more rhetorical, more contextually bound than it is often assumed to be. My own account of this shift—shift, rather than reversal, for we are dealing here with a developing stance, not a repudiated one—would focus on Wordsworth's evolving understanding of the relation between the epic genre and his own changing poetic project. Abrams's now-standard account of Wordsworth's *Prelude* as a lyrical epic[20]—an epic of the poet's intellectual and moral growth—is useful here for suggesting implicitly the following question: having written such an epic, to what literary tradition is Wordsworth to appeal in a long poem concerned with the nation and its past? It seems clear that to return to the conventions of epic would be problematical; it would suggest palinode, or at least some striving against an earlier poetic self.

But beyond this difficulty, in two crucial respects the epic tradition—a tradition in which the virile mind at once espouses nature and subdues it—sorts ill with Wordsworth's particular concerns in *The Excursion*. First, Wordsworth's concept of nation is decentered and indirect, evoked by means of local, communal, rural experience. The Burkean figure of concentric social circles speaks directly to Wordsworth's concept of nation, as does Burke's insistence on the centrality of land as opposed to the urban, commercial crux. True, Burke and Wordsworth understood the meaning, the *power* of land differently; but for both the heart of the nation beat ubiquitously, not simply in the commercial center. Similarly, the nation's people are not assembled for inspection and instruction; the poem concerns not a people, but diverse people within and without the bounds of the churchyard. National institutions, likewise, are broached by means of their excrescences in the locality. There is something distinctly minor and domestic about Wordsworth's evocation of the nation; something, within the discourse of early nineteenth-century social practice, insistently feminine.

And nation is not the only term approached through feminine tropes by Wordsworth in *The Excursion*; the past is similarly broached. In this poem, Wordsworth seeks to write a poetry of the past that acknowledges the discontinuity between present and past, the need to invent the past for a present audience; in short, a poetry that acknowledges the fictivity of history. It is Wordsworth's splendid insight that such an acknowledgment need not entail an elegiac lament for a lost, better age, but rather that it might celebrate the moral power revealed in the act of bringing the past to life. And for that act of conception, I have been arguing, Wordsworth uses the maternal trope of conceiving and bringing forth a discourse of the past.

These remarks may raise as many questions as they address. Is *The Excursion*, then, a feminine epic? Is Wordsworth's feminization of such terms as "nation" and "past" symptomatic of his attachment of the feminine to the public sphere? Or does the conjunction of the feminine and the public work against such exposures of the feminine? Is Wordsworth's *Excursion* yet another taking up of epic concerns within the private sphere? Let me approach these issues by comparing *The Excursion* with the epic poetics of Elizabeth Barrett Browning, who published the first self-proclaimed feminine epic—*Aurora Leigh*—in 1857:

> Never flinch,
> But still, unscrupulously epic, catch
> Upon the burning lava of a song
> That full-veined, heaving, double-breasted Age:
> That, when the next shall come, the men of that
> May touch the impress with reverent hand, and say,
> "Behold,—behold the paps we all have sucked!
> This bosom seems to beat still, or at least
> It sets ours beating: this is living art,
> Which thus presents and thus records true life.[21]

For Wordsworth's "pregnant spot of ground," Barrett Browning substitutes a "heaving, double-breasted Age." For her the epic is not, however, the nurse of heroes, but a palimpsestic "impress" of these breasts. Like Wordsworth, Barrett Browning argues that the epic is not a repository of the past; what it makes known is the *absence* of the past that has given life to the present and sustained it. But by causing a quickening in the present, the epic summons the influence of the past. Again like Wordsworth, Barrett Browning celebrates not epic continuity, but the birth of historical consciousness that makes epic poetry possible. The feminized epic, here, is linked to a particular kind of history, in which consciousness re-creates that which we know—or come to know—to have created us. Whereas Johnson associates "fiction" with the unserious ornamentation of Classical allusion (just as Milton associates classical mythology with "fable"), Wordsworth and Barrett Browning alike recognize that history is an imaginative fiction; it is what we *make* of the dead.

If Barrett Browning celebrates this kind of history, Wordsworth's poem creates it through the person of the Pastor. And yet the Pastor is no epic poet. The Pastor's "pure eloquence" may ascend to "a higher mark than song can reach" (7:24), but he is identified, persistently, as the poem's *historian*. However sublime the effect of his eloquence—his rhetoric of virtue—Wordsworth would have us understand that the Pastor is no rapt bard, but a self-conscious maker of narratives rooted in the ground of his researches. His historical "remedy" for the Solitary's solipsism—Wordsworth's alternative to Schiller's theory of the idyll—is to recognize the gap between what we are and what we cherish in his images of the dead.

Moreover, the Pastor's "authentic epitaphs" recognize that history is not a single epic stance taken on the dead, but a peripatetic sojourn among them. History, on the Pastor's premises, becomes a network of narratives, as single traces of narrative accumulate, cross, and generate, in turn, other narratives. Historical "faithfulness" appreciates difference by valuing it; thus, history becomes multiple, not monolithic. It is the cumulative "biography" of a community, and its praxis consists in the imaginative acts of telling that make tradition possible. The Pastor's closest literary affinities are neither with the expansive national epic nor with the contracted epitaph, but rather with a nineteenth-century fictional form that modulates between biography and history, between the personal and the communal; in this respect, *The Excursion* brings to mind such Victorian fictions as George Eliot's *Middlemarch*, Elizabeth Gaskell's *Cranford*, and Margaret Oliphant's *Chronicles of Carlingford*.

Hence, the Pastor's historicism, a counterpoint, even a challenge to epic history, is identified with the feminine in several ways: through tropes of conception, pregnancy, parturition, and nursing; through figures of minority and domesticity; through a sense of indirect connection with the nation's institutional heritage. If the Pastor's "authentic epitaphs" are figured as the feminine complement of patriarchal institutions, then "bearing the dead," means nothing less than giving birth to history. But the Pastor's role in the poem is hardly exhausted by the "benign observances" through which he acts as historian. For the Pastor himself is a crucial mediating figure between the masculine heritage of embodied institutions and the feminine process of making history. In the closing section of this chapter, I want to examine Wordsworth's alignment of these two senses of the past; his insistence on them as complementary. Let us attend to a narrative "authentically" concerned with the bearing of the dead: the story of Ellen.

"Home to Her Mother's House": The Story of Ellen (6:778–1052)

The story of Ellen is framed on both ends by references to the tale of Margaret, which by 1809[22] had come to serve as the initial passage of *The Excursion*. By recalling Margaret, Wordsworth aligns the story of Ellen with the intense pathos of *The Ruined Cottage*. At the same time, he seeks to link the Pedlar's (now the Wanderer's) tale, with its advocacy of a complex and ambiguous "natural sympathy," to the more orthodox moral instruction delivered by the Pastor. In large measure, both narratives are taken up with a tension between the individual's power both to imagine and to remedy its own suffering and the necessity that compels individuals to suffering and anguish. The difference between the tales is epitomized by that between Margaret and Ellen—a difference between a suffering mind conscious only of pain and the hope of its dismissal, and a suffering mind supremely conscious of its own responsibility and intent on discerning meaning within suffering. I would argue, however, that the story of Ellen completes that of Margaret—not by exemplifying a higher level of moral development, nor, particularly, by demonstrating the role of revelation in the endurance of suffering.[23] If the Pastor plays Beatrice to the Wanderer's Virgil in this *Excursion*, it is because his historicism accommodates both the powers of mind and nature, of the imagined past and the received past. In the story of Ellen, the two faces of grief in *The Ruined Cottage* become one.

The story's opening allusion to the tale of Margaret places emphasis on the moral consciousness of both the Pastor and Ellen. The "cottage bench" on which the Pedlar lay asleep, his face "dappled" by "the shadows of the breezy elms above" has become a "long stone-seat, fixed in the Churchyard wall;/Part shaded by cool sycamore" (6:779–80); here the Pastor's moral alertness is signaled by his wakefulness. Similarly, whereas Margaret "sleeps in the calm earth," the death of Ellen bespeaks disturbance, the fate of "them/Who seek" (even if they do not reach) "the House of Worship" (6:782). What concerns the pastor is not Ellen's proximity to the Church—her grave, of course, lies in the churchyard—but her anxious striving toward it.

Whereas Margaret's story emerges spontaneously from the Wanderer's painful comparison of past and present, Ellen's begins with a Pastoral meditation on the moral necessity of narrative. Whereas "the small heap/Speaks for itself; an Infant there doth rest" (6:790–91), it is not enough simply to recognize "the sheltering hillock" as "the Mother's grave":

> "Ah! what a warning for a thoughtless man,
> Could field or grove, could any spot of earth,
> Show to his eye an image of the pangs
> Which it hath witnessed; render back an echo
> Of the sad steps by which it hath been trod!
>
> . . . . .
>
> [T]he swelling turf reports
> Of the fresh shower, but of poor Ellen's tears
> Is silent; nor is any vestige left
> Of the path worn by mournful tread of her. . ."
>
> (6:806–20)

For Ellen's mute, imageless grave to supply a "warning for a thoughtless man," the Pastor must evoke the sound of Ellen weeping over the child's grave, and the sight of her kneeling form. Here, Wordsworth connects the narrator's power to provide the senses images and sounds with his power to provide the understanding a moral interpretation of sinful acts. Like many of the tales, in which "elements of virtue" "Are oft-times not unprofitably shown/In the perverseness of a selfish course" (6:667–68), the story of Ellen poses a moral paradox. If we are to seek for Ellen's virtues, we must look first to her sins:

> And if religious tenderness of heart,
> Grieving for sin, and penitential tears
> Shed when the clouds had gathered and distained
> The spotless ether of a maiden life;
> If these may make a hallowed spot of earth
> More holy in the sight of God or Man;
> Then, o'er that mould, a sanctity shall brood
> Till the stars sicken at the day of doom.
>
> (6:798–805)

The "spotless ether of a maiden life" offers no resistance to "the clouds" which "had gathered and distained" it; but the conspicuous "spot" of earth in which Ellen lies buried—a "spot" that raises her distaining as the central fact in her life—is nonetheless, hallowed. The moral meaning of Ellen's "spot"—both her grave and her sin—is invoked through the ensuing narrative. Whereas the Pedlar's tale of Margaret advocates moral vision through, or *beyond* images, the Pastor's story of Ellen advocates moral vision through, or *by means of* images. The imagination and the senses alike become moral agents.

The Pastor's narrative begins by evoking an unfallen Ellen in "virgin fearlessness":

> The form, port, motions, of this Cottage-girl
> Were such as might have quickened and inspired
> A Titian's hand, addrest to picture forth
> Oread or Dryad glancing through the shade
> What time the hunter's earliest horn is heard
> Startling the golden hills.
>
> (6:826–31)

This image of earliness, set in a "Prime hour of sweetest scents and airs" entails an allusion to a crucial moment in *Paradise Lost* at the threshold of the fall; for Titian, read Milton.[24] As Eve, having decided to work separately from Adam, withdraws her hand from Adam's, Milton describes Adam's last glance at the unfallen Eve:

> Thus saying, from her Husband's hand her hand
> Soft she withdrew, and like a Wood-Nymph light,
> *Oread* or *Dryad*, or of *Delia's* Train,
> Betook her to the Groves, but *Delia's* self

In gait surpass'd and Goddess-like deport,
Though not as shee with Bow and Quiver arm'd
But with such Gardn'ning Tools as Art yet rude,
Guiltless of fire had form'd, or Angels brought.
To *Pales*, or *Pomona*, thus adorn'd,
Likest she seem'd, *Pomona* when she fled
Vertumnus, or to *Ceres* in her Prime,
Yet Virgin of *Proserpina* from *Jove*.

(*PL* 9:385–96)

The simile can barely keep pace with Eve as she rushes into the grove, let alone capture her. Milton's overwrought simile, which figurally imports guilty fire, arms, lust, seduction, and rape into Eden, suggests the inescapability of the fallen consciousness through which Milton narrates. Thus, while the Pastor attempts to represent Ellen in her unfallen existence—she cannot (to use Wordsworth's painterly metaphor) be framed within it; Wordsworth's allusive simile both links Ellen's fall to the Fall in Eden, and places the innocent Ellen firmly within the context of her subsequent history. A diptych of elegiac images, employed here to provide a narrative "epitome," follows; Ellen's fall is framed by two different images of "THE JOYFUL TREE." In the first, Ellen dances "hapless" around "THE JOYFUL TREE"; in the second, she dances round it bearing "a secret burden."[25]

Once Ellen loses her innocence, the Pastor's narrative comes increasingly to focus on the workings of her own consciousness.[26] Alienated from the blithe natural world, reflecting on her own mental pain, Ellen is easily recognized as a sentimental mourner. Like the poet of the "Intimations Ode," she feels isolated in the renewing world of "unfolding leaves/. . . And small birds singing happily to mates/Happy as they" (6:855–88). And like that poet also, she contrasts her own sense of lack with the plenary birdsong she hears. But Ellen is not content simply to long for the naive unconsciousness of nature; a sentimental poet of lamentation, she writes a lyric in "the blank margin of a Valentine,/Bedropped with tears" (6:891–93). At the same time, wishing to avoid company, she seeks refuge "in lonely reading":

"[S]tudiously withdrawing from the eye
Of all companionship, the Sufferer yet
In lonely reading found a meek resource:
How thankful for the warmth of summer days,
When she could slip into the cottage-barn,
And find a secret oratory there;
Or, in the garden, under friendly veil

Of their long twilight, pore upon her book
By the last lingering help of the open sky
Until dark night dismissed her to her bed!"

(6:894–903)

Notably, Wordsworth associates Ellen's burgeoning powers of mind—
her creation of poetry and her intensive reading—with her advancing
pregnancy. While the Pastor suggests that this information "[will] please
you to be told," the analogy marks her developing mind as transgressive:
Ellen's reading, writing, and pregnancy alike are secret, marginal pursuits, conducted "under friendly veil/Of their long twilight." Moreover,
the analogy feminizes Ellen's mental inner life. The transgressive and the
feminine merge in the mention of "waking fancy," suggesting the potential dangers of Ellen's mental development, though fancy enters here not
to fan love's flame, but to quell "the unconquerable pang of despised
love."

The birth of Ellen's child may appear to suggest a traditional Christian plot of loss and consolation, particularly in light of the Miltonic
echoes raised by Ellen's "fall." Indeed, Ellen views the child as a heaven-
sent comforter, through whom God "made/Unlooked-for gladness in
the desert place,/To save the perishing" (6:921–23). But within a sentimental context, the child figures as Ellen's supreme imagining: motherhood is Ellen's redemptive idyll. The fatherless child, like the "un-
fathered vapour" of imagination in *Prelude* 13, is Ellen's imagination
incarnate; it plays the role of comforter only insofar as Ellen interprets
it as one. In fact, the succor offered Ellen by the child reciprocates the
mother's suckling of the child, a reciprocity that strongly suggests an
identification between mother and child.

But this identification also betrays a rift within the idyll of motherhood. Like Margaret's child, Ellen's infant child seems to have caught
"the trick of grief" from its mother; its instinctual life is fraught with
sorrow, "Like a poor singing-bird from distant lands." The child's
nascent melancholia anticipates its failure to redeem Ellen's sins and
console her sorrow. Into the idyll of motherhood intrude Ellen's anxieties in a world of want and narrowed opportunity: "scruples rose;/
Thoughts, which the rich are free from, came and crossed/The fond
affection" (6:940–42). Divided between her duty as a mother and her
duty as a daughter, Ellen forfeits her idyll of motherhood, as she exchanges mothering for foster-mothering. The child who was to bring
"unlooked-for gladness in the desert place" is, by Ellen's own account,
"deserted."

Forbidden the "communion" of freely suckling her child, Ellen is
thrust within the "enforced mandate" of her employers; she retreats into

the painful condition of yearning: "So near! yet not allowed, upon that sight/To fix her eyes—alas! 'twas hard to bear!" (6:963–64). And as the idyll of motherhood fails, so fails the child, succumbing to disease. Unable to nurse the child with her milk, Ellen is similarly unable to nurse it through its final illness: "Once, only once,/She saw it in that mortal malady" (6:969–70). The scene of mourning that follows cruelly parodies the scene of nursing:

> "She reached the house, last of the funeral train;
> And someone, as she entered, having chanced
> To urge unthinkingly their prompt departure,
> 'Nay,' said she, with commanding look, a spirit
> Of anger never seen in her before,
> 'Nay, ye must wait my time!' and down she sate,
> And by the unclosed coffin kept her seat
> Weeping and looking, looking on and weeping,
> Upon the last sweet slumber of her Child,
> Until at length her soul was satisfied."
>
> (6:973–82)

Ellen's "commanding" demand for more time ironically reflects the bondage which, in her own mind, doomed her child. Where once she took succor from her child, now she hungrily absorbs the sight of its corpse, leaving off only in satiety. Similarly, the milk which once flowed from her to the child is replaced by tears; that which had sustained the child's life is replaced by that which will sustain, after death, its memory.

Ellen's complex identification with her child in this exquisite scene of mourning anticipates the course her mourning will take. For Ellen is both mourning mother—continuing to "nurse" her child's memory with tears, returning to its grave whenever possible—and mourned child, her sorrow expanding to embrace her own virginal self and the "transgression"(VII:990) that doomed her. Unlike the mourning of the Solitary, however, Ellen's mourning simultaneously deepens her self-consciousness and keeps faith with the dead; she turns *to* the grave, not away from it. Like the child who succumbed to "mortal malady," Ellen gradually succumbs to the malady of mortality: "the green stalk of Ellen's life was snapped,/And the flower drooped; as every eye could see,/It hung its head in mortal languishment" (6:1000–1001). Her illness literally "releases" her from "the bounds" and "bonds" of service, and figuratively liberates her into a life of the mind as she returns "Home to her mother's house."

This is the house both of Ellen's mother, and of her mothering. Just as Ellen's reading was identified with her pregnancy, her intensive self-scrutiny takes place in a maternal space:

"—The bodily frame wasted from day to day;
Meanwhile, relinquishing all other cares,
Her mind she strictly tutored to find peace
And pleasure in endurance. Much she thought,
And much she read; and brooded feelingly
Upon her own unworthiness.

(6:1024–29)

Unlike the "tall woman" whose story immediately precedes hers, Ellen does not read to satisfy a "keen desire of knowledge" (7: 700). Her studies do not produce pleasure, but rather self-mortification, "the sting of self-reproach" (6:1033). The maternal location casts an ironic pall over meditations that the Pastor recognizes as self-destructive.

But whereas she once studied under cover of darkness, Ellen now decides to "open her heart" to the Pastor. The narrative she brings forth—a narrative of sins, sorrows, and suffering—constitutes Ellen's last maternal act. Through the Pastor, Ellen provides an occasion for the community to join together "In due observance of her pious wish" to pray for her soul. While Ellen remains "by her lonely hearth," in the heart of her mother's house, she manages to unite the community "within [the] walls" of the church. Like the diffusive life of George Eliot's Dorothea Brooke, Ellen's nursing of the dead and mourning of herself come to nourish and sustain the community. It is hardly surprising that Ellen is intolerant of pity, for in objectifying her, pity negates the mind with which she manages to endure. Reproving those who pity her, she proclaims, "He who afflicts me knows what I can bear." For Ellen, "bearing the dead" entails bearing the enduring pain of enduring loss. But in "bearing the dead," Ellen also becomes her own historian; as her bodily "flower" droops, her mental life finally flourishes within the narrative that she entrusts to the Pastor.

It is significant that Ellen delivers her burdens to the Pastor, who moves easily between the patriarchal space of the Church and the maternal space of the churchyard. We need to consider what happens when the story of Ellen—that is, *Ellen's story*—becomes taken up into the Pastor's "history" of the churchyard. As retold by the Pastor—here called the "Vicar"—the story of Ellen does indeed culminate in the sublime Christian deliverance of the "Sufferer": "So, through the cloud of death, her Spirit passed/Into that pure and unknown world of love/Where injury cannot come" (6:1049–51). Transmitted as a moral tale of endurance and faith, the Pastor's story evokes the moral "nature"—what Burke liked to call "our natural entrails" (99)—common to all three listeners: ". . . [D]owncast looks made known/That each had listened with his inmost heart" (6:1053–54). Even the Solitary's "cheek," having so often betrayed "the power of nature" now "Confesse[s]" it.

Yet even as Ellen's story is appropriated for the Burkean ends of promulgating the values of tradition, church, community, and a universal moral "nature," it conjures in the Poet's mind the image of a woman:

> For me, the emotion scarcely was less strong
> Or less benign than that which I had felt
> When seated near my venerable Friend,
> Under those shady elms, from him I heard
> The story that retraced the slow decline
> Of Margaret, sinking on the lonely heath
> With the neglected house to which she clung.
>
> (6:1053–63)

While the Pastor's words supply the images and sounds of Ellen's story, his *silence* allows the Poet's mind to conjure not Ellen, but the haunting image of Margaret. Like Lycidas, "sunk low, but mounted high," the image of Margaret "Sinking on the lonely heath" is countered by the buoyancy with which she rises into the poet's mind. Though she may "[sleep] in the cold earth," the image of Margaret lives on in the Poet's mind to witness her endurance, her preternatural watchfulness, her ordeal of hope and pain. If Ellen recalls Margaret, it is because the story of one recalls the tale of the other; and in that recollection the complexity, the multiplicity, the *process* of history is brought to life. Even the Wanderer responds to the story of Ellen by calling not for the consolations of "natural sympathy," but for "the bones of Wilfred Armathwaite" and the vivid history they harbor. "Bearing the dead," like bearing a child, means finally allowing them to make their own way in the world.

The response to the story of Ellen, which insists simultaneously on a shared moral "nature" and on the urgency of imaginative response—recalls another moment in which the Poet responds to the Pastor:

> While thus from theme to theme the Historian passed,
> The words he uttered, and the scene that lay
> Before our eyes, awakened in my mind
> Vivid remembrance of those long-past hours;
> When, in the hollow of some shadowy vale. . . .
>
> . . . . . .
>
> A wandering Youth, I listened with delight
> To pastoral melody or warlike air,
> Drawn from the chords of the ancient British harp
> By some accomplished Master. . . .

．　．　．　．　．

> And, when the stream
> Which overflowed the soul was passed away,
> A consciousness remained that it had left,
> Deposited upon the silent shore
> Of memory, images and precious thoughts,
> That shall not die, and cannot be destroyed.

(7:1–30)

The Pastor's history, his "words" and "scene[s]," causes the Poet to turn inward, reflecting on his own "wandering Youth." But Wordsworth takes pains to establish that the Pastor's words harmonize with recollected "chords of the ancient British harp/By some accomplished Master." In this recollection, the Pastor's precise words fade within their historical resonance, immediately intuited by the Poet as ancient, British, and masterful. Implicitly, the Poet identifies the Pastor's history with his own British heritage; but it is a Britain of "pastoral melody or warlike air," carried in the mind from childhood—a Britain inherited not from the "wise forefathers" but *from a younger self*. In these crucial lines, Wordsworth conflates an archaic British "nature" with the interiority of reflection and memory. In the figure of the shoreline—itself borrowed from the "Intimations Ode," where it evokes the equivocal relations between fate and memory—Wordsworth celebrates the meeting places of nature and the imagination. Here, the moral value of the affections lies not in the depth and power of oceanic "stream[s]" of feeling, but in the detritus they leave behind in the mind—the valuable "deposit[s] upon the silent shore/Of memory, images and precious thoughts,/That shall not die, and cannot be destroyed."

．　．　．　．　．

In the *Reflections on the Revolution in France*, Burke writes:

> We do not draw the moral lessons we might from history. On the contrary, without care it may be used to vitiate our minds and to destroy our happiness. In history a great volume is unrolled for our instruction, drawing the materials of future wisdom from the past errors and infirmities of mankind. (155)

Burke's caveat on the use and abuse of history is embedded in a trenchant account of the Revolutions's users and abusers. In it, as I have argued in chapter 3, Burke fills "the shell and husk of history" (157) with his own moral imaginings. In *The Excursion*, Wordsworth shares Burke's conviction that "the past errors and infirmities of mankind" are rife with moral instruction. But whereas Burke, despite his intuition of distance from the past, purports to read the "great volume" of history, Wordsworth gives us the making of history. It is this process that stands as the corrective for the Solitary's solipsism, for the temptations of a transcendentalism that denies history. Of all the "authentic epitaphs" related by the Pastor, the two that leave the Solitary visibly moved—that move him closer to his expected conversion to history—are the stories of Ellen and that of young Oswald. If the conservative heroics of young Oswald's story pays homage to the institutions of Burkean patriarchy, the story of Ellen fills Burke's "shell and husk of history" with human images and sounds. In *The Excursion*, the meaning of history lies somewhere between Oswald and Ellen, between patriarchy and maternity, church and churchyard, institution and imagination. In the poem of Oswald and Ellen, the Janus-face of grief shows us two faces of Wordsworth's Burke: Oswald's, gazing heavenward with "patriotic confidence and joy"; and Ellen's, weeping for the dead within the mother's house.

SIX

A NATION'S SORROWS, A PEOPLE'S TEARS:
THE POLITICS OF MOURNING
PRINCESS CHARLOTTE

The preceding year [1816] had afforded a happy augury to the nation, in the union of the daughter of the Prince Regent to Prince Leopold of Saxe Cobourg, which promised a lasting source of domestic felicity. The connexion was blest with a hope of progeny, which was brought to maturity early in November; but, to the unspeakable disappointment of the general expectation, the Princess sunk under the effort, and after having been the mother of a dead child, became herself the victim.

(*Annual Register. . .for the Year 1817*)

Now should a Nations Sorrows flow!
  For lo! tremendous cause appears,
When public grief and private woe,
  Combine to ask a people's tears.
(Thomas Beck, "An Elegy on the Lamented Death of Her
      Royal Highness the Princess Charlotte")

"Catastrophe at Claremont"

AT 9:00 P.M. on November 5, 1817, after fifty hours of labor, Princess Charlotte Augusta was delivered of a stillborn male infant. The child, had it lived, would have been third in line for the crown after its maternal grandfather, the Prince Regent, and its mother; attempts to "reanimate" the "perfectly formed," nine-pound infant with mouth-to-mouth insufflation, salt and mustard rubs, chest pressure, and brandy were futile.[1] The exhausted Princess is said to have remarked, "It is the will of God," taken some nourishment, and tried to sleep. But toward midnight she complained of a ringing in her ears and vomited; forty-five minutes later her pulse became weak and irregular, her breathing labored; she was extremely agitated and restless and could not be made comfortable. At 2:30 A.M. on November 6, the Princess died in childbed.

In this chapter I am concerned not with the death of Princess Charlotte (the medical causes of which continue to be debated to this day in the obstetrical literature)[2], but with the documentary evidence of Britain's response to it. The nation's mourning following the "catastrophe at Claremont"[3] is made known to us in nearly two hundred extant documents published within weeks (or in some cases, months) of November 6, 1817: pamphlets on Princess Charlotte's life, death, and funeral; sermons delivered on Sunday the 16th, and on the funeral day; discourses; memoirs; and a myriad of dirges, monodies, elegies, and epitaphs, several swiftly collected as *A Cypress Wreath, for the Tomb of her Late Royal Highness the Princess Charlotte of Wales.*[4]

The national shock and sorrow recorded in these documents seem uncannily familiar now when media coverage gives an entire nation—and, indeed, the world—instant access to the most tragic of events. Princess Charlotte's expectations had been those of the kingdom; when the morning papers appeared with black borders, the British nation was stunned. Bonfires stacked to celebrate the birth of a presumptive heir to the throne were dismantled; shops and theatres were closed, and official business suspended.[5] Mourning was worn by aristocrats and laborers alike. On Sunday, November 16, memorial sermons were given in all corners of the kingdom, and on the following Wednesday, November 19, the day of the funeral, all commercial activity ground to a halt. Services were held, and if not held, demanded, in Anglican churches, Dissenting meeting-houses, Roman Catholic chapels, and synagogues; Coleridge himself translated Hyman Hurowitz's "Hebrew Dirge." Southey, the poet laureate, elegized the Princess, whose death, in the words of memorialist Robert Huish, "called into action all the poetical talent of the country."[6] Bells tolled from Edinburgh to Dover to Dublin. In France, Germany, and Holland, journalists and rulers alike published condolences; from Venice, Byron wrote, "The death of the Princess Charlotte has been a shock even here, and must have been an earthquake at home."[7] And Napoleon, in his cell at St. Helena, is reported to have said, "What has happened to the English that they have not stoned her accoucheurs?"[8]

Because of the dearth of legitimate issue among the Prince Regent's siblings, the death of the Princess was swiftly understood as a monarchical crisis. On the demise of the Princess and her baby, the crown was in jeopardy of falling into the hands of a foreign ruler.[9] Overnight, alarmist pamphlets appeared raising the threat of Jerome Bonaparte acceding to the British throne; others dwelled on the feeble-minded, adolescent

Duke of Brunswick; still others exhorted the Dukes of Clarence, Kent, and Cambridge to marry. The Reverend Samuel Woolmer lamented that, "In her whose loss we so grievously deplore, every thing was regular and clear, and promised indubitable permanency."[10] But in a decade of Luddite actions, working-class revolts, and reformist agitation—a decade of unrest that would culminate at Peterloo—the threat of a foreign ruler probably seemed remote compared to the looming spectre of a fragile, indeed dubious and impermanent, crown.

While most of the Princess's mourners proclaim the catastrophe to be "above" politics—indeed, adduce the moral benefits to the nation of a mourning that transcends politics—I will demonstrate here that a variety of political tensions are inscribed within these documents. In sermons, memoirs, and elegies, we can glimpse clearly the contours of such contemporary issues as the pressure for reform; workers' uprisings; Dissenters' liberties; the emerging distinction between masculine and feminine "spheres"; the role of women in the home and in society at large; and the character and function of the royal family. To find such a constellation of issues is hardly surprising in documents that urgently attempt national self-definition at a moment of supreme monarchical crisis. Echoes of Burkean and, occasionally, Jacobin rhetoric link Britain's national soul-searching explicitly to an earlier moment of monarchical crisis: the controversy over the French Revolution.

My argument, in brief, is that the national mourning for Princess Charlotte issues in a paradoxical politics. On the one hand, these documents conscript the Princess in death for the marshaling of a national moral consensus that would conceal fissures in the body politic. Such an appeal is based on a conservative, Burkean ideology equating nation and nature. On the other hand, Burke's trope of the patriarchal family—a metaphor Burke uses to bridge the realms of nature and culture—becomes revised in accordance with the emerging middle-class meaning of "family"—a group of contemporaneous individuals related by blood or marriage residing within a household, usually under a male head. This revision of Burke not only produces a new and enduring idealization of the monarchy on the model of the middle-class family; it also envisions a strong, popular female monarch on the British throne.

Before analyzing the politics of mourning Princess Charlotte, let me place this argument in the context of the present study. As I have argued in chapters 1 and 2, a dominant strain in Enlightenment moral theory sought to derive public morals from individual affections. Conceptualizing public morals as an economy of the affections, moral philosophers such as Hume and Smith described the relations between private affections and public morality as a phenomenon of exchanged and circulated affections, or sentiments, kept current by a shared dead. This sentimental theory, already recognized as tenuous in the 1780s, was over-whelmed by the intense factionalism of the Revolution controversy. Thereafter, economic and moral theory began to part company, and in the period we now call "Romantic," the task of theorizing morals fell to the writers of poetry and *belles lettres*. Whereas the Enlightenment had accorded public significance to the private sphere of moral judgments, Romantics such as William Wordsworth probed the private sources and meanings of the complex, conflicting, and often unfathomable arena of public morality.

Wordsworth's *Excursion*, however, stands in a complex relation to the late-eighteenth-century doctrine of "separate spheres"—public and private, or domestic—for men and women, respectively. Certainly Wordsworth's poem, in its invocation of both patriarchal institutions and feminine domesticity, sustains the gendering of public and private spheres as masculine and feminine. I have already argued that these designations, as they are elaborated in the poem, subvert the gendering of mind and nature as masculine and feminine, respectively, in Words-worth's inaugural poem of *The Recluse*. But such designations are heter-odox also in relation to the larger cultural assumptions behind the doctrine of the "separate spheres," assumptions that link masculinity with civilization and femininity with a natural morality. Of particular note is Wordsworth's representation of the public and private less as physical spheres of activity than as complementary modes of evoking the past. Wordsworth's dualistic approach to history combines a reverence for the "wise forefathers" who saw fit to erect and sustain institutions with a celebration of those maternal presences who conceive and bring forth the historical. In quite a different sense than the "Prospectus" intends, *The Excursion* is indeed a spousal verse.

The "authentic epitaphs" surrounding Princess Charlotte's death, I argue in this chapter, exceed Wordsworth's own intuitions of intimate relations between the public and private spheres. A central theme in the documents that mourn the Princess is the conflation of public and private grief. The private and public realms are not simply shown to complement one another; nor are they construed as cooperating toward a larger, national goal. Instead, they are *identified* with one another expressly to argue for the necessity of domesticating the nation's rulers. As a consequence of this upheaval in the relations between the public and private realms following the death of the Princess, the public would lay claim to the private lives of its monarchs. Even as these documents appear to equate femininity, domesticity, and morality, they complicate the equation by reviving the sentimental precept that private affections are constitutive of public morality and national character. Paradoxically, the doctrine of the "separate spheres" both underwrites these documents and is laid bare by them; they lend strong support to Colley's assessment of this doctrine as "more didactic than prescriptive."[11]

While one might read these documents for their striking, often moving expressions of grief (as contemporary readers no doubt did), my focus in this chapter, necessarily, is on the rhetorical *uses* of grief. My rhetorical approach to the culture of mourning surrounding Princess Charlotte's death will show a certain skepticism. I do not deny the dignity and sincerity of the grief that pervades these writings; rather I hope to make audible the political undertones of the general lamentation, and those eloquent, if isolated, dissenting voices that proclaim the occasion no less tragic for warranting political debate, and no less political for being tragic. Let us turn first to the resonant protest of Percy Bysshe Shelley.

Pitied Plumage, Dying Bird: Shelley's *Address to the People on the Death of the Princess Charlotte*

Within days of the Princess's death, Shelley drafted a pamphlet entitled *"We Pity the Plumage, but Forget the Dying Bird": An Address to the People on the Death of the Princess Charlotte*. Writing in the heat of discussions with the Hunt brothers, William Godwin, and Charles Ollier[12] Shelley invokes the Jacobin rhetoric of a previous generation to raise again several radical (and unresolved) issues of the 1790s: the rights of man, the nature and function of government, and the necessity of reform. Shelley's title quotes Paine's skeptical attack on the elegiac Burke. If Paine exposes Burke, Shelley imitates him by seizing upon the Princess's demise as an occasion for political rhetoric. But whereas Burke invokes pathos to gain sympathy for the British monarchy, Shelley, using the pseudonym under which he had already published a reformist pamphlet, invokes pathos in order to undermine the institution of monarchy itself.

In the *Address*, Shelley compares the Princess's death on November 6 to the November 7th execution of three Derbyshire laborers—Jeremiah Brandreth, a knitter; Isaac Ludlam, a stonemason; and William Turner, a quarryman and dissenting preacher.[13] A few words on the abortive Pentridge revolt of June 1817 will provide the necessary context for Shelley's remarks. A crowd of three hundred laborers marching toward Nottingham was summarily dispersed by a squad of dragoons; in the melee, Brandreth killed a farm servant. Some three dozen laborers were brought up on charges of high treason. One week after the incident, the Leeds *Mercury* exposed the intervention of a spy for the crown, Robert Oliver, and accused Sidmouth's government of fomenting the uprising in order to cripple the reform movement and garner support for its three-month-old suspension of habeas corpus. The exposure of Oliver, though he was never acknowledged by the government, led eventually to a plea bargain with eighteen or nineteen prisoners, who were eventually released; fourteen others were transported. Brandreth, having killed a person, was not permitted to bargain his plea; Ludlam and Turner, "devoted"[14] to the end, refused to make deals. The three received the traitor's sentence and the traitor's execution of hanging, drawing, and quartering.

Juxtaposing the coincidental deaths of the Princess and the laborers, Shelley argues that the true national calamity lies not in the deaths of the throne's heirs, but in the laborers' brutal execution. It is an ambitious argument, mounted, as others have observed, within a flamboyant rhetorical performance.[15] A catalogue of rhetorical figures of speech and thought used by the classically trained Shelley would include antithesis, epanaphora, antistrophe, paralepsis, ocular demonstration, vivid description, periphrasis, and interrogation. Shelley shrewdly sizes up the opportunities for pathos in representing the suffering of the dead and the grief and horror of their kindred.

But while emphasis on Shelley's appeal to pathos has aligned the *Address* with the beginnings of sensational journalism,[16] I would like instead to examine Shelley's appeal to logos, linking it with an oral rhetorical tradition: the classical funeral oration. According to Nicole Loraux's *Invention of Athens*, the funeral oration was an occasion publicly to rehearse—or, in her phrase, "invent"—the founding, history, and civic values of the Athenian polis. Women, and families more generally, were largely excluded from the "male assembly that met to honor its dead."[17] Where a "compromise" was reached between the public concerns of the polis and the private concerns of the bereaved families:

> civic values were uppermost: they unquestionably dominated the most solemn moments of the funeral, the cortège and the burial. . . . [T]his predominance of the city determined the very structure of the oration, in which the consolation offered the grieving relations usually culminates in an exaltation of civic honors and of the benevolence of the polis.[18]

While Shelley does represent grieving relations to evoke pathos, the argument of the *Address*, like the classical funeral oration, hinges upon a strict distinction between public and private mourning. Adverting to the Athenian practice of publicly mourning "the death of those who had guided the republic with their valor and their understanding, or illustrated it with their genius"(164), Shelley boldly defines the Princess's death as an occasion of private mourning, and the laborers' death as one warranting public mourning. In large part, Shelley's *Address* is a commentary on the *inappropriateness* of offering the British people an address on the death of their Princess. But it is also a brilliant attempt to turn the resources of the democratic funeral oration toward eulogizing three unknown Derbyshire laborers as martyrs to British liberty.

From the beginning of the *Address*, Shelley asserts the ordinariness of the circumstances in which the Princess died. Like so many of her mourners, Shelley acknowledges how much "the death of the Princess Charlotte has in common with the death of thousands. How many women die in childbed and leave their families of motherless children and their husbands to live on blighted by the remembrance of that heavy loss?(163)" But Shelley's comparison between the Princess and "the poorest poor"(163) has a bitter edge when he asks, "Are they [the poor] not human flesh and blood? Yet none weep for them—none mourn for them—none when their coffins are carried to the grave (if indeed the parish furnishes a coffin for all) turn aside and moralize upon the sadness they have left behind"(164). Later in the *Address*, Shelley likens the Princess to "thousands of others equally distinguished as she for *private* excellencies who have been cut off in youth and hope" (165; my emphasis). Moreover, Shelley denounces the institution of royalty for disallowing the Princess accomplishments worthy of public recognition: "Such is the misery, such the impotence of royalty. Princes are prevented from the cradle from becoming anything which may deserve that greatest of all rewards next to a good conscience, public admiration and regret"(165).[19] Ironically, the very "accident of her [royal] birth" renders the Princess *unworthy* of public mourning. Though Shelley does not detract from the Princess's "domestic virtues," he takes the opportunity to observe that "the regulations of her rank had held [her family] in perpetual estrangement from her. Her husband was to her as father, mother, and brethren"(165).[20]

Conversely, the moral stature of Brandreth, Ludlam, and Turner is *enhanced* by their "low station"; in a Wordsworthian gesture, Shelley considers whether their status "permitted the growth of those affections in a degree not consistent with a more exalted rank"(165). While Leopold's mourning is not described, that of Turner's brother attests to a depth of familial attachment denied to monarchy. Shelley uses the figure of paralepsis to bypass the gruesomeness of the execution, focusing instead on the anguish of Turner's brother, who "shrieked horribly and fell in a fit and was carried away like a corpse by two men"(165). Rather than indicate the tender age of the Princess to enhance the tragedy of her death, as so many would, Shelley evinces the maturity of Ludlam and Turner to demonstrate that "the affections were ripened and strengthened within them"(166). But having argued that the deaths of the laborers were felt more deeply within the private sphere, Shelley next asserts that the laborers' deaths are not "a mere private or customary grief": "[T]heir death by hanging and beheading, and the circumstances of which it is the characteristic and the consequence constitute a calamity such as the English nation ought to mourn with an unassuageable grief"(166).

With these words, Shelley cues himself to begin the funeral oration's required recitation of the history and ideals of "the English nation." According to Loraux, the historical events narrated in a funeral oration were selected not because they changed the course of Athenian life, but because they ostensibly demonstrate the transcendental nature of Athenian valor and the endurance of the polis beyond the particular lives of its residents and soldiers.[21] Shelley offers a nineteenth-century answer to the funeral oration's required recitation of the polis's history and ideals: a thumbnail sketch of British political economy from antiquity to the present. But his post-Enlightenment substitution of economic history for military exploits is a skeptical gesture, suggesting that money, not ideals and morals, unifies the nation. Because of the greed of "Kings and their ministers"—greed nationally subsidized by a running up of the public debt—money does not in fact provide the nation with liquidity; on the contrary, a swollen national debt has produced "such an unequal distribution of the means of living as saps the foundation of social union and civilized life"(166):

> [O]ne man is forced to labor for another in a degree not only not necessary to the support of the subsisting distinctions among mankind but so as by the excess of the injustice to endanger the very foundations of all that is valuable in social order and to provoke that anarchy which is at once the enemy of freedom and the child and the chastiser of misrule. (167)

Money, when it is hoarded by a bloated "double aristocracy," "saps" the "foundations" of civil society instead of nourishing them. We notice, in passing, that Shelley's complex figure appeals to Enlightenment metaphors of commercial and affectional circulation, while insisting, in line with the Athenian tradition, on the "foundational" quality of the social order such circulation makes possible.

Hence, instead of praising the moral unity of the community, Shelley describes "a nation tottering on the brink of two chasms"(167). Whereas the funeral oration primarily celebrates the perseverance of the city against enemies from without, Shelley's *Address* exposes the enemy *within*. Robert Oliver, denounced by name, is recognized as the incarnation of a much larger, more potent, and more vicious enemy, a government that would conspire against the populace:

It is a national calamity that we endure men to rule over us who sanction for whatever ends a conspiracy which is to arrive at its purpose through such a frightful pouring forth of human blood and agony. But when that purpose is to trample upon our rights and liberties forever, to present to us the alternatives of anarchy and oppression . . . to maintain a vast standing army, and add year by year to a public debt . . . ; to imprison and calumniate those who may offend them, at will; when this, if not the purpose, is the effect of that conspiracy, how ought we not to mourn? (168)

Only by appealing to the model of the funeral oration does Shelley convey how short "the English nation" falls of the example of Athenian democracy.

How is Shelley to speak, then, of an "English nation"? The success of Shelley's *Address* depends on his ability to identify his reader—a reader conversant with classical Athens, British history, Milton, Rousseau, and Voltaire as well as principles of political economy—with the horror-struck "crowd," the "multitude" that bears witness to the execution:

How fearful must have been [the agony of the laborers' kindred], sitting in solitude on that day when the tempestuous voice of horror from the crowd told them that the head so dear to them was severed from the body! Yes—they listened to the maddening shriek which burst from the multitude; they heard the rush of ten thousand terror-stricken feet, the groans and the hootings which told them that the mangled and distorted head was then lifted in the air. (165)

Unlike tragedy, in which spectators understand their immunity from the travails they witness, this scene instills terror in its observers. The mob's sympathetic identification initiates a chain of sympathies leading outward from the suffering laborers, through the screaming mob, through the stricken, corpselike form of Edward Turner, and finally to the reader.

Enjoining the people to mourn—"mourn then, . . . Clothe yourselves in solemn black. Let the bells be tolled"—Shelley transgresses the funeral oration's traditional injunction to cease mourning and "return to political life."[22] In urging a national mourning, Shelley seeks to transform the crowd's "tempestuous voice of horror" into a self-conscious voice of lamentation. Those already mourning the Princess are to take up the cry of the multitude and rededicate their mourning to the slain figure of "LIBERTY":

LIBERTY is dead. . . . If One has died who was like her that should have ruled over this land, like Liberty, young, innocent, and lovely, know that the power through which that one perished was God, and that it was a private grief. But *man* has murdered Liberty, and while the life was ebbing from its wound, there descended on the heads and on the hearts of every human thing the sympathy of an universal blast and curse. (168–69)

By replacing the mutilated corpses of Brandreth, Ludlam, and Turner with the exalted figure of "Liberty," Shelley sharpens his comparison between the death of the Princess and the executions. With a single masterful stroke, he summarizes, elevates, and aestheticizes the deaths of the laborers by abstracting the moral import of their sentence. At the same time, what has been called a "national" calamity is now extended beyond both Derbyshire and Britain to become a "universal blast and curse" descending on all humanity. Having replaced the dead Princess with the slain Liberty, Shelley closes by awaiting the apocalyptic resurrection of Liberty as a "glorious Phantom."[23] Thus his response to a crisis in the monarchy is to envision its dissolution in the universal identification of "the Spirit of Liberty" with "our Queen."

. . . . .

In Shelley's hands, the meaning of "public mourning" is radically expanded to embrace a revolutionary vision. Indeed, the *Address* closes by invoking familiar Jacobin images: the injured figure of "Liberty"; the "dungeon more pestilential than damp and narrow walls, because the earth is its floor and the heavens are its roof"(169); the "fetters heavier than iron . . . because they bind our souls"(169). Such images, as I have already argued, emerge from a sentimental recognition of continuity between the private and the public realms, a recognition of the personal as political. Notably, Shelley's own exposition of mourning conflicts with the classical premise of his argument, with its distinction between the public and private realms.

According to Shelley, the moral benefits derived from public and private mourning differ in degree, not in kind:

> Men do well to mourn for the dead: it proves that we love something besides ourselves; and he must have a hard heart who can see his friend depart to rottenness and dust and speed him without emotion on his voyage to "that bourne whence no traveller returns." To lament for those who have benefited the state is a habit of piety yet more favorable to the cultivation of our best affections. (164)

He defines the proper occasion for public mourning as an event "which make[s] all good men mourn in their hearts"(164); like Hutcheson, he defines public affections as a critical aggregate of private sympathies.

Public mourning, then, is merely the public erection of signs of private sympathy, "the external symbols of grief" that indicate "the sorrow and the indignation which fill[s] all hearts." Like Hume and Smith, however, Shelley also describes public mourning as the flowing of affections throughout a society, citing "those fertilizing streams of sympathy which a public mourning should be the occasion of pouring forth"(164). By this means, public mourning "helps to maintain that connection between one man and another, and all men considered as a whole, which is the bond of social life"(164).

A somewhat different phenomenology of public mourning appears later in the same passage. Mourning, by Shelley's lights, is a "habit of piety," a "cultivator" of affections which promote social bonds. "The great secret of morals is love"—so Shelley would recast Enlightenment theories of sympathy in the *Defence of Poetry*. If the phenomenon of "public mourning" in the *Address* entails a leap of imagination cognate with that involved in love, it also recalls Adam Smith's theory of sympathy as a phenomenon of identification:

> We cannot truly grieve for every one who dies beyond the circle of those especially dear to us; yet in the extinction of the objects of public love and admiration and gratitude, there is something, if we enjoy a liberal mind, which has departed from within that circle. (164)

Sympathy, theorizes Smith, results from our tendency to imagine ourselves in the place of the suffering. If we seem to experience "true grief" for those beyond our circle, it is because we habitually imagine "the objects of public love and admiration and gratitude" as our familiars; in order to sympathize with them (or grieve for them) we identify ourselves with *an imaginary figure erected in the place of those close enough to warrant our sympathy*. This phenomenon, which we might call "celebrity," is actually a second-order sympathetic identification.[24] This phenomenon calls forth intense affections for remote figures, even to the point where our sympathy rivals the "true grief" we bear for "the circle of those especially dear to us." Shelley's theory of celebrity is that "public mourning" is simply mourning for the imaginary, intimately known simulacrum of a public figure.

Whether Shelley defines public mourning as an aggregative, morally beneficent surplus of private affections, as a phenomenon of morally "fertilizing" grief, or as a sympathetic imposture of the affections, his sentimental concept of mourning blurs the sharp distinction between public and private mourning on which his argument depends. If Shelley's reformist argument, heralded with a quotation from Paine, makes his an isolated voice in the lamentation following Princess Charlotte's death, his unexpectedly sentimental conflation of public and private mourning in certain passages precisely indicates the discourse within which the conservative, Burkean response to the Princess's death would occur. Seizing on a historical coincidence for the sake of reform, Shelley urgently enjoins the nation to dedicate its mourning to the spirit of Liberty. But the fabulous mourning that ensued would have quite another provenance.

"Tears of Patriotism"

Toward the beginning of the *Reflections on the Revolution in France*, Burke announces that "All circumstances taken together, the French Revolution is the most astonishing that has hitherto happened in the world"(21). Burke sweepingly denounces the Revolution as a historical aberration, while emphasizing, from a panhistorical perspective, the decisiveness of the present moment. In the wake of Princess Charlotte's death, Burke's urgent cadences are widely echoed. The Preface to the *Annual Register* for 1817 notes that "the public feeling was scarcely ever marked by a more universal mourning";[25] a thousand years of British history are scanned for precedent, to no avail. One memorialist, J. Coote, notes that "History . . . does not afford us an instance of such unequivocal heartfelt and universal tribute to the shade of any prince or potentate."[26] Several ministers, such as the Reverend W. Thorpe, interpreted the Princess's death as "the visitation of an angry God"—angry with Britain, in particular, about the "revolutionary mania" of the 1790s and its legacy in the reform movements of a tumultuous decade.[27] Such documents focus less on the events of November 6, than on the popular *response* to this event, a spectacular demonstration of the British moral "nature." Whereas Burke contrasts the astonishing, unnatural French Revolution with the naturalness of the British people, these documents echo Burke to render the very *naturalness* of the British people astonishing.

This sublime heightening of Burke's trope of British "nature" is designed to weather a domestic crisis of succession, rather than to execrate a foreign crisis of revolution. A desire for such "indubitable permanency" as Woolmer laments recalls Burke's conceit of the body politic in the *Reflections* as:

> a permanent body composed of transitory parts; wherein, by the disposition of a stupendous wisdom, moulding together the great mysterious incorporation of the human race, the whole, at one time, is never old, or

middle-aged or young, but in a condition of unchangeable constancy, moves on through the varied tenour of perpetual decay, fall, renovation and progression. (46)

But a crisis in the succession puts Burke's faith in the regenerative powers of the body politic in some doubt; the figment of a headless body politic calls into question precisely those powers which Burke celebrates. In the wake of Princess Charlotte's death, the transcendental continuity of the body politic is reasserted with a vengeance, but also with a difference: while Burke emphasizes *diachronic* continuity—the enduring membership of the dead in the body politic—these documents emphasize the *synchronic* continuity of the British people. The "uniting sensibility" displayed in the nation's response strongly recalls Burke's allegorization of the body politic: "The whole nation felt as one man"(576), writes Huish, who goes on to describe "that grief which vibrated through seventeen millions of human beings, as if their blood had circulated from a single heart, and their tears were shed from the same fountain"(615–16).[28] As in Burke's *Reflections*, the conceit of moral "nature" points not only toward that which is innate, but also toward that which is culturally acquired. The danger of accepting a foreign heir to the British throne, for example, is readily phrased in terms of Burkean "prejudice": "It is difficult to our British prejudices to look with confidence to a foreigner at the head of our government. . . . We must still conceive it hard, nay, almost impossible, for a person not bred up and educated amongst ourselves to identify himself with our feelings. . . ."[29] Even as such pamphleteers acknowledge "prejudices" to be the effect of learning, they place this learning so "early" as to deny the capacity for a foreign ruler ever to become a "naturalized" Briton.

In many instances, the celebration of British moral nature generates a scruple to link this spectacular display of the affections with publicly sanctioned codes of behavior. As a consequence, the nation's outpouring of grief becomes rationalized in various ways. Huish, on the one hand, denies that the rationalist French, seeing but " 'the spectacle of a nation deeply impressed with the salutary doctrines of legitimate succession' "(616), can properly understand the meaning of "our unfeigned and universal grief"(615). On the other hand, Huish insists anxiously that "the *principles* of an Englishman are the preceptors of his heart; . . . if we mourn our lost Princess as they see we mourn, it is as well for her virtues, as her birth"(617; my emphasis). Elsewhere, Huish appeals to the sanction of religious awe, questioning "whether the annals of any country can produce the record of a scene so morally sublime, as England on this day offered to the world"(608). Others cast the nation's grief as a sign of its loyalty and allegiance to the British crown. As the illustrious Reverend Thomas Chalmers puts it, "is it possible . . . that tears of pity can, on such an emergency as the present, be other than tears of patriotism?"[30]

This insistence on sanctioning the nation's grief, whether by appeal to reason, religious authority, or patriotic values, recalls Burke's disdain for the unregulated flow of sentiments through a society by means of private events of sympathy. Calling the tragic theater "a better school of moral sentiments than churches"(94) in the *Reflections*, Burke well understood the uses of tragedy in establishing and transmitting moral authority. Presenting the French Revolution as a full-dress tragedy, Burke arranges his scenes as authorized tragic spectacles heading inexorably toward the French King's demise, scenes designed to train the "well-placed sympathies in the human breast" toward their appropriate object and sanctioned end: the retention and support of British monarchy. Tragic theater, in Burke's view, mediates between the dispersed authority of private affections and the centered authority of government; it provides a public space in which individuals are transformed into a corporate audience for a ruling authority.

Burke's theory of tragedy will assist us in interpreting the highly dramatic events of November 19, 1817, the day of the Princess's funeral in Windsor.[31] On that day, by many accounts, the nation spontaneously channeled its sorrows into a nationwide observance of funeral services for the Princess. Ministers of every denomination held services, preaching sermons that reviewed pathetic scenes of the preceding week—the Princess's suffering and death, the anguish of Prince Leopold, the spreading of the fatal news—and conjured the events of the royal funeral.

In point of fact, most of these sermons were preached *earlier* than the royal funeral, which only began after dark. This fact simply underscores the pains such preachers took to give their audience the illusion of attendance at the obsequies. Within a few days, journals and pamphlets had begun to supply in rich, sensational detail the events of the interment. It is hard, even today, to imagine a more graphic account of the proceedings than appears in the pamphlets that follow the Princess's body onto the embalmers' table and into the coffins; its brain and viscera into an urn; both urn and coffins into the hearse and then into the vault where the coffin lay in state until the 19th.[32] In addition to supplying the customary diagram of mourners at an aristocratic funeral, pamphleteers meticulously described and profusely depicted the funeral procession of nearly three hundred; also described was the "imperceptible" machinery that dramatically lowered the coffin into the mausoleum when the Priest intoned the words, "man that is born of woman."[33] Many ministers repeated their sermons for the 19th on the following Sunday, when details of the funeral had already reached into the remotest corners of the realm. By creating an illusion of simultaneous witness, ministers across the kingdom created the powerful fiction of a national audience for a national tragedy.

In an irony widely noted in these pamphlets, however, the tragic staging of the funeral day occurred in a nation sophisticated in the art of theatrical marketing. At St. George's Chapel, Windsor, writes Coote, "the prices were regulated as at a theatre, or a shew. The gallery so much, and the pit so much. Ten guineas were taken for a seat in the organ loft, and from five to seven guineas for a standing place in the aisle."[34] He continues:

> The sordid system of calculation, on which many of the tickets were issued, had nearly created a riot. In an hour of universal affliction, when every class of our population merged their worldy interests in the nobler impulse of national sensibility, here a traffic was opened within the sacred precincts of the mausoleum. . . —and when our Exchanges, Banks, Shops, and Theatres were shut by inclination and duty, the aisle of St. George's Chapel became an object of venal calculation.[35]

Extortionary rents were charged at inns along the procession route; one could even hire window space to watch it from private homes. And such profiteering was not limited to Windsor; the London clergy charged admission to packed churches and ushers accepted bribes for seating. At St. Paul's the impatient crowd charged the doors, overturned the toll-takers and broke windows, and a similar commotion occurred at Westminster Abbey. In such highly publicized incidents, funereal theater became, in Coote's phrase, "sepulchral pageant."

Despite the aggressive marketing of the funeral spectacle, most accounts of the funeral day celebrate it as a sublime showcase for British morals. The insistence on the *naturalness* of the nation's response often involves the adamant denial of religious, gender, class, and party differences. Chalmers notes that "The novel exhibition is now offered, of all party-irritations merging into one common and overwhelming sensibility";[36] in the words of the Reverend Charles Hoare, "[W]hatever minor differences may sometimes unhappily divide us as fellow-citizens and fellow-Christians" are erased by "feelings and principles . . . that do honour to human nature, in which we all agree."[37] One pamphlet meticulously describes the different mourning costumes worn by orphans, shopkeepers, ladies-in-waiting, and the chief mourner, Prince Leopold, even while marveling that the voluntary wearing of mourning levels class distinctions.

In such testimonies, the denial of sectarian distinctions is a major theme. The devotions of the funeral day are said by Huish to affirm an essentially *British* religiosity:

> Uncalled by any spiritual ordinance, unbidden by any mandate of temporal authority, but prompted only by their own unfeigned sorrow, and their profound reliance upon the consolations of religion, [the people] voluntarily desisted from public affairs, and with humble, awful earnestness, filled our sacred temples, to supplicate the throne of mercy. A whole people thus prostrate before God, that they may tell the anguish of their hearts, implore forgiveness for the past, and mercy for the future, has in it something so holy, so majestical, so edifying, that we would blush for ourselves, if we hesitated to acknowledge the motions of piety with which we are inspired. (608–9)

In particular, many accounts stress the participation of Dissenters in the national day of mourning. In Kingston according to Coote, "there was the most numerous congregation ever seen in the memory of the oldest inhabitants, [D]issenters of all descriptions, even Quakers";[38] nor, according to Huish, "were the Protestant Dissenters [at Deal] less forward in testifying their grief and respect; their meeting-houses were clothed in the garb of woe, and the solemn services of the day were performed in the midst of lamentations fervent and sincere"(630). In their sermons, Dissenting ministers warmly but anxiously recalled the cordial reception a delegation of their leaders had recently enjoyed at the behest of the Princess. At London's Old Jewry Chapel, the site of Richard Price's famous sermon *On the Love of Our Country*, the Reverend Abraham Rees noted that "We augured the continuance and enlargement of our liberty, in connection with the permanent prosperity of our country."[39] The Reverend John Pye Smith, another London Dissenter, recalled that "With regard to the Protestant Dissenters, [the Princess] declared . . . that she felt the respect and would shew the honourable treatment, which her august Grandfather and his two predecessors of the house of Brunswick, had uniformly demonstrated."[40] That Dissenters saw the "continuance and enlargement" of their liberties to be less assured upon the Princess's death may help us to see why, if these accounts are to be trusted, their participation was so ardent, even ostentatious.[41] At the same time, the widespread tendency to vouch for the Dissenters's conformity with the funeral day observances suggests an urgent need to portray the Dissenters's devotions as continuous with the pieties of the nation. Certainly the Dissenters were not alone in recognizing the political ramifications of their participation. If the spectacle of a "nation's tears" was to augur the durability of the monarchy, then the critical success of that spectacle depended on the role played in it by religious Dissenters.

The "Discussion in Edinburgh"

To discern more clearly the political tensions focused upon Dissenters, let us consider the texts of a controversy over Presbyterian involvement in the funeral day observances in Edinburgh. The "discussion in Edinburgh," as this pamphlet war came to be known, arose when the Presbyterian minister of St. George's Chapel, Edinburgh, refused to offer services on the funeral day, against the demands of his congregation. A pamphlet by the pseudonymous "Lucius" violently attacked Thomson, igniting an explosive debate focused first on the meaning of Thomson's refusal, and ultimately on the meaning of the national observances beyond the chapel at Windsor. But these pamphlets pale in comparison to the magisterial essay that responds to them: Thomas M'Crie's *Free Thoughts on the Late Religious Celebrations of the Funeral of Her Royal Highness the Princess Charlotte of Wales.*

M'Crie's essay, said by his son to have been "considered so conclusive . . . that the voice of censure was hushed, and nothing more was heard on the subject,"[42] is best approached in the context of its provocation. "Lucius," writing an open letter to Thomson, sets the terms of the debate by denouncing Thomson's act as an isolated aberration:

> At a moment, when all party feelings were at rest—when distinctions were forgotten—when every heart was sorrowful, and every knee was bent— you, Sir, you alone, in this wide and extended realm, have the satisfaction of reflecting that you singly withheld the meet tribute of regret . . . that you have outraged the pious loyalty of your charge—that you have, as far as in you lay, insulted a nation's grief, and a monarch's tears—that you have deserved, and incurred, the censure and indignation of every generous heart.[43]

As Burke attacks Price's heart, "Lucius" attacks Thomson's, which has led him to betray both the trust of his congregation and the moral consensus of the nation. While "Lucius" appears to have launched the first salvo, he claims to express "the censure and indignation of every generous heart." Moreover, he portrays Thomson as a figure of prejudice and bigotry who exercised a heartless prudence at a moment in which "Presbytery is triumphant."[44] Despite his optimistic estimation of the fortunes of Presbyterianism, "Lucius" frames the discussion that follows by identifying Thomson's refusal to preach as an unwillingness "to sanction the Episcopalian service for the dead."[45]

Thomson's first defenders raise the issues that would be elaborated, historically framed and politically pointed by M'Crie. Predictably, the first pamphlets defending Thomson advance ad hominem attacks on "Lucius" and his "bombastic," "raving," and "unhinged" rhetoric.[46] Typically, he is alleged to be an Anglican minister; "Scotus" suggests that Lucius seeks anonymity because he covets a bishopric, "looking forward to the lawn sleeves."[47] Beyond such personal attacks, however, lies a vigorous assault on the Anglican church, its clergy, and its rhetoric: "This constitution of our [Presbyterian] Church tends to form clergy-men to an independence in sentiment, which would be accounted indiscreet and fatal to the hopes of any English churchman who would conspire even to the moderate elevation of a rectory."[48] The crucial phrase "independence of sentiment" refers not only to Thomson's freedom of conscience, but also to the Presbyterian church's distance from the "sentimental" practices of the Anglican church. "Candidus" writes:

["Lucius'"] remarks upon the funeral service of the Church of England are beautiful, and written in the true spirit of that sentimental religion, which is so imposing and yet so useless; it is easy to preach an affecting funeral oration,—it is easy to call forth the tear of sympathy, and, by painting the virtues of the deceased, the loss sustained, and the uncertainty of life, to awaken all the benevolent affections of the mind, and a firm conviction of the truth of what is advanced:—But such orations are more beautiful than useful—they are productive of that sort of feeling and commiseration which are felt in reading the details of fictitious woe, but quite distinct from the practical exercise of virtue and benevolence, founded upon principle.[49]

An "independence of sentiment," then, is not only freedom of conscience; it is also a freedom to resist and expose the moral claims of sentimental rhetoric. What "Candidus" impugns in the passage just quoted is the ethical pretense of such rhetoric, which he circumscribes within the realm of the aesthetic; the ethical usefulness of such "benevolent affections" is comparable to that evoked "in reading the details of fictitious woe." His criterion for judging ethical value is one of principled, rational action, "the practical exercise of virtue and benevolence, founded on principle." From this perspective, Anglicanism itself is disparaged as "that sentimental religion"—in his admirable phrase—"so imposing and yet so useless."

By and large, Thomson's initial supporters frame his refusal in the context of the ongoing struggle for Presbyterian liberties. "Scotus" asks facetiously, "is 'Lucius' so uninformed as not to know, that the forms of service of the burial of the dead are of no more authority or respect with us than the service of the mass which the Roman Catholics perform for the salvation of souls[?]."[50] To "Candidus," Thomson's own enigmatic silence ennobles him as a hero of conscience:

Is there no such thing as a point of conscience? Is it impossible for a Presbyterian, who looks back to the struggles that his church has had for liberty, and the final adjustment of the Covenant, to see it right to put his foot against every encroachment, however trifling. . . . Whether right or wrong it is in Mr. Thomson a point of conscience,—and being so, in place of being accused for obstinancy, he ought to be commended.[51]

For "Scotus," Thomson's act places him among the spiritual heroes of Presbyterian liberty: "[I]t is to this same tenderness of conscience in our ancestors, that we are indebted for our present civil and religious freedom."[52]

M'Crie's *Free Thoughts*, a pamphlet more than five times longer than its predecessors, resonantly criticizes the fiction of a British moral nature. M'Crie, who held a Chair of Divinity at Edinburgh University, was a man accustomed to controversy. In 1804, as minister of Potterow Chapel, he had refused to endorse a major revision in the Presbyterian Testimony, claiming that its complete separation of church and state violated the Covenanters's intentions; after two years of debate, he was deposed by the Synod, and finally ejected by lawsuit from Potterow Chapel. Biographer of Knox and Melville, historian of reform movements in Italy and Spain, and contributor to *Blackwoods*, M'Crie in 1813 had become the first Scottish Dissenter to receive the Doctor of Divinity degree from Edinburgh University. Passionate in his defense of Thomson (a colleague and personal friend) and temperate in his censure of the minister's opponents, M'Crie advances a sober, eloquent critique of the nation's sublime and "natural" devotions on November 19th.[53]

Calling himself "Scoto-Britannus," M'Crie begins by charging that "the religious movement which lately took place may be traced to a paragraph in a *newspaper*"(5). In a footnote to this claim, M'Crie prints six announcements from the *London Courier*, "the organ of the court," in which an initial suggestion "to have divine service performed" throughout the land on the 19th becomes, over the course of four days, increasingly more definite and prescriptive.[54] Without fingering any conspirators, M'Crie strongly implies that agents of the crown sought to leave the impression of a spontaneous, growing movement to nationalize the funeral proceedings. Coote's wonderstruck observation that "it seemed as if there had been a preconceived agreement that Divine Service should be attended at all the Churches"(57) takes on a certain irony.[55]

The analogy between government intervention (as alleged by M'Crie) and the provocations of Oliver in the Pentridge revolt remains implicit but suggestive: M'Crie plays the role of the whistle-blowing Whig press to the *London Courier*'s insidious Robert Oliver. The Pentridge affair encouraged the kind of skepticism with which M'Crie pondered the mysteries of "spontaneous" mass responsiveness, whether of grief or of rage. Like the Whig journals that exposed the Oliver scandal, M'Crie does not portray the people as passive and malleable; on the contrary, he seeks to demonstrate that the people's demands were in part shaped and maneuvered by the government's interests. Arguing that such an observance is wholly unprecedented, M'Crie writes:

> If religious assemblies shall be called in compliance with the irregular impulse of popular feeling, or at the dictation of political, perhaps hireling journals;—if the worship of God must be celebrated at the cry of the mob;—if every anonymous scribbler in the newspaper, and every forward demagogue in an assembly, shall assume a right to call for a preacher and religious service as he would call for an actor or a song at a theatre—must not divine ordinances be profaned, and the Majesty of Heaven grossly insulted, under the pretence of honouring him? (6–7)

Exposing the *staged* quality of the observances, M'Crie denounces as blasphemous both the exploitation of the clergy and its complicity in this *coup de theatre*. Establishing that "a funeral sermon . . . is a sermon preached at a funeral,—the day of the funeral, or so connected with it as to form a part of the funeral service"(15), M'Crie deems the services held on the funeral day to constitute funeral services. Hence, reviewing in exquisite detail the "solemn and express stipulations" in the First Book of Discipline that prohibit funeral services, he admonishes the participating Presbyterians, lay, and clergy: "Those who assembled for worship that day transgressed the laws and violated the principles of our Church"(8).

But M'Crie is not content simply to note the transgressed prohibition; he reads that prohibition as a sign of the Presbyterian church's continuity with both the purity of the Apostolic church and, moving further back in history, the austere Judaic tradition: "He who provided that Moses should be interred secretly, so that 'no man knoweth of his sepulture to this day,' lest the Jews should have abused it to idolatry, wisely and graciously guarded against a practice which he foresaw would easily degenerate into superstition"(17). Christ himself, claims M'Crie, was buried without a religious service, but in time the church would adopt a variety of heathen practices governing burial: sacrifices, oblations, the invocation of manes, the ringing of bells, the carrying of torches, and funeral orations. The funeral service, M'Crie concludes, is "a powerful institution in the hands of superstition and priestcraft"(17).

At the core of M'Crie's essay lies an extended comparison between the failed Reformation of Anglicanism and the achieved Reformation of Presbyterianism. M'Crie represents the Reformation as a movement of both progressive enlightenment and fundamentalist return to the original "purity" of the apostolic church; but while the Scottish, Dutch, and French churches struck "at the heart of these [superstitious] observances"(25), Anglicanism sustained them:

> The service of the Church of England is addressed to the senses and the fancy. The service of the Church of Scotland is addressed to the understanding and the conscience. The former endeavours to produce its effects, by pleasing the eye and gratifying the ear. The latter borrows sparingly from the senses, and calls in their aid only so far as they are connected with it by nature or by divine institutions. By the external decoration of its temples, by the gaudy attire of its priests, the pomp and variety of its musical entertainments, and by frequent festivals, celebrated with all the parade of forms and gestures, the Episcopal Church strives to excite the imagination, and thus to make an impression on the heart—to fix the attention of the careless worshipper, and to make up for the radical defect in the bosom of the indevout. (28)

Whereas "Candidus" charges Anglicanism with uselessness, M'Crie charges it with hypocrisy and fraud; the broad, aesthetic appeal of the Episcopal church leaves unaddressed "the radical defect in the bosom of the indevout"—a defect, apparently, that goes deeper than both the senses and the heart. The critique of "Candidus" is essentially ethical; M'Crie's absorbs the ethical into the theological. His charge, in brief, is that the Church of England would rather keep the populace in its thrall—"fix their attention"—than secure their salvation.

M'Crie's strong implication is that such aesthetic enthrallment habituates a population to political enthrallment, jeopardizing the full range of their liberties. By contrast, Presbyterianism is portrayed as a religion of Enlightenment that promotes liberty:

> This thorough reform constitutes the high distinction of Scotland among the Protestant Churches. Its beneficial influence has extended to all departments of society—it has improved our temporal as well as our spiritual welfare—it has freed us from many galling impositions, which diminish the comforts and fret the spirits of other nations: it may be seen as the superior information of our people, in their freedom from childish fears and vulgar prejudices, in the purity of their morals, and in their practical regard, which, unconstrained by forms, and unattracted by show, they voluntarily pay to the ordinances of religion. (22)

What M'Crie rejects is the habit of locating the proof of a nation's enlightenment in its moral homogeneity. For M'Crie, who had paid a steep personal price for dissent within his own church, the crowning glory of enlightened Presbyterianism remains its insistence on freedom of conscience, its noble resistance to homogeneity—moral, political, or theological:

> [T]o the unfettered genius of our worship—to our exemption from the benumbing bondage of recurring holidays, political or religious, and from forms of prayer dictated on particular occasions by the Court, and to the freedom of discusssion yet retrained in our Ecclesiastical Assemblies, we hesitate not to ascribe, more than to any other cause, the preservation of public spirit and independence, which many things in our political situation and local circumstances have a powerful tendency to weaken and to crush. (36)

Pausing to imagine the lot of a Scottish people "loosened" from Presbyterianism, M'Crie argues that their enlightened religion—their freedom to dissent—provides both the basis for an ethics of community and, in the context of Anglo-Scottish relations, the political salvation of the Scottish people. For M'Crie, who had broken with his Church rather than sever Presbyterianism from the Scottish government, the civic culture of Scotland is continuous with the "public spirit and independence" fostered by its religion. Only in the final pages of *Free Thoughts* does M'Crie defend Thomson, suggesting that his political opponents—both among the burgher Seceders of the Presbyterian church and among the Edinburgh Tories—may have been behind the attack.

The best remedy for sentimental novels, wrote Wollstonecraft, is criticism; M'Crie's essay concludes with a critical reading of the texts that had already begun to turn the Princess's obsequies into funereal romance. In these paragraphs, M'Crie cuts to the heart of both sentimental discourse and its Burkean critique in the mediations of tragic theatre. Blasting a collection of sermon extracts published in the *Courier*, M'Crie denounces the pride taken in the national mourning, said by one minister (who, in M'Crie's words, "placed his confidence not in God, but in national humiliation"[41]) to be the nation's "'assured means of divine grace'" (39). In several sermons, M'Crie notes disgustedly, the Princess's death becomes "a propitiatory sacrifice for our sins," a primitive satisfaction of divine bloodlust. Reviewing accounts of the proceedings at St. Paul's—torchlit procession, rung bells—he asks, "Did all this take place at London, or was it at Rome or Madrid?" (45).

As a historian, M'Crie understood this much: that the historian's power to focus posterity's attention is precisely the power to make history meaningful. Writing the history of Edinburgh's involvement in the death of Princess Charlotte, M'Crie emphasizes not Thomson's refusal, nor the compliance of the other Presbyterian ministers, but the ensuing "discussion in Edinburgh"; what wanted preserving were both the "free thoughts" of the debate and the freedom to think them. "The late service," writes M'Crie ". . . has been gloried in as the spontaneous effusion of the people's loyalty and affection. What has taken place in Edinburgh is a commentary on this text"(69). With these words, the most eloquent skeptic of the national mourning topples the myth of a British religion squarely upon the issue of religious liberties.

"One Family Mourning"

Both Shelley's *Address* and M'Crie's *Free Thoughts* argue on behalf of a distinction between the realms of the public and the private. Both designate the highest moral plane as a realm other than the domestic. For Shelley, the highest moral virtues inhere in the public realm; M'Crie, by contrast, designates the individual conscience—what Godwin had called the "right of private judgment"—as more resistant to corruption than the morals of the community. Though they value and define the public and private realms differently, both writers stand apart from the sentimental strain that predominates in the mourning documents, a strain that conflates the public and private realms.

The central metaphor through which the nation meditated on its monarchy in November 1817 is an institution that itself conflates the public and private realms: the family. The sentimental myth of the nation's moral unanimity—a myth that M'Crie's "commentary," well before mine, insists is textual, not natural—derives much of its force from figurations of the nation as a family: "For fourteen days successively," writes Coote, "the nation has resembled one family mourning over a favourite child."[56] Numerous accounts compare the loss of the Princess to "the most woeful domestic visitation":[57] in Felicia Hemans's words, "All deeply, strangely, fearfully serene,/As in each ravaged home th'avenging one had been."[58] John Pye Smith testified that "no event, not immediately personal or domestic, has ever made on my mind an impression of sorrow, so deep seated, so abiding as the present."[59] According to Huish, "the mother looked as if she had lost her child—the husband as if he had lost his wife,—the brother as if he had lost a sister,—and all looked as if they had lost a friend"(536). To the generation of the Prince Regent, the Princess was a "blooming daughter"; to that of the Princess herself, "a beloved sister"(vii).

To probe the rich implications of this ubiquitous metaphor, let us first scrutinize its relation to Burke's figure of the nation's "family affections." In the *Reflections*, Burke places emphasis on the affections and attachments formalized in the practice of inheritance, the institution by virtue of which we "adhere . . . to our forefathers": "In this choice of inheritance we have given to our frame of polity the image of a relation in blood; binding up the constitution of our country with our dearest domestic ties; adopting our fundamental laws into the bosom of our family affections. . . . (46)" The "great primaeval contract of eternal society"(110), Burke argues, is not to be regarded as a business contract to be drawn up or dissolved by its partners, but as a familial contract, "a partnership not only between those who are living, but between those who are living, those who are dead, and those who are to be born"(110). As I have already suggested, Burke's insistence on the diachronic continuity of the nation is adapted in the mourning documents to express the nation's synchronic continuity at a moment of crisis. By the same token, Burke's emphasis on patriarchal inheritance—our adherence to "our forefathers"—is transformed into an emphasis on affections among the *contemporaneous* members of a family.[60] "Family," in the discourse of these documents, does not signify a multi-generational, transhistorical lineage, but a household of parents and their children; it signifies, in other words, the *domestic* rather than *patrilineal* family.

An account of this cultural and historical shift in the meaning of "family" lies beyond the purview of this study. Lawrence Stone, in *Family, Sex and Marriage in England 1500–1800* traces the emergence of the "closed domesticated nuclear family" between 1620 and 1800. According to Stone, the chief factors in this emergence were decreasing allegiance to lineage or patron in favor of allegiance to nation or sect; declining absoluteness of patriarchal authority within the family; and increasing emphasis on spousal intimacy, marital happiness, and the cult of manners.[61] More recently, in *Family Fortunes*, a study of the English middle class from 1780 to 1850, Leonore Davidoff and Catherine Hall emphasize the influence of commerce and Evangelicalism; they trace the rise of the domestic family to the middle-class "rejection of landed wealth as the source of honour and [the] insistence on the primacy of the inner spirit," an emphasis that "brought with it a preoccupation with the domestic as a necessary basis for a good Christian life."[62] Domesticity, no longer the exclusive prerogative of the gentry, became democratized in the middle-class household.[63]

The changing contours of the family, in other words, gave rise to an emerging culture of domesticity that was registered in the character of the British monarchy itself. As Colley has argued, the latter portion of the reign of George III saw a popularization of the monarchy without precedent since the Renaissance[64]; central to this increase in popularity was "a steady background of domestic responsibility and, preferably, domestic bliss. The royal *family* and not just the monarch had acquired increased currency and popularity in this period."[65] As women came increasingly to assert their support of the monarchy, the prolific Queen Charlotte, faithful companion to George III and mother of fifteen, became an object of admiration unto herself. After 1811, however, the troubled, embittered marriage between the Prince Regent and Caroline, Princess of Wales—compounded by the Regent's scandalous habits— threatened the gains of the Hanoverian monarchy within the middle class; at stake was the nationalistic, symbolic power that had accrued to the monarchy during the Napoleonic Wars even as it relinquished a good measure of political influence. The death of Princess Charlotte in childbirth, even more than her marriage, allowed the populace to reassert its identification with the Hanoverian monarchy, that is, with the *idea* of a royal family; moreover, this assertion was a strong warning to the Regent—and, as the furor over the Regent's attempt to divorce Queen Caroline in 1820 would show, not the last[66]—that the monarchy would become increasingly unpopular unless it at least appeared to resume its stable, domestic character.

In these years between the French Revolution and the accession of Victoria, it is as though the monarchy assumed its most sympathetic face when the frailty of the royal family was revealed[67]; weakness, whether expressed in the King's pathetic madness or the Princess's pathetic death in childbed, empowered the Hanovers by endearing them to wider portions of the public. In a revealing passage, Huish links the posthumous Princess, now an ethereal spirit, to her destitute grandfather:

> How pure a spirit is then gone before him, to minister peace to him in his hermit hours on earth; and to give him a foretaste of that bliss to which he must soon be called! That being, whom on earth he so ardently loved, may now be the visitant of his nightly watchings, and in the darkness of his state he may hear the whispers of consolation from those lips, which to us on earth are henceforth closed for ever. (ix–x)

With the Prince Regent conspicuously absent, Princess Charlotte reaches across two generations to reassert the domestic affections of the Hanovers. As the Princess comforts her grandfather, Huish comforts his readers with an emblem of monarchical continuity, and the power that resides in royal frailty.

But Princess Charlotte, in death, does not simply revive the popular Hanoverian monarchy of her grandparents; she also powerfully anticipates the rise of Victoria. There is an important difference, I would argue, between the stolid, patriarchal domesticity of George III, Queen Charlotte, and their fifteen children; and the maternal, feminized images of domesticity projected in the mourning documents for the Princess. Such documents do not simply emphasize the Princess's domestic, feminine virtues; they explicitly link such virtues to the character of her anticipated reign. The death of Princess Charlotte, by evoking fantasies of a maternal female monarch, projects the image of a woman who would simultaneously play roles that were ostensibly public *and* private.

The difference between these two versions of domesticity illuminates the influence and function of what Davidoff and Hall have called the "potent imagery of 'separate spheres.'"[68] The doctrine of "separate spheres," articulated in Evangelical texts regarding distinct roles for men and women, was popularized and secularized during the last two decades of the eighteenth century. Women, ostensibly confined to the domestic sphere, were compensated with a myth that their rearing of children and performance of charitable works constituted a potent moral influence on society.[69] Davidoff and Hall urge a certain skepticism regarding the separate spheres; the so-called public and private realms stipulated and definitively gendered as masculine and feminine by this doctrine, they claim, are "ideological constructs with specific meaning which must be understood as products of a particular historical time."[70]

But the documents that mourn the Princess do not simply suggest the rhetoricality of the doctrine of separate spheres; they lend support to Colley's contention that this doctrine could and did license the greater national influence of women, provided they did not identify themselves with the cause of enhancing female liberties.[71] What these documents reveal is that certain features of this doctrine, in particular its elaboration of "natural" qualities peculiar to each gender, were exploited to the end of complicating—even undermining—the very separateness of masculine and feminine domains. For all their ardency, the Princess's mourners give us a glimpse of the complex lived experience that the doctrine of separate spheres was designed to order and regulate. And they do so in the course of reflecting upon the strained relations between the monarchy and its subjects. In the final section of this chapter, I examine how the mourning for Princess Charlotte complicates—indeed, criticizes—the emerging doctrine of the separate spheres. I then consider the consequences of this merging of the so-called public and private realms.

. . . . .

Because Princess Charlotte was a young woman who had only recently emerged from childhood, her public persona had always been defined in terms of her domestic roles. Known for many years as the spirited daughter of an embittered marriage between the Regent and Princess Caroline, she had survived a difficult childhood to become in 1816 the wife of Prince Leopold of Saxe-Coburg, and within several months, an expectant mother. According to her memorialists and biographers, the Princess and her consort were admired for their evident compatibility, for their avoidance of the frivolous court life enjoyed by the Prince Regent, for their seemly retirement in Claremont, and, not least, for their expeditious conception of an heir to the throne. In the words of one anonymous pamphleteer, "Perhaps there never was a Royal match formed in which political considerations had less influence upon the parties themselves, and in which the feelings of the heart were more deeply engaged. . . . [T]he illustrious pair, during their short connubial life, were the very model of domestic harmony."[72]

While the Princess was known to be congenial to Whigs and Dissenters, Shelley's account of her tenuous grasp of "those great political questions which involve the happiness of those over whom she was destined to rule"(165) seems fairly accurate. On the other hand, Shelley's claim that "for the public she had done nothing either good or evil" (which suggests Shelley's co-optation of classical Athens for the emerging doctrine of the "separate spheres") is ardently contradicted in the majority of mourning documents. The Princess's benevolence is generally viewed as a reciprocation of "the homage which was paid to her rank"; by many it is considered continuous with the virtues desired in a reigning monarch. Her reputation for supporting local charities is accounted a symptom of her "deeply felt alliance with the universal family of the earth." To be thus charitable, even within the local sphere, constituted, in part, the performance of her public role as a female member of the royal family.

Not surprisingly, several poems in *A Cypress Wreath* celebrate the Princess's combination of "manly" and "feminine" qualities: "Her *manly* sense, her sweetness, void of art,/Made her the idol of each British heart."[73] In such poems, gender epithets do not refer to the Princess's sexuality so much as encode the sphere in which such qualities are generally practiced: "Tell how to more than manly sense/She join'd the soft'ning influence/Of more than female tenderness."[74] One anonymous poet, in a footnote, cites the Princess's intercession in 1812 on behalf of a young woman, sentenced to death for theft "after having been seduced and deserted." The poet notes that the Princess's "death is, we fear, the grave of *Britain's hope* and fondest expectation of a *female* succession, which bade fair to eclipse the far-famed aera of *ELIZABETH.*"[75]

Saliently, this fantasy of a female monarch's reign invokes the glory of the "Virgin Queen" while insisting that that of a *maternal* queen would "eclipse" it. In many eulogies, the Princess's "feminine" virtues are difficult to extricate from her "masculine" ones:

> The liberal principles which she professed as to state affairs,—her spirited espousal of her calumniated mother,—her determination not to enter into a matrimonial union but with one to whom she could give her heart along

with her hand;—the amiable picture of domestic felicity which she exhibited from the moment of her being united with the object of her affections
. . . all concurred to cherish the fondest expectations in the breast of those
who thought themselves destined to be her future subjects.[76]

Hemans devotes an entire stanza to the Princess's powers of mind:

> We watched her childhood from its earliest hour,
> From every word and look blest omens caught;
> While that young mind developed all its power,
> And rose to energies of loftiest thought.
> On her was fixed the Patriot's ardent eye,
> One hope still bloomed—one vista still was fair;
> And when the tempest swept the troubled sky,
> She was our dayspring—all was cloudless *there*;
> And oh! how lovely broke on England's gaze,
> E'en through the mist and storm, the light of distant days.[77]

Like so many of the Princess's eulogists, both Coote and Hemans place
her virtues—whether "masculine" or "feminine"—in the context of her
anticipated reign. Significantly, the very virtues that Shelley had read as
"domestic" were adduced by ministers as a moral pattern for congregants—particularly children—of both sexes. As Woolmer put it, "The
example of our much lamented Princess was loyalty, discretion and
moderation."[78] Rudge informs his congregants that "a pattern of all that
was good and lovely to look upon in the endearing relation of a wife . . .
was complete in other parts. . . . [S]he felt for the woes and wretchedness
of the distressed; and whenever a well-authenticated case of human suffering was submitted to her, the ear was as open to hear, as the heart was
ready to receive it."[79]

The crux in this joining of public and private lies in the representation
of the Princess's pregnancy. On the one hand, the Princess had conducted herself with the modesty and decorum that would beseem any
aristocratic woman of her day, continually contracting her sphere of activity as her pregnancy advanced.[80] On the other hand, the Princess had
carried within her the heir to the crown; the sorrow her death evoked is,
in part, a measure of the nation's vested interest in her "interesting condition." To many, doubtless, the Princess's most important public role
until assuming the crown was her service as a vessel for monarchic continuity—in other words, her conception, pregnancy, and birthing of a
royal heir. Widely viewed as a martyr to the preservation of the monarchic line, this madonna of the Hanovers was represented in both words
and sculpture (as M'Crie notes with chagrin); she was sculpted, according to Huish, as "our departed Saint"(630).[81]

Other accounts, as if loath to expose the pregnant body of the Princess by representing it, allude obliquely to the "pregnancy" of her death, the "promise" of her reign, the "pangs" of her mourners, and the thwarted "expectations" of her subjects. In Coote's eyes, the stillbirth of the child—a male heir—elevated the tragic death in childbed into the realm of the sublime: "The death of Nelson had its consolations. He was a great spirit released after he had gone his round of glory. . . . But this fair and gentle being lived only in promise . . . like infancy with its bloom and softness to be stricken before our eyes into frightful decay. . . ."[82] Coote's juxtaposition between the death of Nelson and that of the Princess is a comparison, not a contrast. They are two public figures: one who survived his own glory, and one whose early death wasted the potential of her "public heart." The Princess's much-discussed pregnancy becomes figured as her "promise," the stillborn child an emblem of the blighted infancy of her public career. In lamenting the public worth of the Princess—and in fantasizing the reign she would never have—the mourning documents reconfigure the Princess's ostensibly private virtues of benevolence, modesty, charity, and sympathy within the public sphere.

Even the most pathetic of the mourning documents, the elegiac poems, directly relate the Princess's domestic conduct to her national esteem.[83] Even as the Princess becomes everywoman—everydaughter, everywife, every expectant mother—her versatility is predictive of her royal abilities:

> No pomp of birth, no pride of rank had she,
> Her beauty, graced by sweet humility,
> Endeared her to the *good* in private life,
> And stamped her fame, as Daughter, Friend, and Wife.[84]

In "The Last Pious Aspirations of the Idolized Princess Charlotte," the Princess herself is shown mourning her stillborn child. The scant hours between the stillbirth and the Princess's death are seized upon to create a pathetic fiction of the bereft mother:

> Must I weep for thee, Babe? Nor shall my *single sorrow*
> In fast falling currents thy obsequies lave?
> For o'er thy hapless fate ere the night of *to-morrow*,
> The sorrows of *millions* shall stream o'er thy grave![85]

Here the Princess's short-lived maternity is a showcase for her renowned powers of sympathy. Her imminent expectation of death is more a function of her sympathetic identification with her dead child than the physiological consequence of childbirth. But such powers of sympathy are also the basis for the "sorrows of *millions*" which are to follow hers.

Whereas Wordsworth's Ellen arrests the public funeral with an intensely private pause for mourning, Princess Charlotte is shown implicitly to instruct the entire nation in the moral affections of mourning.

In such representations of the Princess, her femininity is shown to support, rather than undermine, her anticipated performance of the monarch's public role. To lend further support to the fantasy of a female monarch, the image of the mourning royal family is, accordingly, domesticated:

> There is an outward pomp, a garb of woe,
>   That sometimes follows Sovereigns to the tomb;
>   There is a soul-felt grief that sighs at home,
> And presses on the heart. The great, the low,
>   Alike feel this: and, oh lamented shade:
> To thy dear loss shall every rite be paid,
> And the sad tear of fond affection flow![86]

Whereas Shelley holds the extensiveness of public grief to be the highest test of virtue, such poets hold the test of moral worth to be the depth of private grief within the circle of intimates. The equipoise between the masculine role of monarch and the Princess's feminine virtue is so exquisite that the masculinity of the bereaved consort Prince Leopold is persistently minimized. In "Fair Promise of Britannia's Powerful Realm," Leopold is said to "[claim] a double sympathy from those/Who feel the stranger's grief—the widow's woes." Attending the royal childbed, Leopold is recognized in the maternal role left absent by Princess Caroline; after the Princess's death, Coote describes him "rush[ing]" into Lord Lauderdale's arms for comfort, at which point "he was unmanned and burst into a flood of tears."[87] In the final stanza of "The House of Mourning," the testimony of their "private sorrows" is predicted to outlast that of "public grief":

> Nor less do these more humble sorrows tell,
> How great their rev'rence and deserved how well.
> Oh, these are records high, that shall not fade,
> When lost is public grief, its grandeur and parade."[88]

The conflation of the "separate spheres" in these documents not only reveals the arbitrariness of their gender codings; it also permits an unusual fluidity in the representation of social class. Shelley, of course, had observed the "commonness" of the Princess's death and noted the "thousands of others equally distinguished as she for private excellencies who have been cut off in youth and hope"(165). But whereas Shelley quickly turns his argument toward the difference between the impoverished and aristocratic classes, many funeral sermons reverently acknowledge the human sameness before death. "No man can die by proxy," declares the Reverend William Newman:

> Let us learn that Death levels all ranks, making no distinction. The body of the Princess, and the body of the poorest young woman in this congregation, are framed and fashioned out of the same British clay. The materials, the fabric, the workmanship are the same. They are nourished by the same grass—they breathe the same air—they are cheered by the same sun—They are exposed to the same diseases—they are under the same sentence of death. There is no essential difference.[89]

The moral of "no essential difference," however, is not simply the medieval moralists' lesson of death as the great equalizer. If the difference of rank or class is inessential, then the essence of this similarity lies in "the same British clay" of which this society is fashioned. In such hands as Newman's, the mortal lesson about human sameness before death becomes another lesson about the difference being British makes.

• • • • •

The rhetoric of universality that emerges, in part, from the conflation of the public and private spheres was turned to three distinct *British* political purposes. Shelley, as we have seen, maneuvers the "commonness" of the Princess's death to gain attention and sympathy for the lowest ranks of society; for those who return unmourned and even uncóffined to the earth. But whereas Shelley asks his educated reader to identify with the "multitude," Chalmers uses the trope of universality to cultivate middle-class sympathy for those, like the Princess, in the *highest* echelons of the social order. Urging "the desirableness of a more frequent intercourse between the higher and lower orders of society,"[90] Chalmers takes the opportunity to disarm the agitation for reform:

> Let the rich, instead of being viewed by their inferiors through the dim and distant medium of that fancied interval which separates the ranks of society, be seen as heirs of the same frailty and as dependent on the same sympathies with themselves—and, at that moment, all the floodgates of honest sympathy will be opened—and the lowest servants of the establishment will join in the cry of distress which has come upon their family—and the neighboring cottagers, to share in their grief, have only to recognise them as the partakers of one nature, and to perceive an assimilation of feelings and of circumstances between them.[91]

While Chalmers's exhortation for the "lower order" to sympathize with the rich suggests condescension, it also suggests how much was at stake in how the laboring class conceived of itself. Just as the rhetoric of the

universal mourning focuses anxiously on Dissenters, Chalmers's rhetoric of universal mortality is intended to foster a sympathetic identification between the laboring class and the upper classes. For Chalmers, the
way to strengthen the upper classes' grasp of political and financial
power, paradoxically, is to portray these classes as frail and deserving of
pity. By offering the upper classes to the "lower order" as an object of
pity, Chalmers implicitly compensates the working classes for their
disenfranchisement. Like women, the "lower order" are granted the elevating power of sympathetic benevolence. But Chalmers's distinction
between the rich and their "inferiors"—between the gentry's domestic
"establishment" and its "lowest servants" and "neighboring cot-
tagers"—hardly describes the emerging culture of middle-class domesticity during the second decade of the nineteenth century; it even accords
poorly with the urbanized culture of his native Glasgow. Such elevation
as Chalmers condescends to offer was simply claimed by the Princess's
mourners, who overwhelmingly and confidently identify the institution
of royalty with that of the home.[92]

What still needs elaboration is the third end to which the conflation of
the public and private realms was turned: the prescription of middle-
class domestic morals for the royal family. In the documents that mourn
the Princess, the domestic family becomes the favored context in which
to render a moral judgment on the crisis within the Hanoverian monarchy. While the decadent state of the royal family is observed implicitly
in every account of the royal crisis, a few explicitly note the Princess's
isolation from her family—or, in Shelley's mordant words, the "perpetual estrangement" of the royals from one another.[93] As one pamphlet
put it:

> Not one female relative was with her Royal Highness at the time of her
> accouchement and death; not a human being with whom she was connected
> by blood, assisted that moment, when, of all others, a female is surely an
> object of female sympathy and attention. She, the presumptive heiress to the
> British throne, in the hour of childbirth, was left as if she had no kindred.
> Her mother, the Princess of Wales, long separated from the Prince Regent,
> was on the Continent; her father, the Prince Regent, was on a shooting-
> party at the Marquis of Hertford's in Suffolk; her grandmother, the *Queen*,
> was at Bath, taking the waters, none of her aunts, the Princesses, either
> married or unmarried, were present.[94]

This is a stinging attack not on the deathbed, but on the childbed; as
such it focuses on the Princess's betrayal by female relatives. Women are
alerted that if the family is to be the moral guardian of the society at
large, it is for them to be the moral guardians of the family. In such
pamphlets, the dashed dream of a female monarch not only prescribes a

certain moral role for women; it defines with startling clarity the role of a female monarch in the nineteenth century.

When Edmund Burke sought to defend monarchy in 1790, he entreated his readers to identify with the royal lineage because it personified the nation's inheritance. Nearly thirty years later, these documents seek to salvage an endangered monarchy by identifying it with the sympathetic "family" of Britain—and by extension, with Britain's families. By 1817, "an old, mad, blind, despised" King; a frivolous, scandal-ridden Regent; a dissolute Princess of Wales in exile; and an ill-assorted group of royal siblings who seemed indifferent to the nation's need for legitimate heirs; had strained the symbolic embodying function of the royal family to the breaking point. In Princess Charlotte, who had forsworn the Prince of Orange to remain in Britain; who had made a splendid match "in which the feelings of the heart were . . . deeply engaged";[95] radiated connubial bliss during the couple's retirement at Claremont house and engaged in charitable works; who had, to crown her virtues, conceived an heir to the crown—in such a Princess, the British nation had finally the promise of a domesticated royal family. On the night of November 5, 1817, this expectation was dashed. The Princess's mourners could not know that eighteen months later, with the birth of Princess Alexandrina Victoria to the Duke of Clarence and the sister of the Princely widower Leopold, the possibility of domesticating the royal family would be reborn.

More in her death than in her life, Princess Charlotte was the crucial figure of monarchical continuity between the declining years of George III and the accession of Victoria. But she is as much a figure of transition as of continuity. In the documents that mourn her death, the character of the monarchy shifts from the patriarchal domesticity of George III to a newly feminized monarchy with a maternal, female ruler. Like the institution of the family, the documents that mourn Princess Charlotte lie between the private and public spheres; between the inchoate fantasy of a reformed, moralized monarchy and the rhetorical forms in which that fantasy was made vivid. The mourning documents do not only show that the domestic ideology of the "separate spheres" was never simply a repressive cult of the private sphere; beyond this, they suggest how the moral ground held by femininity could be annexed to increasingly larger spheres of influence for women. This is by no means a story of steady gains; a century after the Princess's death, suffrage was still not achieved. Still, the salient figure of a female monarch would be crucial to the developing arena of women's rights during the century of Victoria.

Queen Victoria was conceived as a result of Princess Charlotte's death. But as a cultural phenomenon, Queen Victoria was born in the documents with which a middle-class public definitively and self-consciously laid claim to the private lives of their monarchs. As Robert Huish observed, the death of Princess Charlotte bore more lessons for "the governing [than for] the governed!":

> May it teach the former that a constant and sacred regard for the nation's rights, as well as for public and private morals, presents to them the only chance of being loved in life, and lamented in death! The country has shewn, by its acute grief on this occasion, that it is capable of the highest and most disinterested affection for the family of its rulers: but it is not for the trappings of royalty that they have this veneraton: this tribute is reserved for virtue; and may the people ever make this discrimination! (vi)

In the nation's mourning for Princess Charlotte, the family became the moral measure of the state.

EPILOGUE

"Leisure and Money": Mrs. Pullet's Mourning

> "Sophy," said Mrs Glegg, unable any longer to contain her
> spirit of rational remonstrance—"Sophy, I wonder *at* you
> fretting and injuring your health about people as don't belong
> to you. . . ."
>
> Mrs Pullet was silent, having to finish her crying, and rather
> flattered than indignant at being upbraided for crying too
> much. It was not everybody who could afford to cry so much
> about their neighbours who had left them nothing; but Mrs
> Pullet had married a gentleman farmer, and had leisure and
> money to carry her crying and everything else to the highest
> pitch of respectability.
>
> (George Eliot, *The Mill on the Floss*, 1860)

LET US COMPARE Eliot's epigraph above to the 1711 quotation from Richard Steele that stands as an epigraph to chapter 1. Both writers satirize an instance of mourning by raising a question of propriety: when is the connection between mourner and mourned too remote to be worthy of the reader's (or in Steele's case, questioner's) sympathy? Steele ridicules the notion of a tradesman's wife grieving for an aristocrat; a lower-class origin, it would seem, can disallow the moral dignity implicit in the act of mourning. Foreignness ("one of the house of Austria") serves here as a metaphor for a social incongruity and remoteness that belies the woman's pretense of belonging, along with Austrian aristocrats, to a human family. In the passage from *Mill on the Floss*, however, the mourner is *higher* in social class than the person she mourns—and from whom she expects no inheritance. What Eliot mocks is not Mrs. Pullet's sympathy, but rather the manner in which Mrs. Pullet parlays mourning into a display of precisely what she can "afford"; her grief shows her to have the "leisure and money" with which, by grieving, she *purchases* respectability. Her grief is a display not of moral elevation, but of affluence and high social status.

Where mourning was, during the Enlightenment, a figurative moral currency for the nation, it becomes in the Victorian period virtually a form of legal tender negotiable for "respectability"; thus, in a metonymic, rather than metaphorical sense, Mrs. Pullet's mourning is a type of currency. The proffering of sympathy, in other words, no longer promotes the vitality of a moral economy within a community, but rather signifies an amassment of wealth sufficient to purchase social status. The appropriate metaphor is not circulation but striation; the axis of figuration has become vertical, not horizontal. Social historians of the Victorian era enumerate the myriad accoutrements required for a "respectable" mourning—the crepe gowns, black silk bonnets, and jet ornaments; the black-edged mourning cards; the miniatures; the mourning tea sets for entertaining; the commemorative ceramics, medals, and memorials.[1] Besides milliners and haberdashers devoted exclusively to purveying varying gradations of mourning wear, there arose a thriving, notoriously corrupt industry in the furnishing and direction of funerals. Never accepted into the guildhall—for they had usurped upon the business of the cabinetmakers—the "United Company of Undertakers" actually comprised three distinct and strictly hierarchical trades: in ascending order of status, coffinmakers, undertakers, and funeral furnishers.[2] Their ranks—and their prices—were bloated by the presence of middlemen who simply served as brokers for the providers of goods and services. One historian of the funeral trade estimates that grieving families paid markups of between 200 and 500 percent.[3]

The famed "Chadwick report" of 1843—*A Supplementary Report on the Results of a Special Inquiry into the Practice of Interment in Towns*—details these and other abuses, laying the groundwork for legislation limiting the amount of debt one could legally incur in planning a funeral. Most strikingly, the report laid bare the elaborate aping of the heraldic array of baronial funerals for the middle and laboring classes. The charade of a full-dress baronial funeral made literal the desire to purchase rank through funereal expense. The funerals of the aristocracy were unprecedently elaborate, the most expensive and well-attended of the century being that of the Duke of Wellington in November 1852; a triumphal "funeral car" costing some 11,000 pounds was built to usher his remains to the vault. Nearly seventy thousand people paid their respects as the body lay in state and an estimated one and a half million watched the procession, which was virtually devoid of Christian symbolism.[4]

There was, however, a more private mode of ostentation, one that exhibited the expenditure of time rather than money. The converse of Mrs. Pullet's high mourning—its negative correlative on an imaginary vertical axis—was the "deep" mourning of Queen Victoria in the years following the death of her Consort, Prince Albert, in 1861.[5] Technically, "deep" mourning refers to a code of behavior and dress to be observed during the initial, most stringent, period of mourning; within a few months, the rules relaxed as the family (and often its servants) donned the more moderate costumes of "half-mourning." The Queen and her household observed deep mourning for an entire year, after which she permitted her servants to wear white, mauve, and grey. Though the royal household would observe at least three gradations of mourning (finally abandoning armbands in 1869),[6] the Queen would not allow grief to relinquish its hold on her; except to attend memorial ceremonies, she refused to appear in public for nearly two years and made constant reference in letters and interviews to her great loss. Her baroque domestic observances—for example, the daily laying out of the Prince's clothes— have become legendary. By 1863 sporadic criticisms of the Queen's withdrawal in such journals as the *Times* had gained momentum, provoking her to write an unsigned letter of self-defense which the *Times* duly published.[7]

Like Queen Victoria, who remained in seclusion at Osborne during the obsequies for her late husband,[8] Alfred Lord Tennyson did not attend Arthur Hallam's funeral.[9] But the 131 lyrics he composed between Hallam's death in 1833 and 1850 became a consoling witness to the sense of deep, boundless grief articulated by Queen Victoria and countless other mid- and late-Victorian mourners. While Tennyson's *In Memoriam* provides a grave countertext to George Eliot's satirical leveling of Mrs. Pullet's mourning, his investment in grief outdoes Mrs. Pullet's by a considerable margin.

What put many readers on intimate terms with the poem, paradoxically, was Tennyson's extreme sense of the mourner's isolation. Other human figures—usually types, not persons—are invoked as analogues to support the poet's explication of his grief. The poet is preoccupied with his relations to Hallam, God, and nature, but not with fellow mourners or comforters. His verse, he declares repeatedly, is designed to bring himself relief (lyrics 5, 75), not to move his reader. He considers and rejects the discourse of eulogy (lyric 75) because he despairs of a receptive audience for Hallam's youthful promise. Where Milton entreats "May some Gentle muse/ With lucky words favor my destin'd Urn,/And as he passes turn,/And bid fair peace be to my sable shroud" (*Lycidas* 19–21), Tennyson mortifies his "lullabies of pain" (lyric 77); he predicts that "A man upon a stall may find,/And, passing, turn the page that tells/A grief, then changed to something else,/Sung by a long-forgotten mind"(lyric 77). Like Gray in the "Sonnet [on the Death of Mr. Richard West]," he laments the death of conversation with Hallam: "We cannot hear each other speak"; yet in lyric 85, he designates Hallam's "being working in mine own" as his best comforter. The same lyric voices compunctions about excessive mourning, declaring it a "crime/To mourn for any overmuch"; he considers engaging with a lesser substitute for

Hallam—but only after allowing Hallam, so to speak, to raise the issue. Having questioned the propriety of his extended mourning, his "parade of pain," in lyric 21, he later voices his disgust with the reflexivity of mourning:

> What find I in the highest place,
>> But mine own phantom chanting hymns?
>> And on the depths of death there swims
> The reflex of a human face.
>
> (lyric 108)

Tennyson chooses his elegiac pretexts carefully; unlike the poet in Shelley's *Alastor*, Tennyson turns from his melancholy reflection with some horror, echoing Wordsworth's "Peele Castle": "I will not shut me from my kind." The entire poem, famously, turns toward the social by concluding with the marriage of the poet's sister Cecilia. But though Tennyson was to marry within months of the poem's publication—and though his bereaved sister Emily, Hallam's fiancée, had married several years earlier—neither the poet nor his sister becomes espoused in the poem's conclusion. It is as though Tennyson, having espoused Sorrow in lyric 59, cannot renounce her.

Beyond representing the depths of grief as isolation, Tennyson also links the Victorian figure of deep grief with tropes of sublimity. Such tropes verge alternately—sometimes simultaneously—on Romantic profundity and on a celestial, Christian transcendence. In lyric 41 ("Thy spirit ere our fatal loss"), the poet seems to prefer the sublimity of intellectual and spiritual striving—Hallam's rise, in life, "from high to higher"—to the sublime change that has "turn'd" Hallam "to something strange." At the same time, the exertions of the poet's "upward mind" are enfeebled by a wild desire:

> that this could be—
> That I could wing my will with might
> To leap the grades of life and light,
> And flash at once, my friend, to thee.
>
> (lyric 41)

Such a desire is not quited until the climactic lyric 95 ("By night we lingered on the lawn"), in which the poet reads "the noble letters of the dead" and enjoys an insistently "strange" experience of communion:

> So word by word, and line by line,
>> The dead man touch'd me from the past,
>> And all at once it seem'd at last
> The living soul was flash'd on mine,

> And mine in this was wound, and whirl'd
> About empyreal heights of thought,
> And came on that which is, and caught
> The deep pulsations of the world. . . .
>
> (lyric 95)

Whether this "trance" is a sublime experience of preternaturally close reading or an ecstatic communion with Hallam's spirit is left tantalizingly uncertain; the poet journeys to "empyreal heights," but they are "heights of thought"; on the other hand, what seems a Wordsworthian "flash" does not "fade into the light of common day" but is, like a religious vision, "cancell'd, stricken thro' with doubt." The equipoise between two types of sublimity is itself sublime, and it persists in the paradoxical conclusions of lyric 130, which establish Hallam's immortality as simultaneously immanent and transcendent. The lyric ends with a hymn to Hallam's immortality, which suffices here to provide a measure of solace for loss:

> Far off thou art, but ever nigh;
> I have thee still, and I rejoice;
> I prosper, circled with thy voice;
> I shall not lose thee tho' I die.
>
> (lyric 130)

Tennyson's conviction of Hallam's enduring presence reveals the most striking difference between Enlightenment and Victorian death and mourning: the character of the dead. Even as Adam Smith theorizes that the living identify with the dead, the import of that identification is an abyss between the living and the dead, a sense of what differentiates us from them—a piquant sense, in other words, of the moral life we live to carry on. Ironically, I would argue, such a difference is obscured within the Victorian cult of death and mourning, whose lyrics and narratives lay emphasis on all manner of interpenetration between the worlds of the living and the dead: intuitions of the beyond, visitations by the dead, and, most pervasively, the fantastic drama of mortal transition performed on the deathbed.[10] As Elisabeth Jay has observed in *Religion of the Heart*, the focal deathbed scenes in Evangelical biography, anthologized in such volumes as *The Family Sepulchre*,[11] had a profound impact on novelists of the Victorian era, Evangelical and otherwise. The deaths of Milly Barton, Paul Dombey, Helen Burns, and especially Little Nell all depend to varying degrees on the conventions of the Evangelical deathbed: the dying words (often laboriously taken down), the beatific smile, the ministering of comforters. Whereas the High Church placed emphasis chiefly on the salvation of the dying person, Evangelicals, according to Jay, emphasized the impact of the death on witnesses.[12] Such an emphasis on the witnessing of death led novelists to emphasize the perception of the deathbed scene, and deemphasize (or crudely insist upon) the metaphysical state of the dying. Evangelical critiques of such "vulgarization" took issue not only with the aestheticization of the dying, which masks the corruption of all flesh, but also with the encroachment of a secular, sentimental discourse of sympathy upon a religious discourse of salvation. To the Evangelicals, the dead are not our moral debtors, but rather our predecessors on line to receive the fine reward of salvation. Paradoxically, the Victorian ghost story, installing pale apparitions in all the familiar places, is the premier example of how the dead as such come to *disappear* in the later nineteenth century.

To put it more emphatically, the living dead of pietistic Victoriana and the rotting dead of the skeptical Enlightenment are not the same dead.[13] The grave was one kind of place to Adam Smith and quite another to John Keble.[14] Is there, then, no afterlife for the dead of the Enlightenment; the dead who motivate the life of morals; the dead of Smith and Gray? To what discursive destination are *those other* dead borne? In the remainder of this epilogue, I want to turn from Victorian death and mourning to consider an allegory of *their* fate in Mary Shelley's 1826 novel *The Last Man*.[15] Writing between the tumultuous decades of revolution and war, and the rise of Victoria, Shelley provides an uncannily shrewd account of the fate of the Enlightenment culture of mourning—in her century and afterwards.

The Death of Morals and the Birth of Aestheticism

> Such as he had now become, such as was his terrene vesture, defaced and spoiled, we wrapt it in our cloaks, and lifting the burthen in our arms, bore it from this city of the dead.
>
> (Mary Shelley, *The Last Man*)
>
> Death is the mother of beauty. . . .
> (Wallace Stevens, "Sunday Morning")

Mary Shelley's allegorical point of departure in *The Last Man* is the failure of sentimentalism to move beyond an ethics of moral value to become an ethics of moral action.[16] In the characters Raymond and Adrian, Mary Shelley creates an opposition between the political man of action and the philosophical man of sympathy and reflection:

> [Raymond's] passions were violent. . . . He looked on the structure of society as but a part of the machinery which supported the web on which his life was traced. . . .

Adrian felt that he made a part of a great whole. . . . His soul was sympathy, and dedicated to the worship of beauty and excellence. . . . Adrian despised the narrow views of the politician, and Raymond held in supreme contempt the benevolent visions of the philanthropist.[17]

But Adrian's sublimation of ego drains him of sufficient political will to assume a role on the public stage—even an inherited and effectively abdicated role. The Last Man, in large part, explores the political, social, and moral consequences of a polarity between sympathy for suffering and the will to ameliorate it; crucially, the deterioration of civic order—under the ironically titled "Protectorate" of Raymond—precedes the advent of the Plague. Raymond's depravity resides not in his passions, but in his casuistry, his use of language to "contaminate" the moral categories of good and evil; "contagion" makes its first appearance in the novel as a figure for moral corruption. Such casuistry pervades as well Raymond's panhellenic heroics, which Adrian denounces as a corrupt "[dream] of massacre and glory"(117). It is for the sympathetic Adrian to remove the "turban" of "Mahometanism" to reveal the essential humanity of the Turkish "foe": "The Turks are men; each fibre, each limb is as feeling as our own, and every spasm, be it mental or [bo]dily [sic] is as truly felt in a Turk's heart or brain, as in a Greek's"(116).

If Raymond's moral corruption is a metonym for the Plague, Adrian's powers, surprisingly, are closely linked to it as well. For the Plague finally brings about Adrian's ascendancy to political power. Adrian's strategy is to counter and contain the circulation of disease through the circulation of sympathies, but in fact sympathy, by placing human beings in intimate contact, ironically serves to foster the spread of Plague. Adrian's effort to resist the plague through sympathy, then, is complementary, not oppositional; the apotheosis of sympathy over which Adrian presides is but a struggle between the nature within and the nature without.

In this "struggle" of nature against nature, I would suggest, Mary Shelley allegorizes a debate between two concepts of nature: the benevolent nature of Shaftesbury, Hutcheson, and Smith, and the malevolent, amoral nature of Malthus. In the world of The Last Man, Mary Shelley looks forward and back; hers is a world in which two cultures of nature compete for dominance. But Mary Shelley's pronounced ambivalence to the remedy of Adrian—that is, to the culture of sentimentalism—must give us pause. In The Last Man—in the Protectorate of the sublimely sympathetic Adrian—Mary Shelley dramatizes the manner in which sentimentalism derives a moral life from the predicament of the dead. Specifically, she exposes the Enlightenment myth of a "natural" morality to be a cultural artifact. Precisely what motivates Shelley's deeper discontent with the Enlightenment culture of mourning is difficult to say. It may be the secular erection of the dead in the place of a divine moral authority; or the exploitation of the dead to fund the circulation of morals with "natural" value; or it may be a stinging sense of the ambiguous moral legacy left by her own great dead, Percy Shelley and Lord Byron. But it seems clear that though Mary Shelley has been repeatedly faulted for writing a romance caught between sentimentalism and nihilism,[18] she has done no such thing. *The Last Man* offers a scathing critique of Enlightenment sentimentalism for conscripting the dead to serve its invention of a "natural" morality. As for Mary Shelley's putative "nihilism," I would suggest that the novel, both through the morally confounding plague and the moral confusions of casuistry, implicitly adumbrates a sane and positive morality: the *unnatural*—that is, human, cognitive and linguistic—power to draw and articulate the distinction between good and evil. Such a morality—not the moral benevolism of sentimentalism—is implicitly the conceptual, allegorical opposite to the Plague.

In the final phase of the novel, Mary Shelley writes the obituary of the British nation-state. Within months, the circulation of the Plague brings an end to the "circulation of property"(230): "Commerce had ceased" (188). And with the fall of the market, comes the fall of the nation: its commercial capital "pulseless," the body politic of England is moribund. To take leave of England, as Lionel, the narrator, and Adrian recognize, is to bid farewell not only to a dead England, but also to the English dead. Such a recognition raises numerous pointed allusions to Burke—and unwitting echoes of his Jacobin critics: "Yet let us go! England is in her shroud,—we may not enchain ourselves to a corpse"(237). As Wordsworth does in the unpublished "Letter to the Bishop of Llandaff," Mary Shelley figures the Burkean attachment to the dead as a perversion.

A profounder critique of Burke, however, comes when the Plague confounds the very temporal order on which Burke stakes the survival of the English nation: "The world had grown old, and all its inmates partook of the decrepitude. Why talk of infancy, manhood, and old age? We all stood equal sharers of the last throes of time-worn nature"(231). Such a recognition underlies the declaration with which the surviving remnant leaves England: "England, no more; for without her children, what name could that barren island claim?"(300). Mary Shelley's nationless dead, then, ironize Burke's scruple for the fate of the *English* dead: "[W]hen any whole nation becomes the victim of the destructive powers of exterior agents," observes Lionel, "then indeed man shrinks into insignificance, he feels his tenure of life insecure, his inheritance on earth cut off"(167).

Undoing—even as it bids "farewell" to—"the giant powers of man," the Plague returns humanity to the state of its "first parents." And in unmaking history, it reduces the human to an animal-like existence. Comparing the remnant to "the cattle that grazes in the field," Lionel exhorts the "deserted one" to indulge in an animal-like unconsciousness: "[L]ie down at evening-tide unknowing of the past, careless of the future, for from such fond ignorance alone canst thou hope for ease!"(234). Mary Shelley's "last man," then, is the human disjoined from both social and moral life; the human who survives "the snapping of dear affinities"(191). Just as the Plague turns the clock of human history back to the liminal moment of the expulsion from Paradise, Mary Shelley turns the history of morals back beyond Smith and Hume to a moment between Shaftesbury and Hobbes—a moment, that is, between the erection of human perception as the cornerstone of a "natural" moral order and the reduction of humanity to an eternal present of animal passions. This, it would seem, is the moral impasse to which Mary Shelley's novel delivers humanity in the winter of "2100, last year of the world"(340).

And yet precisely by arresting the history of morals at this liminal moment, Mary Shelley accords a particular emphasis—a particular *value*—to the phenomenon of perception. With the recognition that "We became ephemera, to whom the interval between the rising and setting sun was as a long drawn year of common time"(198), comes a sensation of intensity in the act of perception: "I know not how to express or communicate the sense of concentrated, intense, though evanescent transport, that imparadized us in the present hour. Our joys were dearer because we saw their end; they were keener because we felt, to its fullest extent, their value. . . ."(198). Quite remarkably, the death of morals in Mary Shelley's *Last Man* brings about the birth of aestheticism: a privileging of aesthetic perception as that which alone accords value to the fragility of human existence.

To support this argument, I want to observe how closely Mary Shelley's account of the last man's days resembles Walter Pater's famous eulogy of "the individual in his isolation, each mind keeping as a solitary prisoner its own dream of a world."[19] Accordingly, Pater's point of departure in the "Conclusion" to *The Renaissance*—"that strange, perpetual, weaving and unweaving of ourselves"(188)—evokes the concluding recognitions of Mary Shelley's novel, the survivor Lionel's poignant sense of the ephemerality of human existence. Pater, valuing "experience"—"Not the fruit of experience, but experience itself"(188)—as "the end" of human existence, recalls both Mary Shelley's human remnant, committing "the precious freight of their hopes" to "the present, as an unalienable possession"(197); and Lionel's vow "not [to] lose the end of life, the improvement of my faculties"(338). In the final pages of the novel, Mary Shelley fills the last man's "journal of death" with exquisite—one wants to say *Paterian*—appreciations of nature. Lionel finds the time to notice, in Pater's words, "some tone on the hills or the sea . . . choicer than the rest" (188):

> A robin red-breast dropt from the frosty branches of the trees, upon the congealed rivulet; its panting breast and half-closed eyes shewed that it was dying: a hawk appeared in the air; sudden fear seized the little creature; it exerted its last strength, throwing itself on its back, raising its talons in impotent defence against its powerful enemy. . . . [T]he scene is still before me; the snow-clad fields seen through the silvered trunks of the beeches,—the brook, in days of happiness alive with sparkling waters, now choked by ice—the leafless trees fantastically dressed in hoar frost—the shapes of summer leaves imaged by winter's frozen hand on the hard ground—the dusky sky, drear cold, and unbroken silence. (225)

Even Mont Blanc, which a decade earlier had served the fictions of both Mary and Percy Shelley as the sublunary seat of sublimity, now becomes a sign of the beauty to which death gives birth: " 'Why,' cried [Adrian], at last, 'Why, oh heart, whisperest thou of grief to me? Drink in the beauty of that scene, and possess delight beyond what a fabled paradise could afford"(305). For Pater, such moments of aesthetic experience are all that stand between ourselves and death: "Not to discriminate every moment some passionate attitude in those about us, and in the very brilliancy of their gifts some tragic dividing of forces on their ways, is, on this short day of frost and sun, to sleep before evening"(189). In such stavings-off of death, Mary Shelley anticipates Pater's famous quotation of Hugo: "[W]e are all under sentence of death but with a sort of indefinite reprieve"(190).

And yet neither the journey nor the "journal" comes to rest in such visions of nature. Moving south toward Italy—toward the precise locations of Pater's *Renaissance*—the last man repudiates nature in favor of the ruins of human civilization: "I will seek the towns—Rome, the capital of the world, the crown of man's achievements. Among its storied streets, hallowed ruins, and stupendous remains of human exertion, I shall not, as here, find every thing forgetful of man. . . ."(335). The perception of art, then, is at once a cult of human presence and a preservation of the human past.

Perhaps the consummation of this aesthetic creed lies in its eroticization of art:

Each stone deity . . . looked on me with unsympathizing complacency, and often in wild accents I reproached them for their supreme indifference—for they were human shapes. . . . [O]ften, half in bitter mockery, half in self-delusion, I clasped their icy proportions, and, coming between Cupid and his Psyche's lips, pressed the unconceiving marble. (338)

"Unconceiving," the marble statues tacitly admonish Lionel that "experience," "not the fruit of experience," is the end of human life. In *The Last Man*, the *art* of the dead inherits the moral role of the dead themselves: to convey value upon human life.

Which returns us to the query with which we turned to Mary Shelley: What is the fate of the dead? In *The Last Man*, Mary Shelley responds to the legacy of the Enlightenment by responding to the last Enlightenment man: William Godwin. For Lionel's ironic inscription of his narrative "to the Illustrious Dead," explicitly parodies the subtitle of Godwin's 1809 *Essay on Sepulchres: A Proposal for Erecting Some Memorial of the Illustrious Dead in all Ages on the Spot where their Remains have been Interred*. Godwin's essay, a polemic urging the moral value to society of "affectionate recollection and admiration of the dead"[20] was ridiculed at the time of its publication, and by 1826 had long since fallen into oblivion; as such it stood as an ironic testimony to the demise of the Enlightenment dead by the early nineteenth century. But Mary Shelley's grim allegory of the death of morals foretells the rebirth of secular morals in the aestheticist creed. It is not the ghostly dead of Victoriana, but the still life of art—the "unconceiving" marble statues of the dead—that Mary Shelley prophesies as the modern legacy of the Enlightenment theory of sentiment.

Aestheticism, as it emerges in Mary Shelley's allegory, may seem an odd culmination of this history of the dead; the course I have been traversing has reached from Pope to Pater. In a certain light, aestheticism appears more an inversion than a legacy of sentimentalism: while the latter boasts a morals without religion, the former boasts a religion without morals.[21] But these are boasts, and boasts invite quarrels; Mary Shelley, as I have argued here, quarreled—and quarreled well—with sentimentalism. I would insist that the aestheticist valuing of human life through the mediating perception of art gives the lie to Pater's boasting "'children of this world'"; "the world," in Mary Shelley's words, "has grown old," and we have lived to see even Wilde become a moral hero.[22] If the Enlightenment failed to will us an enduring legacy of moral communion, it perhaps leaves our own brutal, troubled century something more precious: the inseparability of value and human life itself.

NOTES

INTRODUCTION

1. In addition to Philippe Ariès's landmark study, *The Hour of Our Death*, trans. Helen Weaver (New York: Vintage, 1982), the post–World War II explosion of thanatology includes Ernest Becker, *The Denial of Death* (New York: Free Press, 1973); Geoffrey Gorer, *Death, Grief, and Mourning* (Garden City: Doubleday, 1965); Elisabeth Kübler-Ross, *On Death and Dying* (New York: Collier, 1969); Robert Jay Lifton, *The Broken Connection: On Death and the Continuity of Life* (New York: Basic Books, 1979); and Jessica Mitford, *The American Way of Death* (New York: Simon and Schuster, 1963). Stanley B. Burns's *Sleeping Beauty: Memorial Photography in America* (Altadena, Calif.: Twelvetrees Press, 1990) is a stunning historical anthology of mortuary photography.

2. Sigmund Freud, "Mourning and Melancholia," trans. Joan Riviere, in *General Psychological Theory*, ed. Philip Rieff (New York: Collier, 1963), 164–79. A lucid explication of the psychoanalytic approach to the elegy may be found in "Interpreting the Genre: The Elegy and the Work of Mourning," chapter 1 of Peter Sacks's *The English Elegy: Studies in the Genre from Spenser to Yeats* (Baltimore: Johns Hopkins Univ. Press, 1985), 1–37. While I find Sacks's readings in the elegiac tradition compelling, even their considerable force is often curtailed by the Procrustean bed of the Freudian paradigm.

3. Michel de Certeau, *The Writing of History*, trans. Tom Conley (New York: Columbia Univ. Press, 1988), 46.

4. J. B. Schneewind, "The Divine Corporation and the history of ethics," in Richard Rorty, J. B. Schneewind, and Quentin Skinner, eds., *Philosophy in History* (Cambridge: Cambridge Univ. Press, 1984), 173–92.

5. Ariès, *The Hour of Our Death*, 322–406.

6. J.G.A. Pocock, "Virtues, rights, and manners: A model for historians of political thought," in *Virtue, Commerce, and History* (Cambridge: Cambridge Univ. Press, 1985), 37–50. For a discussion of commerce and gentility in the Enlightenment ("le doux commerce"), see Albert O. Hirschman, *The Passions and the Interests: Political Arguments for Capitalism Before its Triumph* (Princeton: Princeton Univ. Press, 1977), 56–66.

7. Pocock, "Virtues, rights, and manners," 48.

8. Ibid., 48–49.

9. The received history of Enlightenment moral philosophy, dating back to the Victorians Leslie Stephen and Henry Sidgwick, gives Hume, rather than Smith, pride of place. My account of Smith's *Theory of Moral Sentiments* as a response to Hume (and other moral sense philosophers) does, however, intersect with Stephen's and Sidgwick's respective accounts of Hume in important ways. Stephen criticizes Hume for lacking a "conception of a social organism" and for "an inadequate view of history," endemic to his atomistic view of society. But by

dwelling on Smith's conceit of the "impartial spectator," Stephen bypasses Smith's attempt in his discussion of sympathy at the grave to address Hume's inadequacy as a social theorist; see *English Thought in the Eighteenth Century* (London, 1881), 2:70–80. Sidgwick, revising his account of Hume and Smith in the third edition of 1892, focuses on Hume's failure to theorize a link between the moral sense and duty. In Smith's theory of sympathy, Sigdwick senses an incipient sense of justice; in his theory of conscience, an appeal to general rules of conduct. In both respects, Smith seems to be addressing the sociology, rather than the psychology, of morals; see Sidgwick's *Outlines of the History of Ethics* (London: Macmillan, 1902), 204–18. Interest in Adam Smith's moral philosophy has been stimulated recently by political and economic historians; see n. 6 above and chapter 1, n. 22.

10. Pocock, "Cambridge paradigms and Scotch philosophers: a study of the relations between the civic humanist and the civil jurisprudential interpretation of eighteenth-century social thought," in Istvan Hont and Michael Ignatieff, eds., *Wealth and Virtue: The Shaping of Political Economy in the Scottish Enlightenment* (Cambridge: Cambridge Univ. Press, 1983), 251.

11. Such an emphasis on the intellectual and affectional underlies what Christopher Herbert calls "the increasing displacement of the biological model of physical *function* in the name of the philological and linguistic model" in which culture is understood as " 'a system of signs.' " See Christopher Herbert, *Culture and Anomie: Ethnographic Imagination in the Nineteenth Century* (Chicago: Univ. of Chicago Press, 1991), 19; "a system of signs" is drawn (by Herbert) from Foucault's *Order of Things: An Archaeology of the Human Sciences* (New York: Vintage, 1973), 357.

12. For a discussion of English Romanticism and the New Historicism see Jon Klancher, "English Romanticism and Cultural Production," in H. Aram Veeser, ed., *The New Historicism* (New York: Routledge, 1989), 78–82.

13. As an example, consider Leslie Stephen's 1881 definition of sentimentalism: "the name of a kind of mildew which spreads over the surface of literature . . . to indicate a sickly constitution. It is the name of the mood in which we make a luxury of grief, and regard sympathetic emotion as an end rather than a means—a mood rightly despised by men of masculine nature"; see Stephen, *English Thought*, 2:436. The *Oxford English Dictionary* records the degradation of "sentimental" as follows: "Originally in favourable sense: Characterized by or exhibiting refined and elevated feeling. In later use: Addicted to indulgence in superficial emotion; apt to be swayed by sentiment."

14. "The [eighteenth-century] emphasis on manly emotion faded and the development of a rational outlook increasingly restricted the expression of men's feelings"; see Leonore Davidoff and Catherine Hall, *Family Fortunes: Men and Women of the English Middle Class, 1780–1850* (Chicago: Univ. of Chicago Press, 1987), 451.

15. Joshua Scodel's *The English Poetic Epitaph* (Ithaca: Cornell Univ. Press, 1991), a notable exception to this generalization, is based on the premise that the epitaph "participates in the social, and therefore historical, construction of the dead"(1). The period Scodel assigns to the decline of "the epitaphic project of

defining the public significance of the dead"(11) coincides more or less with the purview of this study. Scodel, however, confines his study to examining the literary form of the epitaph; he is not concerned with how this "epitaphic project" is taken up within other literary forms and discursive modes.

16. Paul de Man, "The Rhetoric of Temporality," in *Blindness and Insight: Essays in the Rhetoric of Contemporary Criticism* (Minneapolis: Univ. of Minnesota Press, 1983), 206.

17. Ibid., 207.

18. Walter Benjamin, *The Origin of German Tragic Drama*, trans. John Osborne (London: NLB [New Left Books], 1977). In the third section of the treatise, Benjamin contrasts a theological concept of temporality—"a progression of events which is . . . redemptive, even sacred" with an ethical and historical concept of temporality; see 159–67.

19. H. Aram Veeser, Introduction, *The New Historicism*, xii.

20. Louis Montrose, "Professing the Renaissance: The Poetics and Politics of Culture," in Veeser, ed., *The New Historicism*, 15–36. See also Hayden White's shrewd discussion of Montrose's historicism in "New Historicism: A Comment," in Veeser, ed., *The New Historicism*, 293–302.

21. Montrose in Veeser, ed., *The New Historicism*, 20.

22. Ibid., 17.

23. Stephen Greenblatt, "Towards a Poetics of Culture," in Veeser, ed., *The New Historicism*, 1–14.

24. Writing a cultural history of mourning is not simply a matter of situating mourning within a specific social and historical context—in this case, Britain during the eighteenth and early nineteenth centuries. For I suspect that this study of mourning has implications for the developing idea of culture itself. During the period which this book studies, according to Raymond Williams, the meaning of "culture" evolved from the process of training natural proclivities—human or otherwise—into the notion of a highly developed realm of intellectual and artistic life; see *Culture and Society 1780–1850* (New York: Columbia Univ. Press, 1958), xvi. Historians of the idea of culture generally identify the modern concept of culture—the immaterial complex of customs, values, and beliefs that defines a social group—with the rise of Victorian social anthropology; see Fred W. Voget, *A History of Ethnology* (New York: Holt, 1975), 114–64. But the modern concept of culture has older and less scientific origins than Voget's account implies. In *Culture and Anomie*, Herbert argues persuasively that "the idea of culture has been in crisis from the moment it began to take distinct shape and that it has embarrassed as much as it has empowered its users" (17). The logical incoherence of the "culture thesis," Herbert writes, lies in its claim "to ground itself in minute observed detail [while moving] in a realm of pseudoentities where 'no positive terms' are to be found"(21). Among the most acute embarrassments of culturalist argument, he locates Herbert Spencer's notion that "life in the present is in fact secretly dictated by past generations" (15); "It has turned out," remarks Herbert, " . . . that the persecution of the living by predatory spirits is no primitive delusion after all, but a basis of scientific sociology!"(15). I understand the "provocative symmetry" between the role of the dead in modern soci-

ology and in so-called primitive society as something more than an embarrassment; for as the argument of this book suggests, Spencer's notion of the dead as a vital force in the acculturation of the living is an idea he inherits from the skeptical British Enlightenment.

CHAPTER ONE
ELEGIA AND THE ENLIGHTENMENT

1. Scott Elledge, ed., *Milton's "Lycidas"* (New York: Harper, 1966), xxx.

2. Samuel Johnson, *Lives of the English Poets*, ed. John Wain (New York: Dutton, 1977), 88. All subsequent quotations from Johnson's *Lives*, unless otherwise noted, are drawn from this edition; citations appear in the text.

3. See Sacks, *The English Elegy*, 90–116. In the *ottava rima* envoi of the poem, Sacks finds that "The way in which the elegist preempts the rising of the sun reflects back on Christ's power to effect a spiritual sunlike rise for man. But Milton has calmly assumed that power himself: *he* makes the uncouth swain rise, and he himself has risen, as though he were another sun. . . . The frame of fictionality encompasses even [the raising of Lycidas]; which brings us to the disquieting region of conjecture, so important to Milton, of whether Christianity may be no more than a superior product . . . of man's imagination" (116).

4. Ariès, *The Hour of Our Death*, 346. Ariès moves from this observation to a discussion of two consequences: first, the diffusion of death "over the whole length of a life," and second, the widespread fascination with "the dead body, macabre eroticism, and natural violence"(353).

5. A notable exception is Dryden, who would domesticate the passions of Pindar in fashioning his elegiac ode for Anne Killigrew. For a discussion of the relations between ode and elegy, see Paul Fry, *The Poet's Calling in the English Ode* (New Haven: Yale Univ. Press, 1980), 13.

6. In defining the terms *elegiac* and *elegy*, the *Oxford English Dictionary* distinguishes between metric and thematic definitions of elegy. But because many of the Latin elegies are plaintive, the distinction can be misleading; it is difficult to ascertain exactly when the term *elegy* comes to be used for plaintive verse independent of its meter, though the Renaissance vogue for funeral elegies most likely dates the strict association between elegy and lamentation to this period. It is also difficult to establish when the term "elegiac" is applied to poems not derived from the Latin distich. Weever's *Ancient Funeral Monuments* (1631), quoted by Wordsworth, refers to "an Elegiacall or sorrowfull Epitaph." Apart from the phrase "elegiac knell" attributed to Bulwer (1644), the *OED* cites Gay (1720) for the line "He might sweetly mourn in elegiac verse" (though the line was not published until 1745). A century later, the elegy, except in literary-historical discussion, had become primarily identified with the elegiac *mode*. In the 1830s Coleridge would remark that the elegy "may treat of any subject, but . . . of no subject for itself . . . always and exclusively with reference to the poet"; Carlyle would refer to Rousseau's *Confessions* as an "elegiaco-didactic poem." By 1846, Landor would refer offhandedly to "this higher elegiacal strain" in Shakespeare; and Kingsley in 1859 would write of Burns writing in the "subjective and reflective" "domain" of elegy. Occasionally, Latin elegy be-

comes more salient for its thematics of lament than for its meter; the Victorian classicist Thirlwall (1839) refers to the Latin elegy as "the organ of . . . voluptuous melancholy."

7. Joseph Trapp, *Lectures on Poetry . . . Translated from the Latin* (London: 1742), 6. All subsequent references to Trapp's *Lectures on Poetry* are drawn from this edition; citations appear in the text. Trapp's polemical *Lectures* are an English translation of his Latin *Praelectiones Poeticae*, delivered at the Schools of Natural Philosophy at Oxford in 1712. For bibliographical suggestions concerning the poetics of elegy in the eighteenth century, I am indebted to Stuart Curran's *Poetic Form and British Romanticism* (Oxford: Oxford Univ. Press, 1986), 14–28, and to Roger Lonsdale's introduction to Thomas Gray's *Elegy Written in a Country Church-yard* in his edition of *The Poems of Gray, Collins and Goldsmith* (London: Longman, 1969), 103–17.

8. Trapp is at pains to describe the mechanism by which tragedy can provide pleasure and yet conduce to virtue. His explanation combines the Aristotelian theory of tragic *katharsis* with moral sense theory. First, he suggests that pleasure arises from comparisons of our own lot with that of the tragic hero. If we are better off, we become "sensible of our own Happiness" (324); if we are similarly afflicted, "the Representation of the like Miseries make our own more supportable." In addition, Trapp observes that "[a]nother cause of this Pleasure is, the Operation of the Mind upon itself, or (what the Schools call) its *reflex Act*. It contemplates that generous and human Disposition, which inclines it towards others, and is conscious that this Commiseration does, in some Measure, arise from it. Perhaps it may be objected, that these two Principles are not consistent, since the one is an Evidence of Self-love, the other of a great and generous Mind. . . ."(325). Expanding upon these remarks in his commentary on the fourth book of the *Aeneid*, a book of "Heroick Tragedy," Trapp remarks: "[W]e may talk as long as we will of a noble disinterested Spirit; still all our Passions, and Actions too, will be found ultimately to resolve into *Self-Love*: I mean as that implies the *Desire of our own Happiness* . . . and the Mind does but flatter herself if she thinks otherwise." Unlike Shaftesbury, Trapp does not view the preservation of the social system as the object of the moral sense. In light of this fact, Trapp's antithetical gendering of tragedy and elegy in the *Lectures* becomes specious: to follow Trapp's tragic logic, the erotic, effeminate temptations of elegy must be compared not to tragedy's heroic virtues, but to its autotelic self-interest. See Trapp, *The Works of Virgil: Translated into English Blank Verse*, 3d ed. (London: 1735), 196.

9. William Shenstone, *Works in Verse and Prose* (London: 1764), 1:3–4. All subsequent references to Shenstone's writings are drawn from this edition; citations appear in the text. Though published in 1764, the "Prefatory essay on Elegy" (3–12) appears to have been written during the mid-1740s *before* the publication of Gray's *Elegy*. See J. Fisher, "Shenstone, Gray and the 'Moral Elegy,'" *Modern Philology* 34 (1935): 273–94. Shenstone's essay bears the following note: "This essay was written near twenty years ago." Because of this note, and because the essay refers to the recent death of Pope, which occurred in 1744, Fisher concludes that "the essay was written in 1745 or soon after" (276).

10. Alexander Pope, *Poems*, ed. John Butt (New Haven: Yale Univ. Press, 1963). All subsequent references to the writings of Pope are drawn from this edition; citations appear in the text.

11. In "A Discourse on Pastoral Poetry," which he claimed to have written at age sixteen, Pope writes that pastoral, "by giving us an esteem for the virtues of a former age, might recommend them to the present"; see *Poems*, 119. He lists among those virtues simplicity and tranquility, but Pope's chief concern in the preface is with his own poetical apprenticeship; the discourse mainly ekes out precepts from the pastorals of Theocritus, Virgil, and Spenser.

12. Trapp's comments on the elegy in Lecture xiii begin by quoting Horace's *Ars Poetica*: "But to whose Muse we owe that Sort of verse, is undecided by the men of skill"; see Trapp, *Lectures on Poetry*, 163.

13. Recently three full-length works have studied the relations between moral sense theory and literature. David Marshall's *The Figure of Theater* (New York: Columbia Univ. Press, 1986) and *The Surprising Effects of Sympathy* (Chicago: Univ. of Chicago Press, 1988) both subtly relate moral sense theory to the culture of theatrical representation (rather than to drama per se) in eighteenth- and nineteenth-century France and England. Marshall's two books mirror one another. *The Figure of Theater* traces "the interplay between the threat of the theatrical position of appearing as a spectacle before spectators; the protection of dramatic impersonations that would conceal the self from those who would see, name, or know it; and the dream of an act of sympathy. . . ." (2). *The Surprising Effects of Sympathy*, on the other hand, takes sympathy as its governing figure, examining its duality as both an aesthetic and epistemological problem. John Mullan's *Sentiment and Sociability* (Oxford: Oxford Univ. Press, 1988) studies how "the increasing difficulty . . . of conceiving of society as a community of moral and material interests, and the resultant premium upon models of social understanding" (4) is represented in the novels of Richardson and Sterne. For a linking of eighteenth-century moral philosophy with Victorian sentimentality, see Fred Kaplan, *Sacred Tears: Sentimentality and Victorian Literature* (Princeton: Princeton Univ. Press, 1987).

14. Anthony Ashley Cooper, 3d Earl of Shaftesbury, *An Inquiry Concerning Virtue, or Merit*, ed. David Walford (Manchester Univ. Press, 1977), 35. All subsequent references to Shaftesbury's works are drawn from this edition; citations appear in the text. Walford claims that a draft of the *Inquiry* was completed in 1691; John Toland published an unauthorized edition of it in 1699. In 1711, one year before Trapp delivered his *Praelectiones*, the first authorized edition of the *Inquiry* appeared in volume 2 of the first edition of the *Characteristicks*. A revised edition of the *Inquiry* appeared in the second edition of the *Characteristicks*, published posthumously in 1714.

15. On the parochialization of "interest" and "the interests," see Hirschman, *The Passions and the Interests*, 31–48.

16. Francis Hutcheson, *Illustrations on the Moral Sense*, ed. Bernard Peach (Cambridge: Harvard Univ. Press, 1971), 261. All subsequent quotations from Hutcheson's *Illustrations* are drawn from this edition; citations appear in the text.

17. David Hume, *Treatise of Human Nature*, ed. P. H. Nidditch (Oxford: Oxford Univ. Press, 1978), 320. All subsequent quotations from Hume's *Treatise* are drawn from this edition; citations appear in the text.

18. Pocock elaborates on the ascendancy of social, rather than political, connections due to the increasing specialization and diversification of labor in "Virtues, rights, and manners," 48–49.

19. "Metaphors . . . to do the work of argument": I have borrowed this phrase from David Bromwich.

20. The *Oxford English Dictionary* lists as the fifth sense of "contagion," "The contagious or 'catching' influence or operation of example, sympathy, and the like," but the predominant use of the word in the eighteenth century was to connote contamination.

21. Adam Smith, *Theory of Moral Sentiments* (Edinburgh: 1813), 1:9. All subsequent references to Smith's *Theory of Moral Sentiments* are drawn from this edition; citations appear in the text.

22. Alan Bewell, *Wordsworth and the Enlightenment* (New Haven: Yale Univ. Press, 1989), 190. The quotation continues: "To decipher religious myths about death and immortality, then, we need only recognize that the nexus of all spiritual imagery is the corpse; all narratives about life after death can be reduced to and derive their formal organization from a primary confrontation, which every culture and every individual repeats, with the bodies of the dead. The history of death, then, is the history of our organization, displacement and metaphorical embellishment of this encounter, through language and funerary rituals" (190); see chapter 5, "The History of Death," 187–236.

23. Ariès devotes an entire chapter to such imaginings as Smith describes; see chapter 9, "The Living Dead" in *Hour of Our Death*, 396–401. He discusses numerous accounts of calamitous live burial, and notes that many wills of the period provide for a waiting period or physical tests such as scratching of the feet to prevent live burial.

24. In chapter 11 of *The English Poetic Epitaph*, Scodel cites this passage to develop affinities between the dead and the poor in Smith's *Theory of Moral Sentiments* and *The Wealth of Nations*. Scodel's emphasis falls, in this chapter, on sentimental attempts to reestablish bonds with the poor; my own argument about Smith pursues the relations between society and the dead more generally. For other discussions relating the *Theory of Moral Sentiments* and *The Wealth of Nations*, see Stephen, *English Thought*, 2:319–22; Hirschman, *The Passions and the Interests*, 100–113; Patricia H. Werhane, "The Role of Self-interest in Adam Smith's *Wealth of Nations*," *The Journal of Philosophy*, 86:11 (Nov. 1989), 669–80; and, in the same issue of the *Journal of Philosophy*, Charles L. Griswold, Jr., "Adam Smith on Virtue and Self-interest," 681–82.

25. "The mind, therefore, is rarely so disturbed, but that the company of a friend will restore it to some degree of tranquillity and sedateness. . . . We are immediately put in mind of the light in which he will view our situation, and we begin to view it ourselves in the same light"; *Theory of Moral Sentiments* 1:37. In Smith's formulation, the very act of imagining another's sympathy itself provides the wanted abatement of violent passions of grief.

26. Ibid., 1:39.

27. In using the term "moral economy" to designate Smith's theory of sympathetic circulation, I stand at some distance from E. P. Thompson's use of the same term in "The Moral Economy of the English Crowd in the Eighteenth Century," *Past and Present* 50 (Feb. 1971): 76–136. For Thompson, Smith's *Wealth of Nations* entails "a demoralizing of the theory of trade and consumption" (89) which is at odds with the paternalistic traditions governing prices, supply, and profiteering; such traditions Thompson understands to constitute the "moral economy" of a nascent working class.

28. Smith, *An Inquiry into the Nature and Causes of the Wealth of Nations*, ed. Edwin Cannan (Chicago: Univ. of Chicago Press, 1976), 1:341.

29. Linda Colley, *Britons: Forging the Nation 1707–1837* (New Haven: Yale Univ. Press, 1992), 66.

30. Ibid., 67.

31. Sterne's novel offers spectacular examples of this cultural debt to death. For Tristram Shandy, writing later volumes of his *Life and Opinions* in full view of cartloads of unsold earlier volumes, his own *Life* becomes a sign of his authorial demise.

32. Those who have read Gray's *Elegy Written in a Country Church-yard* as a transition between Augustan and Romantic values have claimed that among the poem's "versions" of selfhood can be detected a prototypical Romantic self. For a discussion of proto-Romantic selfhood in Gray's *Elegy*, see Lonsdale, "The Poetry of Thomas Gray: Versions of the Self" in Harold Bloom, ed., *Thomas Gray's "Elegy Written in a Country Church-yard"* (New York: Chelsea House, 1987), 19–38; and Anne Williams's "Elegy into Lyric: *Elegy Written in a Country Churchyard*" in Bloom, 101–18. Treatments of Gray's *Elegy* in a generic context may be found in Eric Smith, *By Mourning Tongues* (Ipswich: Boydell, 1977), 40–54 and Sacks, *The English Elegy*, 133–37. Conversely, those who have read the *Elegy* in a generic context have been struck by its generalized, somewhat hollow moral concerns, which seem only tenuously related to what is now considered the "traditional" elegiac occasion, a specific and significant death.

33. Lonsdale, ed., *Poems of Gray*, 112–13.

34. Henry Weinfeld, *Poet Without a Name: Gray's "Elegy" and the Problem of History* (Carbondale: Southern Illinois Univ. Press, 1991), 1. In the first full-length study of the poem, Weinfeld notes that the poem's popularity has long been a problem for its critics, many of whom have recognized that the poem's most popular features—its oft-acknowledged universality and quietism—are at odds with its sharp recognitions of class difference.

35. See Fisher, "Shenstone," 193n. 63.

36. In *Poet Without a Name*, Weinfeld places the poem in the tradition of pastoral, arguing that "the *Elegy* represents the symbolic dissolution of the pastoral in what one might call its transcendental formulation. For if the problem of history [both a sense of deprivation and the burden of overcoming it] *emerges* in the *Elegy*, this is because it had previously been submerged in the pastoral. . . ." (xii). Chapter 3 offers a penetrating reading of the poem in this context, though

Weinfeld's claim that the poem "bears an antithetical relationship to the . . . elegiac" tradition (xix) accounts for his surprising indifference to elegy in his discussion of genre (119–22). His discussion of the poem's relation to elegiac poetry is hampered by an anachronistic sense of the funeral elegy (as opposed to the love elegy, retirement elegy, or graveyard meditation) as the preeminent type of elegiac poetry in the period. On the poem's title, Weinfeld quotes Gray's letter to Walpole of February 11, 1751: " '& the Title must be, Elegy wrote in a Country Churchyard' " (121).

37. James Hervey, "Meditations Among the Tombs," in *Meditations and Contemplations*, 2 vols. (London 1803).

38. All subsequent quotations from Gray's poems are drawn from Lonsdale, ed. *Poems of Gray*; citations apear in the text.

39. Weinfeld quotes at length Gray's 1742 letter to West identifying himself with " 'a White Melancholy, or rather leucholy for the most part, which though it seldom laughs or dances, nor ever amounts to what one calls Joy or Pleasure, yet is a good easy sort of state' "; see Weinfeld, *Poet Without a Name*, 219n. 105. Weinfeld finds Gray alluding to Milton's *L'Allegro* and *Il Penseroso*, as I do, but finds him distinguishing after Milton between two views of melancholy, Galenic and Aristotelian. I would suggest, alternatively, that Gray's poem would influence a shift in the second half of the century from the former model of melancholy to the latter.

40. Johnson's citation, through a letter by a Reverend Temple, of Gray's " 'affectation in delicacy, or rather effeminacy,' " is partly responsible for Gray's marginalization after his death; in any event, it made Wordsworth's complaints about Gray's diction tantamount to minimizing the earlier poet's stature. During the last few decades Gray's putative effeminacy has been reappraised as repressed homosexuality. Lonsdale, in a 1973 address before the British Academy (anthologized by Bloom as "The Poetry of Thomas Gray"), poignantly relates Gray's "versions of the self" to a reflexivity and self-consciousness incurred through decades of homoerotic repression, or what Lonsdale calls "a private predicament." Curran claims that Gray wrote the "Sonnet [on the Death of Mr. Richard West]" (he titled it simply "Sonnet") "in the encoded tradition of Renaissance love sonnets, suppressing the record of his emotional life until after its cessation"; see *Poetic Form*, 30. As Lonsdale's essay suggests, Gray's homoerotic emotional life—or at least his desire for one—did not cease with the death of West.

41. See Alexander Welsh, *The City of Dickens* (Oxford: Oxford Univ. Press, 1971), 180–212.

42. If I understand Weinfeld correctly, he takes Gray's own identification with the nameless dead as a synecdoche for identifying "the problem of history" with the predicament of those buried in the country churchyard; these identifications, for Weinfeld, inhere in the poem's "[deep commitment] to the Enlightenment ideal of progress"; see *Poet Without a Name*, xviii. Reading Gray through Edmund Burke's *Reflections on the Revolution in France*, however, it is impossible to ignore the difference it makes that the residents of the churchyard are dead. I am suggesting not that the poem is not progres-

sive, but that in the course of its reception during the second half of the century, it would be seen to swerve to the right. See my reading of Charlotte Smith's "Press'd by the Moon" as a revision of Gray in chapter 2 (65–66).

43. Just as Johnson sought the identity of Pope's "Unfortunate Lady," readers from Gray's day onward have sought to identify the poem's motive as a personal loss: Mason suggests the death of Richard West in 1742; other suggestions include the death of an uncle in 1742, the death of an aunt in 1749, and, less personally, the execution of three rebel Scotsmen in 1746. For a discussion of dating the *Elegy*, see Lonsdale, ed., *Poems*, 104–8; F. H. Ellis, "Gray's *Elegy*: The Biographical Problem in Literary Criticism" *PMLA* LXVI (1951): 971–1008; and Fisher, "Shenstone," 288–92.

44. Gray's stinging comments on Shaftesbury, as quoted by Johnson in *Lives*, are made redundant by the ironic conclusion to the *Elegy*: " 'You say you cannot conceive how Lord Shaftesbury came to be a philosopher in vogue; I will tell you: first, he was a lord; secondly, he was as vain as any of his readers; thirdly, men are very prone to believe what they do not understand; fourthly, they will believe anything at all, provided they are under no obligation to believe it; fifthly, they love to take a new road, even when that road leads nowhere; sixthly, he was reckoned a fine writer, and seems always to mean more than he said. Would you have any more reasons? An interval above forty years has pretty well destroyed the charm' " (465–66).

45. John Newbery, *Art of Poetry* (London, 1762), 72. All subsequent quotations from Newbery's *Art of Poetry* are drawn from this edition; citations appear in the text.

46. Edmund Burke, *Reflections on the Revolution in France* and Thomas Paine, *The Rights of Man* (Garden City: Doubleday, 1973), 46. All subsequent references to the works of both Burke and Paine, unless otherwise noted, are drawn from this edition; citations appear in the text.

47. In his final chapter, "Hypochondria and Hysteria: Sensibility and the Physicians," Mullan discusses the paradoxes of sensibility: It "elaborates society as a capacity of the self—a moral as well as semantic potential for which my approximate word is 'sociability'—and, in the end, this capacity can achieve no expression which is not private and exceptional. There is no social space for sensibility. Illness is its appropriate metaphor"; see Mullan, *Sentiment and Sociability*, 239–40.

CHAPTER TWO
WRITTEN WAILINGS

1. "An Essay on Elegies," *Annual Register, or a View of the History, Politics, and Literature for the Year 1767* (London, 1786), 2:221. All subsequent quotations from this anonymous essay are drawn from this edition; citations appear in the text. As an incidental point of interest, this volume of the *Annual Register* contains meticulous diagrams of the funeral procession for the Duke of York, who died in Monaco on September 17, 1767.

2. George Campbell, *The Philosophy of Rhetoric* in James L. Golden and Edward P. J. Corbett, eds., *The Rhetoric of Blair, Campbell, and Whately* (Car-

bondale: Southern Illinois Univ. Press, 1990), 211–12. All subsequent quotations from Campbell's *Philosophy of Rhetoric* are drawn from this edition; citations appear in the text.

3. Smith, *Lectures on Rhetoric and Belles Lettres*, ed. John M. Lothian (Carbondale: Southern Illinois Univ. Press, 1971). Smith's lectures exist in a transcription by an anonymous student written in 1762–63. According to the transcription, Smith begins his "*History of historians*" in Lecture 19 by claiming that "the poets were the first historians of any" (100). In Lecture 21, he pronounces the superiority of poetic over prose compositions "in beauty and strength" (113): "For what it is that constitutes the essential difference betwixt a historical poem and a history? It is no more than this, that the one is in prose, and the other in verse" (113). Smith's examples, whether he is discussing demonstrative, deliberative, or judicial composition, are derived from a range of literary sources including Homer, Virgil, and Ovid; Spenser and Milton; and Swift, Pope, Addison, Thomson, Swift, Temple, Gray—and even Colley Cibber.

4. In Book 1, chapter 1 of *The Philosophy of Rhetoric*, Campbell asserts that the faculties are addressed "in a regular progression" from understanding, to fancy (imagination), to the passions, to the will (146). In chapter 7, citing the centrality of the passions, Campbell contradicts his own ordering of the faculties: "[I]n order to persuade, there are two things which must be carefully studied by the orator. The first is, to excite some desire or passion in the hearers; the second is to satisfy their judgment that there is a connexion between the action to which he would persuade them, and the gratification of the desire or passion which he excites. This is the analysis of persuasion"(210).

5. John Young, *A Criticism on the Elegy written in a Country Church Yard, Being a Continuation of Dr. J——n's Criticism on the Poems of Gray* (London: 1783; reprt. New York: Garland, 1974), 9. All subsequent quotations from Young's *Criticism* are drawn from this edition; citations appear in the text.

6. Oliver Goldsmith, *The Vicar of Wakefield* (New York: New American Library, 1961), 82.

7. For discussion of the cult of simplicity in the latter half of the eighteenth century, see Marilyn Butler, "The Arts in an Age of Revolution: 1760–1790," in *Romantics, Rebels, Reactionaries* (Oxford: Oxford Univ. Press, 1981), 11–38.

8. Newbery, *Art of Poetry*, 70. Newbery links the elegy with sonorousness, but casts the issue of poetic "Harmony" in gendered terms: "It would not be unseasonable to make some observations . . . by way of advice to many of our present writers, who seem to lay the whole Stress of their endeavour upon the *Harmony* of words: like *Eunuchs* they sacrifice their manhood for a voice, and reduce our Poetry to be like an *Echo*, nothing but *Sound*" (vi).

9. Johnson, *Lives*, 88. In his "Life of Hammond," Johnson writes, "But the truth is these elegies have neither passion, nature, nor manners. Where there is fiction, there is no passion; he that describes himself as a shepherd and his Naeara or Delia as a shepherdess and talks of goats and lambs, feels no passion"; see "Life of Hammond" in *Lives of the English Poets*, ed. George Birkbeck Hill, vol. 2 (Oxford: Clarendon Press, 1905), 315.

10. My idiosyncratic use of the Aristotelian term *logos* warrants some explanation. Aristotle defines *logos* as a mode of persuasion effected "through the

speech itself when we have proved a truth or an apparent truth by means of the persuasive arguments suitable to the case in question"; see Patricia Bizzel and Bruce Herzberg, *The Rhetorical Tradition* (Boston: St. Martin's, 1990), 154. The appeal to *logos* is traditionally associated with proof through logical argument. My desire to apply *logos* to the phenomenon of textual allusion, however, hinges on Aristotle's designation of enthymeme, rather than syllogism, as the argumentative technique of rhetoric. Enthymeme differs from syllogism in two ways: its major premise is probable, rather than certain; and one of its two premises is implied, rather than stated. Enthymeme is, I would argue, a structure of textual allusion; it depends on a relation between a stated premise and an unstated one to which it points, and through which it issues in a logical conclusion.

11. I am indebted to Richard Kroll for suggestions along these lines.

12. Thomas Warton, *History of English Poetry* (London[?], 1775), 1:ii.

13. Henry Headley, *Select Beauties of Ancient English Poetry* (London, 1787), 1:xii. All subsequent quotations from Headley's *Select Beauties* are drawn from this edition; citations appear in the text.

14. Curran, *Poetic Form*, 30. Ironically, the poem that might be said to have sanctioned a decisive break with the traditional elegiac object and occasion was itself written to mourn such an occasion and such an object—the premature death of Gray's literary schoolfriend, Richard West.

15. William Wordsworth, *Prose Works*, ed. W.J.B. Owen and Jane Worthington Smyser (Oxford: Oxford Univ. Press, 1974), 1:132. All subsequent quotations from Wordsworth's prose, except where otherwise noted, are drawn from this edition; citations appear in the text.

16. "Praise," writes Joel Fineman on the reflexivity of epideixis, "is an objective showing that is essentially a subjective showing off"; see *Shakespeare's Perjured Eye* (Berkeley: Univ. of California Press, 1986), 6.

17. John Milton, *Paradise Lost* in *Complete Poems and Major Prose*, ed. Merritt Y. Hughes (Indianapolis: Bobbs-Merrill, 1957). All subsequent quotations from Milton's works are drawn from this edition; citations appear in the text.

18. Curran, *Poetic Form*, 30.

19. For a lucid discussion of the significance of Coleridge's collection, of which three copies survive, see Curran, *Poetic Form*, 34–39. The collection and preface are reprinted in Paul M. Zall, ed., *Coleridge's "Sonnets from Various Authors"* (Glendale, Calif.: La Siesta Press, 1968). I have quoted the preface from Samuel Taylor Coleridge, *Poetical Works* (London: Macmillan, 1938), 543. All subsequent quotations from Coleridge's works are drawn from this edition; citations appear in the text.

20. Quotations from the works of William Lisle Bowles are drawn from *Fourteen Sonnets, Sonnets Written on Picturesque Spots, etc.* (Bath, 1789; reprt. New York: Garland, 1978); citations appear in the text. Unless otherwise noted, I refer to Bowles's sonnets by the number in the second edition of 1789.

21. Curran, *Poetic Form*, 32. Quotations from the works of Charlotte Smith are drawn from *Elegiac Sonnets and other Poems*, (London: 1811). Unless otherwise noted, I refer to Smith's sonnets by the number in the tenth edition of 1811.

My understanding of Smith's rhetorical strategies has been enhanced by chapters 1 and 2 of Sarah Zimmerman's "Lyric Realism, Romanticism and History," diss., Princeton Univ., 1992. Zimmerman studies the dialectic between the literal and the literary in Smith, setting her sonnets in the context of their prefaces, notes, and revisions, on the one hand, and their literary allusions, on the other. Whereas I study some of these relations in the context of elegiac rhetoric, Zimmerman studies how they create what she calls "a strain of lyric realism" in the works of Smith, Dorothy Wordsworth, and John Clare. I am also indebted to Sarah Zimmerman for sharing with me her records of Smith's revisions to *Elegiac Sonnets*.

22. Even the elegiac epics of Byron and Keats a generation later, epics unteth-ered to an English landscape, recall the sonnet cycles of Bowles and Smith. In Byron's *Childe Harold's Pilgrimage*, the Bowlesian elegist-traveler becomes his own hero-in-exile; in Keats's Hyperion poems, Smith's "cause," a relentless cycle of oppression, becomes the sublime yet poignant "first cause" of progress.

23. Curran, *Poetic Form*, 33.

24. For a discussion of Wordsworth's juvenilia in the context of sentimental-ism, see chapter 1, "The Sentimental Background" in James Averill, *Words-worth and the Poetry of Human Suffering* (Ithaca: Cornell Univ. Press, 1980), 21–54; and chapter 1, "Hawkshead: 1785–1787" in Paul Sheats, *The Making of Wordsworth's Poetry, 1785–1798* (Cambridge: Harvard Univ. Press, 1973), 1–42.

25. In "Romantic Elegy: The Consolations of Transcendence in England and America," diss. Yale Univ., 1985, 13–20, I discuss "The Dog" as a paradigm for the autonomous consolations of Romantic elegies.

26. Wordsworth, *Poems*, ed. John O. Hayden (Harmondsworth: Penguin, 1982), 1:47. All excerpts from Wordsworth's poems, with the exception of *Salisbury Plain*, *Adventures on Salisbury Plain*, and *The Prelude*, are drawn from the two volumes of this edition; citations by line number appear in the text.

27. Averill, *Wordsworth*, 37. Averill's reading of the sonnet on Williams is informed by his assertion that "What distinguishes the sentimentalist is his pro-found interest in the man looking at the sorrow, in a word, himself. . . . [T]he central drama of sentimental fiction and poetry lies in reflection, the mind turn-ing from externals to the exciting things happening within" (24–25). Averill understands what he calls the "bipolarity" of sentimentalism not as a fruitful dialectic, but as an elaborate attempt to camouflage literary sophistication and self-consciousness in the "platitudes of sentimental morality" (38). Response, for Averill, is simply reflection; chapter 3 below studies the political advantages that accrue to writers who manipulate the dialectic of reflection and response through the alternative strategies of collapsing them or keeping them apart. My readings of the *Salisbury Plain* poems reveal my strong disagreement with Aver-ill's statement that "Only with *The Ruined Cottage* and *Peter Bell* does [Words-worth] begin to emphasize a connection between sympathetic emotion and moral improvement" (38).

28. Because both sympathy and sensibility develop from sentimentalism (or "sentimentality"), it is difficult to draw a strict distinction among these overlap-

ping terms. Kaplan, in *Sacred Tears*, makes a useful distinction between "sentimentality as an expression of the doctrine of the moral sentiments and sensibility as a register of the capacity to respond to external stimuli" (32). "Sentimentalism" is defined too narrowly as either a literary movement or as philosophical moral sense theory (also referred to as "sentimental theory"); the term bridges literature and philosophy by yoking the literary representation of the moral sentiments with the theoretical construction of a society's normative morality, in which literature plays a crucial role. As the previous chapter suggests, sentimental theory entails both an ethics of social responsiveness and a psychology of reflection. The term "sensibility" privileges the psychologism of sentimental reflexivity, while the term "sympathy" privileges the ethics of sentimental response.

CHAPTER THREE
BURKE, PAINE, WORDSWORTH, AND THE POLITICS OF SYMPATHY

1. Laurence S. Lockridge, *The Ethics of Romanticism* (Cambridge: Cambridge Univ. Press, 1989), 27. Emphasizing the dialectical nature of Romantic ethics, Lockridge criticizes Jameson's "blanket characterization of [ethics] as binary and exclusivist" (32). For a discussion of relations between the ethical and the political in literary texts, see 23–33.

2. Comparing Wordsworth's sonnet on Williams with another sonnet on Williams published in the *Gentleman's Magazine*, Averill notes that Wordsworth, unlike "E.," who cites Williams's long poem *Peru*, declines to mention the particular tale of distress that occasions the poet's weeping; see *Wordsworth and the Poetry of Human Suffering*, 35.

3. Edmund Burke, in a letter to Calonne, October 25, 1790; quoted in Ronald Paulson, *Representations of Revolution (1789–1820)* (New Haven: Yale Univ. Press, 1983), 67.

4. James K. Chandler reads in Burke's title a refusal to "speculate" through letters; see "Poetical Liberties: Burke's France and the 'Adequate Representation' of the English," in François Furet and Mona Ozouf, eds. *The Transformation of Political Culture 1789–1848* (Oxford: Pergamon, 1987–89), 48.

5. In the *Convention of Cintra*, such "sympathies" are also described in the discourse of the "affections," as when Wordsworth notes that there were many "whose affections . . . were, in the former part of the contest [between England and France] . . . for a long time on the side of their nominal enemies" (1:226).

6. The political history of such rifts may be found in chapters 9 and 11 of Pocock's *Virtue, Commerce, and History*; Pocock discusses the complexities of conservatism in "Josiah Tucker on Burke, Locke, and Price: A study in the varieties of eighteenth-century conservatism"(157–92); and those of Whiggism in "The Varieties of Whiggism from Exclusion to Reform: A history of ideology and discourse"(215–310).

7. Discussions of British Jacobinism and Tory reaction in their historical context may be found in James Boulton, *The Language of Politics in the Age of Paine and Burke* (London: Routledge and Kegan Paul, 1963); Carl B. Cone, *The English Jacobins* (New York: Scribner's Sons, 1968); J. E. Cookson, *The*

Friends of Peace: Anti-War Liberalism in England, 1793–1815 (Cambridge: Cambridge Univ. Press, 1982); Albert Goodwin, *The Friends of Liberty: The English Democratic Reform Movement in the Age of the French Revolution* (Cambridge: Harvard Univ. Press, 1979); and E. P. Thompson, *The Making of the English Working Class* (New York: Random House, 1963). Two excellent recent treatments of Wordsworth in the 1790s—James K. Chandler's *Wordsworth's Second Nature* (Chicago: Univ. of Chicago Press, 1984) and Nicholas Roe's *Wordsworth and Coleridge: The Radical Years* (Oxford: Oxford Univ. Press, 1988)—pursue, respectively, his affinities to Burke and his involvements with radicals and radicalism. Studies setting British Romanticism in the context of the Revolution controversy are Butler's *Romantics, Rebels and Reactionaries*; and Carl Woodring's *Politics in English Romantic Poetry* (Cambridge: Harvard Univ. Press, 1970), 1–48; a brief treatment appears in Iain Robertson Scott, "'Things As They Are': the Literary Response to the French Revolution 1789–1815," in H. T. Dickinson, ed., *Britain and the French Revolution, 1789–1815* (London: Macmillan, 1989). Two introductory anthologies of prose of the 1790s are Marilyn Butler, ed., *Burke, Paine, Godwin and the Revolution Controversy* (Cambridge: Cambridge Univ. Press, 1984), which includes an excellent introduction; and Stephen Prickett, *England and the French Revolution* (London: Macmillan, 1989).

8. See chapter 4, "The Uses of Second Nature," in Chandler, *Wordsworth's Second Nature*, 62–92: "Burke's use of 'nature' is peculiarly problematic because he employs the word differently according to the needs of two very different kinds of claims. These are claims on the one hand about the timeless and universal condition of things (including human beings) and on the other about what human beings acquire as a result of their particular times and places; claims about matters often represented, in other words, by such oppositions as 'nature' and 'nurture.' Nor is this duplicity merely grammatical, as becomes clear if we recall Burke's metaphor of the rays of light piercing into a dense medium. The metaphor gains its force from its analogy with Newtonian 'laws of nature.' In this respect, there is one nature and one set of laws. But the 'dense medium' is made to correspond to 'man's nature' in this account, as if it were a nature within nature. The metaphor ultimately insists on having it both ways: there is Nature and there is a second nature which is at once within Nature yet parallel to it. Second nature is at once metaphorical and metonymous with Nature" (67). Chandler contrasts Burke's dialectical model with Rousseau's oppositional one, arguing that "Wordsworthian 'nature' typically operates according to Burke's dialectic of second nature and not according to the Rousseauist model of nature to which, either implicitly or explicitly, it is most often likened" (74).

9. In light of Price's own carefully articulated critique of Hutcheson in his rationalist *Review of the Principal Questions in Morals* (London, 1758), one can only imagine how Price would have shunned Burke's identification of him with the social legacy of moral sense philosophy. Price even discriminates between good and benevolent actions; in making this distinction, he anticipates Kant. In Price, Burke seizes on a figure in whom rationalist and rhetorical menace are conjoined, despite the illegitimacy of charging Price with the secular heresy of moral sense sentimentalism. In sum, Burke's rather perverse insistence on attack-

ing Price as a sentimentalist might well suggest his familiarity with, rather than ignorance of, Price's *Principal Questions*.

10. Edmund Burke, *Philosophical Enquiry into the Origins of our Ideas of the Sublime and the Beautiful* in *Works* (Boston, 1806), 1:x (92). All subsequent quotations from Burke's *Enquiry* are drawn from this edition and appear in the text; for convenience, the *Enquiry* is cited by part and section number in the text.

11. See Hannah Arendt, *On Revolution* (London: Penguin, 1963), 59–114. In her discussion of revolutionary terror in chapter 2, "The Social Question," Arendt takes as her point of departure this same misplacement of pity from the individual to the group. Arendt's and Burke's analyses diverge on the interpretation of the terrorist act. Burke attacks revolutionary pity for withering (or, alternatively, eviscerating) the heart; for him, the "perversion" of "well-placed sympathies" would make possible the widespread, coordinated performance of pitiless acts. Arendt's account associates the Terror with the desire to close a widening gap between feeling, rhetoric, and act. The cult of revolutionary pity—which Arendt, but not Burke, associates with sensibility—promotes a culture of suspicion about the rhetoricality of revolutionary acts and avowals. Violence offers a simulacrum of certainty when it is interposed between private belief and public rhetoric, thus preempting acts that might otherwise follow directly from concealed counterrevolutionary beliefs rather than from revolutionary rhetoric. Where Burke examines the role of revolutionary rhetoric in displacing the sympathies, Arendt goes further in analyzing terrorist desperation itself as a rhetorical problem.

12. See David Bromwich, "Burke, Wordsworth, and the Defense of History" in *A Choice of Inheritance* (Cambridge: Harvard Univ. Press, 1989), 43–78. Bromwich analyzes Burke's *Reflections* as a "defensive" (in both the political and rhetorical sense) rather than "reactionary" argument, assuming that "Burke supposes that he himself has helped to make the order he admires," even as he recognizes that "the rebels whom [he] deplores are, in his own eyes, candidates for success as plausible as himself. . . . One effect of seeing Burke like this is to make his defense of an establishment more a matter of active resistance, less a matter of intellectual police-work, than it can ever be for historians who picture him as a master rhetorician of orthodoxy. . . . When nothing supports a sense of the past other than the reiterated words and repeated actions of people like Burke; when the very definition of human nature depends on the victory of such people, and their victory is not engraved in all our hearts—then for the first time, a general defense of history can take on an air of heroic defiance" (56). Generally speaking, my reading of Burke's rhetoric of sympathy accords with Bromwich's activist view of Burke. Oddly, a passage central to this defense both supports and unsettles Bromwich's view; this doubleness revolves upon Burke's slippery use of "analogy." The "permanent body composed of transitory parts," of course, is Burke's own analogy for "our political system"; but Burke's contention is that the political system is continually reproduced by those whose political choices are "guided . . . by the spirit of philosophic analogy." Against the appearance of the system's contingency, Burke insists on the mediating term "spirit"; what guides, then, is not an analogy, but a spirit. If there are no analogizers but those "inspired" to do so, has not the matter of agency been transcended?

13. I am indebted to Susan Wolfson for noting the gendering of Paine's figures.

14. Edmund Burke, "Letter to a Noble Lord," in Butler, ed., *Burke, Paine, Godwin*, 55.

15. My discussion of tragedy, theatre, and history in Burke and Paine is indebted to the insights of Victoria Kahn, with whom I taught the *Reflections* and *The Rights of Man* at Princeton in a course called "Rhetoric, Politics and Theory" (Spring 1992).

16. Richard Price, "A Discourse on the Love of Our Country," in Butler, ed., *Burke, Paine, Godwin*, 32.

17. Shelley's translation of this epigram:

> To Stella
> Thou wert the morning star among the living,
> Ere thy fair light had fled—
> Now, having died, thou art as Hesperus, giving
> New splendour to the dead.

See Percy Bysshe Shelley, *Complete Poetical Works*, ed. Thomas Hutchinson with notes by Mary Shelley (London: Oxford Univ. Press, 1929), 712. For Tennyson's allusion to "Sweet Hesper-Phosphor, double name" see Alfred Lord Tennyson, *In Memoriam*, ed. Susan Shatto and Marion Shaw (Oxford: Oxford Univ. Press, 1982), lyric 121. All subsequent quotations from Tennyson's *In Memoriam* are drawn from this edition; citations by lyric number appear in the text.

18. On Burke's correspondence with Philip Francis regarding the lament for Marie Antoinette (which Francis called "pure foppery"), see Conor Cruise O'Brien, *The Great Melody: A Thematic Biography of Edmund Burke* (Chicago: Univ. of Chicago Press, 1992), 407–12.

19. In the *Vindication of the Rights of Woman* (Harmondsworth: Penguin, 1986), Mary Wollstonecraft comments on the dangers of such transient idealization: "The passions of men have thus placed women on thrones, and till mankind become more reasonable, it is to be feared that women will avail themselves of the power which they attain with the least exertion, and which is the most indisputable. They will smile—yes, they will smile. . . . But the adoration comes first, and the scorn is not anticipated" (146).

20. "Prejudice renders a man's virtue his habit; and not a series of unconnected acts. Through just prejudice, his duty becomes a part of his nature"; see Burke, *Reflections*, 101.

21. Such a merging of ethos and style is implicit in Aristotle's admonition that *ethos* "should be achieved by what the speaker says, not by what people think of his character before he begins to speak"; see Aristotle, *Rhetoric* in Bizzell and Hertzberg, *The Rhetorical Tradition*, 153. *Ethos*, as a means of persuasion, is constituted through language, not through reputation.

22. Boulton, in a discussion of Paine's "vulgar style," considers his references to popular forms of entertainment—"farces, ballad-operas, 'entertainment,' pantomime," etc.; see Boulton, *The Language of Politics*, 143. Boulton maintains that "Paine's theatrical allusions are invariably used for the purpose of

attack"(143). Burke, on the other hand, refers to the drama "to arouse the emotional fervour normally associated with serious drama and to suggest that the proper state of mind for observers of the French Revolution is that appropriate to watching a tragedy" (144). I would amend Boulton by insisting that Paine represents his "history" of the revolution in terms of a popular form of entertainment—cinema—that would not be invented for another 110 years.

23. William Wordsworth, *The Prelude: 1799, 1805, 1850*, ed. Jonathan Wordsworth, M. H. Abrams, and Stephen Gill (New York: Norton, 1979), 9:94–108 (1805). All subsequent quotations from Wordsworth's *Prelude* are drawn from the 1805 version in this edition; citations appear in the text.

24. See Roe, *Wordsworth and Coleridge*, 58–63.

25. The editors of the Norton *Prelude* suggest that "the completion of Book VI in late April 1804 was followed by composition of IX, 18–293, 556–end, plus a version of X, 1–566, and . . . at a final stage ca. early June (or conceivably at the beginning of October) IX, 294–555 [the lines on the hunger-bitten girl] were inserted" (519). See section ii, "Composition and Texts: *The Prelude* of 1805 and 1850," in *The Prelude*, 517–20.

26. David Hume, *Treatise*, 265.

27. Ibid., 153.

28. Ibid.

29. I am grateful for Susan Wolfson's observation of the earth's *partnership* in this enterprise.

30. R[ichard] Watson, Lord Bishop of Llandaff, "Appendix to a Sermon Preached Before the Stewards of the Westminster Dispensary," in William Wordsworth, *Prose Works*, ed. Alexander Grosart (London, 1876), 1:25.

31. William Wordsworth, "Letter to the Bishop of Llandaff," in *Prose Works*, ed. Alexander Grosart, 1:32. All subsequent quotations from Wordsworth's "Letter" are drawn from this edition; citations appear in the text.

32. Chandler explores "striking parallels" between the lament for Marie Antoinette and Wordsworth's tribute to Burke himself in *The Prelude* 8 (1850); see *Wordsworth's Second Nature*, 72–74.

33. Edward Said, *Orientalism* (New York: Vintage, 1979), 2. As Said points out, the late eighteenth century is a historical watershed after which "Orientalism can be discussed and analyzed as the corporate institution for dealing with the Orient—dealing with it by making statements about it, authorizing views of it, describing it, by teaching it, settling it, ruling over it: in short, Orientalism as a Western style for dominating, restructuring, and having authority over the Orient" (3).

34. The brooding Spenserianism of the Salisbury Plain poems has persuaded many critics to read them as allegories of a crux in Wordsworth's own developmental journey. Geoffrey Hartman's, *Wordsworth's Poetry 1787–1814*, rev. ed. (New Haven: Yale Univ. Press, 1967), 116–25 allegorizes *Salisbury Plain* as "a purgatory, a strait between states of being," and, as well, a crossroads in Wordsworth's own development: "He comes a step closer to the separation of his imagination from nature or to interpreting that apocalyptically as involving a *death* of nature" (122); see also 116–25. Enid Welsford's full-length study, *Salisbury Plain: A Study in the Development of Wordsworth's Mind and Art* (Oxford:

Blackwell, 1966) relates the Salisbury Plain poems to *The Borderers, The Prelude,* and *The Excursion.* Sheats's perspicuous readings in *The Making of Wordsworth's Poetry* (83–94, 108–18) trace in the Salisbury Plain poems the decline of Wordsworth's revolutionary optimism and the (here rejected) possibility of reconciling the mind to nature. More recently, Chandler in *Wordsworth's Second Nature* views *Salisbury Plain* and *The Ruined Cottage* as emblematic of "Wordsworth's moral positions in 1793 and 1798," respectively (136); whereas the narrator of *Salisbury Plain* expects "enlightened action" to follow from the narrative, the latter poem suggests that the " 'purposes of Wisdom' " can be fulfilled "without having to traffic in the methods and procedures of enlightenment" (138); see 130–39. See also John Williams, "Salisbury Plain: Politics in Wordsworth's Poetry," *Literature and History* 9 (Autumn 1983): 164–93; and, more recently, Andrea Henderson, "A Tale Told to be Forgotten: Enlightenment, Revolution, and the Poet in *Salisbury Plain,*" *Studies in Romanticism* 30 (Spring 1991): 71–84.

35. William Wordsworth, *Salisbury Plain* in *The Salisbury Plain Poems,* ed. Stephen Gill (Ithaca: Cornell Univ. Press, 1975). All subsequent quotations to *Salisbury Plain* (*SP*) and *Adventures on Salisbury Plain* (*ASP*) are drawn from this edition; citations appear in the text.

36. In *The Making of Wordsworth's Poetry,* Sheats observes that "Although [the female vagrant] attacks both war and economic exploitation of the poor, her story pays less attention to the social causes of suffering than to its psychological effects. It is in fact Wordsworth's first attempt to place the trauma of separation and loss in a chronological perspective, his first history of an individual mind" (86–87).

37. In *Salisbury Plain,* the vagrant's seaward gaze is broken by the ship's return: "To break my dream the vessel reached its bound" (385). In Coleridge's *Rime of the Ancient Mariner,* the breaking of the gaze occurs metaphysically, through the spontaneous blessing of the water snakes. To Wordsworth's seagoing vagrant in *Salisbury Plain* can be traced not only Coleridge's Mariner, but Herman Melville's observation that "as every one knows, meditation and water are wedded for ever"; see *Moby Dick* (Indianapolis: Bobbs-Merrill, 1964), 25.

38. William Godwin, Preface to *Caleb Williams* (Harmondsworth: Penguin, 1988), 3.

39. My reading accords with Sheats's sense of "the fragmentation of both technique and identity" in *Salisbury Plain;* see *The Making of Wordsworth's Poetry,* 94. Whereas I emphasize discrepancies between the female vagrant and the narrator, Sheats emphasizes discrepancies between narrator and traveler, in whom Sheats finds a "voice [that] would become that of Wordsworth's mature poetry and would eventually find philosophic justification in Coleridge's version of transcendental idealism" (94). I disagree with Sheats's opposition of the narrator's closing heroics to the "unheroic feelings" of the vagrant; on the contrary, her sentimental heroism competes stiffly with the rationalist heroics of the narrator.

40. Stephen Gill, *William Wordsworth* (Oxford: Oxford Univ. Press, 1989), 97. Wordsworth's much-quoted letter to Francis Wrangham (Nov. 20, 1795) sets the second version in the context of political developments since 1793: "I

have a poem which I should wish to dispose of provided I could get any thing for it. I recollect reading the first draught of it to you in London. But since I came to Racedown, I have made alterations and additions so material as that it may be looked on almost as another work. Its object is partly to expose the vices of the penal law and the calamities of war as they affect individuals"; see William and Dorothy Wordsworth, *The Early Letters*, ed. de Selincourt (Oxford: Oxford Univ. Press, 1935), 145. For discussions of Wordsworth's revisions to *Salisbury Plain*, see also Gill's "Introduction" to Wordsworth, *The Salisbury Plain Poems*, 3–16; Sheats, *The Making of Wordsworth's Poetry*, 108–18; and Roe, *Wordsworth and Coleridge*, 127–34.

41. In his "Introduction" to Dickens's *Dombey and Son* (Harmondsworth: Penguin, 1970), 11–34, Raymond Williams distinguishes between two kinds of moral analysis in the novel: "There is a kind of moral analysis in which society is a background against which the drama of personal virtues and vices is enacted. There is another kind—increasingly important in the development of nineteenth-century literature—in which society is the creator of virtues and vices; its active relationships and institutions at once generating and controlling, or failing to control, what in the earlier mode of analysis could be seen as faults of the soul" (16). Williams's comments suggest a transitional role for such Jacobin fictions as *Adventures on Salisbury Plain*, which present in a realistic mode an argument that society creates vices that militate against the explicit sentimental ideals of the natural soul and natural human relations.

42. *In Adventures on Salisbury Plain* Sheats finds "the ethical perspective of the poem . . . deeply ambiguous" because the sailor's inexplicit guilt for deserting his wife is displaced onto his explicit, but mitigated, guilt for the murder; see *The Making of Wordsworth's Poetry*, 112–14.

43. In *Wordsworth and the Poetry of Human Suffering*, Averill links the sailor's trance to that experienced by the female vagrant on board ship, reading both as part of a pattern of suffering and calm (or, alternatively, excitement and tranquility) indicating tragic catharsis. His concluding discussion in chapter 3, "Excitement and Tranquillity," distinguishes between the pathetic and the sublime: "Although almost any object, if rightly considered, can provide sublime experience, the object of pathos is another human being, usually one more unfortunate than the poet and reader" (115). As my reading of the gallows passage suggests, I find Averill's sublime reading of this episode suggestive for its psychologism, but I disagree with his sense that Wordsworth only in the *late* nineties "self-consciously explores the problematic moral and psychological questions" this sublime response raises. In my view, Wordsworth regards this response, when enacted in the realm of human relations, as morally, as well as rhetorically, dysfunctional.

44. A similar conjunction is noted in general terms by Garrett Stewart in *Death Sentences: Styles of Dying in British Fiction* (Cambridge: Harvard Univ. Press, 1984): "[D]eath in the Victorian novel can be taken to mark something like the intersection between (and at the same time final divergence of) sociology and psychology in their mutual plotting of identity within community" (50).

45. Nathan Drake, *Literary Hours* (London, 1804), 1:61. All subsequent quotations from Drake are drawn from this edition; citations appear in the text.

CHAPTER FOUR
"THE IMPOTENCE OF GRIEF": WORDSWORTH'S
GENEALOGIES OF MORALS

1. Since *The Ruined Cottage*, in its several phases and versions, was circulated privately until its publication as Book I of *The Excursion* in 1814, the contemporary response is largely anecdotal. James Butler, in his Introduction to the Cornell *Ruined Cottage and The Pedlar* (Ithaca: Cornell Univ. Press, 1979), notes that both Coleridge and Lamb were impressed by the poem as early as 1797 (10–14). When it appeared in 1814 as part of *The Excursion*, Francis Jeffrey paid the poem a backhanded compliment: "[T]here is very considerable pathos in the telling of this simple story; . . . they who can get over the repugnance excited by the triteness of its incidents, and the lowness of its objects, will not fail to be struck with the author's knowledge of the human heart, and the power he possesses of stirring up its deepest and gentlest sympathies"; see John O. Hayden, *Romantic Bards and British Reviewers* (London: Routledge & Kegan Paul, 1971), 44. Since Wordsworth's death, the poem has often appeared sprung from *The Excursion* (though sometimes with late, pious revisions). Jonathan Wordsworth's *Music of Humanity* (London: Nelson, 1969), a critical edition of both the MS D text of *The Ruined Cottage* and of fragments on the Pedlar, prompted a revival of interest in the 1970s in the poem's complex development: see Reeve Parker's " 'Finer Distance': The Narrative Art of Wordsworth's 'The Wanderer' " in *ELH* 39:1 (Spring 1972), 87–111; Peter J. Manning's "Wordsworth, Margaret, and the Pedlar" in *Studies in Romanticism* 15 (Spring 1976): 195–220; and James Averill's "Pleasures of Tragedy, 1798," chapter 4 in *Wordsworth and the Poetry of Human Suffering*. Frank Jordan, in *The English Romantic Poets* (New York: Modern Language Association, 1985) notes that *The Ruined Cottage* has been elevated to inclusion (on its own) in both the Oxford and Norton anthologies of English literature (289).

2. All quotations from *The Ruined Cottage*, unless otherwise noted, are drawn from the MS D (1799) version in the Cornell edition of *The Ruined Cottage and the Pedlar*; citations appear in the text. This version omits the biography of the Pedlar that appears in MS B (1788); lines D73–84 ("The Poets in their elegies and songs"), D362–75 ("Sir, I feel/The story linger in my heart. . . ."), and the Pedlar's concluding consolation first appear in this manuscript. An elaborate account of the poem's compositional history appears in James Butler's Introduction (3–35) to the Cornell edition.

3. In *Romantic Ecology* (London: Routledge, 1991), Jonathan Bate opens his discussion of *The Ruined Cottage* with DeQuincey's utilitarian reading: " 'It might be allowable to ask the philosophic wanderer who washes the case of Margaret with so many coats of metaphysical varnish, but ends with finding all unavailing, "Pray, amongst your other experiments, did you ever try the effect of a guinea?" ' "(quoted in Bate, 13). Bate likens this response to the less "playful" readings of McGann, Levinson, and others, who also concentrate on Wordsworth's evasions of social realities. My own approach is to find Wordsworth displacing the question of use onto the matter of grief; a *fruitful* displacement, I

would add, for the philosophical character of the poem, if not for the poetical character, Margaret.

4. While Wordsworth did not write a pastoral elegy, as Sacks notes, the "Intimations Ode" would link him closely to this tradition in the minds of the younger Romantics, the Victorians, and even the Modernists; see Sacks, *The English Elegy*, 138–45. By and large, the term "elegy" is used by Wordsworth in a characteristically loose way. In the *Essays on Epitaphs* III, he distinguishes "monody" from epitaph by its accommodation of the "poignant and transitory"(2:83), although in Essay I he quotes Weever's observation that in ancient Greece, epitaphs " 'were first sung at burials, after engraved upon the sepulchres' " (2:50). His emphasis on the critical criterion of epitaphic "sincerity" follows closely eighteenth-century canons of elegiac taste. In the Preface of 1815, Wordsworth classes the elegy, along with the hymn, ode, song, and ballad under the rubric of the "lyrical," "in all which, for the production of their *full* effect, an accompaniment of music is indispensable" (2:27); and the epitaph, along with the inscription, sonnet, first-person epistle, and loco-descriptive poetry under the rubric of the "idyllium"; here the epitaph, rather than the elegy, is closely linked to pastoral. From 1815, when Wordsworth roughly organized his collected poems according to the phases of life from youth to age, the grouping "Epitaphs and Elegiac pieces" follows "Poems Referring to the Period of Old Age." They, in turn, were followed by the Ode, standing by itself. See also Frances Ferguson, "Wordsworth's Classification of His Poems," chapter 2 of *Wordsworth: Language as Counter-Spirit* (New Haven: Yale Univ. Press, 1977), 35–95. For a discussion of Wordsworth's relation (broadly conceived) to the Greek elegiac diptych, see Abbie Findlay Potts, *The Elegiac Mode: Poetic Form in Wordsworth and Other Elegists* (Ithaca: Cornell Univ. Press, 1967), 9–35 and passim.

5. Shelley slightly misquotes Wordsworth: " 'The good die first,/And those whose hearts are dry as summer dust,/Burn to the socket!' "; see Percy Shelley, Preface to *Adonais*, in *Shelley's Poetry and Prose*, ed. Donald H. Reiman and Sharon B. Powers (New York: Norton, 1977), 69–70.

6. In *Modern Painters* 3, chapter 12, Ruskin defines the term as "the extraordinary, or false appearances, when we are under the influence of emotion, or contemplative fancy; false appearances, I say, as being entirely unconnected with any real power or character in the object, and only imputed to it by us"; cited in John Ruskin, *Literary Criticism*, ed. Harold Bloom (Gloucester: Peter Smith, 1969), 62.

7. See chapter 1, n. 3.

8. In *Placing Sorrow* (Chapel Hill: Univ. of North Carolina Press, 1976), Ellen Zetzel Lambert defines the presence of death in Arcadia as a definitive feature of pastoral. Hence, she finds Christian pastoral offering a distinctly different mode of consolation: "The reminder that the one we mourn, though he no longer lives *here* with us, still lives in some better world elsewhere, may be consoling; but it is not in itself a pastoral consolation" (xix). Renato Poggioli, in his famous essay, "The Oaten Flute," declares that "[T]he critical mind can only treat as failures all attempts to Christianize the pastoral, or to translate Christianity into pastoral terms"; see *The Oaten Flute* (Cambridge: Harvard Univ. Press, 1979), 19.

9. I thank Paul Fry for putting it this way.

10. See Annabel Patterson, *Pastoral and Ideology: From Virgil to Valéry* (Berkeley: Univ. of California Press, 1987), 1–17.

11. Poggioli, *The Oaten Flute*, 110.

12. Samuel Taylor Coleridge, *Specimens of the Table Talk* (New York, 1835), 2:137.

13. Recent bibliography for all three poems may be found in Jordan, ed. *English Romantic Poets*: for "Tintern Abbey," 305–6; for the Ode (which receives its own brief but lucid bibliographical essay), 299–303; for "Peele Castle," 312–13. In the same volume, Karl Kroeber raises the chastening "question . . . of whether the proliferation of criticism [of the Intimations Ode] serves a worthwhile purpose" (302). The question might be asked as well of "Tintern Abbey" and, to a lesser extent, "Peele Castle." If my own reading veers away from "careful historical reconstruction of the circumstances" (300) in which these poems were written (of which a fine recent example is Gene Ruoff's *Wordsworth and Coleridge: The Making of the Major Lyrics, 1802–1804* [New Brunswick: Rutgers Univ. Press, 1989]), it does so, finally, to tease out the historicism implicit in Wordsworth's narratives of moral development. I read these poems as closely linked meditations on the mediating role of images in the relation between the experience of loss and the attainment of ethical consciousness.

14. See Helen Vendler, "Lionel Trilling and Wordsworth's Immortality Ode," in *The Music of What Happens* (Cambridge: Harvard Univ. Press, 1988), 93–114.

15. Shelley, *Defence of Poetry* in *Poetry and Prose*, 502.

16. See Friedrich von Schiller, *On Naive and Sentimental Poetry*, trans. Julius A. Elias (New York: Ungar, 1975). All subsequent quotations from Schiller's *On Naive and Sentimental Poetry* are drawn from this edition; citations appear in the text. The conclusion of the Ode—the disposition of nature's "remains"—is suggestive of Schiller's contrast between the naive and sentimental conceptions of nature. With respect to the naive, "Nature . . . is for us nothing but the voluntary presence, the subsistence of things on their own, their existence in accordance with their own immutable laws" (84). Viewed sentimentally, "nature" is an aesthetic, not a moral phenomenon, a perception of the physical world unmediated by moral ideas. The conclusion to the Ode strives to argue that a sentimental view of nature can indeed be morally mediated through the sympathetic imagination.

17. Several poems treat John Wordsworth's drowning—among them "To the Daisy" and "When, to the Attractions of the Busy World"—without naming him more specifically than "My Brother," the "cherished Visitant," or "the lamented Person." John Wordsworth *is* named, however, in the "Elegiac Verses In Memory of My Brother, John Wordsworth": "He who had been our living John/Was nothing but a name"(39–40). Bearing that name, the poem is charged with an epitaphic function: "Brother and friend, if verse of mine/Have power to make thy virtues known,/Here let a monumental Stone/Stand—sacred as a Shrine"(61–64). Unlike *Lycidas*, where only the "frail surmise" of a bier stands between the poet and the lost body, here Wordsworth designates his poem to monumentalize the place at which the brothers had parted—now the grave of his "earthly hope, however pure."

18. James Butler, "Introduction," *The Ruined Cottage and The Pedlar*, 17.

19. Jeffrey's review of the 1814 *Excursion* (minus his quotations from the poem) appears in Hayden, *Romantic Bards*, 39–52: "[T]he wilfulness with which he persists in choosing his examples of intellectual dignity and tenderness exclusively from the lowest ranks of society, will be sufficiently apparent, from the circumstance of his having thought fit to make his chief prolocutor in this poetical dialogue, and chief advocate of Providence and Virtue, *an old Scotch Pedlar*"(43).

20. Francis Jeffrey: "Did Mr Wordsworth really imagine, that his favourite doctrines were likely to gain any thing in point of effect or authority by being put into the mouth of a person accustomed to higgle about tape, or brass sleeve-buttons?. . . A man who went about selling flannel and pocket-handkerchiefs in this lofty diction, would soon frighten away all his customers; and would infallibly pass either for a madman, or for some learned and affected gentleman, who, in a frolic, had taken up a character which he was peculiarly ill qualified for supporting"; see Hayden, *Romantic Bards*, 52.

21. *The Ruined Cottage and The Pedlar*, 121, 123.

22. Ibid., 261.

23. Ibid., 263, 265.

24. While Wordsworth's diction anticipates Shelley's observation that poets are "unacknowledged legislators," he sidesteps the issue of law in this fragment from the Alfoxden notebook to take up that of scientific reform. The impulse of science as practiced, claims Wordsworth, is to "pore & dwindle as we pore/For ever dimly pore"; what he urges instead, is to "enlarge our sphere of pleasure & of pain" through enlightenment: "Let us rise from this oblivious sleep, these fretful dreams/Of feverish nothingness." Here, at last, is an awakening, which "quicken[s]" and "rouzes" the mind. For sense to be subservient to "moral purposes," the intellect, apparently, must mediate: "For thus the senses & the intellect/Shall each to each supply a mutual aid." In its broad gestures, then, this passage offers a remedy for "naked hearts" and "naked minds" "left to mourn/The burthen of existence"—a faith that such mourning was never necessary: "Whate'er we see/Whate'er we feel by agen[c]y direct/Or indirect shall tend to feed & nurse/Our faculties. . . ." See *The Ruined Cottage and The Pedlar*, 267, 269, 271.

25. These lines are excerpted from a fragment ("We live by admiration and by love") found in MS Y. It appears in "MS Drafts and Fragments, 1798–1804" in the Norton *Prelude: 1799, 1805, 1850*, 504.

26. The phrase "tale traditionary" appears in Wordsworth's elaboration of the Pedlar's childhood in MS B; see *The Ruined Cottage and The Pedlar*, 163. In *Wordsworth's Second Nature*, Chandler observes that the contemporary use of the term "tradition" referred specifically to unwritten traditions; "Wordsworth proves to be an even more thoroughgoing traditionalist than Burke in some ways, since, unlike Burke, he embraces 'tradition' with an explicit awareness of its roots in illiterate forms of cultural life"(160). In chapter 6, "Natural Lore," Chandler discusses the Pedlar's imaginative "nourishment" by such tales (120–24).

27. For a discussion of Wordsworth's troping of fancy as feminine from *The Prelude* to *The Excursion*, see Julie Ellison, " 'Nice Arts' and 'Potent Enginery':

The Gendered Economy of Wordsworth's Fancy," *Centennial Review* 33 (Fall 1989): 441–67.

28. On my use of the term "moral economy," see chapter 1, n. 27.

29. Lockridge, *The Ethics of Romanticism*, 45.

30. Friedrich Nietzsche, *The Birth of Tragedy and The Genealogy of Morals*, trans. Francis Golffing (Garden City: Doubleday, 1956), 158.

31. David Hartley, *Observations on Man, His Frame, His Duty and His Expectations* (London, 1749), vol. 1, prop. 99.

32. The task of assessing relations between British and continental influences (through Coleridge) in Wordsworth's poetry remains to this day a staple of Wordsworth criticism—and of Romantic studies more generally. In *The Ethics of Romanticism*, Lockridge argues that "the oppositional character of European moral schools as they develop historically is inscribed internally in the Romantics's augmented conception of human personality, action, and moral value"(42). As against Grob's view in *The Philosophic Mind: A Study of Wordsworth's Poetry and Thought 1797–1805* (Columbus: Ohio State Univ. Press, 1973) that Wordsworth "progresses" from empirical premises through a "Middle Phase" and finally into a mature transcendentalism, most commentators have accepted Hartman's sense of an ongoing dialectic between British and Continental philosophical traditions. Kenneth Johnston discusses this dialectic as it informs the changing conception of *The Recluse* in *Wordsworth and "The Recluse"* (New Haven: Yale Univ. Press, 1984), 16–17. Lockridge claims that Wordsworth "and DeQuincey after him, in weakening the voluntarism of Blake and Coleridge, see the force of circumstance—both natural and social—as exerting greater power over the moral agent. In this they are more indebted to the empirical and associationist model of mind, with the reduction of human freedom that vulnerability to environment usually implies. . . . [De Quincey] and Wordsworth, in making greater concessions to circumstance, natural process, and loss, challenge the high estimate of potential power the self-originating moral agent is granted within the ideology of Romantic humanism" (206–7). Lockridge debates Hartman's post-Kantian emphasis on the preeminence of mind in the dialectic between mind and nature. My argument in this chapter concerns not the balance of power in the dialectic, but rather Wordsworth's search for a moral discourse adequate to the complexity of his dialectical perspective. Whereas Lockridge finds Wordsworth most successful in that search in *The Prelude*, I argue in the following chapter that he meets with greatest success in *The Excursion*.

CHAPTER FIVE
"THIS PREGNANT SPOT OF GROUND":
BEARING THE DEAD IN *THE EXCURSION*

1. Hayden, ed., *Romantic Bards*, 42. Jeffrey's review, published in the *Edinburgh Review* XXIV (Nov. 1814), may be found in Hayden, 39–52. Lamb's review, published in the *Quarterly Review* XII (Oct. 1814) also appears in Hayden, 53–61. In a paper delivered at the 1991 MLA convention, Peter Manning compares Jeffrey's reading—or misreading—of Wordsworth's *Excursion* to his treatment of Scott's *Waverly* in the same issue of the *Edinburgh Review*.

2. For a discussion of clinical diagnosis in the Romantic period—and a rich treatment of contemporary medical culture more generally—see Hermione de Almeida, *Romantic Medicine and John Keats* (New York: Oxford Univ. Press, 1991). In *The Ethics of Romanticism*, Lockridge echoes Jeffrey by dismissing *The Excursion*: "It has the effect of making one doubt, retrospectively, the profundity of the earlier work and should probably be read, beyond Book One and a few other passages of great power, only for diagnostic purposes" (245).

3. J.G.A. Pocock, "The Political Economy of Burke's Analysis of the French Revolution," in *Virtue, Commerce, and History*, 211.

4. For a detailed discussion of the *Edinburgh Review* and its developing critical elaboration of Smith's *Wealth of Nations*, see chapter 2 of Biancamaria Fontana, *Rethinking the Politics of Commercial Society: The "Edinburgh Review" 1802–1832* (Cambridge: Cambridge Univ. Press, 1985), 46–78.

5. See William Hazlitt, "Observations on Mr. Wordsworth's Poem The Excursion," in *Complete Works* (London: Dent, 1932), 4:111–25. In his "Observations," Hazlitt dissents from Wordsworth's conclusion "that one day *our* triumph, the triumph of humanity and liberty, may be complete. For this purpose, we think several things necessary which are impossible. It is a consummation which cannot happen till the nature of things is changed, till the many become as united as the *one*, till romantic generosity shall be as common as gross selfishness, till reason shall have acquired the obstinate blindness of prejudice, till the love of power and of change, shall no longer goad man on to restless action, till passion and will, hope and fear, love and hatred, and the objects proper to excite them, that is, alternate good and evil, shall no longer sway the bosoms and businesses of men"(4:119). Hazlitt's skepticism evolves into an elegy for the early days of the Revolution, "that glad dawn of the day-star of liberty; that spring-time of the world, in which the hopes and expectations of the human race seemed opening in the same gay career with our own; when France called her children to partake her equal blessings beneath her laughing skies. . . ." (4:119–20).

6. In Jeffrey's day, as in ours, the dominant critical response to *The Excursion* comprises the twin claims of poetic decline and ideological conservatism (with exceptions often made for the tale of Margaret in Book I). Hartman in *Wordsworth's Poetry* (292–323) and Lockridge in *The Ethics of Romanticism* (244–48) find the poem betraying the sublime and the ethical, respectively. Responding to Hartman, Ferguson finds Wordsworth *characteristically* betraying the sublime in a work that "dramatize[s] the essential reserve of Wordsworth's poetry that refuses to allow any 'erected spirit' to believe that he can ever renounce enough to stand beyond language or the world"(241); see *Wordsworth: Language as Counter-Spirit*, 195–241. The strongest answer to such claims remains Johnston's in *Wordsworth and "The Recluse"*: "The true, blind sublimity of Wordsworth's egotistical genius . . . was its wish to ignore its own prerogatives in order to write the redemptive poem he felt modern man needed: democratic, necessarily unheroic, lost to the admirations of traditional genius"(287); see also 263–329. In particular, see Johnston's discussion of the Solitary (268–80) and his reading of the Wanderer's "eloquent harangue" in Book 4, as the passage most keenly relevant to Wordsworth's ambitions for *The Recluse* (280–84). Chandler, in *Wordsworth's Second Nature* uses the "tales traditionary" of *The*

Excursion as a context in which to argue for the "implicit traditionalism" of Wordsworthian "spots of time"; see 206–15.

7. See Pocock, "The Political Economy," in *Virtue, Commerce, and History*, 210. Pocock closes the essay by observing that "An author is not necessarily read as he intended" (211); he calls for inquiry into "the reception of Burke's anti-revolutionary writings by his English readers, rather especially those sympathetic to them" (211). My reading of Wordsworth's Burkeanism focuses not on hints about Burke's tentative comments on a "bourgeoisie," perhaps the prime source of interest for Pocock, but on Burke's historicism.

8. In *Wordsworth's Second Nature*, Chandler usefully glosses this passage with excerpts from Burke "to construct a working notion of Burke's doctrine"; see 32–39.

9. Jeffrey in Hayden, ed. *Romantic Bards*, 49.

10. Edmund Spenser, *The Faerie Queene*, ed. Thomas P. Roche, Jr. (Harmondsworth: Penguin, 1979), I x 48. All subsequent quotations to *The Faerie Queene* are drawn from this edition; citations by line number appear in the text.

11. A note on nomenclature: in *On Naive and Sentimental Poetry*, Schiller uses the term "elegiac" to refer to the poet who sets "nature and art, the ideal and actuality, in such opposition that the representation of the first prevails and pleasure in it becomes the predominant feeling"(125); and "elegy" for poems in which "nature and the ideal are an object of sadness if the first is treated as lost and the second as unattained"(125). For clarity's sake, I have used the word "lamentation" for Schiller's "*elegy* in the narrower sense" and "lamentational poet" to mean a poet who produces lamentational "elegies." In a footnote, Schiller stresses that he uses generic and formal terms to refer to "the mode of perception predominant in these poetic categories," rather than to the categories themselves (125).

12. It may appear that this vision, insofar as it discovers sublime architecture amid the mist, is a conservative corrective to Wordsworth's (as yet unpublished in 1814) vision atop Snowdon; all that is "lodged" in "*that* breach/Through which the homeless voice of water rose" is "the soul, the imagination of the whole" (my emphasis). I would argue, however, that the Solitary does not replace the mist with the heavenly city, but instead draws that city out of it—out of the same mind, in other words, that had supposed spirit to reside in nature. Hazlitt's memorable commentary generalizes the Solitary's egotism to embrace the entire poem: "An intense intellectual egotism swallows up every thing. Even the dialogues introduced in the present volume are soliloquies of the same character, taking different views of the subject. The recluse, the pastor, and the pedlar, are three persons in one poet"; see Hazlitt, *Complete Works*, 4:113.

13. Since Hazlitt's observations on the poet's egotism, numerous critics have aligned the Solitary's history with Wordsworth's own. The Solitary's self-silencing seems a classic symptom of sublimation, one that brings to mind David Bromwich's description of "Tintern Abbey" as "a poem about the peace and rest that one can know only by a sublimation of remembered terror"; see Bromwich, "The French Revolution and 'Tintern Abbey,'" *Raritan* 10 (Winter 1991): 3, 1–23.

14. Wallace Stevens, "Final Soliloquy of the Interior Paramour," *The Palm at the End of the Mind*, ed. Holly Stevens (New York: Vintage, 1972), 367–68.

15. Paul Fry sees the Solitary's failure to reach conversion as an analogue for the metonymic structure of the epitaph: "Thus while the weak dramatic structure of the poem, based on opposition, calls in vain for the conversion of the Solitary, the dominant topographical structure, based on metonymy, prefers him just as he is, a half-deadened link between life and the insensate. . . ."; see "The Absent Dead: Wordsworth, Byron and the Epitaph," *Studies in Romanticism* 17 (Fall 1978): 420. Annabel Patterson discusses the poem's metonymic structure in terms of the georgic tradition: "Readers of *The Excursion* are not required to select, but to mediate between Wordsworthian epic and pastoral" (145); see "Wordsworth's Georgic: Genre and Structure in *The Excursion*," *Wordsworth Circle* 9 (Spring 1978): 2, 145–53.

16. Ferguson writes, "One of the most striking features of *The Excursion* is the proliferation of near-poets. The Wanderer (that poet sown by Nature), the Solitary (a former preacher and political rhetorician), the Pastor (the pronouncer both of sermons and of 'authentic epitaphs'), and the Poet overpopulate the rhetorical field"; see *Wordsworth: Language as Counter-Spirit*, 208. Schiller's theory of the "sentimental" affords a framework within which to compare these "near-poets."

17. The allegory of two parents lies in some tension with Wordsworth's suggestion that the dead are conceived by a feminine principle through divine inspiration. The "wise Forefathers" who enshrined the past in enduring institutions are perhaps the prudent stepfathers of a moral tradition.

18. Johnston finds the epitomizing narratives of *The Excursion* 6 and 7 to epitomize *The Recluse*: "each of them is in effect an epitaph, the smallest compression of the fullest story, a direction in which *The Recluse* was always tending once it began its dialectical relations with *The Prelude*, the fullest expansion of the most individual story"; see *Wordsworth and "The Recluse,"* 287. A dissenting opinion can be found in Scodel, who finds these narratives a curtailment of the public epitaph in favor of a more personal poetic mode: "The epitaph seems doomed in Wordsworth's hand either to minimum gestures or to complete absence, both of which can stimulate the poet's and—so Wordsworth hopes—his reader's reflections"; see *The English Poetic Epitaph*, 398.

19. Scodel, in chapter 10 of *The English Poetic Epitaph*, discusses the incursion of the personal—including the concern for authorial sincerity regarding the dead—into epitaphic poetry during the latter half of the eighteenth century. Whereas Johnson's writing on elegy hovers over the issue of sincerity, Scodel finds his writing on the epitaph to worry over the uncertainty with which epitaphs are encountered by their readers (332–44).

20. See M. H. Abrams, *Natural Supernaturalism* (New York: Norton, 1971), 17–140. While Abrams's reading of *The Prelude* stresses its affinities with the *Bildungsroman* and the *Künstlerroman*, he notes of the Prospectus, "The unparalleled density of the Miltonic reminiscences suggests what the explicit argument of the Prospectus confirms, that Wordsworth is setting out to emulate his revered predecessor—and rival—by writing the equivalent for his own age of the great Protestant English epic" (21–22).

21. Elizabeth Barrett Browning, *Aurora Leigh* in Sandra Gilbert and Susan Gubar, eds., *The Norton Anthology of Literature by Women* (New York: Norton, 1985), 5:396–405 (287).

22. Gill, *William Wordsworth*, 282.

23. While Jeffrey locates Margaret as the pathetic center of the poem, Lamb cites the story of Ellen: "We might extract powerful instances of pathos from these tales—the story of Ellen in particular—but their force is in combination. . . ."; see Hayden, ed., *Romantic Bards*, 59.

24. For a discussion of other Miltonic allusions in *The Excursion*, see Stuart Peterfreund, " 'In Free Homage and Generous Subjection': Miltonic Influence on *The Excursion*" in *Wordsworth Circle* IX (Spring 1978): 2, 173–77.

25. A discussion of botanical metaphors in *The Excursion* may be found in Geoffrey Durrant, "The Elegiac Poetry of *The Excursion*," in *Wordsworth Circle* IX (Spring 1978): 2, 155–61.

26. I agree with Johnston that such strength of mind is emphasized throughout the poem: "The Pastor's flock certainly led lives based on Christian assumptions, but their author stresses their paramount virtue as strength of mind. . . . This primacy of mind over faith makes *The Excursion* a meditative rather than a devotional work and accounts for its extremely tough, relentlessly cold comfort. . . ."; see *Wordsworth and "The Recluse*," 286. Ellen is distinguished among the poem's many tough-minded protagonists, however, by her exquisite self-consciousness.

CHAPTER SIX
A NATION'S SORROWS, A PEOPLE'S TEARS:
THE POLITICS OF MOURNING
PRINCESS CHARLOTTE

1. For a modern biography of Princess Charlotte Augusta, see Thea Holme, *Prinny's Daughter* (London: Hamish Hamilton, 1976) and, more recently, Alison Plowden, *Caroline and Charlotte* (London: Sidgwick and Jackson, 1989). Modern medical accounts of Princess Charlotte's death appear in Franco Crainz, *An Obstetric Tragedy* (London: Heinemann Medical Books, 1977), a critical edition of several documents concerning the incident; and Henry Vincent Corbett, *A Royal Catastrophe* (Worcestershire: Roman Press, 1985). An account of attempts to revive the infant, written by Sir Richard Croft, the Princess's accoucheur, can be found in Crainz, 13. Modern medical reappraisals were largely stimulated by Sir Eardley Holland's 1951 William Meredith Fletcher Shaw memorial lecture before the Royal College of Obstetricians and Gynaecologists. Corbett reprints the text of Holland's lecture on pages 21–37.

2. Crainz's bibliography in *An Obstetric Tragedy* lists two calls for a medical investigation issued by a Jesse Foot, Esq., as well as separate medical reports by Rees Price and Anthony Todd Thomson, both MRCS. At issue was Croft's decision to manage the labor, which was two weeks postmature, without forceps. Croft was exonerated of wrongdoing. Croft, still reeling from the tragedy three months later, fatally shot himself while attending a patient in labor. Holland's opinion confidently blames the Princess's hemorrhage on "uterine inertia"

rather than malpractice, noting that "for those who believe in the psychologic aetiology of this condition, there is the life-long emotional stress from which Charlotte suffered"(37). Other physicians have suspected "a pulmonary embolism or thrombosis associated with possible mitral stenosis, and . . . an acute attack of porphyria"(58). Corbett, though loath to blame Croft, observes nonetheless in *A Royal Catastrophe* that forceps might well have helped avert the tragedy. The foremost accoucheurs in Britain at the time of the Princess's death looked askance at forceps, though female midwives appeared to have endorsed their use. By the time Princess Alexandrina Victoria was born less than two years later, obstetrics had entered a period of activist practice and forceps became widely used once more; see Corbett, 12–19.

3. James Rudge, *A Sermon on the Much-Lamented Death of Her Royal Highness the Princess Charlotte Augusta* (London, 1817), 39.

4. The catalogue of the British Library lists some fifty-odd individually published poems or collections, half of which are anonymous; nearly ninety sermons; and forty miscellaneous documents, nearly half of which are anonymous. A number of the poems and miscellaneous pamphlets appear to be pseudonymous; a large number of pamphlets contain unattributed passages lifted from journals and other contemporary accounts.

5. Felicia Hemans's "Stanzas on the National Calamity, the Death of the Princess Charlotte" begins with the tragic reversal from joy to mourning:

> Marked ye the mingling of the city's throng,
> Each mien, each glance, with expectation bright?
> Prepare the pageant and the choral song,
> The pealing chimes, the blaze of festal light?
> And hark! what rumor's gathering sound is nigh?
> It is the voice of joy, that murmur deep?
> Away, be hushed! ye sounds of revelry!
> Back to your homes, ye multitudes, to weep!
> Weep! for the storm hath o'er us darkly past,
> And England's royal flower is broken by the blast.

See *Poetical Works* (Philadelphia, 1844), 294.

6. Robert Huish, *Memorials of her Late Royal Highness Charlotte Augusta, Princess of Wales* (London, 1818), 647. All subsequent references to Huish's *Memorials* are drawn from this edition; citations appear in the text.

7. George Gordon, Lord Byron, *"So late into the night": Byron's Letters and Journals*, ed. Leslie A. Marchand (London: John Murray, 1976), 5:276 (Dec. 3, 1817).

8. Corbett, *A Royal Catastrophe*, 17.

9. Corbett reprints Holland, synopsizing the Hanoverian marital mess: "One wonders if ever there could have been, maritally, so tragic a family"; ibid., 23–24.

10. Reverend Samuel Woolmer, *A Tribute of Respect to the Memory of the Late Princess Charlotte Augusta* (Salisbury, 1817), 6.

11. Colley, *Britons*, 281.

12. Percy Bysshe Shelley, *An Address to the People on the Death of the Princess Charlotte* in *Shelley's Prose*, ed. David Lee Clark (New York: New Amsterdam, 1988), 162–69. For background, see Clark's headnote (162). All subsequent quotations from Shelley's *Address* are drawn from this edition; citations appear in the text.

13. For a fuller account of the Pentridge revolt, see Thompson, *The Making of the English Working Class*, 649–69. Thompson calls the incident "one of the first attempts in history to mount a wholly proletarian insurrection, without any middle-class support"(668).

14. An account of the "special commission held at Derby" appears in the *Annual Register . . . for the Year 1817* (London, 1818), 102.

15. See, for example, Stephen C. Behrendt, *Shelley and His Audiences* (Lincoln: Univ. of Nebraska Press, 1989), 33–38. Behrendt emphasizes the "apocalyptic" quality of Shelley's discourse: "The considerable variety of voices, stylistic features, and rhetorical devices Shelley employs in *An Address* suggest not a disordered rhetorical patchwork quilt but the heterogeneity associated with literature of prophecy"(37).

16. Ibid., 37.

17. See Nicole Loraux, *The Invention of Athens: The Funeral Oration in the Classical City*, trans. Alan Sheridan (Cambridge: Harvard Univ. Press, 1986), 24.

18. Ibid., 24–25.

19. Shelley's republican rhetoric, as Behrendt notes in *Shelley and His Audiences* (31–32; 37), contrasts with the gradualism of his earlier "Hermit" pamphlet urging a national referendum on reform.

20. In the *Address*, Shelley, notably, declines to represent the princely anguish of Leopold, choosing instead to generalize—in pathetic detail—the plight of men who "have watched by the bedside of their expiring wives and have gone mad when the hideous death-rattle was heard within the throat"(163).

21. While Athenian funeral orations have historically been celebrated for their universal conception of humanity, Loraux finds them ideological insofar as they "*conceal* the internal divisions of a society"; the purpose of funereal "history" is ultimately to "[mask] . . . the question of power within and outside the democratic city"; see *The Invention of Athens*, 331. Loraux's own preferred discourse, however, is that of the "imaginary" rather than the "ideological"; see 335–38.

22. The phrase is Garry Wills's; see *Lincoln at Gettysburg* (New York: Simon and Schuster, 1992), 53.

23. Shelley would resurrect the "glorious phantom" in the sonnet "England in 1819." This figural link between the *Address* and the sonnet was brought to my attention by James Chandler.

24. Hume conceptualizes pride along similar lines, deriving it from a "double relation of ideas and impressions." Hence, pride relates to the self through an external object that is at once a part of and apart from the self; see Hume, *Treatise*, 285–90.

25. *Annual Register . . . for the Year 1817*, iv.

26. J. Coote, "Preface" to *A Cypress Wreath, For the Tomb of her Late Royal Highness the Princess Charlotte of Wales* (London, 1817), 78. See also *A Biographical Memoir of the Public and Private Life of the Much Lamented Princess Charlotte Augusta of Wales and Saxe-Coburg* (London, 1817), attributed to Coote.

27. Thorpe invokes "schemes subversive of the constitution handed down to us from our ancestors, under which we have so long enjoyed liberty and happiness; schemes which, putting power into the hands of those incompetent to the rational exercise of it, must have the speedy effect of involving us in all the horrors of revolution"; see Reverend W. Thorpe, *On the Death of Her Royal Highness the Princess Charlotte of Wales* (London[?], 1818), 9. In another sermon, the Reverend John Pye Smith observes that "The taking away of good and valuable and promising characters, especially in high stations and in seats of power, is one of the methods by which the Most High manifests his displeasure against the iniquities of nations. . . . [W]e have Public and National sins which, in formidable array, rise up against us before the judgment of God"; see *The Sorrows of Britian* (London[?], 1817), 14.

28. Not surprisingly, the imagery of responsiveness often suggests ineluctable natural forces: the nation is said to endure a universal "impulse of feeling"; "a sudden . . . and unprepared explosion of grief and esteem"; "warm vibrations of the heart." An "electric spark," notes Coote in *Cypress Wreath*, "has run from mind to mind"(64).

29. *Authentic Particulars of the Death of Princess Charlotte and Her Infant* (London, 1817), 14.

30. Thomas Chalmers, *A Sermon Delivered in The Tron Church, Glasgow on Wednesday November 19, 1817* (Glasgow, 1817), 19.

31. According to Coote, "[T]he strongest and most indubitable display of public feeling in behalf of the deceased Princess was evidently reserved for the day of her funeral. Without any positive obligation of religion; without the least interposition of human authority or even the usual excitation of a party influence, it seemed as if there had been a preconceived agreement that Divine Service should be attended at all the Churches and other places of worship in the metropolis and elsewhere"; see *Cypress Wreath*, 57.

32. See, for example, *A Most Correct Account of the Funeral of the Princess Charlotte in St. George's Chapel, Windsor* (London, 1817).

33. Coote, *Cypress Wreath*, 53. Whereas Shelley focuses on the sympathetic horror and fear of those who witness suffering, Coote highlights the sympathetic sorrow of Prince Leopold, turning from the official mourners to the grieving audience at St. George's chapel: "His Serene Highness never ceased to weep, and the sympathy of the assemblage was heartfelt and universal, especially when the coffin was let down into the vault; then indeed there was no eye without a tear, no heart without emotion"(56).

34. Ibid., 67.

35. Ibid., 48.

36. Chalmers, *A Sermon Delivered in the Tron Church*, 7.

37. Charles James Hoare, *Silent Submission to the Divine Will* (Dorsetshire[?], 1817), 28.

38. Coote, *Cypress Wreath*, 71–72.

39. Abraham Rees, *Sermon, Preached at the Old Jewry Chapel, in Jerwin St. on the Occasion of the Much Lamented Death of the Princess Charlotte Augusta on Wednesday the 19th of November* (London, 1817), 28.

40. John Pye Smith, *The Sorrows of Britain*, 10.

41. See Joseph Ivimey, *Reasons Why Protestant Dissenters Lament the Death of Her Royal Highness the Princess Charlotte Augusta* (London, 1818[?]).

42. Thomas M'Crie [the younger], *Life of Thoms M'Crie, D. D.* (Philadelphia, 1842), 204.

43. "Lucius" [pseud.], *A Letter to the Rev. Andrew Thomson, Minister of St. George's Church, on the Respect due to National Feeling* (Edinburgh, 1817), 19.

44. Ibid., 10.

45. Ibid.

46. See "Candidus" [pseud.], *Observations on a Letter by Lucius to the Reverend Andrew Thomson* (Edinburgh, 1817), 7; and "An Alkali" [pseud.], *An Antidote to the Acid of Lucius' Letter to the Reverend Andrew Thomson* (Edinburgh, 1817), 6.

47. "Scotus" [J. Gibson], *Strictures Upon the "Letter of Lucius" to the Reverend Andrew Thomson* (Edinburgh, 1817), 12.

48. Ibid., 8.

49. "Candidus," *Observations*, 17–18.

50. "Scotus," *Strictures*, 13. Several supporters point out that the original stance of the Presbyterian community was not to participate. But as the funeral day drew near, an edict issued by the Edinburgh magistrates persuaded several ministers to change their minds, unbeknownst to Thomson. Nor was Thomson alone in his refusal; among those who refused, Coote lists churches in Esher, Canterbury, Milton, and Curzon Street (*Cypress Wreath*, 66–67); several accounts mention the lack of services in Oxford. The noncompliant Baptist minister of St. Neot's, Huntingdonshire, is dubiously quoted in Coote as follows: " 'I have no doubt that some persons present have come with expectations of hearing a funeral sermon for the Princess Charlotte; if so, they will be disappointed. She might have possessed some amiable qualifications, for aught I know; but this I can assert, that all who are not converted by the grace of God, will go to hell. Of the Princess Charlotte, I know nothing, therefore can say nothing about her; and if other people choose to preach a funeral sermon for a *cat*, there is no reason I should"(68). Thomson, who did deliver two Sunday sermons on the Princess's death, apparently offered his pulpit to another minister, but a misdelivered note prevented the service from being held.

51. "Candidus," *Observations*, 14.

52. "Scotus," *Strictures*, 16.

53. For biographical information, consult the younger M'Crie's *Life of Thomas M'Crie* and the *Dictionary of National Biography* (New York, 1893), vol. 35, 12–14.

54. "Scoto-Britannus" [Thomas M'Crie], *Free Thoughts on the Late Religious Celebration of the Funeral of Her Royal Highness the Princess Charlotte of Wales and on the Discussion to Which it Has Given Rise in Edinburgh*

(Edinburgh, 1817), 5. All subsequent quotations from M'Crie's *Free Thoughts* are drawn from this edition; citations appear in the text. I excerpt here three of the six *London Courier* announcements reprinted in M'Crie's footnote (71–72):

> " '*Monday, November 10*: In the great number of country papers, we have received this morning, there is the same tone of grief. In every town all amusements have been suspended, all public meetings postponed, except for the celebration of divine worship. We have inserted several accounts from different parts of the country. IT IS PROPOSED to have divine service performed in all of them on the day of the funeral.' "

> " '*Tuesday, November 11*: *It is said*, that in every Church and Chapel throughout the empire, divine service will be performed; and that awful and sublime part which constitutes the funeral service, be read.' "

> " '*Saturday, November 15*: There is no doubt that on Wednesday next, the day of the funeral, all business will be suspended; and that the empire will afford the awful and appropriate spectacle of a whole people spontaneously engaged in religious exercise and devotion.' "

55. In her discussion of royal subsidies for journals—in particular, the *Courier*—Colley cites M'Crie; see *Britons*, 221, 403n. 54. See also Linda Colley, "The Apotheosis of George III: Loyalty, Royalty and the British Nation 1760–1820," *Past and Present* 102 (Feb. 1984): 114–16.

56. Coote, *Cypress Wreath*, 78.

57. Chalmers, *A Sermon Delivered in the Tron Church*, 9.

58. Hemans, *Poetical Works*, 296.

59. John Pye Smith, *The Sorrows of Britain*, 3.

60. Burke's reference to "the little platoon we belong to in society" (quoted in chap. 5) does not explicitly mention the family. By "platoon," Burke appears to refer not to the domestic family but to the local community. His curious use of the military figure "platoon" is cited in the *Oxford English Dictionary* under the figural definition, "A squad; a company or set of people."

61. Lawrence Stone, *The Family, Sex and Marriage in England 1500–1800* (New York: Harper and Row, 1977), 652–58.

62. Davidoff and Hall, *Family Fortunes*, 450.

63. "This democratization of domesticity was solidly rooted in the homes of the middle class and not in the country estates of the minor gentry. It was no longer tied to a desire for a retreat from the development of towns and industries and a return to a patriarchal rural idyll, but located in the towns and villages of England, among middling manufacturers, traders, professionals and farmers"; see Davidoff and Hall, *Family Fortunes*, 184. See also "Domesticity," chapter 3 of Witold Rybczynski, *Home: A Short History of an Idea* (New York: Penguin, 1987), 51–76.

64. In "The Apotheosis of George III," Colley cites six developments in the latter half of the King's reign that contributed to his popularity: "first, increased familiarity with royal *cum* national celebration; second, the reportage and incitement of the London and provincial press; third, an increase in urban affluence

and/or civic pride and emulation; fourth, a growth in the number of voluntary organizations which aided mobilization and control of civic events; fifth, combined clerical, landowner, and employer sponsorship of loyalist displays; sixth and crucially, the wartime context which allowed the king to be celebrated not only for his royalty but also because his uniquely long reign had become the prime symbol of Britain's national identity and, in European terms, her singular success in resisting French domination" (113). On George III and royal domesticity see also Tom Nairn, *The Enchanted Glass: Britain and its Monarchy* (London: Radius, 1988), 163–74.

65. Colley, "The Apotheosis of George III," 124–25.

66. The Queen Caroline affair, treated by Halevy in 1926 in relation to the fortunes of radicalism, has become the centerpiece of two recent discussions of domesticity, gender and monarchy. Colley emphasizes the prominence of women actively taking the Queen's part (*Britons*, 265–68); Davidoff and Hall represent the Queen Caroline affair of 1820 as a decisive moment in the "imprinting" of the domestic on the monarchical (*Family Fortunes*, 152). My discussion of Princess Charlotte offers both a context for the Queen Caroline affair, and a corrective to the huge emphasis the affair of 1820 has lately received. The poor fit between the impassioned defenses of the Queen's feminine virtue and her character suggests that her defense was modeled on the popular image of a virtuous Queen projected in the mourning for Princess Charlotte. Moreover, while the Queen Caroline affair connects femininity with victimization and helplessness—at the hands of the Regent, no less—Princess Charlotte's death evokes images of an empowered, reigning female, images that would gain substance with the accession of Victoria. While Davidoff and Hall mention Princess Charlotte only in passing, Colley places the Princess among a trio of royal females—Queen Charlotte, Queen Caroline, and Princess Charlotte—who implicitly encouraged women subjects of varying ages and social classes to recognize their stake in the monarchy. Among social historians, Colley is alone in giving serious consideration to the aftermath of the Princess's death; by contrast, in Harold Perkin's *Origins of Modern English Society* (London: Routledge, 1969), Michael Reed's *Georgian Triumph 1700–1830* (London: Routledge & Kegan Paul, 1983), and Asa Briggs's *Social History of England* (London: Weidenfeld and Nicolson, 1983), virtually no mention is made of the Princess. See also Elie Halevy, *A History of the English People in the Nineteenth Century, Vol II: The Liberal Awakening 1815–1830*, trans. E. I. Watkin (London: Benn, 1926, rev. 1949), 80–106.

67. In "The Apotheosis of George III," Colley emphasizes, rightly, the combination of royal splendour and royal domesticity in this popularization of the monarchy: "George [III] was, perhaps, the unconscious precursor of that curious blend of assiduous domestic cosiness interspersed with occasional bouts of public splendour which is the current royal trademark in Britain" (108); still, it seems to have been the vulnerability of the royal family that earned them sympathy. As David Bromwich has helpfully reminded me, this was precisely Burke's intuition in dramatizing the assault on Marie Antoinette and the royal family of France.

68. Davidoff and Hall, *Family Fortunes*, 33.

69. For the compensatory myth of moral influence, see Davidoff and Hall, *Family Fortunes*, 183. Hannah More is treated here as a crucial figure in this moral-domestic mythology (167–72). More's 1805 *Hints For Forming the Character of a Young Princess* (New York, 1839) addresses "one of the most momentous concerns which can engage the attention of an Englishman, who feels for his country like a patriot, and for his posterity like a father . . . the education of the Princess Charlotte of Wales"(5).

70. Davidoff and Hall, 33.

71. Colley, *Britons*, 280.

72. *Authentic Particulars*, 12–13.

73. E. Smith, "Elegy," *Cypress Wreath*, 21.

74. "Lord Lyttleton's Monody on his Lady, Who Died in Childbed: Adapted to the Late Melancholy Event," *A Cypress Wreath*, 40.

75. "Lord Lyttleton's Monody," *Cypress Wreath*, 40.

76. Coote, *Cypress Wreath*, 15.

77. Hemans, *Poetical Works*, 295.

78. Woolmer, *A Tribute of Respect*, 8.

79. Rudge, *A Sermon*, 41.

80. Nine letters from Princess Charlotte to Croft concerning the progress of the pregnancy may be found in Crainz, *An Obstetric Tragedy*, 4–9. The correspondence shows the Princess to have been frank in discussions of her body and its functions. Two previous pregnancies that had ended in miscarriage had never been publicized at all.

81. In *Britons*, Colley identifies the "cult of royal women"—not only of Princess Charlotte, but of her grandmother, Queen Charlotte, and mother, Queen Caroline—as a Protestant substitute for a cult of the Virgin Mary; she relates this point to the flamboyant Wyatt monument to the late Princess, originally funded solely by women (272–73).

82. Coote, *Cypress Wreath*, 33.

83. Although only one female author ("Mrs. W. Serres") is explicitly cited in the *Cypress Wreath*, several others are listed as elegists for the Princess in the catalogue of the British Library; they include Mary Cockle, Margaret S. Croker, Harriet English, Mary Stockdale, and Elizabeth Tregar. I suspect that more than a few of the anonymous poems were written by women poets practiced (as was Hemans) at writing both occasional and memorial verse. Even as these poems promote an ideal of feminine domesticity, they strongly assert the compensatory emphasis on women's moral influence discussed by Davidoff and Hall (183).

84. Smith, *Cypress Wreath*, 21.

85. "The Last Pious Aspirations of the Idolized Princess Charlotte," *Cypress Wreath*, 92.

86. "There is an outward pomp," *Cypress Wreath*, 55.

87. Coote, *Cypress Wreath*, 43.

88. "The House of Mourning," *Cypress Wreath*, 29.

89. William Newman, *The British Empire in Mourning! A Funeral Sermon Occasioned by the Death of Her Royal Highness the Princess Charlotte Augusta* (London, 1817), 20.

90. Chalmers, *A Sermon Delivered in the Tron Church*, 30.

91. Ibid., 15.

92. In the *Sermon Delivered in the Tron Church*, Chalmers recommends a scheme that would send the ministry from house to house: "Where without any feverish or distracting variety of labor [the minister] may be able to familiarise himself to every house, and to know every individual, and to visit every spiritual patient, and to watch every death-bed and to pour out the sympathies of a pious and affectionate bosom over every mourning and bereaved family" (33). Under Chalmers's proposal, the house becomes the site of the spirit—not of its salvation, but of its nursing and healing. Even as the nation joined together in funeral services as though in a single "house of worship," Chalmers's scheme literalizes that trope by sending the church into the home. For more details on both Chalmers's campaign against "home heathenism" and his attempts to battle pauperism through voluntarism, see the *Dictionary of National Biography*, 9:449–54.

93. In general, the Princess's isolation redounds in the moral favour of Prince Leopold, whom even Shelley recognized "was to her as father, mother, and brethren"; see Shelley's *Address*, 165. As Coote writes, "In the absence of all who were connected with her by the ties of consanguinity, she had the consolation of finding the gallant stranger, whom she had . . . by her bed-side, smoothing the pillow of affection and at length catching her expiring breath in all the agony of heart-felt grief"; see *Cypress Wreath*, 15.

94. *Authentic Particulars*, 16.

95. Ibid., 12.

EPILOGUE

1. John Morley, *Death, Heaven and the Victorians* (London: Studio Vista, 1971), 14. See also the admirable collection of plates illustrating mourning artifacts following the text.

2. Julian Litten, *The English Way of Death: The Common Funeral Since 1450* (London: Robert Hale, 1991), 26.

3. Ibid., 29.

4. See Morley's account in *Death, Heaven and the Victorians*, 80–90.

5. For a discussion of the Queen's mourning, see Stanley Weintraub, *Victoria: An Intimate Biography* (New York: Dutton, 1987), 302–35. Weintraub notes that Prince Albert's funeral, which took place December 23, 1861, was modest in size, perhaps because it was arranged quickly so as not to interfere with the Christmas holidays (304–6).

6. Ibid., 309.

7. Ibid., 328–29.

8. Weintraub, 326.

9. Michael Wheeler, *Death and the Future Life in Victorian Literature and Theology* (Cambridge: Cambridge Univ. Press, 1990), 222.

10. Ibid., 25–58. See also Elisabeth Jay, *Religion of the Heart: Anglican Evangelicalism and the Nineteenth-Century Novel* (Oxford: Oxford Univ. Press, 1979), 154–68; and Stewart, *Death Sentences*.

11. Jay, *Religion of the Heart*, 162.

12. Ibid., 157.

13. Among the most popular—and the most complex—of the Victorian fictions of *revenants* is Margaret Oliphant's 1880 novella *A Beleaguered City* (New York: Oxford Univ. Press, 1988). See also Esther H. Schor, "The Haunted Interpreter in Margaret Oliphant's Supernatural Fiction," *Women's Studies*, 22:371–88.

14. Keble's "Burial of the Dead" appears in Wheeler, *Death and the Future Life*, 57:

> Far better they should sleep awhile
> Within the church's shade,
> Nor wake, until new heaven, new earth,
> Meet for their new immortal birth
> For their abiding place be made,
>
> Than wander back to life, and lean
> On our frail love once more.

15. As with any allegorical reading of a novel, one regrets the inevitable obscuring of fictive particulars in favor of the argument mounted among and by virtue of them—an especial bane to a novel so explicit in its political satire and so meticulous in its representation of a plague-ridden world. Still, the prophetic coherence of Mary Shelley's allegorical argument is my warrant for such an approach.

16. A brief summary of the novel (still not widely read) is provided by William Veeder:

> Lionel [Verney] narrates the extermination of the human race by plague at the end of the twenty-first century. Two males dominate the action, Raymond and Adrian. Raymond determines to return England to monarchical rule (the last king, Adrian's father, permitted the country to become a democracy). Raymond's energy is dissipated by his untoward passion for Adrian's former beloved Evadne, by his inability to live happily with his devoted but often willful wife Perdita [Lionel's sister], and by his dreams of military glory. Raymond conquers Constantinople, but dies as the plague breaks out. Adrian gradually assumes leadership of the dwindling remnant of the earth's wandering populace. He is reconciled to his dominating mother, the ex-queen, whose willfulness is softened by the life and death of Adrian's exemplary sister, Idris [Lionel's wife]. Adrian eventually drowns, and Lionel is left alone to ponder man's fate.

In this otherwise serviceable summary, I differ with Veeder's statement that both Raymond and Adrian dominate the "action" of the novel. While the flamboyant, charismatic Raymond accedes to political power—the "Protectorate" of republican England—the ethereal, sober bachelor Adrian keeps up a "Cincinnatus-like" retirement that he refuses to relinquish, even when Raymond attempts (for ends of his own) to install him in power. See Veeder, *Mary Shelley & Frankenstein: The Fate of Androgyny* (Chicago: Univ. of Chicago Press, 1986), 223.

17. Mary Shelley, *The Last Man*, ed. Hugh J. Luke, Jr. (Lincoln: Univ. of Nebraska Press, 1965), 31. All subsequent quotations from *The Last Man* are drawn from this edition; citations appear in the text.

18. Often read as a roman a clé about Percy Shelley and Lord Byron, *The Last Man* has been considered a sentimental, elegiac work by such critics as Hugh J. Luke, Jr., editor of the University of Nebraska Press edition; and Jean de Palacio in "Mary Shelley and the *Last Man*: A Minor Romantic Theme," *Revue de Littérature Comparée* 42 (1968): 37–49. For discussion of Mary Shelley as a nihilist, see Robert Lance Snyder, "Apocalypse and Indeterminacy in Mary Shelley's *The Last Man*," *Studies in Romanticism* 17 (1978): 435–52; and (with some qualifications) Jane Aaron, "The Return of the Repressed: Reading Mary Shelley's *The Last Man*," in Susan Sellers, ed., *Feminist Criticism: Theory and Practice* (New York: Harvester/Wheatsheaf, 1991), 9–21.

19. Walter Pater, "Conclusion," *The Renaissance: Studies in Art and Poetry. The 1893 Text*, ed. Donald L. Hill (Berkeley: Univ. of California Press, 1980), 187–88. All subsequent quotations from Pater's "Conclusion" are drawn from this edition; citations appear in the text.

20. William Godwin, *Essay on Sepulchres: A Proposal for Erecting Some Memorial of The Illustrious Dead in All Ages on the Spot Where Their Remains Have Been Interred* (London, 1809), 30.

21. See Leon Chai, *Aestheticism: The Religion of Art in Post-Romantic Literature* (New York: Columbia Univ. Press, 1990), 1–43.

22. "We inherit [Wilde's] struggle to achieve supreme fictions in art, to associate art with social change, to bring together individual and social impulse, to save what is eccentric and singular from being sanitized and standardized, to replace a morality of severity by one of sympathy"; see Richard Ellmann, *Oscar Wilde* (New York: Knopf, 1988), 589.

INDEX